MEMORY, TRADITION,
AND TEXT

Society of Biblical Literature

Semeia Studies

Gale A. Yee, General Editor

Number 52

MEMORY, TRADITION,
AND TEXT
Uses of the Past in
Early Christianity

MEMORY, TRADITION, AND TEXT

Uses of the Past in
Early Christianity

Edited by
Alan Kirk and Tom Thatcher

Society of Biblical Literature
Atlanta

MEMORY, TRADITION, AND TEXT

Copyright © 2005 by the Society of Biblical Literature

Library of Congress Cataloging-in-Publication Data

Memory, tradition, and text : uses of the past in early Christianity / edited by Alan Kirk and Tom Thatcher.
     p. cm. — (Semeia studies ; no. 52)
    Includes bibliographical references.
    ISBN 9781589831490 (pbk. : alk. paper)
    1. Bible—Criticism, interpretation, etc. 2. Church history—Primitive and early church, ca. 30–600. 3. Christianity—Origin. 4. Memory. I. Kirk, Alan (Alan K.). II. Thatcher, Tom, 1967–. III. Series: Semeia studies ; no. 52.
    BR162.3 .M46 2005b
    270.1—dc22   2005010894

13 12 11 10 09 08 07 06 05   5 4 3 2 1

Printed in the United States of America on acid-free, recycled paper conforming to ANSI/NISO Z39.48-1992 (R1997) and ISO 9706:1994 standards for paper permanence.

CONTENTS

RESPONSES

ABBREVIATIONS

AB	Anchor Bible
Ant.	Josephus, *Jewish Antiquities*
Apoc. Ab.	*Apocalypse of Abraham*
AJS	*American Journal of Sociology*
ArBib	The Aramaic Bible
ARW	*Archiv für Religionswissenschaft*
Ascen. Isa.	*Mart. Ascen. Isa.* 6–11
ASR	*American Sociological Review*
AthR	*Anglican Theological Review*
BDF	Blass, F., A. Debrunner, and R. W. Funk. *A Greek Grammar of the New Testament and Other Early Christian Literature.* Chicago: University of Chicago Press, 1961.
BETL	Bibliotheca ephemeridum theologicarum lovaniensium
BEvTh	Beiträge zur evangelischen Theologie
Bib	*Biblica*
BibInt	*Biblical Interpretation*
BTB	*Biblical Theology Bulletin*
CBQ	*Catholic Biblical Quarterly*
CSMC	*Critical Studies in Mass Communication*
CWH	*Civil War History*
Deipn.	Athenaeus, *Deipnosophistae*
DJG	*Dictionary of Jesus and the Gospels.* Edited by J. B. Green and S. McKnight. Downers Grove, Ill.: InterVarsity Press, 1992.
DSS	Dead Sea Scrolls
EEJA	*East European Jewish Affairs*
1 En.	*1 Enoch*
2 En.	*2 Enoch*
3 En.	*3 Enoch*
ETL	*Ephemerides theologicae lovanienses*
ETR	*Etudes théologiques et religieuses*
ExpTim	*Expository Times*
FCNTECW	Feminist Companion to the New Testament and Early Christian Writings

Gos. Thom.	*Gospel of Thomas*
Hag.	*Hagigah*
HNT	Handbuch zum Neuen Testament
HTR	*Harvard Theological Review*
HUCA	*Hebrew Union College Annual*
Int	*Interpretation*
JAF	*Journal of American Folklore*
JAH	*Journal of American History*
JASP	*Journal of Abnormal and Social Psychology*
JBL	*Journal of Biblical Literature*
JC	*Journal of Communication*
JHS	*Journal of Hellenic Studies*
JR	*Journal of Religion*
JRAI	*Journal of the Royal Anthropological Institute*
JRS	*Journal of Roman Studies*
JSJ	*Journal for the Study of Judaism in the Persian, Hellenistic, and Roman Periods*
JSP	*Journal of the Study of the Pseudepigrapha*
JTSA	*Journal of Theology for Southern Africa*
Jub.	*Jubilees*
L.A.B.	*Liber antiquitatum biblicarum* (Pseudo–Philo)
L.A.E.	*Life of Adam and Eve*
LCL	Loeb Classic Library
Liv. Pro.	*Lives of the Prophets*
LXX	Septuagint
1 Macc	1 Maccabees
4 Macc	4 Maccabees
Mart. Ascen. Isa.	*Martyrdom and Ascension of Isaiah*
MTSR	*Method and Theory in the Study of Religion*
Nat.	*Naturalis historia*
Neot	*Neotestamentica*
NICNT	New International Commentary on the New Testament
NovTSup	Novum Testamentum Supplements
NRSV	New Revised Standard Version
NTS	*New Testament Studies*
Pesiq. Rab.	*Pesiqta Rabbati*
QS	*Qualitative Sociology*
RSV	Revised Standard Version
Šabb.	*Šabbat*
SBLDS	Society of Biblical Literature Dissertation Series
SBT	Studies in Biblical Theology
SE	*Studia evangelica*

Sir	Sirach/Ecclesiasticus
SNTSMS	Society for New Testament Studies Monograph Series
ST	*Sociological Theory*
Tg. Onq.	*Targum Onqelos*
Tg. Neb.	*Targum of the Prophets*
TU	Texte und Untersuchungen
VC	*Vigiliae christianae*
VCSup	Vigiliae christianae Supplement Series
Vesp.	*Vespae*
WBC	Word Biblical Commentary
WMANT	Wissenschaftliche Monographien zum Alten und Neuen Testament
ZNW	*Zeitschrift für die neutestamentliche Wissenschaft und die Kunde der älteren Kirche*

SOCIAL AND CULTURAL MEMORY

Alan Kirk

INTRODUCTION

The significance of memory for virtually all research domains relating to emergent Christianity has been gaining at best only slow recognition. Social memory studies are less than a century old, having originated in the writings of Maurice Halbwachs (1877–1945), a disciple of Emile Durkheim. A recent state-of-the-question essay shows their wide diffusion into the social sciences and humanities (Olick and Robbins: 105–40). Bibliographic surveys of the relevant literature reveal that the vast majority of focused studies in social memory have been published within the last two decades. In many ways, then, social memory is a new and emerging field. However, while memory studies have burgeoned in the humanities and social sciences, no comparable effect can be noticed in New Testament scholarship (Kelber 2002:58–59). That this myopia is a problem almost uniquely of New Testament scholarship is due in large part to the continuing influence of classical form criticism, which in the wake of the failure of the nineteenth-century quests for the historical Jesus reconstructed the category "tradition" in such a way as to marginalize memory. Corresponding to this inattention to memory is the absence of analytical approaches able to conceptualize the operations of memory and assess its effects. We will defer further discussion of the roots of these analytical deficits to the companion essay (Kirk and Thatcher) in this volume. For now, a glance at a key text for early Christian memory, the *anamnesis* passage in 1 Cor 11:23–26, shows memorializing practices of early Christian communities implicated in ritual and ethics, in issues of oral tradition and transmission, and accordingly in historical Jesus questions as well.

This essay will outline analytical approaches that are emerging within memory studies and introduce the work of leading theorists.[1]

---

1. "Social memory" is largely the term used in Anglo-American scholarship, while "cultural memory" predominates in German scholarship associated with Aleida and Jan

Contemporary memory studies are diffuse, spread across many disciplines, and so they resist simple systematization. Accordingly, the focus in what follows will be upon major elements from this diverse body of theory that appear to have direct implications for research problems in Christian origins, though for the most part the task of beginning to make those implications explicit has been left for the essays which follow in the volume.

Social Frameworks of Memory

Maurice Halbwachs showed that memory is in determinative respects a social phenomenon. "He was interested in memory as a social reality, as a function of the individual's membership in various social groups" (J. Assmann 1988:47–48). Traditionally, memory has been taken to be the most "purely individual" of human faculties, the "product of an isolated mind," a view, however, that "overemphasizes the isolation of the individual in social life" (Prager: 59–60). Memory is in fact "intersubjectively constituted"; it is inseparable from "the social world ... in which remembering occurs" (213–14). Halbwachs argued that memory is constituted by *social frameworks*, which is to say he focused on the way the structure and inner workings of specific groups shape memory for the people belonging to those groups. Social frameworks of memory are indispensable for the very possibility of remembering, for they give coherence and legibility to memories, arranging them within dominant cultural systems of meaning (Halbwachs 1992:38–43; 1980:54; Namer 1987:37, 56–57; J. Assmann 1992:35; 2000:114). Halbwachs identified and analyzed a number of these group frameworks. Here we shall limit ourselves to spelling out, first, how the patterns impressed upon *space* and *time* by the social configurations of discrete groups act as mnemonic frameworks, and, second, the role *communicative* practices of groups plays in giving substance to memory.

Spatio-temporal frameworks are crucial, for it is not possible to remember apart from memories fastening to definite places and times (Halbwachs 1980:134–40, 157; Namer 2000:50–51; Casey 1987:189). Time and locale act as economizing, organizing principles that condense and render into emblematic composites the memories associated with them (Casey 1987:72–75; Halbwachs 1992:61; 1980:70). Memory attaches to places and landscapes, and likewise survives, erodes, or perishes along

---

Assmann. Though clearly embodying differences of approach and focus, "social memory" and "cultural memory" analyses have a great deal in common, and this essay will seek to bring out a number of these points of intersection.

with them (Farmer: 101–3, 199–205; Jing: 170–73). The space within which memory is plotted is a *social* framework because space is conceptualized, organized, and shaped by the group inhabiting it (Halbwachs 1980:156–57; Fentress and Wickham: 80; Namer 2000:230; Gillis 1994a:6). The same holds true of the framework of time. Calendar organizes duration, and so it is the essential scaffolding both for situating and reconstituting memories. However, there are as many calendars as there are groups. A community organizes its calendar in accordance with group-specific commemorative concerns and activities, and so freights it with religious, political, and social meanings (Halbwachs 1980:88–89, 111–12; see also Burkert: 225–26). In villages the rhythms and recurrences of the agricultural cycle (marked calendrically), bisected by the ritually marked biographical trajectory of the life cycle, specific to individual households and their constituent members, act as accretion points and organizing grids for memory, while reciprocity networks among households connect individual household memory into the communal memory of a village (Zonabend: 142, 197–200; Halbwachs 1992:63–73). Calendrical innovations in a community may, on the one hand, be driven by memorializing concerns and, on the other, obliterate memories accumulated upon the obsolescent calendar. With time as with space, memory is enframed within the social and cultural dynamics of groups. The mnemonic effects of social frameworks, however, do not entail cryogenic preservation of discrete memories. Rather, "all memory transmutes experience, distils the past rather than simply reflecting it" (Lowenthal 1985:204).

Communication is essential for the formation of memory. Memory emerges in coherent, durable form to the extent remembrances find articulation and reinforcement in communicative interaction within a group, and conversely, a person's remembrances fade to the extent they are not taken up in the groups with which he or she is affiliated (e.g., Halbwachs 1992:173). It is through communicative discourse that otherwise ephemeral, disconnected remembrances are given connection, stability, and coherence (Halbwachs 1992:53). Gérard Namer refers to this as "a *sociability of speech* [his emphasis] that permits the discontinuities of remembering [*souvenir*] to be woven into a living memory [*mémoire vécue*]" (1987:142–43). Concentration camp survivors (by way of a diagnostic example) constructed a coherent memory of their experiences, so horrible as to be *incommunicables*, only through the formation of survivor groups. In these groups was forged the collective discourse that integrated fragmented, individualized remembrances into a coherent, communicable memory of the camps (Namer 1987:140–57). Articulation of memories through discourse in a community is simultaneously the urgent articulation of the meaning of those memories, which if left in fragmentary form would be at best ambiguous as regards their significance

(Namer 1987:154–55; Fentress and Wickham: 73). Roy Rosenzweig and David Thelen in a major survey of popular uses of memory report of their respondents that "with individuals they trusted ... they probed experiences and constructed the traditions they wanted to sustain. In these relationships they ... shaped and reshaped memories into trajectories ... and generally created the perceptual world they wanted to inhabit" (196). On the basis of her fieldwork in Hutu refugee camps in Tanzania, Liisa Malkki characterizes this face-to-face discussion of remembrances as "an intensively signifying context," whose effect is to weave memory into semantically dense narrative patterns (140).

MEMORY AND COLLECTIVE IDENTITY

"Memory is *embedded* ... the rememberer remembers in a contemporary world, peopled by others who collectively contribute to the construction of memory and help determine the importance that the past holds for an individual in the present" (Prager: 70–71). For its part, a community bears a complex of memories constitutive of its very existence (Olick 1999a:342). Accordingly, "genuine communities are communities of memory that constantly tell and retell their constitutive memories" (344; also E. Zerubavel 1996:289; Coser: 22; Schwartz 1998b:67; Zonabend: 203). Individuals come to participate in these memories by virtue of their incorporation into the group, a process Eviatar Zerubavel describes as the "existential fusion of our own personal biography with the history of the groups or communities to which we belong" (1996:290; see also Halbwachs 1980:51–53, 68; Schwartz 2000:294; Shils: 51, 212; Lowenthal 1985:196–97; Rosenzweig and Thelen: 198; Jing: 78–79). Indeed, "familiarizing new members with its past is an important part of a community's effort to incorporate them" (E. Zerubavel 1996:290; see also Schudson 1989:111; J. Assmann 2000:108). Ritual and other commemorative activities bring individuals into vital connection with that memory and its associated norms (J. Assmann 1992:16; 2000:22–23). The locus of the collective memory is the memory of individuals whose identity is bound up in the group (Assmann and Assmann 1988:27; J. Assmann 2000:19). "Memory is produced by an individual, but it is always produced in relation to the larger interpersonal and cultural world in which that individual lives" (Prager: 70).

Individual identity is "constituted by a train of events and experiences" (Schudson 1989:111), constantly being linked together in meaningful patterns by the work of memory (Casey 1987:290; Lowenthal 1985:41, 197; Olick and Robbins: 133–34; Prager: 91, 123–25; Shils: 50). This process never reaches stasis; rather, it is a matter of constantly correlating past, present, and the anticipated future to achieve a sense of personal coherence and continuity. Social memory exercises a role analogous to that played by individual memory: "Social memory defines a group, giving it a sense of its past and defining its aspirations for the future" (Fentress and Wickham: 25; see also Lowenthal 1985:198; J. Assmann 1992:89; Halbwachs 1992:83; 1980:126; Rosenzweig and Thelen: 172).

A community *marks* certain elements of its past as being of constitutive significance. Both identity and continuity, in fact the very survival of a community, depend upon its constant revitalization of these memories (J. Assmann 1992:30, 132–33; Schwartz 1998b:67). These are memories of the community's origins—"the event that marks the group's emergence as an independent social entity"—and other landmark events in its history (Y. Zerubavel 1995:4–7; see also Zonabend: x; Rosenzweig and Thelen: 172). These memories are shaped into a community's "master commemorative narrative"; moreover, through recitation of its master narrative a group continually reconstitutes itself as a coherent community, and as it moves forward through its history it aligns its fresh experiences with this master narrative, as well as vice versa (Y. Zerubavel 1995:7).

COMMUNICATIVE MEMORY AND CULTURAL MEMORY

We can better grasp dynamics of social memory by focusing on emergent communities still close to their origins. Jan Assmann uses the term "communicative memory" (*kommunikative Gedächtnis*) for this period, characterized as it is by face-to-face circulation of foundational memories (1992:50–56). These memories are biographically vested in those who experienced originating events; it is the time of "eyewitness and living memory" (J. Assmann 1992:32; 2000:88). Lowenthal points out that the period after the American Revolutionary War was characterized by "the prolonged survival of the actual fathers, living memorials to their own splendid deeds for half a century beyond the Revolution" (Lowenthal 1985:118). The outer limit of "communicative memory" is the passing of those able to claim living contact with the original generation, hence three to four generations, that is, eighty to one hundred years (J. Assmann 1992:56; 1995b:127; 2000:37–38). Bodnar uses the term "vernacular memory" for this phenomenon and observes that "much of the power of vernacular memory [is] derived from the lived or shared experiences of small groups.... vernacular interests [lose] intensity with the death and demise of individuals who participated in historic events" (1992:247).

Thus, communicative memory cannot sustain group-constitutive remembrances beyond the three to four generations able to claim living contact with the generation of origins (J. Assmann 1992:50). Assmann argues that the limitations of communicative memory force themselves upon an emergent community as a *crisis of memory* at approximately the forty-year threshold, the point at which it becomes apparent that the cohort of living carriers of memory is disappearing (1992:11; 2000:29; also Farmer: 197–213). It is at this threshold that the community, if it is not itself to dissolve along with its memory, must turn toward more enduring media capable of carrying memory in a vital manner across generations, that is, toward forms of "cultural memory" (*kulturelle Gedächtnis*) (J. Assmann 1992:218–21; 2000:53–54), though lineaments of such forms may begin to appear even during the high period of communicative memory (Farmer: 100–123).[2] "If we conceive of the typical three-generation time framework of communicative memory as a synchronic space of memory, then cultural memory forms a diachronic axis, by virtue of tradition which extends far into the past" (J. Assmann 2000:30).[3] Assmann isolates this phenomenon—transition from communicative to cultural memory—to secure an analytical standpoint from which he can gain a broad perspective upon the dynamics of culture, viewed as the constellation of the "means of collective mnemo-technique" (1992:218; 1995b:129; 2000:117).

Writing is "an extraordinarily efficient medium of symbolic objectification" (J. Assmann 2000:54). In societies with scribal technology, writing takes on particular importance in the event of a "breakdown in tradition" (*Traditionsbruch*). For emergent groups, this refers to the point of serious breakdown of communicative memory. Analogously, at the level of long-established societies, it indicates crisis times when historical disruptions and changes suddenly problematize the immanent, organic connections of a society with its past, as well as the smooth functioning of usual forms (including oral) of transmission. In such cases a society is confronted with loss of connection to memory and so turns more intensively to writing as a means of stabilizing group memory, of working out connections to the past in the midst of drastically altered circumstances (J. Assmann 2000:87–88; 1992:165).

---

2. A case in point is the formation of "master commemorative narratives," which on the one hand are forged in group communicative contexts, and on the other operate as durable cultural artifacts.

3. Jan Assmann expressly draws here upon Aleida Assmann's *Zeit und Tradition: Kulturelle Strategien der Dauer* (Köln: Böulau, 1999).

COMMEMORATION

Discussion of the artifactual forms of cultural memory leads on to commemoration. Viable communities are at pains to commemorate their pasts. Commemoration, in Savage's apt characterization, is the "effort to fix the meaning and purpose ... [of crucial memories] in an enduring form" (127). Commemoration renders constitutive memories into durable forms; it creates what Namer calls "the material basis of memory" (2000:157). In public monuments, for example, "the very hardness and hardiness of granite or marble" evidences the concern to fix and make constantly available constitutive memories (Casey 1987:227). Commemoration is a culture-formative impulse that ramifies into a wide range of artifacts, commemorative narratives, and ritual practices (Y. Zerubavel 1995:5; J. Assmann 2000:19–20; 1995b:130–31; Casey 1987:218). These densely sedimentize memory into various material and visible formats that function to make the past immanent in the present (Savage: 132; J. Assmann 2000:19; Casey: 218-19, 273; Farmer: 123). Commemorative practice of all sorts attempts to counteract the danger of rupture, the possibility of a fatal disconnect between a community and its past, the loss of memory that spells unraveling of identity in the present and future. It seeks to bridge the problematic, ever-widening gap that opens up between formative events and a community's ongoing historical existence (J. Assmann 1988:55; Coser: 25; Casey 1987:224–25, 237; Yerushalmi 1982:94; Connerton: 70). As a "making-present of the founding past" commemoration aims to ensure the continued vitality of collective memory. It "has the goal of rendering visible and stabilizing collective identity by presenting it in symbolic and dramatic form" (J. Assmann 2000:28).

Remembering together common *commemoranda*, present in mediating artifacts and practices, serves also to incorporate new members through communication of a group's constitutive memories and socialization into the corollary norms—what Assmann refers to as the "formative and normative" dimensions of cultural memory (2000:20; see also Schwartz 2000:10; Duchesne-Guillemin: 19; Georgoudi: 89; Casey: 247–51; Warner: 279, 305–6; Rosenzweig and Thelen: 45). In other words, the past is exemplary for the group that commemorates it. Schwartz states that "commemoration lifts from an ordinary historical sequence those extraordinary events which embody our deepest and most fundamental values" (Schwartz 1982:377). This in turn means that commemoration has a mobilizing effect, or stated differently, is oriented toward the future as well as the past (Namer 1987:211; Casey 1987:256; Duchesne-Guillemin: 13).

At its core commemoration is a hermeneutical activity: to return to Savage's definition, it is the "effort *to fix the meaning and purpose*" of the past (emphasis added; see also Farmer: 78). Commemoration picks up "bedrock events experienced with powerful immediacy" but whose meaning and significance must be discerned, precisely through commemorative activities (Rosenzweig and Thelen: 67). This entails, though, that "commemoration is a way of forming its object in the process of representing it" (Schwartz 2000:306). By the same token, commemoration shapes memory, for a community impresses its present identity upon its "collective re-presentations" of its past (Burke: 101). To adapt Warner's characterization, in commemoration a community states symbolically what it believes and wants itself to be (Warner: 107; see also J. Assmann 1988:55–56). Social tensions erupt in struggles over defining and interpreting a salient past, which is to say that "commemorative efforts are often punctuated as much by conflict as consensus" (Farmer: 4; see also Peri: 121).

Commemorative ritual sustains memory by reenacting a community's "master narrative," itself the product of commemorative impulses (Connerton: 70; Casey 1987:224–25). Farmer notes in the case of the Oradour-sur-Glane massacre by the S.S. that "the events ... had to be removed from their historical context and dramatized, visually and in narrative, to be rendered suitable for telling the archetypal story of innocence and victimization" (Farmer: 55). Translation into ritual transfigures the way salient events are represented. Meaning and significance are distilled out and concentrated into sacralized, highly symbolic words, gestures, and objects (Halbwachs 1992:116). Historical detail recedes to the minimum required to support the symbolic appropriation, with this remainder conformed to the tight structure of the ritual (Yerushalmi 1982:40), and with historical recitation itself coming to be affected by the contours of the ritual. A complex history is thereby precipitated out into a stable ritual artifact, bearer of dense symbolic meaning, with enormous capacity to perdure in multiple enactments through time (Halbwachs 1992:116; Yerushalmi 1982:40, 51–52). In the creation of a commemorative calendar events deemed memorable are extracted from their historical context and replotted within a cyclical commemorative sequence that foregrounds the symbolic significance these events bear for the identity of the community. Calendrical transposition reflects the way group-formative events have come to be arranged within the master commemorative narrative, now traversed cyclically throughout the course of the year (Y. Zerubavel 1995:218–19). "Historical time is thus transformed into commemorative time" (Y. Zerubavel 1995:225; see also Yerushalmi 1982:11, 41–42; Valensi: 286).

The mnemonic effect of ritual resides not just in its concentration of meaning in material signs and gestures that stimulate recollection, but also in its incorporation of the kinetic, emotional, and sensory capacities

of the bodies of participants into the ritualized act of remembering
(J. Assmann 2000:21). The community is literally incorporated—as it
were, fused—with the constitutive past during the time frame of the cer-
emonialized action through participation in its re-presentations.
Simultaneously the community as "conjoined participants acting
together" is dramatically reconstituted and manifests its identity and solidarity (Casey: 227, 253–54; also J. Assmann, 1992:21, 143; Zerubavel
1996:294; Warner: 432).

"Memory flowed [in Judaism] . . . through two channels: ritual and
recital" (Yerushalmi 1982:11). Both along with and independent of rituals and material artifacts groups make use of the verbal arts, oral or
written, for commemorative purposes. Commemorative ritual draws the
community together on a regular basis, which in turn supplies the context for utterance of group memory through genres appropriate to a
given setting (Assmann and Assmann 1983:274; Casey: 235; Warner:
114–16). Verbal elements may occur either correlated with the choreog-
raphy of ritual, or else in genres less directly implicated in ritual
enactment itself but nevertheless appropriate to the commemorative,
incorporative objectives of the ritual setting. One example is the "*logos
épitaphaios*," a genre that emerged in fourth-century B.C.E. Greece "to
commemorate combatants who had died in battle and which was pronounced at their tombs in the course of public funerals" (Simondon: 99).
Instruction, drawing upon the normative elements of the salient past,
will be an essential dimension of rituals that initiate new members into a
community (Ben Yehuda: 152–53).

It is only a step to the emergence of texts themselves as autonomous
commemorative artifacts (Simondon: 105). Oral tradition has enormous
tenacity, but written texts possess material ingrediency that enables diffusion and storage if not permanency and are accordingly less
dependent upon oral ritual settings for their transmission, though they
may initially have been produced for such settings (Casey 1987:227;
Shils: 91). Connerton points out that "whatever is written, and more
generally whatever is inscribed, demonstrates, by the fact of being
inscribed, a will to be remembered " (Connerton: 102; also Assmann
and Assmann 1988:48). Texts may be a response to the crisis of memory
arising in the wake of a *Traditionsbruch* as described by Assmann, which
leads to the articulation of memory in durable cultural artifacts and
practices (1992:218–21). Biographical writing and historiography are
obvious cases, but a community "arranges its social memory into different genres" (Fentress and Wickham: 78, 162–63; also Valensi; Simondon:
105; Namer 1987:157– 58), and nonhistory genres may in fact be suf-
fused with memory (Yerushalmi 1982:14–15, 31, 45–46). We see
confirmed Halbwachs's point that memory takes coherent shape to the

extent that it finds articulation in typical social practices and aligned genres of discourse.

MEMORY AS CONSTRUCTION

That memory is *constructive* activity should now be clear, but it needs emphasis to counter what Casey labels the "passivist" model for memory, namely, "the view that all memories of necessity repeat the past in a strictly replicative manner [and that] the contribution of the remembering subject ... is nugatory" (1987:269). We have already seen that memories are products of coherence-bestowing activities such as conceptualization, schematization, and interpretive articulation in shared forms of discourse. Memory "acts to organize what might otherwise be a mere assemblage of contingently connected events" (291). Memory formations, however, do not thereby assume static, immobile forms. The activity of memory in articulating the past is dynamic, unceasing, *because it is wired into the ever-shifting present.* The remembering subject, from his or her situatedness in the present, interacts with a formative past to relate it meaningfully to contemporary exigencies and to the ongoing project of negotiating continuity and change in personal identity (292; Prager: 11–12, 214–15; Lowenthal 1985:206; Gillis 1994a:3; Zelizer: 218; Rosenzweig and Thelen: 196). In Prager's words, "it becomes nearly impossible to parse out memories of the past from the categories of experience available in the present" (5). Precisely the same holds true for collective memory of communities, where "to remember is to place a part of the past in the service of the needs and conceptions of the present" (Schwartz 1982:374). Halbwachs argued that to remember is not to *retrouver*, but to *reconstruire*, to align the image of the past with present social realities (1992:40).[4] A group will conform its past to shifts in its present realities, group morphology, and moral self-conceptions (Namer 1987:53; Prager: 82). Differential attribution of meaning to the past, a basic feature of memory, proceeds from and serves the conditions of the present. Present social realities and "les pensées dominantes de la société" act therefore as *semantic* frames of memory (J. Assmann 1995a:366; Halbwachs 1992:183; Handler and Linnekin: 288).

We have seen that a community situates its past, self-constitutively, in its present. Frameworks of memory are current social and ideological

---

4. "Les cadres collectifs de la mémoire ... sont ... les instruments dont la mémoire collective se sert pour recomposer une image du passé qui s'accorde à chaque époque avec les pensées dominantes de la société" (cited from Namer 1987:34).

structures through which the past is retrieved and interpreted in a community's incessant activity of self-constitution. Current needs and preoccupations determine what elements of a community's past are awarded prominence, that is, commemorated, or, conversely, are "forgotten" in the unceasing construction of the past that is a community's social memory. The present itself is hardly static; memory frameworks are thus themselves constantly subject to renovation, gradual or radical, as external and internal factors in the group's existence change. Accordingly, the way a community "remembers" and "forgets" its past changes as well (Halbwachs 1992:114–15, 123–24, 172–73, 188–89; Namer 1987:41, 74–75; see also Fentress and Wickham: 73; Lowenthal 1985:362; J. Assmann 1992:224). Research in social memory "shows how beliefs about the past are shaped by the circumstances and problems of current society and how different elements of the past become more or less relevant as these circumstances and problems change. Memory thus becomes a social fact as it is made and remade to serve changing societal interests and needs" (Schwartz 1996a:909). Hence immutability in representation of the past is never achieved; rather, "the past is continually being reorganized by the constantly changing frames of reference of the ever-evolving present" (J. Assmann 1992:41–42). Stated differently, "a charismatic epoch is not a fixed entity which imposes itself on the present; it is a continuously evolving product of social definition" (Schwartz 1982:390). However, it is by constantly bringing its salient past into alignment with its open-ended series of "presents" that a community maintains continuity of identity across time, a sense of always being vitally connected to its past (J. Assmann 1992:40, 88; Namer 1987:224). In some cases we see the past rendered virtually isomorphic with a community's present social perspectives. Joan of Arc, for example, was viewed as an "unfortunate idiot" by Voltaire, by nineteenth-century French republicanism as prefiguring "the heroic rising of the Third Estate," and by French socialists as a protoproletarian "born into the poorest class of society," while Vichy France commemorated Joan's resistance to the English (see Winock). In John Thompson's words, traditions can "become increasingly remote from their contexts of origin and increasingly interwoven with symbolic contents derived from the new circumstances in which they are re-enacted" (103).

POLITICS OF MEMORY

The malleability of memory requires us to be more specific about the nature of the very powerful forces at work in the present to shape particular versions of the past. The past is appropriated to *legitimize* particular sociopolitical goals and ideologies and to *mobilize* action in accord with these goals. Yael Zerubavel puts it bluntly: "The power of collective memory does not lie in its accurate, systematic, or sophisticated mapping of the past, but in establishing basic images that articulate and reinforce a particular ideological stance" (1995:8; also Connerton: 3; Lowenthal 1990:302; Bodnar 1992:134–37). Hence, "interpretations of the past ... are, in important respects, political acts" (Schwartz 2000:12). Zionist commemoration of ancient Jewish resistance movements such as the Zealots, for example, was aimed at legitimating the Zionist political program as well as activist countermodels for Jewish identity, while its breath-taking diminution of the exile to a point of virtually no magnitude signified its repudiation of the stereotypically passive, sighing Jew of the *Galut*. Zionist memory, in other words, was a matter of the "ideological classification of the past" (Y. Zerubavel 1995:32–33; also Ben Yehuda: 139).

A number of theorists go so far as to suggest that constructions of the past may in all important respects be understood as projections of the political struggles and ideological contests of the present. In this view, "public memory speaks primarily about the structure of power in society" (Bodnar 1992:15). Memory is shaped—and contested—by moral entrepreneurs, identified with particular interests, focused in a programmatic fashion upon shaping values and maintaining or achieving power (Gero and Root: 19). The task this kind of analysis sets itself is to deconstruct given versions of the past by exposing the ideological, hegemonic interests that inhere in them.

The ideological appropriation of the past becomes visible in commemorative activities and artifacts. As a hermeneutical act, commemoration attempts "to impose interpretations of the past, to shape memory" (Burke: 101), but from the perspective of the strong constructionist view, "the facts of history become symbolic products of present meanings" (Warner: 159). Halbwachs observed that monumental commemoration of constitutive Christian memories in the physical features of the Holy Land was always reflective of "the needs of the contemporary belief system" (1992:234). The same forces are influential in a community's creation of its master commemorative narrative—its "molding the past into certain types of symbolic texts"—that selectively assigns importance to certain parts of the past, while leaving others "unmarked" (Y. Zerubavel 1995:8, 216). This brings in its wake a corresponding set of commemorative projects that give these memories substance and visibility. The converse effect of this double movement, though, is to marginalize memories of groups allotted either no place or a negatively signed place in the master narrative (Savage: 143; Namer 2000:156; Mikolajczyk: 250; Michnic-Coren: 75).

The tendentious appropriation of the past by the social and political forces of the present has given Eric Hobsbawm and Terence Ranger's pungent coinage, "invention of tradition," particular salience in contemporary discussion. To say that tradition is invented is to claim that much if not most of what goes under the rubric of the venerable past, and thus authoritatively constitutive for the present, is in fact of recent origin and in many cases fabricated, either *de novo* or out of the detritus of the past, by hegemonic interests seeking legitimacy by appropriating the antique aura of "tradition" for new practices, structures, and values (Hobsbawm 5; also Halbwachs 1980:80). A society's continuity with its past, entailed in the notion of tradition, on this view is therefore "factitious" (Hobsbawm 2). In this vein Handler and Linnekin argue that "tradition" and "pastness" are symbolic entities constructed wholly in orientation to the present. Hence the pastness—genuine or spurious—of tradition is of little theoretical interest; the analysis of a given tradition is exhausted upon exposure of its social positioning and symbolic utilization in the present (285–86).

Though "invention of tradition" analysis and its close relative, the "radical social constructionist" (Schudson 1992:54–55) view of social memory, are to be sure indispensable tools for assessing appeals to the past, questions have been raised about whether they can be generalized into paradigmatic models for tradition and memory. Handler and Linnekin, representatives of this view, indiscriminately use with respect to the past the terms "invention," "reinvention," "reinterpretation," "interpretation," and "reconstruction" as though self-evidently conceptual equivalents, when in fact these terms pose a number of complex questions about the relation of past to present. Their discounting the importance of tracing the trajectory of the Quebecois and Hawaiian traditions they analyze backward into the past, focusing instead on the transformation of these traditions for contemporary nationalistic purposes, then concluding that tradition can be understood in all important respects as a symbolic creation of the present, is a textbook case of circular reasoning. It has been suggested that the radical constructionist approach at times seems less argued for than it is taken as an axiomatic point of departure. What have the appearance of corroborating results are products of a theoretical perspective fixated on the synchronic factors of the present, and that *a priori* excludes reciprocal inquiry into the diachronic question, namely, how the depth of the past might inform, shape, support, not to say constrain the dispositions, interests, and actions of those situated in the present (Schwartz 1996a:910, 2000:ix). This tendency to locate all decisive causal variables in social life in the present may owe something to a theoretical orientation in which "attitudes [are] seen as epiphenomenal, as mere expressions of (or at the very least tools for) the more real—that is, *objective*—social structure" (Olick and Levy: 922).

MEMORY AS A SOCIAL FRAME

Schwartz argues that with their exclusive focus on *change*, radical constructionist theories of social memory have difficulties delivering a satisfactory account of how a society establishes the *continuity* indispensable to its cohesion and survival as it traverses time (2000:20; also Coser: 25–28; Connerton: 103). Constructionists would argue that the sense of continuity with the past is itself fabricated by the ideological and hegemonic interests that produce the constructed past (Handler and Linnekin: 286–87). Yael Zerubavel notes, however, that "invented tradition can be successful only as long as it passes as tradition" (1995:232). Hence this approach must assume that most members of society, save the elites, are incorporated into a false consciousness manifest in their naïve acceptance of a fabricated social memory, a view that if for no other reason falters on the fact that subordinated groups are demonstrably and robustly (if discreetly) capable of contesting elite constructions of the past and shaping alternatives (Schwartz 2000:204; 1998a:23; also Scott).

Accordingly we turn now to memory theories that—without falling back upon the indefensible view that "the past" refers to an objective something that exists apart from its perception and interpretation—take stock of the "presence of the past" in the midst of intensely constructive, ever-fluid, and open-ended social milieux. Strong constructionist theorists acknowledge that ideological interests work with debris from the past to fabricate their syntheses. So even in this modest respect the past supplies the materials and thus sets some limits and terms for its appropriation (Schudson 1989:107–8). But the past is not just "a limitless and plastic symbolic resource, infinitely susceptible to the whims of contemporary interest and the distortions of contemporary ideology" (Appadurai: 20). The fact that "no strict correspondence exists between the conditions of any era and the objects of its memory" suggests that the past cannot be reduced to a mythical projection of the present (Schwartz 2000:6, 297; see also Schudson 1992:218). "Tension, not easy compatibility, defines the relation between memory and [present] experience" (Schwartz 1996a:922). Moreover, "as the Holocaust makes evident" (Zelizer: 224)—a case that "levers us quickly back into a reality without quotation marks" (Wagner-Pacifici: 302; also Malkki: 239–40)— competing versions of the past are hardly to be placed on the same level, as though each is indifferently nothing more than a successful or less successful strategy for political advantage. Hegemonic memory falsifies, fabricates a past, whereas antihegemonic memory exposes this mendacity, and it is antihegemonic precisely because it utters a true past. "Secret graves in Yugoslavia could not be lit by private candles without dimming the bright light of socialist optimism" (Schwarz: 9), and "spontaneously erected vernacular memorials labeling the Katyn massacre of Polish army officers in 1940 a Russian atrocity are regularly replaced by official plaques designating the Germans as villains, only to surface elsewhere" (Lowenthal 1990:307; also Hayden: 167–84; Jing: 73–74, 168–71).

Despite its fluidity and contingency, the present is always emerging from its own past. A number of memory theorists, therefore, reverse the variables and explore ways in which the past affects the present. It is true that present identity is the perspective from which individuals—and groups—view and shape the past. But present identity configurations are always emerging from the variegated experiences of ever-deepening pasts. Fentress and Wickham note that "if Welsh miners remember past struggle so clearly, it is because they define themselves through it" (126; also Rosenzweig and Thelen: 66). It is this identity, understood as a diachronic process, that orients to the experiences of the present, and that encompasses the *pre*dispositions for the continual reassessment of its own past. Memory, in other words, is itself a social frame (Schwartz 1996a:908; 1995:266).

We might express this state of affairs as follows: the past, itself constellated by the work of social memory, provides the framework for cognition, organization, and interpretation of the experiences of the present. The salient past,[5] immanent in the narrative patterns in which it has become engrained in social memory, provides the cognitive and linguistic habits by which a group perceives, orients itself, and has its "being in the world" (Fentress and Wickham: 51; Connerton: 2; Hjärpe: 333–34; Schwartz 2000:225–30; Y. Zerubavel 1995:229; Schudson 1992:2; 1989:112; Casey 1987:284–85; Burke: 103; Rosenzweig and Thelen: 68). Master commemorative narratives that have achieved secure status in the cultural memory are not inert, museum-piece representations of the past; rather, they vitally shape perception and organization of reality. They are cognitive schemata, "nuclear scripts" for interpreting and processing streams of experience (Bonanno: 177–82; also Prager: 200–209; Malkki: 53, 105). It is precisely because of the orienting, stabilizing effect of memory that free, innovative action in the present becomes possible (Casey 1987:150–53). However, if the past is not inert, neither is it impermeable:

---

5. By "salient past" is meant the past as it has been marked by a community through the hermeneutical operations of commemoration.

present events and experiences have the capacity to affect decisively the configurations the salient past assumes in the cultural memory (Malkki: 241–42; Prager: 186–87).

"'Frame' ... is a shorthand reference to the way invocations of the past confer meaning on present experience" (Schwartz 1998a:1; also Zonabend: 2). Social memory makes available the moral and symbolic resources for making sense of the present through "keying" present experiences and predicaments to archetypal images and narrative representations of the commemorated past. These semiotic connections "define the meaning of present events by linking them to great and defining events of the past" (Schwartz 2000:232). Further, "frame images are in this sense pictorial counterparts of 'emplotment,' defining the meaning of problematic events by depicting them as episodes in a narrative that precedes and transcends them" (Schwartz 1998a:8; also Malkki: 107, 134–43). This would entail, in contrast to the extreme constructionist position, that *both* present social realities *and* the salient past are potent variables in these semiotic constructions constantly occurring in social memory. A traumatic past in particular projects decisive influence into the present, acting as what Michael Schudson calls a "pre-emptive metaphor," that is, "a past, traumatic experience so compelling that it forces itself as the frame for understanding new experiences" (1992:167). Olick and Levy draw attention to the effect of traumatic memory upon postwar Germany: "Powerful images of the Nazi past have shaped West Germany. Virtually every institutional arrangement and substantive policy is a response, in some sense, to Germany's memory of those fateful years" (921).

Medieval Jewish chronicles resorted to an archetypal pattern in the cultural memory—the binding of Isaac—to interpret the mass suicides in the eleventh-century Rhineland (Yerushalmi 1982:38–39). In many cases the archetypal past so dominates perception of the present that social memory makes the latter virtually isomorphic with features of the former (Fentress and Wickham: 201). Yerushalmi points out that "on the whole, medieval Jewish chronicles tend to assimilate events to old and established conceptual frameworks.... there is a pronounced tendency to subsume even major new events to familiar archetypes, for even the most terrible events are somehow less terrifying when viewed within old patterns rather than in their bewildering specificity" (1982:36). Fentress and Wickham cite the case of "the inhabitants of the coalfields of South Wales and Durham [who] have a very clear sense of the past as struggle.... The General Strike of 1926 is a common touchstone, and for many miners the strikes of 1972, 1974, and 1984–85 simply replayed the experiences of 1926, with the same *dramatis personae* in each: the community, the employers, and the police" (115–16). Events of the 1979 Islamic Revolution in Iran were assimilated in a recapitulative manner to the archetypal Shiite narrative of the martyrdom of Husayn, Muhammad's grandson, at Karbala in 680 C.E., at the hand of Yazid, an evil Umayyad caliph (Hjärpe: 335–36). It is the reactualization of memory, of "master narratives," in commemorative rituals and artifacts that habituates this salient past and gives it power to affect a community's perceptions of its experiences (Hjärpe: 334; Yerushalmi 1982:49; Valensi: 298).

An important aspect of the past's frameworking function is its capacity to mobilize action in the present (Schudson 1989:111, 1992:3; J. Assmann 1992:296; Rosenzweig and Thelen: 75). Through incorporative activities and artifacts of commemoration the salient past is existentially sedimentized into the identities of persons who are simultaneously actors in the present (Yerushalmi 1982:44). Memorialization shapes dispositions and norms for action, in terms of both possibility and constraint (Olick and Levy: 923–25; Fentress and Wickham: 51). "Collective memory ... shapes reality by providing people with a program in terms of which their present lines of conduct can be formulated and enacted" (Schwartz 2000:18; see also Malkki: 43). Constitutive events of origin, as well as memorialized landmark events in a group's subsequent history, possess an exemplary, monitory character that enables them to exert this kind of influence (Schudson 1989:111; Rosenzweig and Thelen: 174; Shils: 206).

Assmann points to the "Mythomotorik" effect of "founding narratives," meaning that constitutive memories are dynamos that drive a society's social and cultural development (1992:168–69, 296). Commemorations of significant pasts are able to generate political programs and mobilize action accordingly (Schudson 1992:217; Hjärpe: 334; Schwartz 2000:243–44). Subjugated groups cultivate memories of ideal pasts characterized by freedom, memories that have the capacity to inspire resistance to oppressive conditions. Theissen and Assmann designate these "kontrapräsentische" uses of memory (Theissen: 174–75; J. Assmann 1992:72–80, 294–97; also Fentress and Wickham: 108–9; Schwartz 1996a:924). Olick and Levy note that "claim-making by actors in political contexts is conditioned by significant pasts as well as by meaningful presents; it is always path-dependent, though not necessarily in obvious ways. This point calls our attention to historical events of definitive importance, to how broad parameters are fixed at particular moments, and to how those moments manifest themselves or are invoked differently in subsequent contexts" (923).

NORMATIVE DIMENSIONS OF SOCIAL MEMORY

We have referred several times to the exemplary, normative force of a community's salient past. Halbwachs called attention to the fact that the memory of foundational persons and events bears the ethos distinctive to the group's identity: "But these memories ... consist not only of a series of individual images of the past. They are at the same time models, examples, and elements of teaching" (1992:59). In short, the social memory has an indelible ethical coloring; its images of archetypal persons and events embody a group's moral order (Schwartz and Miller: 96). Master commemorative narratives recast the past in "fundamentally moral terms"; they are "moral and cosmological ordering stories" (Malkki: 54).[6] The images that exist in the social memory are thus a mnemonic of the group-defining norms thereby embodied (Halbwachs 1992:59; Namer 1987:58; J. Assmann 1992:16–17; 2000:127– 28). It is by virtue of its normativity that the past makes programmatic, urgent moral claims upon a community (J. Assmann 1992:76–80). The salient past, with its corollary virtues, is a "model for society," which is to say that it "shap[es] the moral character [of its members] and orient[s] the way they interpret and engage the world" (Schwartz 2000:xi, 304). The normative critical mass of the past is central to the "mythomotorik" effect of the cultural memory—energizing and driving a community's continual articulation of itself along the lines of its constitutive norms, in the midst of changing realities and in the face of emerging crises (J. Assmann 1992:79–80, 168–69). But this is hardly uni-directional. Present social realities drive the enterprise of seeking moral guidance and legitimacy from the salient past. Political and social movements must claim authorization from the past; they must find and, as necessary, conform the normative profile of past events to current ideological and identity-formation goals (Y. Zerubavel 1995:68; Ben Yehuda: 264–65). Exploitation of the moral resources of the past is a project of moral entrepreneurship, though hardly, as we have seen, an unconstrained one.

Halbwachs went so far as to suggest that the social memory "retains only those events that are of a pedagogic character" (1992:223; also Fine: 1176). It is through inculcation of its distinctive norms that a community incorporates its members and forms, or as the case may be, transforms

---

6. "The narratives of the camp [Hutu] refugees were centrally concerned with the ordering and reordering of sociopolitical and moral categories; with the construction of a collective self in opposition and enmity against an 'other'; and ultimately, with good and evil. Thus, the mythico–historical narratives ingested events, processes, and relationships from the past and from the lived conditions of the present and transformed them within a fundamentally moral scheme of good and evil. These were moral ordering stories on a cosmological level. In the mythico–history, all protagonists are categorical, and they are attributed essential, constitutive characteristics, much as in other classifying schemes" (Malkki: 244).

their identities (J. Assmann 2000:17; also Y. Zerubavel 1994:111; 1995:28, 44; Ben Yehuda: 238–39). The normative dimension of social memory is, accordingly, brought to bear in a community's instructional *Sitze im Leben*, distilled into various commemorative artifacts—the paraenetic genres and media appropriate to the socialization goals of those settings (Schwartz 2000:249; Y. Zerubavel 1995: 138–42; Simondon: 102–4; J. Assmann 1992:141–42; 2000:127).

Hence a synergistic connection exists between *commemorative* and *instructional* activities. Ceremonial holidays frequently are instituted precisely for purposes of inculcating values viewed as inhering in the heroic persons and events commemorated, and to mobilize people to act in accordance with those values (Bodnar 1992:121, 153, 173; Y. Zerubavel 1995:139; Hjärpe: 340). Monuments may bear exhortative inscriptions making their moral lessons explicit, for example, ancient funerary epigrams calling attention to the virtues of the departed (Simondon: 100). Ritual, as discussed earlier, brings about a close identification of the participants with the *commemoranda*. Participants absorb at the deepest existential level of personal identity the normative elements that are immanent in the commemoration.

Deaths of significant persons call forth commemorative activities focused in a particularly intense way upon the norms and virtues these individuals embodied in life and in their death. Halbwachs noted that society "pronounces judgment on people while they are alive and on the day of their death" (1992:175; see also Rosenzweig and Thelen: 147–48). Martyrs, by definition heroic persons who have displayed steadfast commitment—to the death—to a set of emblematic virtues, attract intense cults of commemoration. The martyr's death itself is instrumental in establishing the urgent normative claims of the virtues he or she embodied and died exemplifying, and in mobilizing a social movement cohering around those norms. A community's ritualized activities commemorating martyrs, accordingly, become occasions not just for narrative recitations of the martyr's life and death, but also for instructional activities aimed at inculcating and securing commitment to those emblematic norms (see Y. Zerubavel 1995:148, also 28–29, 41, 91, 108; Connerton: 43; Warner: 265–68). Recitational and instructional impulses that converge around cults of commemoration find expression in respectively differentiated genres. Assmann captures this phenomenon with his rubric *Formative* and *Normative Texte. Formative* texts refer to narrative genres of constitutive histories and myths, while *Normative* refer to instructional genres calibrated to inculcate the cognate norms (2000:53, 127; 1992:141–42; 1995b:132).

MEMORY AND CULTURE

Commemorative activities are central to formation of culture, the latter understood as "an organization of symbolic patterns on which people rely to make sense of their experience" (Schwartz 1996a:908–9, referencing Clifford Geertz). Social memory fashions a "Symbolsystem," which is to say that in commemorated persons, commemorative narratives, and related artifacts and practices, it objectifies a community's archetypal, axiomatic meanings and values (J. Assmann 1992:58–59, 139–40; Schwartz 2000:17–18, 252; Farmer: 78–83). Through commemorative transposition (we might say apotheosis) social memory elevates to symbolic, culture-constitutive status marked elements of a community's past. The "symbolische Figuren" of culture are in effect "*Erinnerungsfiguren*" (memory configurations) (J. Assmann 1992:52, 168; also Assmann and Assmann 1983:266–67; Schwartz 2000:x–xi; 1998a:25–26; Olick 1999b:400; Fentress and Wickham: 59; Warner: 4; Halbwachs 1992:188–89). Lincoln and Washington, for example, "have become national symbols which embody the values, virtues, and ideals of American democracy" (Warner: 268). What Zerubavel refers to as "master commemorative narrative" is a case of the transfiguration of the past into "certain kinds of symbolic texts" (Y. Zerubavel 1995:8–9, 216; see also Connerton: 42; J. Assmann 1992:52; Burke: 103–4). Rituals reenacting and recitations recounting these events, for example the Passover Seder, affect the entire stance of a culture (Yerushalmi 1982:44). These symbolic patterns are connected meaningfully to the experiences of the present through the unceasing operations of "framing" and "keying" discussed above (Schwartz 1996a:910–11).

The semiotizing dynamic of memory is energized by the present realities and crises of the commemorating community. As deep reservoirs of meaning (Connerton: 56), commemorative symbols seem inexhaustibly responsive hermeneutically to complexity and change in a community's social realities (Schwartz 1996b). The revisionist and socialist camps within early Zionism, for example, debated fiercely whether the martyrdom of the settler Trumpeldor authorized the sword or the plough, armed resistance or settlement and agriculture, as a program for national revitalization, each group excavating the narrative to find support for its program, each laying claim to the image of Trumpeldor. "It was not the historical event per se, but rather the encoding of its symbolic meaning, that provided fuel to this controversy" (Y. Zerubavel 1995:157; see also Peri: 113–14, on Yitzak Rabin).

It is this hermeneutical responsiveness of commemorative symbols that gives rise to the sentiment that salient pasts are little more than ideological projections of the present. However, commemorative projects are dependent upon the core realities they take up, though the nature of this dependence from case to case cannot be prescribed ahead of time. Robin Wagner-Pacifici points out that it is "ordering" persons and events, "fraught with conflict and significance" on the larger social scale, that is, crisis persons and events that have broken into "'normal time' by stopping the flow of the everyday," that ignite memorializing activities (301–9). Persons and events of this sort form the "adamantine core" of commemorative interpretation, generating and shaping the interpretations that can be produced upon them across time (Schwartz 2000:309; 1995:270; 1990:103–4; 1982:396; Casey 1987:286; Peri: 113). As the history of the memory of Confucius shows, these salient persons and events are to a significant extent resistant to whimsical make-overs into the image of shifting ideological forces (Zhang and Schwartz: 1997). Wagner-Pacifici argues that the operations of social memory may be understood as the interaction among three factors: "the social realities of empirical events, the cultural realities of modes of generic encodings, and the political and aesthetic realities of the work of translators," the latter being those who effect the transformation of empirical realities into the various forms of cultural memory (Wagner-Pacifici: 308–9). Schwartz points out that "Lincoln was a credible model for the [Progressive] era because his life, as it was imagined, was rooted in his life as it was actually lived" (2000: 174, 254).[7] Further, the complexity of the *commemorandum* itself is a factor in the emergence of multiple meanings in commemoration. "Lincoln himself was ambiguous, complex, and many-sided, and ... different communities, according to their experiences and their interests, saw one side more clearly than others" (Schwartz 2000:223; see also Connerton: 55–57). In short: "the real Lincoln could not determine, but did limit, the range and quality of his representations" (Schwartz 2000:187; also 1996a:922; 1990:104; Ben Yehuda: 278–306).

Social memory, therefore, to borrow Arjun Appadurai's phrase, is the "symbolic negotiation between 'ritual' pasts and the contingencies of the present" (218; also Valensi: 291). Olick and Levy express this principle as follows: "Collective memory *is* this negotiation, rather than pure constraint by, or contemporary strategic manipulation of, the past.... The relationship between remembered pasts and constructed presents is one of perpetual but differentiated constraint and renegotiation over time, rather than pure strategic invention in the present or fidelity to (or inability to escape from) a monolithic legacy" (934; also Prager: 186–87). Schwartz

---

7. Casey notes that memory "is enmeshed in its origins even when it seems to be functioning independently of them" (1987:280).

uses the imagery of "mirror" and "lamp" to encompass the work of social memory: "As a model *of* society, collective memory reflects past events in terms of the needs, interests, fears, and aspirations of the present. As a model *for* society, collective memory ... embodies a *template* that organizes and animates behavior and a *frame* within which people locate and find meaning for their present experience" (2000:18). Moreover,

> the distinction between memory as a "model of" and "model for" society is an analytic, not empirical distinction; both aspects of it are realized in every act of remembrance. Memories must express current problems before they can program ways to deal with them. We cannot be oriented by a past in which we fail to see ourselves. On the other hand, it is memory's programmatic relevance that makes its expressive function significant: We have no reason to look for ourselves in a past that does not already orient our lives. Still, that analytic distinction is important because it underscores memory's intrinsic dualism. In its reflective (model *of*) aspect, memory is an expressive symbol—a language, as it were, for articulating present predicaments; in its second (model *for*) aspect, memory is an orienting symbol—a map that gets us through these predicaments by relating where we are to where we have been. (Schwartz 1996a:910)

Jeffrey Olick points out that this interaction between the salient past and the present stands in vital, though not necessarily slavish, relation to the ever-lengthening tradition, we might say regress, of prior hermeneutical transactions of this nature under differing circumstances, that is, the community's "history of representations over time.... [I]mages of the past depend not only on the relationship between past and present but also on the accumulation of previous such relationships and their ongoing constitution and reconstitution" (Olick 1999b:382). Thus the past, both generating and absorbed into resilient commemorative images, narratives, rituals, and texts, flows with its own *energeia* into the ongoing, creative formation of the life of the community.

Memory, Gospel Traditions, and Early Christian Texts

Memory theory establishes multiple points of departure for fresh examination of a wide range of research problems in the field of New Testament studies and Christian origins. The essays in this volume each follow one or more of these trajectories of exploration, and taken in aggregate they outline a research agenda for memory-oriented analysis of the beginnings of Christianity and its literature.

In "Jesus Tradition as Social Memory," Tom Thatcher and I suggest that memory theory entails a reassessment of the models of tradition inherited from the classical form critics and still influential in Gospels research. This reassessment, in turn, has significant historiographical implications for reconstructions of Christian origins and for historical Jesus research. Thatcher's essay, "Why John Wrote a Gospel," further applies memory theory to the dynamics of tradition in order to describe the transition from oral tradition to written Gospels, arguing that the Fourth Gospel was written to exploit the inherent changes in the shift from group memory to written history book. By moving from fluid memory to written narrative, Thatcher argues, John could freeze one particular image of Jesus and appeal to the mystique of written documents to add authority to that presentation. Holly Hearon's "The Story of 'the Woman Who Anointed Jesus' as Social Memory" likewise engages the interface between memory and tradition, exploring through this case study how social memory dynamics help account for transformations within Jesus traditions.

Two essays in this volume explore the intersection of social memory and social identity. Philip Esler's "Collective Memory and Hebrews 11" approaches Heb 11 as an attempt to enhance group identity by formulating a new collective memory that draws upon, yet at the same time contests, Israelite tradition. Esler argues that the author succeeds in substantially detextualizing the Israelite works he cites as a way of detaching them from Israel and applying them to the Christ-movement, a strategy aided by the fact that the ambient social context was largely oral. In a similar vein, Antoinette Wire's contribution, "Early Jewish Birth Prophecy Stories and Women's Social Memory," examines how early Jewish women grounded their social identity by bringing their important stories into essential connection with birth prophecy stories, a narrative pattern deeply embedded in the cultural memory of early Judaism. Wire argues that the circle of women at birth became a "framework of memory" both for recalling birth prophecies fulfilled by great liberators of the past and for shaping prophecies of liberators now being born. Wire thus brings into clear view the *future*-oriented, programmatic functions of memory.

Arthur Dewey, in his essay "The Locus for Death," initiates a long overdue exploration of the possible relevance of the *ars memoriae*, in this case, to the formation of the Passion Narrative, and just as significantly opens up the all-important question of how the social dynamics of memory may come to be manifested in the rhetorical deployment of the technical "art of memory." Ritual, viewed as a commemorative practice that functions to incorporate others into salient pasts, is applied to the problem of the sources of Paul's knowledge of Jesus in Georgia Keightley's "Christian Collective Memory and Paul's Knowledge of Jesus." Keightley argues that this memory/knowledge was mediated to Paul by, among other things, his ongoing participation in Christian ritual. This experiential, affective knowing of Christ as apprehended in and through ritual proved to be foundational for Paul's theologizing.

An important debate in contemporary memory studies is the nature of the relationship between salient pasts and present social realities in the constructive activities of memory. In "The Memory of Violence and the Death of Jesus in Q," I argue that Q is an artifact of commemoration generated in response to Jesus' death in a ritualized act of political violence. Through commemorative "keying," the community mastered this traumatic event by linking it to images and narrative scripts that had achieved archetypal status in the cultural memory of ancient Judaism. This inquiry is brought to bear upon the problem of Q's genre by demonstrating the essential connection that exists between commemoration and moral exhortation. April DeConick's essay, "Reading the *Gospel of Thomas* as a Repository of Early Christian Communal Memory," likewise explores the impact a community's present crises have upon its memory, as deposited in its tradition, and the emergence of new textual artifacts from this encounter of crisis with tradition. DeConick argues that the sayings material in *Thomas* has been secondarily developed in order to reformulate older apocalyptic traditions by shifting the ideology of the traditions away from an earlier eschatological emphasis to a mystical one, in order to mitigate the crisis in memory that the community had experienced when the end did not come.

The responses come from two of the most prominent scholars in their respective disciplines. Werner Kelber is a leading voice in New Testament scholarship for the application of cultural-memory approaches to biblical studies. His essay in this volume, "The Works of Memory: Christian Origins as MnemnoHistory," is both an important reflection upon memory and a call to New Testament scholarship to overcome its insularity with respect to developments in the humanities and social sciences. Barry Schwartz is a preeminent sociologist working in the field of social memory studies. His first essay, "Christian Origins: Historical Truth and Social Memory," is an adaptation of a keynote address to a special session on social memory at the 2003 meeting of the Society of Biblical Literature. His second essay, "Jesus in First-Century Memory," is a detailed and programmatic response by a leading expert in the field to the contributors to this volume.

This Semeia Studies volume is offered to reintroduce "memory" to research on intractable problems in our field. The contributors are convinced that the return of "memory" to New Testament and Christian origins scholarship as a serious analytical category will have consequences that will reverberate throughout the discipline.

JESUS TRADITION AS SOCIAL MEMORY

Alan Kirk and Tom Thatcher

For more than fifty years, theorists have been exploring the social dimensions of both the nature and transmission of memory. Such studies have examined cultural variables that impact the formation of memory, various forms of community commemorative activity, and the interface between memory and sociopolitical ideologies. As such, social memory theory naturally intersects with several key issues in Christian origins: the early Christian memory of Jesus; the development and transmission of Jesus traditions; the impact of community experience on these memories and traditions; the commemorative rituals of the early communities; the significance of the shift from tradition to text in the composition of written Gospels; the diversity of early Christian thought; and the implications of all these issues for reconstructions of Jesus, Paul, and other founding figures of Christianity.

In view of these many points of contact, it is surprising that social memory theory has, as yet, made no significant impact on biblical studies. To some degree, this has been the case simply because biblical scholars remain largely unaware of the literature in the field. But this neglect itself reflects a general comfort with the current consensus view of memory in the study of Christian origins, a view so taken for granted and, in fact, so foundational to many cherished methods and conclusions that it could not be abandoned without serious consequences. Biblical scholarship has invested deeply in the traditional understanding of "memory" as an individual faculty of recollection, and, moreover, has tended to discount the possibility of vital connections between "memory" and "tradition." Indeed, a sharp distinction between "memory" and "tradition" is fundamental for most contemporary models of the development of primitive Christian theology and the composition history of the Gospels. This essay will review this consensus approach, exploring its roots and current expressions and noting points where a social theory of memory could open significant new avenues of research into problems of Christian origins.

MEMORIES, TRADITIONS, GOSPELS

From the early centuries of the church, the existence of Gospels has been explained through a broad set of assumptions about the relationship between memory, traditions, and written history books, assumptions that undergird a disarmingly simple story of the composition history of these texts. This paradigm views "the memory" as a filing cabinet for past experience, and the act of "remembering" as a process of retrieving and reviewing bits of data "like checked baggage from storage" (Lowenthal 1985:252). From this perspective, the "memory of Jesus" is "a finite activity" limited to his original disciples and associates, those people who could recall their personal encounters with him (quotation from Zelizer: 218). As such, in any given early Christian community, the memory of Jesus died at the moment of the witnesses' departure.

But over time, the followers of Jesus told stories about him and the kingdom of God that he proclaimed. Second-generation Christians remembered and repeated the information contained in these stories, while being unable to recall personal experiences with Jesus. This gave birth to that elusive entity known as "the Jesus tradition." Most biblical scholars view "the Jesus tradition" as an inherently plastic entity, at least compared to the firsthand remembrances of Jesus' companions. Such a distinction is appropriate, it is argued, because "the Jesus tradition" was shaped under the impulse of shifting social concerns, while memories are connected to personal empirical experience. As such, traditions morph and grow, expanding and contracting to meet the needs of the immediate situation, while memories are of a more solid substance that is either preserved intact, suppressed, or replaced.

Eventually, these admixtures of memory and tradition found their way into writing, resulting in the various Gospels. Under this model, writing is viewed as "an adjunct to memory"—essentially an extension of the early Christian tradition, now preserved in a more permanent form. Because the Gospels are seen as storehouses for memories and traditions, it is possible to subject them to a variety of tests to determine whether they are "authentic, credible recountings of events," the same kind of tests one might use in evaluating any memory of the past (Zelizer: 218). Such an approach assumes that "true history ... is not made but found" (Lowenthal 1996:107)—that is, that there was once a relatively fixed and accurate memory of Jesus against which these written sources can be measured to reconstruct the actual past.

The extensive debates in the last few centuries over the reliability of the episodes in the Gospels have been played out in the arena of this paradigm, the conflict centering on the relative distance between the original memories of Jesus and the documents that are now available. In fact, a sharp theoretical distinction between individual memory and community traditions is perhaps the core value of the recent quests for the historical Jesus. Consistent with this approach, the methods and criteria of the current quest are designed to sift nuggets of genuine memory out of the mass of tradition in which the evangelists have embedded them. But because these nuggets are so few and so small, "memory" has, for all practical purposes, disappeared as an analytical category in Jesus research. A detailed survey of this phenomenon is beyond the scope of this essay, but the trend may be illustrated by a brief review of three prominent voices: Ernst Käsemann; Norman Perrin; and the Jesus Seminar.

Ernst Käsemann's key paper "The Problem of the Historical Jesus," opened the new Quest. Within its own historical context, Käsemann's argument was striking in its challenge to Rudolf Bultmann's skepticism and in its emphasis on the evangelists' sense of continuity with the Jesus of the past. At the same time, however, Käsemann clearly held the social realities of the early Christian communities to be the decisive factor in the formation and development of the Synoptic tradition. The early Christians maintained continuity with Jesus not at the level of memory, but rather at the level of living faith, for "mere history becomes significant history not through tradition as such but through interpretation" (21). As a result of this ongoing interpretive process, Jesus always appears in the New Testament not as a figure from the past but as the Lord of the present community: "The significance of this Jesus for faith was so profound, that even in the very earliest days it almost entirely swallowed up his earthly history" (23, 33–34). The Jesus of the Gospels is, then, a petrified figure: "the community takes so much trouble to maintain historical continuity with him who once trod the earth that it allows the historical events of this earthly life [of Jesus] to pass for the most part into oblivion and replaces them by its own message" (20). The analogy of a petrified Jesus characterizes Käsemann's position in the sense that his understanding of "tradition" entails a gradual and unrestrained replacement of memory with *kerygma*, in the same way that minerals replace wood fibers in a petrifying log.

The tension between the Jesus of the church's memory and the risen Lord of its proclamation was a key theme of Norman Perrin's classic study, *Rediscovering the Teaching of Jesus*. Perrin's skepticism was fueled by frequent and explicit appeal to the theorem that the early Christians invented tradition with little restraint. In Perrin's view, the evangelists had no interest in Jesus as a figure from the past, but instead forged tradition to make Jesus speak directly to the needs of the current community (16). Perrin's comments on the problem of the parables illustrate his approach to the formation of tradition particularly well: "Certainly, every single parable in the tradition has to be approached with the basic assumption that, as it now stands, it represents the teaching of the early church: that the voice is the voice of the risen Lord to the evangelist, and of the evangelist to the church, not that of the historical Jesus to a group of disciples gathered by the sea of Galilee" (22). The phrase, "as it now stands," in the quotation above exposes the breach between "memory" and "tradition" in Perrin's theory. Presumably, the historical Jesus said and did things in the presence of his disciples, things that this group of people could recall from their own empirical experience of him. But the recollections of these individuals were gradually replaced by "the tradition," apparently a combination of these initial memories and the church's developing faith. Throughout Perrin's presentation, it is clear that tradition always has the upper hand over memory, so that the ongoing revision and evolution of the tradition to meet the needs of the church was essentially unrestrained by the memory of the past.

Moving to the current state of research, the Jesus Seminar represents the most sustained collaborative effort to reconstruct the teaching and activities of Jesus. In their introduction to *The Five Gospels: The Search for the Authentic Words of Jesus,* Robert Funk and Roy Hoover outline the Seminar's methodology. As regards the present study, the most notable aspect of *The Five Gospels* is its sharp differentiation between authentic memory and fabricated tradition, characteristic of classical form criticism (see below). This model appears here in a markedly dualistic version that minimizes if not severs semantic connections between reminiscences of Jesus and early Christian production of tradition. As a result, the Seminar seeks, through application of appropriate criteria, to free authentic memories of Jesus—"that cry out for recognition and liberation" (4)—from the husks of the fabricated traditions of the early church. Such work is necessary because the memory of Jesus was suppressed by the early Christians' failure to distinguish between genuine recollections of Jesus and the later accretions of tradition. "Jesus' followers did not grasp the subtleties of his position and reverted, once Jesus was not there to remind them, to the view they had learned from John the Baptist. As a consequence of this reversion ... the gospel writers overlaid the tradition of sayings and parables with their own 'memories' of Jesus" (4). Here again, "memory" is understood as individual acts of recollection, recollections that can be judged "true" or "false" in the sense that they do or do not represent genuine empirical experiences of Jesus. The strength of this approach lies in its ability to produce a definitive database of historical Jesus material, so that one can look at specific sayings in the Gospels and conclude that "Jesus undoubtedly said this" or "Jesus did not say this" (36). The weakness of this approach, however, lies in its elimination of memory as a significant analytical category in the quest for Jesus.

Jesus Remembered

The disappearance of memory as an analytical category in biblical research may be attributed to a number of factors, most significantly the effects of form criticism. Nineteenth-century scholars were confident that the Gospels (especially Mark), minus their obviously mythical and miraculous elements, could be exploited to develop a biography of Jesus, including the course of his ministry and the development of his self-consciousness. This consensus collapsed under the weight of William Wrede's *The Messianic Secret* and K. L. Schmidt's subsequent *The Framework of the Story of Jesus*. Wrede argued that the motif of Jesus' "secret identity"—scenes in which Jesus reveals himself as Messiah to the disciples but forbids them from sharing this information with the crowds—was an innovation of the post-Easter communities that was imported into the earliest written Gospel (see Mark 4:33–34; 5:37–43; 8:27–30; 9:2–10; etc.). This being the case, one cannot assume that passages built on this motif reflect Jesus' own self-consciousness. Schmidt argued that Mark, who had no personal knowledge of Jesus, developed a narrative framework for Jesus' life consistent with his own theological views, and then filled this frame with traditional stories and sayings. Wrede and Schmidt thus effectively set the stage for the elimination of memory from discussion of the Gospels by arguing that the Gospel of Mark was a patchwork of traditional units sewn together by someone whose theological interests were not encumbered by personal recollection.

Under the subsequent influence of the form critics, in particular Rudolph Bultmann and Martin Dibelius, scholars focused their attention on these small units of tradition as possible loci for traces of authentic memories of Jesus. The form critics sharply (if unreflectively) distinguished between "memory," understood as personal recall, and "tradition," a term that comprehended both the "forms" these recollections took in oral preaching and teaching and all the processes by which the Gospel writers patched those pieces together. From the form-critical perspective, memories and traditions are of a different substance, displaying different properties and operating in different ways. By identifying these properties, one could extract kernels of memory from the husks of tradition in which they were now encased in the Gospels, creating a database of recollections from which the true image of Jesus could be reconstituted. For convenience, the remainder of this discussion will focus on the theoretical work of Rudolf Bultmann, whose approach to Gospel traditions continues to exert a monumental influence on Jesus scholarship.

For Bultmann, the decisive generative contexts for individual units of oral Jesus tradition were the social realities of the early communities. His approach to the interface between traditional forms and their social settings was therefore thoroughly synchronic: "The forms of the literary tradition must be used to establish the influences operating in the life of the community, and the life of the community must be used to render the forms themselves intelligible" (1968:5). The shape of the tradition, then, is a product of community life, and the framework of community life is reflected in the shape of the tradition. For this reason, much of Bultmann's form-critical work was given to discussion of the various "life settings" (*Sitze im Leben*) in which the needs of faith operated to create Jesus tradition. By identifying these traditional elements and subtracting them from the texts of the Gospels, it would be possible to isolate individual kernels of authentic remembrance. In assigning crucial importance to present social conditions in conceptualizations of the past, Bultmann anticipated the central postulate of social memory theory. But notably, Bultmann construed the social realities of the early communities not only as the formative *contexts* in which Gospel traditions were shaped and transmitted, but also as the primary *generative force* behind those traditions. Gospel tradition was thus a bifurcated entity: layers of fabricated tradition came to overlay the ever-diminishing traces of memory, which for their part were more or less inert with respect to the traditioning process itself.

The "criterion of dissimilarity," to which Bultmann had frequent recourse, was a corollary of this model of tradition. By identifying and peeling away the specifically "Christian" elements in the Gospels, as well as those with parallels in the Jewish and Greco-Roman *Umwelt*, one might expose the original form of a unit, and perhaps even a historical core (1968:6; 1962:60). This core most often took the form of pithy, memorable sayings that represented the point at which remembrances of Jesus were most likely to be found, because they were uniquely able to perdure through oral storytelling. But Bultmann's conception of the interface between memory and tradition made the recovery of these memorable sayings a complicated operation. In Bultmann's view, when a pressing problem arose in the community, a saying (derived either from the authentic memory of Jesus, prophetic utterances of the Risen Lord, or Jewish wisdom teaching) that spoke to the issue was identified and attached to a fabricated narrative setting. These narrative settings reflected typical (or ideal) situations in the life of Jesus as refracted through relevant points of contact with the contemporary situation of the church. Because some sayings units retained traces of actual remembrances of Jesus at their core, Bultmann could affirm that in these pericopae "the general character of [Jesus'] life is rightly portrayed." He also felt that in many cases the various communities created scenes for these sayings "entirely in the spirit of Jesus"

(1968:50–51). The scholar might gain access to these core memories and their original contexts by subtracting the community's beliefs from the observable units of tradition, producing a base of materials "dissimilar" from the views of the church and, therefore, possibly generated by forces outside the church's life settings—i.e., possibly generated by authentic memories of Jesus.

In a sense, then, Bultmann made authentic memories about Jesus the primary object of his endeavor. But as Werner Kelber has recently noted, "Bultmann's monumental scholarly contributions ... display no sustained reflection on memory. The concept is without mention in his scholarly work.... His focus was entirely on determining the original form of a saying or story and its setting in the life of the community" (2002:65). Specifically, Bultmann failed to articulate a working conception of a community's constitutive orientation to memory, or of the wide range of memorializing activities practiced within viable communities. This made it impossible for him to treat either this orientation to memory or these commemorative activities as potentially dynamic variables in a group's traditioning activities. His approach thus effectively eliminated "memory" from the generative equation, in the sense that the images of Jesus' past were passive—shaped by, but much less effectively shaping, the ongoing fabrication of tradition to meet community needs. The "memory" of Jesus was, as it were, swept along by the tide of tradition, incapable of affecting its own revision and expansion in the face of the overwhelming force of the communities' immediate needs. The early communities authorized their rapidly developing doctrines, ethics, and practices by projecting them backward, and in the process significant quantities of material, either created or borrowed from popular wisdom and piety, merged with genuine recollections and were placed on the lips of Jesus.

JESUS TRADITION AS SOCIAL MEMORY

All Gospels scholars assume that a relationship of some sort exists between the memories of Jesus' companions and the reception of those memories in the traditioning activities of the early Christian communities. Bultmann himself stressed that

> though we cannot now define with certainty the extent of the authentic words of Jesus, we are nevertheless able to distinguish the various levels of tradition; and when ... we distinguish the secondary layers in the tradition, what results is not, like the peeling of an onion, a reduction to nothingness—since the farther one goes the nearer one comes to the center, which holds the secret of its historical power. The layers which lie about this center may be viewed as its historical results, either

as its direct consequence or as a partial effect due to its contact with religious material of another kind. (1962:60)

Were this not the case, Bultmann's model of tradition would make any inquiry into the historical Jesus impossible. But while biblical scholars have made giant strides beyond Bultmann's foundational methods of research, they generally have continued to subscribe to his view of the relationship between memory and tradition. As a result, studies of Christian origins and the historical Jesus have remained unable to articulate precisely how this relationship works: What processes lay at the interface between the original memory of Jesus and subsequent traditioning activity of later generations of the church? Answers to this question sometimes take the form of an assertion, stated as an axiom, that early Christian reception stands at odds with the originating events. This view, as noted above, is rooted in a model that locates all decisive factors of the traditioning process in the social realities of various communities and assigns memory an inert status at the origin of a process that unfolds at the primary behest other factors. The remainder of this essay will attempt to show that social memory theory can offer biblical scholars new and helpful ways to reconceptualize the phenomenon of the Gospel tradition.

Consistent with the form-critical model, social memory theory views present social realities as decisive factors in the constant rearticulation of a community's salient past, and it contends that the past is never objectified apart from the frameworks for memory supplied by present circumstances. But social memory theory departs significantly from the form-critical legacy by refusing to authorize any sharp distinction between memory and tradition. Memory is not equivalent to the individual faculty of recall, and the transmission of memories is not an isolated sharing of data between individuals. Instead, cultivation of memory takes place within a number of settings of community life and, correspondingly, across a broad range of memorializing practices. Further, social memory theory indicates that commemorated pasts exercise powerful agency in the community's present life.[1] A group's "social memory" is the constant, creative negotiation of commemorated pasts and open-ended presents. As Jeffrey Prager has argued, "the present and the past are hardly discrete entities in individual consciousness. They converge

---

1. A key concept here is "commemorated past," that is to say, it is not a matter of a so-called empirical past persisting in unelaborated form into the changing present of a community, but a past shaped, sacralized, and interpreted precisely through activities of commemoration. See the discussion of commemoration in the introductory essay to this volume.

through the constitution and continual structuring of the self" (126).[2] From this perspective, "tradition" and "memory" are not elements of the Gospels that can be pried apart through application of particular criteria. Rather, tradition is the indissoluble, irreducibly complex artifact of the continual negotiation and semantic interpenetration of present social realities and memorialized pasts.

Applied to the problem of the Gospel traditioning processes, this approach argues that Jesus was represented through multiple acts of remembering that semantically fused the present situations of the respective communities with their memory of the past as worked out in commemorative practices, with neither factor swallowed up by, or made epiphenomenal of, the other. "Accordingly," Jens Schröter observes, "the appropriation of Jesus tradition can be understood as a process of selection, by which the present situation was interpreted through reference to the person of Jesus" (1997:463). The commemorated past—the memory of Jesus as cultivated by the various communities—was deployed and redeployed in typical situations and new settings. The commemorated past in all its massivity and the exigent demands of the present reciprocally reacted upon each other in the course of this encounter (though the actual relationship of past and present cannot be *a priori* prescribed, but can only be assessed empirically, on a case by case basis). "Tradition" is thus an abbreviation for the countless transactions between sacralized past and actual present vital to the life of a community.

As Maurice Halbwachs argued, in the interplay between the past and the present, current social realities provide the frameworks for the appropriation of the past. The dynamics of this reception are the dynamics of social memory, and the history of the Gospel tradition is in fact the history of the reception of Jesus' image in various contexts. Each act of reception constitutes a discrete episode within that history, affected by the configuration of social and cultural variables inhering in the respective situations (Schröter 1997:141–42). But at the same time, as Jeffrey Olick has shown, characteristics of earlier acts of reception can ripple as factors into subsequent acts of reception (1999b:382). A social memory approach would thus also be concerned with the reception history of Jesus tradition in the early church, as each previous construction of the past becomes an aspect of the overall social setting in which new memories are produced.

---

2. Note that Prager's comment seeks to describe the memory of individuals, illustrating the shift to a more fluid approach to "memory" at all levels (group memories and personal memories) in some circles of experimental psychology.

The dynamic nature of this interplay between past and present complicates attempts to isolate so-called authentic elements of memory from their interpretive reception in any given unit of tradition. The notion that traditional materials embedded in the Gospels can be analytically and cleanly separated into two piles—authentic remembrance and fabricated elements—is predicated upon questionable views of the operations of memory and tradition. Further, our access to actual instances of early Christian reception of tradition is severely limited: largely through Christian writings (primarily the Gospels), themselves artifacts of commemorative enterprises that fundamentally deploy particular interpretive frameworks for their received Jesus traditions. Integration of these traditions into the literary Gospel genre and the corollary reception contexts complicates the project of working back to earlier configurations of the tradition, that is, to earlier contexts of reception (see Schröter 1997:59–60, 82–83, 303). However, while social memory analysis is less confident that a putatively authentic deposit can be cleanly refined out of a given body of tradition, it remains convinced that the commemorated past bore upon the traditioning activities of the early communities in a far more thoroughgoing manner than the form critics envisioned. For this reason, "the more plausible way of proceeding would be to attempt to understand both [memory and present factors of reception] as reciprocally determining elements, which should not be detached from each other, but rather portrayed in their reciprocal inter-connection" (Schröter 1997:485).

Social Memory and the Search for Jesus

The insight that Jesus traditions integrally emerged from the semantic negotiation between salient pasts and open-ended "presents" in ever-changing contexts of commemoration has methodological implications for historical Jesus research. It becomes possible now to challenge scholarship's reflexive methodological recourse to the form-critical model for memory and tradition. A few scholars have begun to move, in varying degrees, beyond this habituated perspective and have endeavored to assess the operations of memory in the formation of Gospel traditions, thus restoring memory as an analytical category in biblical studies. To illustrate this undercurrent of research, the present section will engage, in a manner simultaneously appreciative and critical, the work of Birger Gerhardsson, Burton Mack, John Dominic Crossan, and Jens Schröter.

Gerhardsson

Birger Gerhardsson's model for the operations of memory in the origins and transmission of the Gospel traditions was developed in explicit

opposition to the approach of the German form critics. Gerhardsson readily acknowledged that the Jesus traditions were not so inflexibly
transmitted as to be impermeable to interpretive adaptation in later community settings. But appealing to rabbinic traditioning techniques, he
argued that the decisive factors in the formation of the Gospel tradition
lay in Jesus' own teaching practices and the regulated mnemonic activities of his immediate circle of followers (1998; 2001). Subsequent critique
of Gerhardsson's work has centered, first, on the perception that he aligns
early Christian traditioning practices with rabbinic mnemonic techniques
in a way that he does not adequately justify, and, second, on the claim
that the significant variation within the synoptic tradition cannot be
explained by a model of memorization and regulated transmission.
Moreover, as Gerhardsson acknowledges, the rabbinic parallels are only
one instance of a number of different traditioning practices in the ancient
world.

Nevertheless, Gerhardsson's proposal resonates with social memory
theory in its recognition of the constitutive nature of memory for a community. Also noteworthy in this regard is Gerhardsson's attempt to link
the cultivation of Gospel traditions to specific traditioning practices
attested within the Jewish and Greco-Roman *Umwelt*. "Our point of
departure, then, is the fact that early Christianity was born within a historical sphere in which tradition and transmission had already to some
extent become conscious ideas and distinct activities" (1998:7). His
approach compares favorably to the tendency of the form critics to appeal
to anonymous collectives and immanent tendencies of tradition. Gerhardsson takes the traditioning process—understood as a set of concrete
historical practices by which memory is objectified and transmitted—
seriously, and in this respect aligns with some of Jan Assmann's
conceptions of the workings of cultural memory. At the same time, however, social memory theory also highlights the weakness of
Gerhardsson's model. If the form critics were fixated on present social
realities in the formation of tradition, Gerhardsson severely underestimates the effect of these realities. While acknowledging that Jesus
traditions have been "colored," "marked," and even revised by later
interpretation (2001:27, 56–57), Gerhardsson does not attribute significant
formative effects to social settings of reception, preferring to concentrate
this vital principle within the deposit from the past.

Mack

Burton L. Mack's *A Myth of Innocence: Mark and Christian Origins*
shows keen insight into the ways in which present social forces power-
fully generate images of the past, as well as into the indissoluble

connection between the cultivation of memory and community formation. Mack applies these principles to analyze the formation of the Gospel
tradition, guided by the question, "What if the social circumstances [of
the early communities] were regarded as the generative matrix for a
recasting of the memory tradition?" (16). As this statement indicates,
Mack recognizes that tradition streams are "types of memory" (56), the
ever-changing products of groups reimagining their pasts in light of their
present social realities. Moreover, in an important methodological move,
Mack problematizes the conventional form-critical distinction between
authentic "memory" and layers of "interpretation," pointing out that this
model privileges the originating kernel. Rather, he argues, the so-called
layers of interpretation are in fact "memories" in their own right, that is,
phenomenologically indistinct from the original memory traces (15). In
these respects, Mack's analytical approach aligns closely with constitutive
aspects of social memory theory.

But while Mack's analysis of the dynamics of tradition represents
considerable progress, he ultimately fails to purge his model of the conventional bifurcation of original memory traces and subsequent
developments. In Mack's reading, traces of so-called authentic remembrances lie more or less semantically inert, at worst irrelevant, at best
very tenuously connected with subsequent developments of the tradition.
The social realities of the various Jesus communities constitute the decisive force for the generation of images of the salient past—in particular,
different images of Jesus (166–67). Diverse images of Jesus that emerged
within the different traditions are explained as mythical retrojections of
the responses of the respective communities to their current social realities, as well as projections of the social identities being forged within these
contexts. The semantic forces move monolithically in one direction, from
the present back to a more or less amorphous past. Reacting against the
tendency to explain the development of Gospel traditions wholly from
some secure place of origins in the life of Jesus, Mack finds his
Archimidean point in the social histories of the various early communities.[3]

Also problematic from the perspective of social memory theory is the
opposition Mack sets up between authentic reminiscence and narrative
emplotment. In Mack's view, the conventional narrative motifs evident in
the Gospels are guideposts for the invention of tradition. The Markan
Passion Narrative, Mack points out, clearly is organized along the lines of

---

3. Also dubious is Mack's practice of equating particular "memory streams" with particular genres, and then associating distinct genres with distinct community social identities
(53–56, 96). This association confuses the stylistic distinctives, conventions, and focused
pragmatic objectives of a given genre with a particular group ethos.

the archetypal Jewish wisdom tale of the persecution and vindication of the suffering righteous. This being the case, one must conclude that "this story does not derive from history. History [Mark's account] was written according to the script of the persecution story" (280). Effectively, then, genuine memory cannot be cast in the form of socially relevant narrative structures. In point of fact, however, social memory theorists generally hold that the meaning of landmark events is articulated through emplotment within narrative scripts that have achieved archetypal, symbolic status within a particular culture. By the same token, of course, archetypal narratives have decisive formative effects upon the representation of the events and persons they are adduced to interpret. As such, a social memory approach significantly complicates the equation: historical events and archetypal storylines merge so thoroughly that the problem of extracting so-called purely historical material from the Passion Narrative remains acute. Mark's Passion story is not the sum of memory plus the social frameworks of the present, but rather is memory in the irreducible shape of the commemorating community's social and cultural frameworks.

Crossan

Any review of "memory" and "tradition" in recent studies of the Gospels must include the work of John Dominic Crossan, who, like Mack, has attempted to discuss the implications of memory in his quest for the historical Jesus and, moreover, appeals to experimental studies of memory. Nevertheless, it is clear that Crossan continues to view memory largely as an individual faculty of recollection, a perspective affected by the particular studies of memory he has drawn upon. Crossan's discussion of early Christian memory in *The Birth of Christianity*, for example, appeals to Frederick Bartlett's experiment in the early 1930s, in which a story "was passed along one chain of ten subjects" and in the process experienced significant distortion (Crossan 1998:82). The relevance of Bartlett's laboratory-based experiment to the problem of Gospel traditions is, however, questionable. By its very design, Bartlett's study could only observe memory transmission between isolated individuals who lacked significant social connection to one another, hardly the situation in the early Jesus communities. A similar conception of memory pervades Crossan's appeal to another famous study, which analyzed individuals' recollections (in a controlled sequence of subsequent occasions) of their immediate surroundings when they heard news of the 1984 *Challenger* space shuttle disaster. Crossan observes that "the details got lost and were replaced by mistakes.... But at least the central events actually took place and were remembered" (1998:64). The

"details [that] got lost" were the individuals' recollections of their immediate circumstances at that significant moment, while the "the central
events" that "actually took place and were remembered" remained
secure. This finding is, however, entirely consistent with a social
approach to memory. Recollections of immediate circumstances, which
were either lost or confused, were those most wholly specific to the individual and hence the most fugitive elements of memory, while the
"central events" of the disaster were remembered specifically because
they were taken up in the *social memory* of the community and, in the
process, transcended the empirical experiences of individuals. Details
narrowly tailored to the specific situations of individuals failed to lodge
in either the individual or the collective memory because, having no relevance to the group, they were not assimilated to its shared discourse
and commemorative activities, the crucial supports for memory.

Crossan's analysis of memory in *The Birth of Christianity* is a logical
continuation of his earlier discussions of the interface between memory
and tradition. In these works, Crossan describes the early Christian
memory of Jesus as a three-tiered edifice topped with the production of
written Gospels: "*retention* of original Jesus materials, *development* of those
retained materials, and creation of totally new materials" (1994:xiii;
emphasis original). In Crossan's presentation, these three strata of
memory appear to be arranged in a chronological fashion. "Retention"
refers to personal recall of information, "recording at least the essential
core of words and deeds, events and happenings" and corresponding to
the authentic memories of Jesus' associates (1991:xxxi). "Development"
refers to the application of "such [recalled] data to new situations, novel
problems, and unforeseen circumstances" (1991:xxxi). "Creation" includes
"not only composing new sayings and new stories, but, above all, composing larger complexes that changed their contents," in effect a shift to
fabricated memory. Crossan explains this invention of tradition largely in
terms of the inability of the early Christians to distinguish the Jesus of the
past from the risen Lord of the present. It is therefore not surprising that
he feels that the bulk of the Jesus tradition must be viewed as adaptation
and fabrication. The goal of his analysis, ultimately, remains parallel to
that of Bultmann: to extract elements of pure recall ("retention") from tradition ("development" and "creation") in order to gain access to "what
Jesus actually said and did" (1994:xiii; 1991:xxxi).

Schröter

Jens Schröter has moved the discussion of memory and the Gospels
ahead significantly by his application of Aleida and Jan Assmann's analyses of cultural memory to research problems in Gospel traditions and the

historical Jesus.[4] Schröter views the Gospel traditions as the integral product of remembering Jesus in ever-changing contexts of reception. Because of the integral properties of tradition it becomes extremely difficult to identify a secure deposit of so-called authentic Jesus traditions by bracketing interpretations of original elements that have occurred in various contexts of reception. In Schröter's view, one cannot speak about the historical Jesus apart from the acts of reception: how Jesus was *remembered* in the various social and historical contexts of the early communities (1996:153–58; 1997:465–66, 482–83).

On this basis, Schröter argues for "a quest for the historical Jesus ... that take[s] its starting point in the reception of his preaching in the primitive Christian texts" (1996:165; see also 1997:483–85). Early Christian texts must be the starting point for analysis of reception because the difficulties in establishing preliterary reception contexts for their constituent traditions are often all but insurmountable. Schröter's approach is predicated upon *both* the autonomous semantic vigor of the constitutive past *and* the effect of present social realities that give particular refractions to that past, as well as upon the recognition that the past is accessible only inferentially through those refractions. Comparing the appropriation of shared complexes of material by Mark, Q, and *Thomas*, Schröter works out the reception given to common tradition in these three texts, an analysis that brings to light the social contexts of reception of each. Common traits perduring in these bodies of tradition after reception is accounted for, as well as the acts of reception themselves, become the basis for drawing inferences about the contours of the past that exerts a charged influence upon all three reception contexts (Schröter 1996:155, 163–64; 1997:142, 484). Aware that every act of traditioning is an act of remembering in which past and present semantically interact, Schröter's approach *exploits* interpretive contexts of the tradition to draw inferences about Jesus, rather than trying to *discount* these contexts.

New Directions for Research

As the preceding discussion has shown, social memory theory presents a number of far-reaching implications for the study of the Gospel traditions, the composition history of the Gospels, and the quest for the historical Jesus. Further application of this analytical approach to specific problems in biblical studies promises to raise and answer key

---

4. See also Kelber 2002:55–86. James D. G. Dunn's *Jesus Remembered* (2003) arrives at a model of tradition close to Schröter's and the one argued for in this essay, but via the route of hermeneutical theory and studies of the dynamics of oral traditioning processes.

questions across a broad range of issues. Seven points of intersection of social memory theory and Christian origins will be briefly plotted here in closing.

1. *Memory as an Analytical Category*—Social memory theory rehabilitates "memory" as a relevant analytical term in the study of Christian origins. It stresses memory's inherent agency in group formation, transformations in group identity, and in the broad spectrum of practices and artifacts (verbal, textual, ritual, and monumental) within any cultural formation, established or emergent. Attention to the social dimension of memory does not entail a return to memory understood as an individual faculty of recall that naively captures, stores, and brings forward the past "into the brightly lit circle of perfect presentation" (Casey 1987:219).[5] Instead, social memory theory expressly denies that lines connecting past and present are unproblematic, and highlights the effects of present social realities upon constructions of the past.

2. *Tradition Formation and Transformation*—The concept of "tradition" has long been central to the study of early Christianity and its literature. From the perspective of social memory theory, however, "tradition" is in fact the substance of "memory." Social memory analysis indicates that tradition has its origins in the commemorative activities of communities, and that tradition is continuously generated out of the semantic interaction between salient pasts and the exigencies of current social realities. This approach can thus account for the interplay between stabilizing and transforming forces in traditioning processes without the encumbrance of a distinction between "authentic recall" and "traditional development."

Additionally, social memory theory offers new points of leverage on the old form-critical problem of the connections between memory, early Christian preaching and teaching, and the forms assumed by the oral Gospel tradition. Hints of this type of connection are, for example, evident in Liisa Malkki's description of Hutu refugee camps:

> Accounts of ... key events very quickly circulated among the refugees, and, often in a matter of days, acquired what can be characterized as "standard versions" in the telling and retelling. These "standard versions" were not simply isolated accounts of particular events, told for the sake of telling and soon to be forgotten. Rather, they were accounts which, while becoming increasingly formulaic, also became more didactic and progressively more implicated in, and indicative of, something beyond them. In this sense the "standard versions" acted as diagnostic and mnemonic allegories connecting events of everyday life with wider historical processes impinging on the Hutu refugees. (106)

----

5. Casey is quoting Edmund Husserl.

Also potentially significant is the progress made by experimental psychologists on the neural phenomenology of human memory, which shows that memory resembles not so much a storage bin for data as it does an operating system that works by economizing, condensing, typifying, and schematizing, thereby creating cognitive scripts that give individuals orientation to the world (Bonnano: 175–77; Prager: 207). Descriptions such as these bear obvious similarities to long-observed characteristics of the forms of the oral Gospel tradition. In this respect, memory theory may provide a way through the impasses of form criticism.

3. *Oral Tradition as Cultural Memory*—The premises of social memory theory will immediately resonate with biblical scholars who are familiar with contemporary approaches to folklore and tradition, especially in the line of Parry, Lord, and Foley. According to these theorists, "oral tradition" is not a content but a performance mode, and traditional texts are actualized in contexts of reception under the constraints of the immediate audience's norms and expectations. As such, the dynamics of oral tradition reception are essentially the dynamics of social memory: memory, like oral tradition, arises from the generative encounter of the salient past and the contemporary expectations and social situation of the receiving audience. As such, "oral tradition" and "social memory" are closely related terms, and the connections between them should be explored by biblical scholars.

4. *Written Gospels as Commemorative Artifacts*—In 1975, Graham Stanton observed that "the simple question, 'Why did Mark write his gospel?' has not been answered. The more strongly the role of oral tradition in the early church is stressed, the more difficult it becomes to account for the transition from oral tradition to Mark's comparatively lengthy and not unsophisticated document" (18). At the very least, social memory theory offers new ways to ask the relevant questions. In what ways are the written Gospels artifacts of commemoration? In what ways are Gospels acts of reception, receiving tradition within memory frameworks determined by the social conditions and contestations of the present? How do written texts such as Gospels establish and crystallize the past, functioning as stabilizing points in group memory? For example, Jan Assmann's discussion of the shift from forms of "communicative memory" to the more enduring forms of "cultural memory," and the transformations of representations of the past that may accompany this shift in medium (1992; 2000), provides fresh leverage on understanding the emergence of Gospels as written artifacts and on the transition from orality to writing in early Christianity.

5. *Early Christian Commemoration*—Communities identify, shape, and interpret a salient past across a broad range of commemorative activities and practices. Social memory theory brings the total landscape of early

Christian commemorative activities into high relief, uncovering the sites where communities created their memories and, in many cases, transformed their heritage of ancient Jewish cultural memory and commemoration. As such, social memory theory offers holistic models for analyzing Christian commemorative activities that traditionally have been considered in isolation from one another—instruction, rites, liturgy, creeds, written Gospels, and any other activities through which the memory of Jesus was evoked. Specifically, it provides models that allow memory, tradition, rituals, and written Gospels to be explored as parallel and intersecting venues for early Christian commemoration.

6. *Normative Memory*—Social memory theory posits crucial connections between commemoration and moral formation. This raises the broader issue of the relationship between speech genres and memory, and points to the integrated functions of what Assmann calls "normative" and "formative" texts (2000:127; 1992:141–42). The apparent typification of narrative scenes, for example, and their subordination to sayings and pronouncements in the Gospels may reveal a heavy investment in the normative dimension of commemoration of Jesus. If this is the case, the observable form of the pronouncement story, for example, would be an artifact of this guiding interest in normative memory, and therefore possibly a key to the early Christian construction of ethics.

7. *Continuity and Change in Early Christianity*—Barry Schwartz argues that "the present is constituted by the past, but the past's retention as well as its reconstruction, must be anchored in the present" (2000:302–3). Recognition of this mutually generative relationship has important implications for the intractable problem of accounting for both continuity and change in early Christian communities. Solutions have tended to default to the extremes: either replication of the traditional past in the present, or reinvention of the past within the present. Social memory theory moves toward a more plausible, tightly interactional model that correlates the two factors, analyzing from case to case "how the ... past and present shape each other" (Olick and Levy: 923). Continuity results from the pressure of the sacralized past on the present; change emerges from the pressure of the present on the past; and specific instances of continuity and/or change in a given early Christian community are the evidence of this ongoing dynamic interplay.

CHRISTIAN ORIGINS: HISTORICAL TRUTH AND SOCIAL MEMORY

Barry Schwartz

Christianity begins miraculously—the angel Gabriel appears in Nazareth and announces to Mary that she will bear a son. He will assume David's throne and reign over Israel forever. This astonishing event is the subject of a Jewish joke. Mary asks Gabriel how a virgin can possibly have a child; when God's angel assures her that it will be so, she requests a favor: "If God can do such a thing, would you please ask Him to give me a little girl?" To this Gabriel replies, "Mashele, t'siz nicht ba'shert" (Mary, It's not meant to be). The joke falls flat today, but it was hilarious a century ago. Gabriel, after all, is speaking in Yiddish, not Aramaic or Hebrew. And by saying "It's not meant to be" he is affirming the fate of the Jewish people. "If only God had given Mary the little girl she always wanted! Then our centuries would have been filled with sweetness instead of suffering." And there is a distinct undertone of irreverence and incredulity: irreverence because the joke refers to the Mother of God in the diminutive, "Mashele; sweet little Mary"; incredulity because it affirms that virgins do not have children—period, which makes the issue of Mary's preference irrelevant. The pivotal point, however, is that the joke would not work if the joke-teller and his listener believed in the Annunciation. Many twenty-first century scholars, like the Jewish joke-teller, doubt the Annunciation story; but can such skeptics, however empathetic, grasp the social memory of first-century believers?

Social memory scholarship might help answer this question, but we cannot invoke it rashly; we need to recognize its merits and avoid its pathologies, especially those it shares with biblical studies, lest it certify the very distortions we want to correct. These distortions result from a cynical "constructionist" project rooted in the valuable idea of memory being assembled from parts (Hacking: 49–50), but fixated on the circular

---

[Editors' note: This essay is an adaptation of Professor Schwartz's keynote address to the Special Session on Social Memory at the 2003 Annual Meeting of the Society of Biblical Literature in Atlanta.]

assumption that constructed products are not what they seem precisely because they are constructed. No assumption, in my view, has done more to undermine the foundation of social memory scholarship or hinder its application to biblical studies.

Social Memory

Two models orient social memory scholarship. Neither model describes reality; each is a fictional template in terms of which different relations between social experience and memory can be compared and understood. In the first—presentist—model, social memory is context-dependent and constructed differently as it is invoked in different communities. Whether focusing on the politics of memory (Hobsbawm 1983; Alonso; Tuchman and Fortin; Bodnar 1992; J. Boyarin; Gillis 1994b) or memory over the *longue durée* (Halbwachs 1992; Pelikan; Kammen 1991; M. Peterson; Ben Yehuda), constructionist scholarship endeavors to show how beliefs about the past become hostage to the circumstances of the present, and how different elements of the past become more or less relevant as these circumstances change. Memory thus becomes a social fact as it is made and remade to serve new power distributions, institutional structures, values, interests, and needs.

In the second—culture system—model, society changes constantly, but social memory endures because new beliefs are superimposed upon—rather than replace—old ones (see Durkheim 1965:414–33). "No generation, even in this present time of unprecedented dissolution of tradition," observed Edward Shils, "creates its own beliefs." Generations acquire from the past most of what constitutes them (38). As individuals acquire traditional understandings through forebears (either through oral culture, commemoration, or historiography), common memories endow them with a common heritage, strengthen society's "temporal integration," create links between the living and the dead, and promote consensus over time (Shils: 13–14, 31–32, 38, 327; see also Freud; Bellah et al.; Schwartz 1991; Schudson 1992:205–21). Every society, even the most fragmented, requires a sense of sameness and continuity with what went before.

The presentist model of social memory has become so robust—the culture system model, so feeble—that we have lost sight of the dynamics that sustain the sameness and continuity that make society possible. Stable images of the past are often, but not always, demonstrably true images. Sometimes false ideas are transferred across generations and accepted as if they were true; sometimes true ideas are rejected as if they were false. Truth value and its resistance to revision is one, but not the only, source of the past's stability. The inertia of history (oral and written), commemorative symbolism (icons, monuments, shrines, placenames, rituals), cultural and institutional structures reinforce the continuities of memory. That we should even consider these continuities problematic rather than given is, however, ironic. The pioneers of collective memory research (including Cooley; Czarnowski; Halbwachs 1992; G.H. Mead) surprised the world by demonstrating that a supposedly immutable past is readily and constantly transformed. So abundant has been the evidence of transformation, and so convincing the presentist explanations, that the continuity of memory is now treated as the greatest puzzle of all. Before social memory scholarship can be applied to Christian origins, or to any other problem in biblical studies, that puzzle must be solved, and to do so we must bring the foundational flaws of social memory scholarship into the open.

The Cynical Discipline

"Social memory" refers to the distribution throughout society of beliefs, knowledge, feelings, and moral judgments about the past. Only individuals possess the capacity to contemplate the past, but this does not mean that beliefs originate in the individual alone or can be explained on the basis of his or her unique experience. Individuals do not know the past singly; they know it with and against other individuals situated in diverse communities, and in the context of beliefs that predecessors and contemporaries have transferred to them.

As a branch of the sociology of knowledge, social memory scholarship first assumed pertinence "under a definite complex of social and cultural conditions in which shared orientations diminish and are overshadowed by incompatible differences, where one universe of discourse challenges all others and statements and truth claims are assessed in terms of the social interests of those who produced them" (Merton: 457–60). This new culture of suspicion arose during the post–World War I era of disillusionment, and among its several embodiments, form criticism—a method for analyzing and deconstructing generic oral forms affecting the content of written texts—occupies a prominent place. While Maurice Halbwachs conducted his pioneering work on collective memory, Karl Mannheim (1952; 1936) produced his classic essays on the sociology of knowledge, Carl Becker relativized history in "Every Man His Own Historian," George Herbert Mead defined conceptions of the past uniquely as a way of managing present problems, and Rudolph Bultmann, the most influential form critic, searched for the social roots of the Gospels (1968). The conditions underlying this convergence, however, present us with our greatest obstacle. Social memory scholarship, like the sociology of knowledge and form criticism, has an affinity for cynicism and casual dismissal of conventional belief. It flourishes in societies where cultural values no longer unify, where people have already become alienated from common values, and separate communities regard one another distrustfully. The sociology of memory, like the sociology of knowledge, "systematizes the lack of faith in reigning symbols" (Merton: 459). Biblical scholarship, like social memory scholarship and the sociology of knowledge, frequently despairs over its ability to know events as they actually were and finds its triumphant moments in clever reinterpretations or the debunking of what was once believed to be true. The sociology of memory appeals to the reflexive and hesitant, to those who preface even their own assertions with the disclaimer: "I might be rationalizing, *but*. . . . "

HISTORY, COMMEMORATION, AND MEMORY

Social memory functions differently in traditional and modern societies. The people of traditional societies, whether patriarchal, patrimonial, or feudal, orient themselves to the past and are encompassed by their memories and customs (Weber 1947:341–58; Shils: 9–10). The meaning of everyday practices is based on their conviction that forebears performed them; historical beliefs, on their conviction that forebears embraced them. Modern societies, in contrast, tend toward a traditionless state where practices are assessed according to legal principle and scientific reason; historical beliefs are dissected rather than embraced (Weber 1947: 329–40). Therefore, modern people's breadth of historical knowledge is unprecedented while their identification and continuity with the past steadily declines. Traditional peoples knew much less about the past than we, but they felt a greater sense of identity and continuity with it (see Meyerhoff).

History is absent in traditional society, but social memory flourishes there through oral discourse and ritual observance. Traditional society is a mnemonic garden of Eden in which heroes and miraculous deeds are authoritative, unquestioned, and spontaneously recalled (see Nora). Against this paradise of remembrance stands modern society, the seat of analytic history and self-critical memory.

No pure cases of tradition or modernity exist. Inhabitants of first-century Palestine, largely illiterate, learned from their elites what they needed to know about the sacred past. Historical writing had its roots in the equating of history and theophany, but the result, according to Yosef Yerushalmi, "was not theology, but history on an unprecedented scale" (13). Jesus and his generation saw themselves as part of this history and understood it as a true narrative embodying wisdom, faith, and a law containing the seeds of Western rationality (Weber 1952).

The relevance of social memory scholarship depends on its ability to bring us into contact with first-century Christianity. In our time, a New

History is concerned with ordinary people more than religious and political elites (see Foner). Ironically, biblical scholarship, on the whole, affords the peasants of Jesus' time less emphasis than they deserve, reflects inadequately on the political and economic interests they pursued, and pays too little attention to the traditional worldview, including the social memories, in which they were immersed. For this lapse there are at least two reasons. First, social memory studies—concerned largely with popular memory—did not take root until the early 1980s and only now are beginning to reach a mass critical enough to warrant advance into unfamiliar topical areas. The second answer is prompted by a vaguely felt but definite foreboding that biblical topics are qualitatively different from more recent topics on which social memory scholars feed, in that biblical data are so sparse as to doom a project before it begins. The question of social memory and Christian origins nevertheless remains. Let us explore it.

THE GOSPEL TRADITION

In the literature on the first-century Christian world many themes recur: cultural values, status, kinship, politics, governance, city and rural life, church formation, ritual. Social memory is not among these themes. Yet, memory and commemoration are central to religious life. Georg Simmel's definition of religion includes "the response of souls full of piety to traditions and objects which the past has transmitted to us" (1903:326). In Clifford Geertz's more comprehensive view, religion "is (1) a system of symbols which acts to (2) establish powerful, pervasive, and long-lasting moods and motivations in men by (3) formulating conceptions of a general order of existence and (4) clothing these conceptions with such an aura of facticity that (5) the moods and motivations seem uniquely realistic" (1973:90–91). Applied to Christianity, this symbol system consists exclusively of the history and commemoration of Jesus. No Christianity exists apart from the distribution of beliefs, knowledge, feelings, and moral judgments that define social memory.

The problem is to get from the social memory of Jesus to the establishment of Christianity. Since this problem involves the transition from orality to literacy, we collide with Rudolph Bultmann's presentist approach to memory and Christianity. Seeking to bridge the gap between individual memories and New Testament accounts authenticating specific sayings, Bultmann assumed that oral tradition, the recollection of Jesus' spoken words, could not be trusted to represent Jesus' life. The interests of the early church, not its longing for the truth, shaped its conception of Jesus' life. Bultmann's comment on Mark pertains to all four Gospels: its author is "steeped in the theology of the early church, and he ordered and arranged the traditional material that he received in light of the faith of the early church" (1968:1). Only as it served the needs of the church did elementary forms like parables or sayings become part of moral exhortation, preaching, worship, social control, polemics, apologetics and the other instruments of social memory. The memory of Jesus, thus, becomes little more than a repercussion of the church's search for legitimacy. Many of Jesus' own words may have survived these conditions and this search, but, alas, they remain inert and concealed by fabrication.

Locating decisive sources of memory in social situations, Bultmann reduces the Gospels to an elaborate thematic apperception test: confessional elements, doctrines, values, and practices attain legitimacy in the present as they are projected back to the past. But the problem goes beyond fabrication. Bultmann's theory of memory, if we may so define form criticism, is an instance of what Karl Mannheim (1952) called unmasking, which not only refutes ideas but also undermines them simply by showing what functions they perform. Bultmann was certainly seeking to establish falsehoods in order to peel them away to find the truth, but, notwithstanding his own motive, he could not help but challenge the authority of the past, for once one sees the "extra-theoretical function" of an idea, it loses its efficacy (Mannheim, 1952:140). Claiming that our ideas about the past are construed by elites intent on enlarging the authority of their own institutions, Bultmann's statement above causes the most ardent "politics of memory" scholars to blush.

Form criticism resonates with the constructionist worldview that has been in the air for the past quarter-century (see Hacking), and at its edge dangle the very questions that bedevil constructionism. The first question concerns the relationship between political interests and religious ideas: whether institutional power is the generative matrix for ideas or vice versa. Second, there is the thorny issue of generalization: do the form critics apply to their own work the principles they apply to the Gospels? (To which *Sitz im Leben* are their own insights attributable?) Third, Bultmann and his successors wish to identify fabrications, peel them away, and reveal the core of historical truth. To do so with certainty, however, they must already know or have a way of knowing the difference between the fabricated and the authentic Jesus. Bultmann's method assumes, or, at least, presumes, the very knowledge it seeks to affirm. The fourth problem with form criticism, even in its most diluted and widely accepted forms, is that it asserts what it must demonstrate. "In seeking to bring unity and order to the heterogeneity of the first thirty years," Robert Wilken asserts, Luke "interpreted the material he had inherited to fit into his scheme" (33). Perhaps so, but since no one knows who wrote Luke, Wilken can present no evidence on the author's motives, let alone refute an alternate hypothesis: that the material Luke's author inherited *changed* his scheme. A fifth question concerns continuity and stems from cliché: "Each age has its own responsibility to forge its own distinctive meaning of Christian faith" (Semler, cited in Wilken: 131). Christian origins, it is true, are not fixed but seen differently by successive "period eyes" (Baxandall: 32). Yet, if each generation creates Jesus in terms of its own character and finds in him its own ideals, then why are early accounts recognizable in later generations that see the world through the lens of dissimilar perspectives and ideals?

Perceptions of the past are materialized in monuments, shrines, placenames, and other sites of memory (see Nora). In these sites Bultmann and Halbwachs share great interest, but where Bultmann regards them as one source of information about Christian origins, Halbwachs takes them as the primary source and is determined to demonstrate their capacity to distort. As we consider the question of whether Gospel content reflects or determines popular beliefs about Jesus, therefore, we quickly realize that Maurice Halbwachs, founder of the field of collective memory, provides no help. He says little about the life of Jesus, confining himself instead to the landmarks symbolizing it. He applies to physical sites the same reductionist principles that Bultmann and his followers apply to texts. Halbwachs is a master at demonstrating how events occurring at one site are represented at another and how such "localizations," as he calls them, support the narrative they make concrete. Since Jesus' birth in Bethlehem conveniently connects him to the line of David, Halbwachs dismisses the Nativity as a legend (1992). The logical problem is patent. John F. Kennedy's birthplace, Boston, connects him to the beginning of the American Revolution, but this hardly means that he was not born in Boston. Halbwachs's greatest failure is his inability to see commemoration as anything more than an elaborate delusion. It is not just that localizations distort history; the more they distort the better they work.

Halbwachs advances a pejorative conception of collective memory, one that distrusts and works to undermine established beliefs. He assumes that memory, as opposed to history, is inauthentic, manipulative, shady, something to be overcome rather than accepted in its own right. That commemoration is a selective celebration rather than an inferior version of history escapes Halbwachs. He cannot fully grasp what sacred sites accomplish, how they transmute reality to mobilize and sustain religious sentiment and, above all, elevate Jesus and sustain faith in what he did and represented.

Bultmann's and Halbwachs's common failure is their refusal even to ask how pericopae, texts, and physical sites reflected what ordinary people of the first century believed. Their tactic of invoking extreme instances of construction, including miracle stories, reminds us of

modern investigators invoking the most extreme instances of distortion—
the story of Paul Revere alone alerting thousands of Middlesex County
farmers of the British advance; Betsy Ross making a flag at General
Washington's request; Kentucky farmers defeating the British at New
Orleans—as archetypes of social memory. Although we have little direct
evidence on what or how the people of first-century Palestine thought
about Jesus, we have plenty of indirect evidence, including the Gospels
themselves (see de Jonge). That historical documents reflected and/or
determined what ordinary people believed is an assumption beset with
pitfalls, but it is reasonable and defensible. If we search these documents
for the many ways in which the Gospels could have misrepresented belief
about Jesus, we will surely find them, but we will have failed to meet
what the task at hand—what the Gospels reveal of early Christianity's
social memory—requires.

Gospel writers inscribed not the raw experience of Jesus' life but
what informants led them to understand. As Clifford Geertz has
remarked, however, not everyone is a liar and one need not know everything in order to know something (1973:3–30). The job of social memory
scholarship is to assess what we know: assembling documents like the
Gospels, estimating their meanings and relation to the culture of which
their authors were a part, and drawing conclusions. From the social
memory standpoint, then, our object of study is not the authenticity of
the Gospels; it is rather the Gospels as sources of information about the
popular beliefs of early Christianity. The Gospels are critical to us
because they put us in touch with the way early Christians conceived
Jesus' place in their world, and because without them our understanding
of the social memory of this world would be more shallow. At question,
then, is what popular meanings were conveyed, aspirations satisfied,
fears quieted, by Jesus' invocation. To this end, neither Bultmann's
analysis of isolated verbal forms nor Halbwachs's analysis of physical
sites take us very far.

New Theories

Many past instances can be interpreted in ways to satisfy present
interests. But the problem that Bultmann and Halbwachs fail to address is
whether the interest theory of social memory applies to one set of historical situations or generalizes to all. The distinction is critical. If interest
theory captures the general mindset of elites, then everything known
about the past, not just Jesus, becomes subject to presentist reinterpretation. The stories of Noah, Moses, David, the Exile, etcetera come into
view as projections of religious needs. Form criticism is evidently
grounded in this more general theory. Crossan, for example, declares that

all historical understanding is a "reconstruction" that is "interactive of past and present," and on the question of whether past or present dominates this interaction he leaves little to the imagination. "Positivism or historicism is the delusion that we can see the water without our face being mirrored in it" (1998:3). But can we see any faces besides our own? On the other hand, if the mirror metaphor refers only to early Christianity, what conditions immunize other historical periods from its relevance? That one cannot know the past without interference from one's personal and social situation is certain, but does the past's content have anything at all to do with the way it is apprehended?

Form criticism's inability to answer these questions results from grave doubts about the Gospels' authenticity, which its practitioners have developed ingeniously. Crossan devised a sophisticated stage theory beginning with (1) individuals retaining their original memories of what Jesus said and did; (2) then modifying these contents as they transmit them; and (3) recipients concocting the received episodes as they please (1998). Since the contents of the Gospels are largely derived from the last two phases, they must represent the social conditions in which recipients reside more accurately than the original events they purport to describe. Norman Perrin sharpens this point in his two-step model of information flow: from Jesus to the evangelist; from the evangelist to the church. In the process, almost everything original gets lost (Perrin 1967). Bruce Malina reiterates the idea in terms of levels: "we have an author, such as 'Luke,' (final level of the tradition, level 3), telling us what somebody else said (intermediate level of tradition, level 2) that Jesus said and did (the career of Jesus, level 1)" (2001:198). The movement between levels, according to Malina, is an editing process similar to American newspapers which purport to transmit valid information but actually serve special interests, including pro-Israel lobbies, with "continued material support of Israel." It has been thus since "the Catastrophe, the founding of the Zionist state"(2001:199). Malina's torturous logic would not be worth mentioning were it not so typically distracting. Since Zionist influence has never been strong enough to reduce, let alone deter, anti-Zionist expression, Malina's parallel exemplifies the perils of ransacking the past for far-fetched ideological leverage. Constructionism's pathologies, it is true, must not be mistaken for its paradigm, but the content of these pathologies, dramatized by the failure of peers and editors to challenge Malina, reveal an intellectual climate that gives constructionist assertions more deference than they deserve.

The indirect information flow that Crossan, Perrin, and Malina describe is often compared with the rumor game in which one child whispers a message to a second, the second to a third, and so on until the last child receives a final version totally different from the original. The danger of such a loose analogy is evident in William Herndon's Abraham Lincoln papers (1889), which are based on the same kind of oral tradition from which the Gospel writers drew their accounts of Jesus. After President Lincoln's 1865 assassination, Herndon, his former law partner, began an intense series of correspondences and interviews with people who had known Lincoln between 1831–1837 in New Salem, Illinois—a commercial village which emerged and disappeared in the process of westward population movement. Herndon captured 30 years of Lincoln oral tradition, just as Mark captured approximately the same number of years of Jesus oral tradition. Among the many things Herndon wished to learn about Lincoln's young adulthood was his relation to Ann Rutledge, a New Salem girl who died while young Lincoln was presumably courting her (1889:1.128–42). The question is important not only for its romantic interest but also because, if true, it would demonstrate the contingency of history: Lincoln would have probably not become president if he had married this simple country girl rather than Mary Todd, the well-connected aristocrat. James G. Randall, arguably the greatest Lincoln scholar, prefigured Malina's model when he dismissed one key document suggesting a romantic link: "Here is one person [Level 3] reporting what another person had written him [Level 2] concerning what that person recollected he had inferred from something that Ann [Rutledge] had casually said to him [Level 1] more than thirty-one years before!" (2.328; inserts added). Since the Herndon papers are rife with errors and inconsistencies on other matters, the romance between Ann Rutledge and Abraham Lincoln must be dismissed as legend. Such was Randall's reasonable conclusion.

Weak data, however, trump strong theories. When Douglas Wilson, a contemporary Lincoln scholar, analyzed Herndon's original documents he found all respondents agreeing that Lincoln courted and planned to marry Ann and grieved with unusual intensity after her death (1990). Such testimony, presented by individuals who could have had minimal if any influence on one another, can still be challenged on the grounds that shared beliefs are not necessarily true. But of the infinity of false beliefs that might be held about Lincoln, why was this one held with such tenacity by everyone? Since many, if not, most Lincoln scholars now believe that Lincoln had a romantic understanding with Ann Rutledge, the case is relevant to the social memory of Jesus because it illustrates the cost of setting the bar of admissibility so high that it becomes impossible to accept less than perfect evidence. To assume that evidence is wrong until proven right beyond reasonable doubt would render Lincoln's young adulthood and childhood blank. Instead of a distorted version of those periods of his life we would have no version at all. Indeed, if one applies Bultmann's method of distinctiveness (with due allowance for context) to

Abraham Lincoln's statements, many would have to be discarded because they fail the test.

Presuming that a statement is wrong until proven right beyond a reasonable doubt cuts off most knowledge of Jesus and of what his contemporaries believed about him. It puts the burden of proof on partially documented assertions while allowing skeptics to make undocumented claims about religious writings being weapons in the struggle for dominance. That the church placed on Jesus' lips a decree about forgiveness because it wished to monopolize authority in matters of punishment and pardon is unproven, but its ring of truth is enough to convince any skeptic. Theories that dismiss the Gospels as screens on which church leaders projected their agendas are instances of intellectual dandyism—exercises in creating the impression of efforts to discern meaning without seriously trying—but since they resonate with the taste of a cynical age, their burden of proof is light.

To conceive of Jesus as a mere mirror of reality is to conceive a fiction, for if our changing understanding of his life *uniquely* parallels changes in our society, then the only relevant reality would be the present, and the very concept of social memory would be meaningless. To conceive the meaning of Jesus as fixed is likewise false, since any event must appear differently as perceptual standpoints change. The problem is how to disentangle truth and fiction, and to determine whether historical facts and commemorative symbols affect the way ordinary individuals think about the past. Answering these questions in the case of Jesus, where the best evidence is vague, requires the recognition of different kinds of errors and the estimation of their costs. Those seeking to protect themselves against what statisticians call a Type I error fear to assert that something is true when it may prove to be false. As Norman Perrin would put it, "When in doubt, exclude." In contrast, those seeking to protect themselves against Type II error fear to reject an assertion as false when it may be true. "When in doubt," they would say, "include." Every assertion about Jesus carries the risk of both types of error, and different mentalities have a different tolerance for different risks. The compulsively venturesome cannot bear the thought of ignoring a single truth about the life of Jesus; they set their standards low—so low, sometimes, as to allow the imagination more freedom than it should have. Scholars disdainful of even informed speculation, on the other hand, cannot tolerate the thought of asserting something is true when it may not be; they set their standards high—so high, sometimes, as to paralyze the imagination. They are inclined against even informed speculation on first-century Christian belief. Such is the problem of Bultmann's fatally rigid criterion of dissimilarity.

Since we can arrive at no more than an approximate idea of how Jesus' followers remembered him, we must learn to manage our fear of being wrong. Numerous uncertainties attend answers to the question of how information about Jesus found its way to Mark, Matthew, Luke, and John. We cannot say for sure where or when the Gospels were written, or even who wrote them. Everything is so vague that we would be justified in dropping the whole project; but doing so would substitute total ignorance for partial knowledge, and when we contemplate that choice we realize how precious partial knowledge can be. If we had discovered the Gospels only yesterday, buried in some cave, they would be the objects of great excitement and we would be grateful to possess at last a rich source of evidence putting us into contact with Jesus' contemporaries, if not Jesus himself. I do not propose that first-century written documents be subjected to lower standards of evidence than those applied to data-rich topics. I propose instead that we be aware of the cost of rejecting evidence of which we cannot be totally certain, that uncertain conclusions may bring more net benefit than a studied determination not to reach any conclusion at all—or a determination to believe, aside from cynical claims about the invention of the past, that there is no conclusion to be reached.

SOCIAL MEMORY AS AN ACT OF CREATION AND RECEPTION

Authors and artists who preserve social memory do their work with an audience in mind, and since creators and audiences are members of the same social world, the former know what their work will mean to the latter. Since culture producers, including authors of the Gospels, live under the same roof as their consumers, their relations can be represented in the form of a cultural diamond, as in the figure below.

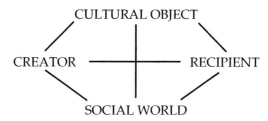

This figure, with its four points (creator, recipient, social world, cultural object) and six connecting links, is no theory because it neither specifies nor explains causal direction. It is simply a model, an accounting scheme, that allows us to keep track of different kinds of data, order their interconnections, and locate gaps in our knowledge (Griswold 1994). Clearly, there exists little evidence about the Gospel *creators'* identities and motives, while evidence on their *recipients'* presuppositions is even weaker. About the first-century Christian *social world* and its *cultural objects,* including the Gospels and Scriptures, much more is known, and since their creators' motives and recipients' reactions are affected by common social experience, recipient beliefs are inferable from an era's texts, symbols, and other cultural objects. The cultural diamond's connecting links furnish the warrant for drawing inferences about memory from knowledge of social worlds and cultural objects, and for embedding changes in the memory of individuals in social change. Such must be our methodological tenet. We cannot imagine ourselves in the shoes of an early Christian listening to an elder reading about Jesus, then try to guess what such a person would think about what she is hearing. We can understand the scene, however, by identifying it, "by searching out and analyzing the symbolic forms—words, images, institutions, behaviors—in terms of which, in each place, people actually represented themselves to themselves and to one another" (Geertz 1983:58). The cultural diamond's logic is identical: we see the world from the "native's point of view" by making contact with the thoughtworld of his community, by reconstructing the context in which its members wrote, spoke, and listened.

CONCLUSION: IN THE GRIP OF MEMORY

Witnesses usually get something wrong, but we depend on them to give us a general idea of what happened in situations where we are absent. Social memory is preserved by witnesses, and the content of the tradition they convey is more than a mere reflection of their needs and troubles. Without the stabilizing force of tradition, Jesus' image would become blurred as new generations replace one another and would eventually cease to be recognizable.

Tradition, strictly defined, is a *traditum,* a thing handed down or transferred across generations. The thing transmitted is nothing concrete; it is a guiding pattern, an abstract conception of an event, object, practice, or person. *Traditum* inevitably changes as it is transmitted, but the receiver gets most of it from what she is given. Thus, successive generations do not create Jesus anew but inherit most of their knowledge, which is why the image of Jesus remains identifiable across generations—and centuries. Whatever the merit of Birger Gerhardsson's comparison of the way rabbis traditionally taught their disciples with the way Jesus taught his, he correctly assumes that Jesus' followers were determined to get his message right (2001). Nothing would have been easier for the early church than to accommodate Gentiles by having Jesus renounce circumcision or to make a statement about the practice of speaking in tongues, the uniting of Jews and Gentiles, whether believers could divorce non-Christian spouses, what role women might play in the ministry (Blomberg: 31–32), but this never happens. Since the past possesses its own authority, it is not always serviceable as a screen for the projection of present issues.

Gerhardsson's analysis of Jesus reminds us of an even less reconstructable man—Confucius. Because the ancient Chinese lacked a transcendental ideal that distanced them from the world, their morality was completely secularized, devoid of prophetic zeal (see Zhang and Schwartz). They were dedicated in their adjustment to the world and relentless in their exaltation of tradition. Reverence for Confucius and the inconceivability of reconstructing him was the very keystone of this tradition, and while his place in China's collective imagination could be officially suspended, as during the Cultural Revolution, it was too deeply installed, too sacred, to be altered fundamentally. This does not mean that Confucius was "the same today and tomorrow as he was yesterday." If his assumed character and teachings had not resonated with China's changing conditions, he could have never been idolized for so long. Progressive intellectuals always criticized Confucius because his doctrines of self-restraint and conformity stand in opposition to ideologies of change (Louie: 1–16); on the other hand, establishments found Confucius necessary to legitimate themselves. The tension has always been resolved by what the Chinese call "critical inheritance"—a form of social memory with no Western counterpart. "Critical inheritance" is a deliberative process whereby positive aspects of historical figures are embraced; negative ones recognized but rejected. Thus, Confucius can be revered—must be revered—by the very institutions and individuals that find his political convictions inconvenient. Might the malleability of Jesus have been similarly, if not identically, limited?

There is no community, past or present, whose true history is a matter of indifference. When Newburyport, Massachusetts celebrated the Tricentennial of its founding, the festival's organizers consulted historians in order to ensure the authenticity of the forty events depicted on floats and in other historical displays (see Warner). Their efforts were part of a secular ritual of consecration that promoted the trust needed to identify with the city and its past. Christians, on the other hand, took most of what they knew about Jesus at face value and felt no need to validate it; for they believed in their Scriptures, despite gaps and contradictions, more strongly than we believe in ours. Our skeptical generation must somehow identify with these strong beliefs—this social memory. I, like a streetsweeper, have tried to clear away some of the intellectual debris that prevents us from doing so.

PROMINENT PATTERNS IN THE SOCIAL MEMORY OF JESUS AND FRIENDS

Richard A. Horsley

> All beginnings contain an element of recollection. This is particularly so when a social group makes a concerted effort to begin with a wholly new start. There is a measure of complete arbitrariness in the very nature of any such attempted beginning.... But the absolutely new is inconceivable.... In all modes of experience we always base our particular experiences on a prior context in order to ensure that they are intelligible at all; prior to any single experience, our mind is already predisposed with a framework of outlines.... (Connerton: 6)

Jesus had little or no memory. At least that is the impression one receives from presentations of prominent members of the Jesus Seminar. More conservative interpreters leave Jesus' memory seemingly intact. There appears to be an irony in the way Jesus scholarship has developed in the last decade or so. Some of the liberal leaders of the Jesus Seminar who further honed the critical methods developed earlier in the twentieth century produce a Jesus who is seemingly detached from his culture. Israelite tradition does not play a prominent role in their construction of Jesus. More conservative interpreters, on the other hand, who give less attention to critical methods, view Jesus as still connected (negatively and/or positively) with Jewish tradition, at least as constructed by Christian theological scholarship. Both, of course, are under pressures, whether those of Christian doctrine or those of marketing a Jesus compelling to contemporary readers, to come up with a distinctively different if not an utterly unique figure.

Research into various concerns of biblical studies and related fields, meanwhile, has problematized a number of the basic assumptions and concepts of standard scholarship on Jesus and the Gospels. Recent exploration of new approaches to and previously unrecognized aspects of the (canonical and noncanonical) Gospels and other texts that provide the principal sources for interpretation of Jesus, moreover, bring new light to old problems and solutions. Scholars in other fields have called attention to "social memory" or "cultural memory" as a historical force that has far more influence on peoples' lives than the ideas and literature of cultural elites. Werner Kelber has pioneered exploration of cultural memory as an important factor in the development of Gospel materials in connection with the interface of orality and literacy. In this volume the younger Gospel scholars Alan Kirk and Tom Thatcher are calling the wider field of New Testament studies to attend critically to the importance of social memory. Recent studies of social memory happen to overlap compellingly with, and to deepen the insights of, other new approaches to Jesus and the Gospels. Critical attention to social memory and how we can get at it might well enable us to discern that Jesus indeed had a memory. Interspersed with discussions of the implications of new research and approaches, I will examine how the highly sophisticated method developed by leaders of the Jesus Seminar, particularly John Dominic Crossan, tends to detach Jesus from Israelite cultural tradition, and then explore how recent studies of social memory can enable us to see Jesus and the early Jesus movement as firmly rooted in Israelite social memory.

New Research and Fresh Approaches

During the last three or four decades a combination of new questions, fresh perspectives, borrowed methods, and expanding research has dramatically changed the way we approach and interpret biblical texts. The standard assumptions, concepts, and approaches of the New Testament field in general and of Gospel and Jesus studies in particular have been challenged and undermined and, to a considerable degree, replaced. The landscape of the historical context of the Gospels has undergone the most extensive change. The way we read texts has also broadened. Most recently extensive new research is undermining standard old assumptions about the cultural context of New Testament texts. Now the introduction of the approach and comparative materials of studies in social memory (or cultural memory—see the introductory essay of this volume) will strongly reinforce some of the most significant challenges to older assumptions and approaches, confirm some of the new approaches, and induce distinctive new insights.

An early and elementary historical opening came with the recognition of the considerable social and cultural diversity in ancient Judea. This recognition gradually cut through the theologically constructed scheme of Christianity developing from and succeeding Judaism that had previously effectively blocked the recognition of that diversity. Standard essentialist concepts such as "Judaism," "normative Judaism," and "Christianity," turn out to have no historical referents. What could be called Judaism or Christianity had not yet emerged in late Second Temple times. The Sadducees, Pharisees, and Essenes together comprised only a tiny fraction of the "Jewish" people. From soon after his crucifixion, followers of Jesus formed differing groups. While some scholars resist acknowledging the diversity, still projecting a monolithic Judaism (see Sanders), and many still write of "(early) Judaism" and "(early) Christianity," others at least take such halfway measures as speaking about "Judaisms" or "formative Judaism."

Such timid scholarly moves, however, still operate on the anachronistic assumption that religion was separate from political-economic structures and institutions. When we deal with the Jerusalem temple and high priesthood, for example, we are dealing unavoidably also with the political-economic institution(s) that headed the temple-state maintained in Judea by imperial regimes as an instrument of their political domination and economic extraction. The high priestly aristocracy was responsible for collection of the tribute to Caesar as well as sacrifices on behalf of Rome and the emperor. The Passover festival celebrated the people's political-economic, as well as religious, deliverance from bondage to Pharaoh, under the watchful eyes of the soldiers that the Roman governor had posted on the porticoes of the temple.

The dominant reality in the political-economic-religious structure was the fundamentally conflictual divide between the imperial rulers and their Herodian and high priestly clients whose wealth and power derived from the tribute, taxes, and tithes they extracted, on the one hand, and the village producers they ruled and taxed, on the other. Nearly all the sources portray this clearly (see Sirach, 1–2 Maccabees, *1 Enoch*, Josephus's histories, Mark). Perhaps the most dramatic illustration of the fundamental political-economic-religious conflict is that the period of the mission and movement(s) of Jesus was framed historically by five major widespread popular revolts against the imperial and Jerusalem rulers: the Maccabean Revolt in the 160s B.C.E., the prolonged resistance to Herod's takeover from 40–37 B.C.E., the revolts in Galilee, Judea, and Perea after Herod's death in 4 B.C.E., the great revolt of 66–70 C.E., and the Bar Kokhba Revolt in 132–35 C.E. The sources also feature division and conflicts between scribal groups and the Jerusalem high priestly rulers and their imperial sponsors (*Psalms of Solomon*, DSS, Josephus).

Compounding the conflictual divide between rulers and ruled were the historical regional differences between Galilee (and Samaria) and Judea/Jerusalem (Horsley, 1995). Galileans, many of whom were presumably descendants and heirs of earlier Israelite peoples, were not brought under Jerusalem rule until a hundred years before Jesus. Interpreters of Jesus, Jesus movements, and the Gospels have barely begun to deal with the implications of these differences.

Simultaneous with these changes in the landscape of the historical context of Jesus, Jesus movements, and the development of the Gospels, some interpreters were learning how to read New Testament literature (Gospels, Acts, Epistles, etc.) as more than the text fragments of isolated sayings and decontextualized pericopae. Especially significant was the recognition that Mark and other Gospels are complexly narrated stories, with plot, subplots, multiple conflicts, and their own narrative styles and agenda (e.g., Kelber 1979; Horsley 2001). More recently some also recognized, for example, that while the *Gospel of Thomas* presents a collection of sayings and parables, the hypothesized document Q is evidently a sequence of speeches rather than a mere collection of sayings (see Kirk's essay in this volume; Horsley and Draper).

Recent research has also decisively undermined some major standard assumptions about the culture of ancient Judea and Galilee, particularly assumptions about literacy and the Hebrew Scriptures. Not only are some scholars now suggesting that the composition of the Torah and Prophetic books should be dated relatively later than previously thought (perhaps in Hellenistic times), those who have closely examined the multiple scrolls of books of the Torah found at Qumran are also concluding that the text of the books of the Torah was not yet uniform or stable. Different textual traditions still existed in the same scribal community (and presumably in Jerusalem as well), each of which was still undergoing development. The Dead Sea Scrolls also supply further examples of alternative Torah (4QMMT; the *Temple Scroll*) and alternative versions of Israelite history and tradition (not rewritten Bible; *Jubilees*, Pseudo–Philo, Biblical Antiquities) that coexisted and competed, at least among scribal circles.

Compounding the implications of such research is the mounting evidence and recognition that literacy was at least as limited in Judea and Galilee as in the rest of the Roman empire (see Harris; Hezser). Oral communication dominated. Indeed, even scribal circles such as the Qumranites apparently recited their texts aloud (see Jaffee). Besides being extremely expensive and therefore rare, scrolls were cumbersome and virtually unreadable to anyone who did not already have the text memorized.

The recent research in these areas thus gives powerful confirmation to hypotheses that only a few interpreters were previously ready to entertain and willing to argue. First, Israelite culture was as diverse as were the groups and communities that comprised Judean, Galilean, and Samaritan society. Different versions of Israelite tradition coexisted and competed. The well-known differences between the Sadducees and the Pharisees can be multiplied.

Second, since they were expensive as well as cumbersome, and few could read them, scrolls of different textual traditions of the Torah and alternative Torah would have existed even in Jerusalem, much less in the villages of Judea and Galilee. That most people were nonliterate, however, does not mean that they did not know and cultivate Israelite tradition. It simply gives powerful reinforcement of the hypothesis that, as in other agrarian societies, popular Israelite traditions paralleled and competed with versions of Israelite tradition maintained in scribal circles and in the temple—for which anthropologists use the terminology "little tradition" and "great tradition" (Horsley and Draper; Horsley 2001; Herzog). It may well be that the Hasmonean insistence that the Galileans accept "the laws of the Judeans" when they took over the area (Josephus, *Ant.* 13. 318–19) meant that they assigned the Pharisees and other scribal retainers to press their own "traditions of the elders" and other officially recognized "(temple-) state law" on the populace. But "the laws of the Judeans" would hardly have replaced the local customs, covenantal teachings, Elijah-Elisha stories, and other Israelite traditions cultivated in Galilean village communities.

Third, whether written copies existed, texts were recited or performed aloud to groups of people, not read silently by individuals. From Judean texts themselves (e.g., 1QS 6:6–8) it is clear that texts were recited in/to groups, almost certainly from the text that existed in memory, not (more than) from a written copy (see Jaffee). Thus even in scribal circles, texts existed more in the memory than written on scrolls, and were learned as well as heard communally by recitation. How much more therefore in village communities that lacked both scrolls and literacy were traditional Israelite materials such as stories of heroes, covenantal laws and teachings, victory songs, etcetera, performed and cultivated orally.

Fourth, in a social-cultural context dominated by oral communication, where even when written scrolls existed, the texts were recited from memory, composition was usually carried out not only for but also in performance. Greek and Latin writers describe how they composed texts in their heads, relying on memory for certain materials, and only later dictated their composed text to a scribe who wrote it down (see Small). The same seems the likely procedure among Judean scribal circles (e.g., for the *Psalms of Solomon, 1 Enoch*, Daniel). If it was the rule among literate circles, then composition in performance is all the more likely for popular literature such as the Gospel of Mark and Q, in communities where literacy would have been even more limited than among the elite.

Recognition that Gospel texts, even if they existed in written form, were performed in groups of people changes dramatically the way they must be understood to have "worked" and therefore the way they should be approached. In standard older biblical studies, the theological interpreter was trying to reconstruct the meaning of a text fragment such as an individual saying or pericope. The text fragment, abstracted from its fuller literary and historical context, was assumed to possess meaning-in-itself.

If the text is rather taken as a complete unit of communication per-formed (regularly) to groups of people in a particular historical situation, then interpreters must try to understand how the story or speech did its work in resonating with the group to whom it was performed. Standard New Testament studies has left us ill-equipped to carry out such a chal-lenging task.

Yet help is now available from other fields that are also just discover-ing oral-derived texts that can, to a degree, be understood in performance. Recent work in social linguistics, ethnography of perform-ance, ethnopoetics, and recent theory of verbal art that draws upon the insights of the others, all draw attention to the special importance of two aspects in particular: the group context in which an oral-derived text was performed, and the cultural tradition that the text referenced metonymi-cally in order to resonate with the community of hearers (Foley 1995; 2002; Horsley and Draper; Horsley 2001). As Werner Kelber has recog-nized, studies of social memory promise to be especially helpful in approaching the relationship of oral-derived texts and the tradition they reference, the cultural "biosphere" in which they do their work (1994).

SOCIAL MEMORY VERSUS ASSUMPTIONS OF JESUS-QUESTERS

There are already some fundamental reasons why the standard pro-cedure used by the Jesus Seminar and before it by form criticism (in which many of us were trained) to identify "data" for reconstruction of the teaching of Jesus is seriously problematic as a method of historical investigation. The Gospels are assumed to be mere containers of data. The data, however, must be removed from the containers for critical eval-uation. Modern rational ("scientific") criteria determine what is potentially good data. While tending to dismiss narratives as too mythic and corrupted by miraculous elements, liberal Jesus-questers in particu-lar tend to focus heavily on sayings. The determinative criteria derive from the dominant modern western literate definition of real knowledge as stated in propositional terms. In contrast to subjective feelings and values, only the sayings material from the Gospels sufficiently resembles this propositional knowledge that it can be relied upon as historical data for Jesus. Accordingly rigorously critical Jesus scholars carefully isolate sayings from their literary contexts that are flawed by faith perspectives in order to evaluate their potential as data.

This procedure is seriously problematic. It is difficult, in the first place, to imagine that anyone anywhere ever communicated effectively by uttering isolated individual sayings. Purposely isolating sayings from their contexts in the ancient texts, moreover, effectively discards the primary guide we might have as historians to determine both how a given saying functioned as a component in a genuine unit of communication (a speech or a narrative) and its possible meaning context(s) for ancient speakers and hearers. With no ancient guide for its meaning-context, then, interpretation is determined only, and almost completely, by the modern scholar, who constructs a new meaning-context on the basis of other such radically decontextualized sayings.

Recent studies of social memory not only confirm those observations, but explain further why and how the standard procedure of form criticism and (some members of) the Jesus Seminar is fundamentally flawed as historical method. A major problem is that these Jesus scholars, along with many others in the New Testament field, are working with a modern (mis-) understanding of memory rooted in the modern western understanding of knowledge. Studies of social memory can help us identify several interrelated aspects of this fundamental misunderstanding. Much of the following discussion engages the work of John Dominic Crossan because his *Historical Jesus,* as the most intensively marketed and most widely read analysis of Jesus sayings, has been highly influential, and because, recognizing memory as a problem, he has seriously grappled with understanding how it works in another methodologically sophisticated and magisterial treatise (1998). But the discussion is also an attempt to grapple critically with what have been standard assumptions and operating procedures in the field of Gospel and Jesus studies that now seem problematic.

The "textual model" of memory: Form critics and their more recent heirs assume that the route that Jesus sayings took from Jesus himself to the literary containers in which they can now be found was oral tradition, that is, the memories of Jesus' followers. As Werner Kelber pointed out over twenty years ago, form criticism depends on the assumptions of modern print culture (1983). The model for how the followers' memory handled Jesus' sayings was how Matthew and Luke handled what they found in Mark and the reconstructed (hypothetical) Q, that is, texts that the modern scholars understood in terms of print culture. That is, not only were the sayings understood as texts, for which Jesus scholars strove to establish the original wording (*ipsissima verba,* or at least *ipsissima structura*), but they worked with a "textual model" of memory.

Students of social memory, however, have explained that this textual model of memory is also an expression of a modern literate definition of knowledge, propositional knowledge that can be separated out as "objective" from the "subjective" aspect of memory (Fentress and Wickham: 2–5). Not only is each piece of knowledge like a text, but the part of memory that carries those pieces is like a text. Thus for the form critics and their successors in the Jesus Seminar, the memory of the Jesus-followers was a container for Jesus-sayings, just like the Gospels into which they fed the sayings. The textual model of memory, however, rests on a fundamental misunderstanding of memory. The reason propositional knowledge in memory seems "objective" is merely that "we can communicate it in words more easily" than we can the memory of "subjective" feelings. "But that has nothing to do with the structure of memory. It is a social fact. What emerges at the point of articulation is not the objective part of memory but its social aspect" (Fentress and Wickham: 6–7). Drawing on Durkheim's insight about the social character of collectively held ideas, Halbwachs recognized that memory is social, the result of social and historical forces. With regard to the Gospels and Gospel tradition as sources for the historical Jesus, the memory involved in oral tradition was not a text–like container but a social process. Moreover, insofar as the Gospels themselves as written texts were almost certainly transcripts of particular performances of the texts, they also were products of social memory. Use of the Gospels as historical sources requires the understanding of social memory.

The "copy-and-save" concept of memory: Closely related to their textual model of memory/ies, form critics and many Jesus scholars also have a "copy-and-save" conception of memory. In the traditioning process, some disciples were able to remember and repeat Jesus sayings. As indicated by the voting by members of the Jesus Seminar, in some cases the copy-and-save mechanism of memory worked well (red and pink), whereas other sayings involved a considerable degree of creativity by the tradents. While assuming the operation of this mechanism, Crossan is skeptical about how accurately it works. He concludes that in many cases the copying reproduces the "gist" of sayings, but not the precise wording of the "text." This modern intellectual (mis)understanding of memory ("copy and save") is illustrated both by Frederic Bartlett's well-known experiments among his Cambridge colleagues and friends in the 1930s and by Crossan's selective use of the results to show how undependable memory is for reliable "reproductions." As Fentress and Wickham see, Bartlett set up the experiment to prove what he suspected about memory in modern intellectual society. Bartlett had his friends read (twice) a story from the Chinook people recorded by the anthropologist Franz Boas and then repeat it soon thereafter and again years later, with mixed and unimpressive results. Crossan takes some of the results of the experiment as applicable to ancient Mediterranean peoples.

Both, however, turn out to be comparing apples and oranges, or rather an apple tree and an orange. As Fentress and Wickham note, Bartlett presented to his friends a story taken completely out of its own cultural context and quite unintelligible to his friends and utterly alien to their own culture. If he had presented them a clever new limerick similar to those commonly shared in Oxbridge culture, the results would have been dramatically different. An appropriate use of the Chinook tale for testing memory, which is social, would have been within Chinook culture. An appropriate illustration of how memory worked among early Jesus-communities would have to come from the culture of those communities. It is Crossan's (very appropriate) distrust of "copy-and-save" memory that leads him to depend so heavily on written-textual containers of sayings as sources for Jesus sayings. But as Fentress andWickham point out, "The ability of society to transmit its social memory in logical and articulate form is not dependent on the possession of writing" (45).

Memory as individual: Like Bartlett, Crossan (like many and perhaps most interpreters) apparently assumes that memory is an individual operation. Given the orientation of modern western culture, particularly in the United States, to the individual, many and perhaps most of us conceive of Jesus' sayings as teachings to individuals remembered and transmitted by individuals. It is true that memory operates through individual consciousness. But the main point that Halbwachs and his successors have been explaining is that memory is thoroughly social, the product of social forces operating through communities, movements, and societies (Fentress and Wickham: 25). Leading historians such as Marc Bloch and Peter Burke have been clear in recognizing this fundamental reality (Burke: 98).

Jesus-sayings as cultural artifacts with meaning in themselves: In accordance with the modern theory of knowledge on which they are operating, Jesus scholars and others assume that the Jesus-sayings transmitted by individual memory have meaning in themselves. That they were operating on this assumption may explain why Crossan and others in the Jesus Seminar were concerned merely to date the documents they took as containers of Jesus sayings. They did not give careful attention to the different meaning contexts and implicit hermeneutics of those different sources. Students of social memory point out that this assumption that a statement has meaning in itself is quite unwarranted. In social memory and social knowledge, a particular statement or tale operates in a larger meaning context. When the context changes, the same statement or tale takes on a more or less altered meaning appropriate to the new context (Fentress and Wickham: 68).

Jesus sayings as "unconventional" or "countercultural": The assumption that Jesus' sayings were text-like propositional statements carried in container-like memory underlies another prominent aspect of Jesus research. Under the old theological imperative to find Jesus distinctively different from "Judaism," an earlier generation of Jesus-questers established the criterion of dissimilarity (from his Jewish cultural context as well as from the early church) as one of the principal measures for the "authentic" sayings of Jesus. While the Jesus Seminar and other scholars have seriously qualified that criterion in the direction of some continuity, some leading members of the Jesus Seminar perpetuate the notion in finding Jesus' sayings to be "unconventional" or "countercultural" (see Crossan; Mack).

As historians, of course, we could immediately ask how Jesus could have become a significant historical player if he had been uttering sayings that were so dissimilar to anything in his cultural context, how anything he said would have been remembered if it had not resonated with followers embedded in a particular culture. Recent theory of performance places great emphasis on how speech works by referencing the hearers' cultural tradition, that is, memory. Studies of social memory strongly reinforce such reactions to the "dissimilarity" criterion and the "unconventional" interpretation. Especially in a new movement, as Connerton emphasizes in the first paragraph of his analysis of social memory, "the absolutely new is inconceivable." The followers of Jesus who remembered his teaching and action were responding from "an organized body of expectations based on recollection" (6). Their experience of Jesus would have been embedded in past experience. Memory represents the past and the present as connected to each other (Fentress and Wickham: 24). This approach closely parallels the recognition of oral performance analysis: tradition is key to the communication taking place (see Foley). More particularly, the images held in social memory are a mixture of pictorial images, slogans, quips, and snatches of discourse. A figure such as Jesus could not have communicated without tapping into those images in ancient Galileans, and others' social memory. Further, the images he used would have communicated effectively only by being "conventionalized and simplified: conventionalized, because the image has to be meaningful for an entire group; simplified, because in order to be generally meaningful and capable of transmission, the complexity of the image must be reduced as far as possible" (Fentress and Wickham: 47). Of course, while Jesus' teaching had to be conventionalized for effective communication with his followers, who were embedded in the Israelite "little tradition" of the peasantry (including fishers and marginalized), it was indeed most likely "counter" to the culture of the elite in Jerusalem and Tiberias. That Jesus' teaching may well have been counter to the elite culture of Jerusalem and scribal circles, who produced the Judean literature that constitutes many of our written sources for late second temple times, should not be mistaken for Jesus' teaching having been counter to Israelite culture generally. It is necessary to be more critically attentive to the differences between the elite and the popular versions of Israelite culture (see below).

The fundamental insight of Halbwachs and his successors that memory is social is simple but profound in its implications for academic endeavors such as studies of Jesus and the Gospels. In order to use the Gospels appropriately as historical sources for Jesus and early Jesus movements, therefore, we have to abandon several interrelated aspects of the modern western misunderstanding of memory, that is, the "textual model," the "copy-and-save" conception, individualization, the notion that Jesus sayings have meaning in themselves, and the presumption that Jesus sayings could have been somehow distinctively different from his cultural context.

WHY AND HOW (STUDY OF) SOCIAL MEMORY IS USEFUL FOR APPROACH TO JESUS AND JESUS-MOVEMENTS

The prominent historian Peter Burke noted some time ago that historians have two principal interests in memory. "In the first place, they need to study memory as a historical *source,* to produce a critique of the reliability of reminiscence on the lines of the traditional critique of historical documents" (99). Against the stiff resistance of their more traditional colleagues, some younger historians of the recent past moved to include "oral history" in their research. Yet historians of earlier periods also need to understand social memory in order to deal with "the oral testimonies and traditions embedded in many written records." Secondly, historians should be concerned with "memory as a historical phenomenon," including the principles of selection, variations by location, and changes over time (100). Given the character of the orally derived texts that they study, biblical historians also have a keen interest in social memory in both of these respects.

It is curious, however, that a social historian of Burke's stature did not mention a third reason for understanding the workings of social memory—for which the two interests he identified would be ancillary. Historians, especially social historians, would presumably have an interest in social movements, particularly popular movements, and, more broadly, peoples' history in general. Social memory is often the most important source for such movements. Indeed, for those popular movements that did not become prominent and gain wide notice, social memory may be virtually the only historical source. More significantly, for movements of mainly nonliterate people, their social memory would have been one of the principal forces driving their collective actions. Burke makes the passing comment that unofficial memories may differ sharply from official memories and "are sometimes historical forces in their own right," offering the examples of the German Peasant War of 1525 and the "Norman Yoke" in the English Revolution (107). Although he does not pursue the implications himself, his passing comment that "unofficial memories" become historical forces themselves leads us to consider how popular Israelite social memory may have played a creative and formative role in the movement resulting from the interaction of Jesus and his followers.

In the academic division of labor, the subject matter that we New Testament scholars deal with provides prime examples of popular leaders and movements that became historical forces that local and imperial "officials" had to reckon with. As suggested above, moreover, given the oral derivation of the Gospels and Gospel materials, the literature we interpret was apparently the product of those movements' social memory. Gospel materials, moreover, mediated both through literature (the Scriptures) and through continuing orally cultivated social memory, comprised an important component of the social memory that motivated both the German Peasant War, the English Revolution, as well as the earlier Hussites and Lollards and many other popular movements. Interpreters of Jesus and the Gospels have compelling reasons to understand social memory.

One of the most important possibilities that social memory studies helps open up for an appropriate approach to Jesus and the Gospels is its critical focus on the diversity and conflict of memories. Students of social memory have long since moved beyond the limitations of Halbwachs's teacher Durkheim, with his emphasis on societal cohesion, to the avoidance of social dissent and conflict (Burke: 106–107). They are as aware as any that the role of professional scholars, like that of schoolteaching and the media, is to reinforce official or established memory more than critically to investigate dissenting memories (Fentress and Wickham: 127). They are aware that the struggle of peoples against hegemonic memory is often the struggle of their memory against enforced forgetting, against the elimination of alternative memory (Connerton: 15).

Study of Jesus, Jesus movements, and the Gospels can learn from these students of social memory. Interpreters of Jesus and the Gospels focus on literature and movements that express opposition to the local and imperial rulers. The latter attempted to suppress those movements and their memory, through the crucifixion of Jesus and subsequent repressive action against his followers. In some cases they apparently succeeded, except that their memory survived in the oral-derived texts they left behind. Ironically, established biblical studies has sometimes effectively suppressed the subversive memory carried in the Gospels that the Roman rulers could not stamp out. This has been done by treating the texts as merely religious and by reducing the focus to Jesus as a teacher and/or to individual discipleship, while virtually ignoring the collective activity and solidarity of a popular movement. Recent studies of social memory can help interpreters of Jesus and the Gospels to appreciate how the adversarial Gospel tradition and literature are rooted not only in the subversive popular memory of Jesus and his movement, but also in the memory of earlier Israelite leaders and movements. Such studies of social memory can help New Testament scholars rediscover the memory of social movements whose voices have been silenced by established scholarship. Like the Gospel literature itself, study of social memory in Jesus movements will be subversive of long-established scholarship, challenging standard assumptions, concepts, and approaches in order to discern oppositional memories and the conflicts they engage.

Crossan declares confidently that what has been discovered about how Balkan bards (their texts and their audiences) are rooted in centuries-old tradition "has nothing whatsoever to do with the memories of illiterate peasants operating within the Jesus tradition," because of the latter's "total newness" (1998:78–79). Indeed, judging from the "data-base" listed in the "Overture" of his Jesus book (1991), the Cynic-like sage he presents is almost completely memory-less. Only one name (Adam) from Israelite tradition remains in the aphorisms and parables that Crossan has declared admissible as evidence. When he comes to presentation and analysis, he does admit to a few other allusions. But we are left wondering what the basis is for concluding that Jesus was a *Jewish* and not just a generic Mediterranean peasant.

Suspicious of the authenticity of most of Jesus' prophetic sayings, he thus eliminates from his data base references to Abraham, Isaac and Jacob, Solomon and the Queen of the South, and Jonah, as well as the traditional Israelite prophetic forms of some of those sayings. Following standard critical criteria in extracting sayings from narrative context, he ignores the prominent references and allusions in Mark and elsewhere to Moses, Elijah, the exodus, the twelve tribes of Israel, and the covenant meal. Because, in standard procedure, he focuses on individual sayings, he does not even notice Jesus' use of traditional Israelite forms and patterns, such as components of Mosaic covenantal patterns and allusions to covenantal teaching.

Although Crossan's procedure tends to eliminate references to Israelite tradition, the "data-base" of the Jesus tradition in which he finds "total newness," if we examine it more closely with "ears to hear," does indeed make numerous references or allusions to Israelite tradition. "Finger of God" refers to the exodus. The issues of adultery and of giving tribute to Caesar are rooted in the Mosaic covenant. "Blessings" and "woes" are components of the Mosaic covenant and "woes" crop up prominently in the prophets. The clever saying about giving one's shift as well as one's cloak refers to Mosaic covenantal law. "Go bury my father" alludes to the story of Elijah's commissioning of Elisha. The parable of the tenants in the vineyard resonates deeply with the song of the vineyard in Isaiah's prophecies. The image of a division of families was used by the prophet Micah. The prophetic action and prophecies against the temple are reminiscent of Jeremiah's prophecies and prophetic actions, etcetera. Moreover, other images (swearing by Jerusalem) and figures (the Samaritan, the Levite and the priest) in Jesus' teaching refer directly to more recent Israelite institutions and history. The "newness" of Crossan's Jesus tradition is in fact not "total." His followers' memory, even when its "copy and save" mechanism is judged dysfunctional, cannot help but carry (Jesus' own?) memory of and allusion to Israelite tradition, including many references to central aspects of that tradition, such as exodus and covenant, Moses and Elijah, prophetic oracle and covenantal teaching.

If we broadened our purview beyond Crossan's critically restricted "data-base" to include the prophetic materials in Q and the narrative in Mark, then the Jesus tradition (however it be judged for "authenticity") is simply permeated with social memory of Israelite tradition. The obvious implication: the Jesus tradition is far from "totally new." It cannot possibly be understood except as rooted in Israelite social memory. That holds even if Mark were "located" in its composition and performance in Syria or even in Rome. Even if the (precanonical) Gospel of Mark belonged to communities of "Gentiles," they apparently identify with and understand the text in terms of its resonance with Israelite tradition. In seeking help from studies of social memory to understand Jesus and the Gospels, therefore, we must focus not only on the Jesus tradition itself but also on its grounding in and continuity with Israelite tradition. That is, we are dealing not only with social memory in the development toward and formation of the oral-derived texts of Gospels themselves but also with the social memory of Israelite tradition that those texts referenced in order to resonate with their hearers (see Foley; Horsley and Draper).

How Do We Gain Access to the Social Memory of Jesus People?

The obvious next question then is how we can gain access to the social memory of the earliest and subsequent "followers" of Jesus, the bearers of the social memory of Jesus' mission and message who were also embedded in Israelite social memory. Students of social memory seek access to it through various kinds of sources, including oral traditions, memoirs and written records (memory transformed through writing), public monuments and other sources of images, places and landscape images, and rituals and other actions. Students of social memory of Jesus tradition and Israelite tradition have only some of these available as sources. How we might be able to use those sources, moreover, requires some critical analysis, given recent research on late Second Temple Israelite society and culture.

For social memory of Jesus tradition itself, we largely lack monuments and landscape images and have minimal access to rituals (Lord's supper, baptism). Recent recognition of the predominantly oral communication environment and the likelihood that texts were orally composed and performed prior to and subsequent to being written down has problematized the use of the Gospels as sources. We must still figure out, and almost certainly will be debating among ourselves for some time, the degree to which the Gospels represent transcripts of oral-derived (performed) texts or written records, that is, memory transformed by written composition.

For social memory of Israelite tradition it can no longer be a matter of consulting the "Old Testament"/Hebrew Bible passages listed in the apparatus of our copy of the Greek New Testament. As recent research has shown, few chirographs existed in ancient Judea (and Galilee), and those few were mainly in scribal circles, where texts were nevertheless recited from memory (see Jaffee). As noted above, moreover, different versions of the Torah and Prophets coexisted even in literate elite circles. The people who responded to Jesus, who participated in Jesus movements, were largely ordinary people who would have had little or no direct contact with written texts, perhaps not even indirect contact. They would have known Israelite tradition through oral communication mainly in their village communities, with perhaps some indirect influence from scribal retainers (e.g., Pharisees) who represented Jerusalem interests in occasional interaction with villagers. We therefore cannot use biblical and other Judean literature as direct sources for the Judean and Galilean "little tradition." Because it was apparently parallel to and in some regular interaction with the "great tradition" represented by the developing texts of the Torah, Prophets, and other versions of Jerusalem-based tradition, however, we can use written biblical and other Judean texts as indirect sources for the Israelite popular tradition, particularly where we have reason to believe there was overlap. We also have other indirect sources. Often we can discern from Josephus's portrayal of popular movements and protests that such actions are informed by Israelite tradition. This seems fairly clear, for example, from his accounts of the popular movements led by "prophets" and popularly acclaimed "kings" and by protests in the temple at Passover. Finally, the Gospels themselves, insofar as they are products of popular circles, provide evidence for Israelite social memory among Galilean (and Judean) popular tradition, both of traditional figures and traditional cultural forms.

The net effect of these critical complications regarding our sources only serves to indicate the historical importance of Israelite social memory for understanding Jesus, Jesus movements, and their literature. Another effect, of course, is to make all the more important and exciting (in anticipation) the help that studies of social memory can provide us, particularly as it appears to dovetail with and supplement the results of recent research that has undermined standard older assumptions, concepts, and approaches in the field of Gospel studies.

THE SOCIAL MEMORY OF JESUS BUILT ON ISRAELITE SOCIAL MEMORY

Finally, the way social memory analysis might contribute to a more defensible approach to the historical Jesus can be illustrated in focusing briefly on two particular complexes of material in the Gospel of Mark that resonate with those same complexes in Israelite social memory: renewal of the Mosaic covenant and renewal of Israel by a new Moses and Elijah. Given the usual orientation in New Testament studies to culture divorced from concrete historical political-economic life, it is important to emphasize that Mark (and Q) were rooted in and reflect the violent domination of the Roman imperial rulers and their client rulers over subject peoples and the continuing struggle of the latter to resist. That struggle, moreover, had intensified in the time of Jesus and his mission, which are so vividly framed by the widespread revolts of Judeans and Galileans in 4–2 B.C.E. and 66–70 C.E. Many recent treatments of social memory may be all the more helpful for investigation of Jesus and the Gospels because they give special attention to subordinate groups and peoples.

In this connection we can perhaps work analogously from Connerton's critique of the approach followed by some oral historians when we focus on Gospel materials and Jesus-followers. In both cases the aim is to open channels for the hearing of voices that are otherwise silenced by scholarly concepts and procedures. Like recent Jesus-interpreters (note the subtitle "The Life of a Mediterranean Jewish Peasant"), however, oral historians approached their sources with the concept of a life history, as if their subjects thought like educated modern people of affairs. This approach, however, may actually impede the aim of the historians.

> The oral history of subordinate groups will produce another type of history: one in which not only will most of the details be different, but in which the very construction of meaningful shapes will obey a different principle. Different details will emerge because they are inserted, as it were, into a different kind of narrative home.... In [the] culture of subordinate groups ... the life histories of its members have a different rhythm ... not patterned by the individual's intervention in the working of dominant institutions". (Connerton: 19)

Analogously, seeking for what Jesus actually said or did, much less his individual "life," will only block access to a Jesus who was historically significant as catalyst of movements who remembered him. Not only was their memory social, but Jesus became significant for his interaction with them in action and speech taken in his and their fundamentally conflictual historical situation. As suggested by this analogy from Connerton, as by all the above discussion, an approach to the historical Jesus and the Gospels must be relational and contextual.

In a complex, multifaceted approach I have recently attempted to understand how we can appreciate certain broad (Israelite) cultural patterns that are discernible in the speeches of Q and in the story of Mark (Horsley and Draper; Horsley 2001). By focusing on individual sayings and narrative episodes extracted from the speeches and overall narrative that formed the units of communication we render them unintelligible, because we decontextualize them. In their own historical communication context, however, what our standard scholarly analytical practices render into unintelligible text fragments were held together intelligibly by cultural patterns or "scripts" derived from Israelite tradition, which constitute/provide the tacit infrastructure as well as the cultural meaning context of the speeches or the broader narrative of which they were integral components. Ancient Judean and other texts may well provide our only sources for and access to these patterns and scripts. Yet their operation in Mark and Q was probably not derived from written texts, but rather from their continuing presence in popular Judean and Galilean tradition. Central among these were the social memory of Mosaic covenant and of popular prophetic and messianic movements. Combined with the recent research and new approaches outlined at the outset above, recent studies of social memory can help open the way to discerning how such popular Israelite social memory was operating in the interaction of Jesus and his followers as represented in Mark and Q.

In the introduction to this volume, Alan Kirk (drawing on several studies of social memory) explains that

> the past, itself constellated by the work of social memory, provides the *framework* for cognition, organization, and interpretation of the experiences of the present. The salient past, immanent in the narrative patterns in which it has become engrained in social memory, provides the very cognitive and linguistic habits by which a group perceives, orients itself, has its "being in the world." ... It is precisely because of the orienting, stabilizing effect of memory that free, innovative action in the present becomes possible. (15–16; emphasis mine; see also Schwartz 2000:225–30; Casey 2000:150–53)

One of the *frameworks* for cognition, organization, and interpretation of political-economic-religious life in ancient Israel, perhaps the principal framework, was the Mosaic covenant. The six-component structure discerned by comparison with second-millennium B.C.E. Hittite suzerainty treaties by Mendenhall and others can be discerned in Exod 20 and Josh 24. From fragments of prophetic oracles such as Mic 6:1–7 and Isa 1:2–3; 3:13–15, it is clear that this deeply rooted framework (that still included the appeal to witnesses) continued to inform prophetic protests (literally in the name of God) against the rulers' oppression of the people. Readers of the Community Rule and Damascus Rule from Qumran can recognize that the framework—in the somewhat simplified three-part form of God's deliverance, commandments to the people, and pronouncement of blessings and curses as sanction on those commandments—continued to inform the organization of dissident movements into late Second Temple times (see Baltzer). Those Qumran texts also demonstrate that the form could be transformed so that the blessings and curses became the new declaration of divine deliverance, with other devices marshaled to serve as sanctions.

This same covenant framework turns out to be prominent in the earliest Gospel texts. As I have argued in larger treatments of the speech in Q/Luke 6:20–49, all those sayings that have been classified into the essentialist category of "sapiental" can be more intelligibly understood as components of a performative speech of covenant renewal (see Horsley and Draper). After declaring God's current/imminent action of deliverance and judgment in the blessings and woes, Q's Jesus pronounces renewed covenantal teachings which make numerous allusions to traditional covenantal principles and exhortations, followed by the double parable of houses built on rock and sand, which serve as sanction on "keeping his word." Similarly, argued in a larger treatment of Mark as a complete story (Horsley 2001), the series of dialogues in Mark 10 which explicitly recite the covenantal commandments, can also be discerned to be a coherent renewal of Mosaic covenant at a crucial point in the narrative sequence, following the announcement and demonstration that the kingdom of God is now at hand. As is particularly clear in Q/Luke 6:20–49, moreover, the covenantal pattern is not simply the framework for organization of sayings and dialogues in the texts of Q and Mark, but the framework of organization of the communities of the movement among whom the speeches and Gospel story were being performed. The traditional covenantal pattern thus becomes the framework of orientation, aiding discernment of what was wrong (people were divided among themselves, not observing the fundamental covenantal principles), and the framework of stabilizing innovation (creatively "updating" the covenantal form and teaching to effect renewal of mutual cooperation, sharing, and solidarity).

In Mark especially, however, the Mosaic covenant pattern extends beyond the covenant renewal dialogues into other episodes (Horsley, 2001). Most prominently, Jesus insists on the basis of the covenantal commandments of God that local economic needs ("honor your father and mother") must take priority, rejecting the pressure on the people to "devote" resources to the temple, as advocated by the Pharisaic representatives of the temple in their "the traditions of the elders" (Mark 7:1–13). And Jesus' final Passover meal with the twelve, and presumably the regular celebration of the Lord's Supper among the Markan communities, was a meal of covenant renewal, as indicated in the allusion that the blood of the covenant makes to Israel's covenantal meal with God on Sinai (Mark 14:17–25; Exodus 24). Less explicitly Jesus' prophetic demonstration against the temple, in reciting part of Jeremiah's oracle against the temple, alludes also to the covenantal basis on which God is condemning it. Studies of social memory thus confirm and further illuminate how the traditional Israelite cultural pattern of the Mosaic covenant, alive and well in the social memory of Jesus' contemporaries, provided a fundamental framework of organization and interpretation in Mark and Q and the movements they addressed.

In the same section of the introductory essay to this volume, Kirk adds: "Social memory makes available the moral and symbolic resources for making sense of the present through 'keying' present experiences and predicaments to archetypal images and narrative representations of the commemorated past" (16). As Fentress and Wickham explain, in popular culture, "stories do more than represent particular events: they connect, clarify, and interpret events in a general fashion. Stories provide us with a set of stock explanations which underlie our predispositions to interpret reality in the ways that we do" (51). The same process happens in the assimilation and interpretation of historical events. What Barry Schwartz calls "frame images" work as "pictorial counterparts of 'emplotment,'" defining the meaning of events by depicting them "as episodes in a narrative that precedes and transcends them" (Schwartz 1998a:8).

Another broad cultural pattern that operates in Mark's story of Jesus is the double sequence of miracle stories (sea crossing, exorcism, healing, healing, wilderness feeding), which in turn appears in Mark's overall story as the "script" of a popular prophet-and-movement, also discernible in the many prophets and their movements that Josephus mentions. The sequence of miracle stories in Mark, of course, may have been semiseparable from the broader "script" of a popular prophetic movement. It is difficult to tell whether the similar sequence of "signs" in the Gospel of John is part of such a larger script that can be clearly identified in the rest of the story. In the main plot of the renewal of Israel in Mark's overall story the double sequence of miracle stories has been interwoven and overlaid with subplots of Jesus' conflict with the disciples and of the women's role in the renewal of Israel. The underlying pattern of "miracle chain," however, remains unmistakable in the duplicated sequence of episodes (see Mack).

Analysis of these episodes in terms of social memory readily confirms and deepens the sense that they are shaped in terms of numerous allusions to the formative events of Israel led by Moses and the renewal of Israel led by Elijah (clinched, in Mark, by the ensuing episode of the appearance of Jesus with both on the mountain before the three disciples). The crossings of the stormy sea are reminiscent of Israel's crossing of the Red Sea led by Moses. Jesus' feedings of the thousands in the wilderness allude to Moses' feeding of the people in the wilderness. By implication, in resonance with the audience's Israelite social memory, Jesus is thus leading a new exodus, a new or re-formed Israel. Jesus' exorcisms and healings in the middle of the sequence of episodes (including a raising of the [almost] dead, and perhaps also the multiplication of food) are reminiscent of Elijah's (and Elisha's) healings in renewal of a disintegrating Israel under the despotic foreign rule of Ahab and Jezebel. The stories to which these episodes in Mark are alluding were basic elements of Israelite popular tradition long before they were taken up into the Judean great tradition, some textual traditions of which developed into the Septuagint and the Masoretic text.

While the allusions these stories make to "scriptural" events have long been recognized, however, standard New Testament scholarship tended not to look for broader patterns of culture. Yet sequences of several incidents in the formative Israelite exodus-wilderness story, such as the sea crossing and the wilderness feeding, appear in any number of Psalms and other passages in Judean literature. The wondrous deeds of Elijah and his disciple Elisha, moreover, were recited in sequences in texts as divergent as the popular stories taken up into the Deuteronomic history (1 Kgs 17–21; 2 Kgs 1–9) and a section of Ben Sira's hymnic "Praise of Famous Men." These sequences appearing in written texts are sufficiently different to suggest not common prototypes but general patterns in Israelite culture, versions of which could be deployed as appropriate in given circumstances. Werner Kelber demonstrated how individual healing or exorcism stories could be understood as orally composed and performed from a standard repertoire of motifs according to a basic three-part narrative pattern (1983). Given evidence of broader patterns of Mosaic or Elijah-Elisha stories, we might build on Kelber's insight to hypothesize that Israelite social memory included a broader repertoire of distinctively Israelite stories and story motifs. Included in that repertoire were several stories organized in sequences. Precisely such resources from Israelite social memory provided the *frameworks* and *frame images* used in emplotting and defining the meaning of Jesus' exorcisms, healings, feedings, etcetera, "depicting them as episodes in a narrative that precede[d] and transcende[d] them" (Schwartz 1998a:8).

It was long since recognized, according to Enlightenment criteria of reliable historical accounts, that there is no point asking whether and how individual miracle stories adequately or authentically represent an incident of healing or exorcism. Studies of social memory confirm that social memory of events is not stable as accurate historical information. Social memory, however, "is stable at the level of shared meanings and remembered images" (Fentress and Wickham: 59). If we focus not on individual stories but on the two parallel sequences of stories, then it is clear that in Mark's story (and prior to and/or independently of Mark) Jesus' followers understand his exorcisms, healings, etcetera, as a renewal of Israel, drawing on and resonating with a deeply rooted pattern of the social memory of Moses and Elijah.

Discerning how Mark and Q are informed by, draw upon, and adapt broader cultural patterns of Israelite social memory, of course, does not constitute direct evidence for Jesus-in-mission. Since we are just beginning to explore the implications of the important insight that memory is social, it would be premature to attempt to draw conclusions about how Israelite social memory functioned in the interaction between Jesus and his immediate followers. Combined with the recent research and its implications sketched at the outset above, however, studies of social memory enable us to begin constructing a far more defensible set of assumptions and approaches than those of form criticism and the Jesus Seminar. Crossan, critical leader of the Jesus Seminar, presents a Jesus whose teaching exhibits little or no Israelite memory that is acknowledged in discussion. In effect we are asked to believe that, historically, Jesus did not operate in Israelite culture in Galilee. (Crossan 1991, of course, suggests that Galilee was "cosmopolitan," including influence from Cynic philosophy.)

The Gospel of Mark, whether written in Syria or even as far away as Rome no later than the 70s, has a rich knowledge of Israelite culture into which Jesus' action and teaching are woven, as is evident in nearly every episode. Similarly the speeches of Q exhibit multiple Israelite figures, motifs, and cultural forms. This may not be a problem for standard New Testament studies: on the assumptions of academic print culture, Mark can be pictured as "composed at a desk in a scholar's study lined with texts" (Mack: 322–23). Recent research, however, has simply pulled the rug out from under such anachronistic assumptions and the resulting procedures. The combination of the recent research cited above and studies of social memory lead rather to the conclusion that there was a far

greater continuity between Jesus in interaction with his immediate followers and emergent texts such the Q speeches and Mark's Gospel. That
continuity is provided by the social memory of Jesus-in-mission, which is
a continuation in key ways of Israelite social memory, including broad
cultural patterns such as those of Mosaic covenant and Moses- and Elijah-
led renewal of Israel. The social memory of Jesus-in-mission accessible in
Q speeches and Markan story does not give us access to exactly what
Jesus said or did, but it does enable us to discern the "shared meanings"
of his typical preaching and practice in the broader cultural patterns
operative in the historical situation in which he worked.

Why John Wrote a Gospel: Memory and History in an Early Christian Community

Tom Thatcher

This article will utilize social memory theory to explain the existence of the Fourth Gospel (FG) as a written document. It seeks to answer the question, What motivated the Fourth Evangelist, "John," to produce a written version of his community's memory of Jesus? Of course, this question has been addressed in every recent commentary on the FG and in a mountain of monographs and articles. Most answers, however, focus not so much on the relationship between fluid traditions and written texts as on the relationship between John's unique theological vision and his life circumstances. Such studies follow the maxim that the content of the FG was developed "in light of the liturgical, polemical, apologetic, and catechetical needs" of John's early Christian community (Culpepper: 58) and assume that the FG was written simply to preserve this unique vision for posterity. While this approach has offered a number of entirely reasonable explanations for the peculiar contours of John's view of Jesus, it is important to stress that it cannot explain why the FG, or any other ancient Gospel, *exists.* In other words, the theorem that the unique theological and literary themes of the FG were developed in the context of specific historical circumstances may explain why John thought about Jesus in the way that he did, but is insufficient to explain why the FG exists today as a written document. The present study, by contrast, will attempt to identify the precipitating causes of literacy in Johannine Christianity by answering the question, Why would any Johannine Christian choose to commit his version of the Jesus story to writing, at a time when it was expensive and difficult to do so and when the vast majority of people could not read?

Social memory theory offers a new approach to this question by providing biblical scholars with valuable tools and terms for the analysis of the interface between orality to literacy in the early church. Essentially, the motives behind the production of documents may be explained through two models of writing, the "archive" model and "rhetorical" model. The archive model treats written texts as filing cabinets, repositories for the storage of important information that might otherwise be forgotten. Following this approach, written documents are viewed as substantially identical to the contents of living memory, and reading a text is seen as parallel to oral discussions about the past. Most scholarship on the FG follows some version of the archive model, assuming that the written text of the FG was produced simply to serve as a more permanent record of the Johannine tradition. The present study, however, will argue that the archive model is inconsistent with John's own understanding of Christian memory and will suggest instead that the FG was written to exploit the symbolic value of written texts. While the production of written histories and biographies, including early Christian Gospels, may itself be considered an act of commemoration and an aspect of a group's memory, the fixing of traditions in writing and the sense of permanence that this technology creates raise several distinct problems. Written histories preserve a group's memory of the past but necessarily freeze that memory in order to preserve it, and all historians and biographers exploit this fact. This essay will explore the transition from group memory to historical document, and will argue that John wrote a Gospel strategically to manipulate the differences between these two ways of recalling the past.[1]

THE FOURTH GOSPEL AS ARCHIVE

Following the seminal work of Milman Parry in the 1920s, a considerable literature has developed on the interface between orality and writing in traditional societies (see Foley 1988). Oral cultures (ancient and modern) adopt and utilize literacy in a variety of ways, depending on the specific society's organization and worldview. In almost every instance, however, it appears that writing develops first and primarily as an aid to memory, a repository of cultural information that might otherwise be forgotten. This phenomenon—the use of documents to store and preserve information—may be referred to as the "archive function" of writing.

---

1. In the discussion to follow, I will focus exclusively on the reasons why "John," the person responsible for the FG as it exists today (or at least for chapters 1–20), might have written a book about Jesus. Of course, many Johannine scholars subscribe to the "developmental" approach, arguing that the current text of the FG is the last of a series of revisions (see summary and documentation in Thatcher 2001:6–7). Space does not permit me to address this theory here, but I will note that my main conclusions would presumably apply to every hypothetical edition of the FG, or at least to every edition whose author/ redactor subscribed to the theory of memory presented in the current Gospel of John and 1, 2, and 3 John. If there were, in fact, multiple editions of the Gospel of John, then the guiding question of this study—What were the precipitating causes of writing in the Johannine context?—must be answered to explain the existence of each of them.

Viewed from the perspective of the archive function, written texts are essentially parallel to memory—or, more specifically, the contents of written texts are essentially synonymous with the contents of memory— and reading these texts is an act of surrogate recall.

Biblical scholars have tended to explain the existence of the Gospel of John—and, indeed, of all written Gospels—in terms of the archive function of written histories. As time goes by, memories falter, witnesses disappear, and oral traditions are distorted through transmission. Writing, however, creates a sense of permanence around its contents, and from this it may be deduced that the Johannine Community adopted writing to create permanence, to archive information about Jesus that might otherwise be forgotten. One could point to the history of writing in support of this conclusion: the earliest written documents in almost every literate culture are generally functional texts, such as business receipts and tax records, that maintain data critical to social interaction and cohesion. Modern readers can easily imagine a similar functional necessity at the origins of the FG. The written text of the FG (and/or its possible literary sources) would help the Johannine Christians remember traditional information about Jesus, thereby preserving his memory against the vicissitudes of amnesia and orality and safeguarding data that was critical to their ongoing community existence. This would be especially true if John 21:20–24 is taken to mean that the Beloved Disciple, a primary authority behind the Johannine Community's memory of Jesus, has died or is about to die. Logically, followers of this individual might feel compelled to preserve the Beloved Disciple's witness, and to produce a written Gospel so that his recollections could continue to inform the community. Viewed from this majority perspective, the FG was a product of necessity in a culture where writing was the only means of preserving the past in permanent form.

The FG, then, may be viewed as a form of surrogate memory, a sacred archive where the Johannine Christians stored traditions about Jesus until needed for later recall, review, and oral performance (i.e., for reading aloud in community gatherings). But this approach runs aground on the fact that it appears to be incompatible with John's own view of memory. First, John does not understand memory as simple autobiographical "recall," at least not the disciples' memories of Jesus; second, he does not seem to believe that written archives would be necessary to preserve such memories. For John, the memory of Jesus is a fluid, dynamic, and charismatic entity that can readily adapt itself to new situations; the fixing of such memory in written form would therefore require a substantial change in the very nature of the recollection. In view of these facts, it seems unlikely that John would feel compelled to write a Gospel primarily in order to create a virtual memory of Jesus for posterity. The following sections will define John's view of "memory" more precisely, then speculate on the possible rhetorical value of a Jesus book in the Johannine context.

John's Memory of Jesus

For John, the memory of Jesus is a complex combination of witness, recall, faith, and Scripture. Of course, many modern scholars would say the same of all early Christian tradition, which is generally viewed as a gradual expansion and elaboration of pristine recollections of Jesus in light of postresurrection faith and ongoing exegesis of the Hebrew Bible. Notably, however, John does not use this model to explain theological developments in the second and third generations of the church, but rather to describe the recollections of the actual associates of the historical Jesus, including those of his own primary witness, the "Beloved Disciple" (John 19:25–35; 21:20–24). For John, even the most primitive memories of Jesus were a dynamic composite entity, and his view of the Spirit suggests that he characterized all later Christian reflection on Jesus in the same way.

John's understanding of Christian memory is perhaps most evident in the FG's version of the temple incident, the story of Jesus' disruption of animal vending and currency exchange in the temple courts during a Passover festival (John 2:13–22). John's account of this episode portrays "the Jews" demanding a miraculous sign from Jesus to authorize his radical actions. Jesus responds by inviting them to "destroy this temple, and in three days I will raise it" (John 2:19). Here, as elsewhere in the FG, the Jews can only point out the absurdity of Jesus' proposition: "This temple has been under construction for forty-six years, and you will raise [ἐγερεῖς] it in three days?!?" The denouement of this heated exchange is, however, truncated, for the narrator is compelled to break in with an explanation of Jesus' words: "But he said this about the 'temple' of his body. Then when he was raised [ἠγέρθη] from the dead, his disciples remembered that he said these things, and they believed the Scriptures and the word that Jesus spoke" (2:21–22). From the perspective of narrative criticism, this explanation is entirely satisfactory, serving as a coherent foreshadowing of John 19:42–20:1. Jesus' dead body will, indeed, lie in the tomb three days—from the Day of Preparation (Friday) until the first day of the week (Sunday)—before being "raised."

One might argue that the Beloved Disciple witnessed both of these events—Jesus' comment about his temple/body and Jesus' subsequent resurrection after three days—and brought these discrete memories together at some later date (see Carson: 182–83; Morris: 201–5). Both the temple saying and the resurrection would theoretically fall within the finite corpus of the Beloved Disciple's autobiographical recollections, the question being whether the FG is an accurate record of a genuine recollection in this particular instance. But this line of inquiry would overlook the fact that John does not portray the disciples' memory of the temple incident as a simple act of recall prompted by the analogy between the number of days Jesus lay in the tomb and his earlier remarks about his body. For this memory was accompanied by the disciples' "belief," a belief not in the veracity of their own recollections but rather in the words that Jesus had spoken on that occasion and "the Scriptures" of the Hebrew Bible (John 2:22). Further, John seems to think that this subsequent "belief" altered the disciples' initial neurological impressions of Jesus' actions, or at least displaced these impressions, for his presentation implies that they were unable to comprehend the true referent of Jesus' words at the time those words were imprinted on their brains. Their initial impression was shaped by one understanding, or misunderstanding, of Jesus' actions and comments, and this impression was later reconfigured in view of the disciples' subsequent understanding of Jesus' identity. In other words, the disciples "remembered" the temple incident in a form clearly distinct from the shape that experience took in their initial consciousness.

The peculiar mode of memory described at John 2:22 reappears in John's portrait of Jesus' triumphal entry into Jerusalem shortly before his death, an event that immediately precedes the temple incident in the Synoptic Gospels but follows it by some ten chapters in the FG (John 12:12–16). As the disciples observe Jesus' journey on the donkey and listen to the crowds proclaiming him "King of Israel," they are apparently at a loss to comprehend what they see and hear. "The disciples did not know [ἔγνωσαν] these things at first," John says, "but when Jesus was glorified then they remembered that these things were written about him and that they did these things to him" (12:16). "At first" (τὸ πρῶτον) here must mean "at the time this happened," and since the disciples later "remembered" the incident, John's assertion that they "did not know these things" must mean that their initial sensory experience differed from their later understanding. In other words, the disciples' initial neurological impressions were flawed, and were reconfigured and corrected in light of subsequent events (see Morris: 587–88).

Here again, John portrays the disciples' "memory" as a complex cognitive interaction of (1) their autobiographical recollections of an ambiguous event involving themselves and Jesus; (2) their subsequent awareness of Jesus' destiny; and, (3) a messianic interpretation of the Hebrew Bible, in this instance Zech 9:9 (loosely quoted at 12:15). Notably, John uses the same verb, μνημονεύω, to describe both the disciples' recollection of the actual event and their subsequent messianic interpretation of the Scriptures that clarified the experience for them. For John, then, the memory of Jesus is not simply a static recall of personal experience that might gradually decay over time; it is, rather, a complex and dynamic entity that combines information about the past with reflection on the ultimate significance of Jesus' death.

It is perhaps not surprising that the memory of Jesus is stamped with faith in the FG, for John portrays Christian memory as a gift of the Holy Spirit, given to believers after Jesus' glorification (John 7:37–39; 20:22). According to John, Jesus made a number of specific promises to the disciples shortly before his death concerning the coming of the Spirit or "Paraclete" (παράκλητος), a unique title that may be variously translated "Helper," "Comforter," "Counselor," or "Advocate" (see Brown 1966– 70:2.1135–43; Turner: 347–51). It is clear from these "Paraclete Sayings," preserved now in the FG's Farewell Address (John 13–17), that John understood the Holy Spirit to be an extension of Jesus' living presence in the community. At John 14:15–17, Jesus tells the disciples that he will send them "another counselor" (ἄλλον παράκλητον) who will "forever ... remain with you and be in you." While commentators are divided on the relationship between the coming of the Paraclete and the reference to Jesus' own "coming" at v. 18, almost all agree that Jesus' subsequent statements indicate that the Spirit will function in the Christian community "as remembrancer and interpreter" (Bruce: 305). The Paraclete will "teach you all things and remind you of all things that I said to you" (John 14:26), "guiding" the disciples "into all truth" by speaking "only what he hears" from Jesus (John 16:13–14). In effect, "the ministry of Jesus is prolonged" through the work of the Holy Spirit because "the Paraclete ... is a parallel figure to Jesus himself," preserving the memory and meaning of Jesus' words and deeds (first quote Barrett: 483; second quote Bultmann 1971:567). Notably, this revelatory memory is the only "gift" that the Johannine Holy Spirit gives to his people, a presentation strikingly different from the pneumatology of Paul.

The passages surveyed above highlight three facets of the Johannine theory of memory that are relevant to a discussion of the reasons why John, or any other Johannine Christian(s), might have written a book about Jesus. First, Johannine memory is not reducible to neurology— that is, memory is not an empirical function of the senses and brain chemistry—so that John's view contrasts sharply with popular modern conceptions of what memory is and how it works. "The classic theory of memory, after a study of the acquisition of memories, studies their preservation [in the brain] before giving an account of their recall," an approach that assumes that "memories as psychic states subsist in the [individual's] mind in an unconscious state, and that they become conscious again when recollected" (Halbwachs 1992:39). In other words, in today's common parlance "memory" is a comprehensive term for all the sensory and intellectual processes by which the brain receives, stores, and later recalls data for review. For John, however, the memory of Jesus is not a simple act of recall, but rather a complex reconfiguration of past experience. This is true not only of the later community's experience of Jesus tradition but also of the first disciples' recollections of their personal experiences with Jesus. In John's view, the memory of Jesus is not static.

Second, for John, memory is a spiritual gift. The memory of Jesus is preserved and enriched by the Paraclete, and is therefore not reducible to the sum total of the sensory impressions that the original disciples stored in their brains. While memory begins with witness it ends with Scripture, Spirit, and faith, so that unaided recall could never fully comprehend Christ. In John's view, those Jews who watched the historical Jesus drive animal vendors from the temple could never truly "remember" that incident, even though they witnessed his deeds and words firsthand.

Third, and most important here, because John does not view memory as a mental archive of information but rather as a complex spiritual experience, it seems unlikely that he would feel compelled to produce a written Gospel in order to preserve traditional material about Jesus for later review and recitation. So long as the Spirit continues to work in the church—and John does not seem to foresee a time when such work would cease—pneumatic memory will continue to sustain and enrich the community's Jesus tradition. As such, there would be no need for a written Gospel that would function as an *aide-mémoire*, the primary assumption of the archival approach to writing. John's motives for writing a book about Jesus must therefore be sought in an alternate model for understanding the relationship between living memories and historical documents such as the FG.

WRITING AS RHETORIC

The Johannine theory of memory weighs against the view that the FG was written primarily as an archive of traditional Jesus material, although it has certainly fulfilled that role in the life of the church for the past nineteen centuries. Viewed from the angle of the Fourth Evangelist's own beliefs and social context, it seems more likely that John wrote a Gospel in order to capitalize on another major function of writing.

Rosalind Thomas has noted that documents can play "monumental" or "symbolic" roles, giving them social values "which take us beyond the message merely contained in the written content" (74). In these cases, the very existence of a written text is of greater social significance than the actual contents of that text, as when we refer to a sales receipt when negotiating with a store manager. Appeals of this kind reflect what may be called the "rhetorical function" of writing, the production of documents in cultural settings where the technology of writing adds special weight or authority to its contents.

The social significance of writing provides a model for explaining why John might have felt the need to produce a written Gospel as a supplement to his community's charismatic memory of Jesus. As a person immersed in an oral culture, John may have felt that a written version of his Gospel message would carry more weight in debates over the correct understanding of Jesus. Of course, oral traditions about Jesus and books about Jesus would function as parallel forms of remembrance in the Johannine community, especially if portions of the text of the FG were sometimes read aloud and discussed in congregational gatherings. Yet these two forms of commemoration would operate under different social and media dynamics. In terms of media, the remembered past of personal reflection and oral discourse is fluid and dialogic, continually re-created in moments when individuals share experiences and common knowledge. History books, however, freeze the past in the fixed form of a written document, giving their account an "immunity to correction"—one can contest the claims of a history book, but such claims cannot be negotiated in the dialogue between text and reader (Lowenthal 1996:146). This key difference in media is reflected in the respective audiences of verbal memory and written memory. Oral memory texts are generated spontaneously for private audiences, either for personal reflection or for consideration by others who are members of the same memory group. As such, oral memories treat the past as "experiences and not events," occurrences with potentially significant implications for personal identity. History books, by contrast, are public, treating the past as an objective, universal phenomenon open to any reader's scrutiny (Rosenzweig and Thelen: 37–38). This basic distinction—that memories treat the past as fluid private experiences while history books treat the past as fixed public events—generates significant differences in the way that living memories and history books conceptualize, organize, and present the past to their respective audiences. The potential social impact of these differences, especially in an oral culture, seems to have been John's primary motive for freezing the charismatic memory of a Jesus in a written Gospel.

THE PAST IN MEMORY

Living memory in the form of group tradition conceptualizes and organizes the past in ways radically different from history books. While histories organize the past along tight narrative schemes, the organization of the past in memory "is not necessarily linear, logical, or rational" (Zelizer: 221). Indeed, "memory retrieval is seldom sequential; we locate recalled events by association rather than by working methodically forward or backward through time" (Lowenthal 1985:208; see also Connerton: 19; Rosenzweig and Thelen: 8–9, 68). Individuals and groups order their images of the past through a continual process of comparison and contrast, analyzing events and people in terms of their similarities to, and differences from, both other past events and present conditions. Because items stored in memory interact on a conceptual level, free from their actual connections in time and space, relationships between images of the past "can be established on any basis" (Fentress and Wickham: 48). As a result, the organizational scheme of social memory is heavily dependent on group logic, language, and experience, making its contours often incomprehensible to outsiders (Halbwachs 1980:86–87; Lowenthal 1985:128–29).

Once a group labels memories and assigns them to ideological categories, the elements within each category tend to blur into larger conflated images, clustering around people, events, or situations that are deemed particularly significant (E. Zerubavel 1991:27–31). Maurice Halbwachs, who discussed this phenomenon extensively, refers to these salient people and things as "landmarks" (*points de repère*) of memory. "In collective memory," Halbwachs notes,

> there are in general particular figures, dates, and periods of time that acquire an extraordinary salience. These attract to themselves other events and figures that happened at other moments. A whole period is concentrated, so to speak, in one year, just as a series of actions and events, about which one has forgotten its varying actors and diverse conditions, gathers together in one man and is attributed to him alone. (1992:222–23)

The conflation of distinct people and events into archetypal landmarks is facilitated by a mental process that Fentress and Wickham call the "conceptualization of memory," "a tendency towards simplification and schematization" in recollections of the past (32). This aspect of memory turns specific images into "generalizable markers about suffering, joy, commitment, and endurance" (Zelizer: 231). Simplified schematic images are easier to remember and to organize, but necessarily make individual persons and events from the past appear less distinct. As a result, in many cases what appear to be discrete memories are actually composite images. Elements of unique events crystallize around the memory of a specific moment, and the traits exhibited by an individual over a period of time are brought together in a unified portrait of that person's character. As such, it is inaccurate to say

> that the [total] remembrance of a period is simply the sum of remembrances from each day. As events grow distant, we have a habit of

recalling them in organized sets. Although certain remembrances stand out clearly, many kinds of elements are included [in those remembered images] and we can neither enumerate each nor distinguish them from one another. (Halbwachs 1980:70)

Living recollections, then, treat the past as personal experience and organize that experience privately, in ways peculiar to the immediate needs of the specific memory group that generates them. As such, when individuals discuss the past with other members of the memory group— as when siblings talk as adults about a remarkable childhood experience at the family breakfast table—they generally assume that the audience has some foreknowledge of the events under consideration, or at least that the audience could predict the outcome by appealing to the group taxonomies by which that version of the past has been meaningfully arranged. Sister may assume, for example, that brother will either recall the specific incident under consideration or will at least remember enough about family meals in general to reconstruct the backdrop and cast of the scene quickly. For this reason, skeptical audiences—people who are not members of the memory group and who are therefore unaware of the categories this group uses to organize the past—may often challenge the remembered past as erroneous, or may question the logic or rationale of the relationship between specific memories (Lowenthal 1996:129). Living memory, presenting the past as private property, can always adapt its presentation to the needs of a sympathetic ear.

The Past in History Books

History books, such as the Gospel of John, differ from other forms of memory (particularly oral tradition and ritual) for two reasons: because they are *histories* and because they are *books*. In other words, history books diverge from living memory in their conceptualization and presentation of the past, and then magnify these differences by committing the historical past to writing.

History books treat past people and events as entities that are public, objective, and fixed. Because individual moments of the past are treated as discrete entities, each history book can present its contents as a demarcated subset within the "universal chronology" of the "total past" (Lowenthal 1996:11; Yerushalmi 1989:95). Histories thereby create the impression that "history is unitary" and that "the historical world is like an ocean fed by the many partial histories": theoretically, it would be possible to combine all the history books that have ever been written and all those that might be written into one massive volume, "the universal memory of the human species" (Halbwachs 1980:84). As a corollary, history books treat all figures and events from the past as essentially equal and worthy of record. While no historian attempts to record every fact and figure from the period under investigation, items are presumably deleted not because they are judged unworthy of attention, but simply because time and space do not permit them to be included in the present study (Halbwachs 1980:83; Yerushalmi 1989:94–95, 114). Thus, while living memory sorts and discriminates information on the basis of the group's present beliefs and needs, histories select and present facts on the basis of "the coherence of the argument, [and] the structure of the presentation" (Yerushalmi 1989:11). Theoretically, the past is finite, the number of histories that might be written is finite, and each history book is a small slice of the larger pie of public facts and figures.

Histories, then, treat moments of the past as distinct, discrete, and neutral, a mass of blank puzzle pieces that the historian must assemble into a coherent image. This task is achieved through the production of a historical narrative, a textual structure that weaves the chaotic fabric of time into a coherent story of causes and effects leading from a marked beginning to a definitive end. Accidents and coincidence are minor themes, as history books are driven by a sense of necessity—moral, natural, economic, divine, empirical—giving the impression that things had to have happened the way they did in order to reach the single point of outcome (Owen: 53–54, 103–4; Lowenthal 1985:218). The past is manageable in history narratives because effects are linked to causes in such a way that the relationship between the two cannot be negotiated, at least not to the extent that members of a group could negotiate their memory of common knowledge. Other historians who disagree might suggest different causes or point out multiple side effects, but critical review of this kind only replaces one narrative with another, thereby affirming the overall logic of historiography.

To achieve this objective vision of the past, the historian must situate herself beyond the conclusion of the story, outside the plot rather than within it. She must, in other words, view the past "as a whole from afar," from a point where the beginning, middle, and end of the cause-effect sequence come clearly into focus (Halbwachs 1980:81). For this reason, David Lowenthal notes that "hindsight as well as anachronism shapes historical interpretations" (1985:217). While history books conceptualize each past moment as discrete and self-contained, as narratives they must shape every event to fit its precipitating causes and subsequent consequences—consequences that might have been guessed by the people living in the time period under consideration but that could not have been known to them. For example, neither John F. Kennedy nor the mob of people gathered at Dealey Plaza in Dallas, Texas on the morning of November 22, 1963, knew that the President would be dead by 1 P.M., but every biographer of Kennedy must know this information and must write the story of a life that could have ended at that fixed point. Similarly, historical Jesus scholars must work backwards, writing the story of a life that could have ended on a cross, an insight that obviously was not shared (or, at least, not fully comprehended) by Jesus' associates at the time.

Unlike living memories, which are theoretically interested in any past event that may offer useful insight into present realities, history books fix precise boundaries for their data pool. While mathematical time moves in "an open-ended historical [= chronological] sequence," "where [the historian decides] to begin and end the story defines what constitutes the relevant event and determines its meaning" (Y. Zerubavel 1995:221). Eviatar Zerubavel refers to this phenomenon as "mnemonic decapitation" and notes that history narratives always operate on an *ex nihilo* principle, pretending that the story was preceded by a historical void and ignoring information that might suggest otherwise (E. Zerubavel 2003:93–97). Histories treat the events and people that fall within their narrative boundaries as uniquely relevant to the topic under consideration, naturally implying that information excluded from this matrix is not worthy of recollection or, at least, not as important to a correct understanding of the past (E. Zerubavel 1991:12–13; Y. Zerubavel 1995:221).

Finally, because they present their contents as public and subject to verification, history books assume a universal audience that transcends the boundaries of any single memory group. "History tells all who will listen what has happened and how things came to be as they are," and invites every reader to review and challenge its claims (Lowenthal 1996:128–29). Histories anticipate an audience that is broad and possibly skeptical, and therefore do not assume the reader's foreknowledge of the events under consideration. Of course, in many cases the reader of a history narrative is aware of the ultimate outcome. The modern American who watches a documentary about Abraham Lincoln at least knows that the subject is dead, and is probably also aware that Lincoln was President during the Civil War and was assassinated. The producer of such a program, however, may not assume this knowledge, and certainly does not assume that the reader could predict the logic of the plot that unites the selected events of Lincoln's life and explains why this life came to a tragic end. Because they are public rather than private, histories must appeal to the lowest common denominator of audience awareness.

As the brief survey above has suggested, while groups use both living memory and history books to commemorate the past, these alternate forms of recollection shape and present the past in distinct ways. Memories order the private past according to the current social and ideological frameworks of the groups that preserve them; histories, by contrast, treat the past as public and organize the objective past within the confines of a fixed narrative. For purposes of the present study, it is important to note that these natural differences would be magnified in John's social setting. The FG was produced in an oral culture and represents a conscious shift from fluid memory to fixed written text. In John's context, the technology of writing would itself further distinguish memory from history, presenting a number of special problems relating to the periodization of the past, the permanence of the written past, and the inaccessibility of the written past. These problems would, for John, enhance the rhetorical force of a written Gospel, making writing an especially appealing medium for his memory of Jesus.

Social memory theorists show a keen interest in the phenomenon of "periodization." Because we always encounter the past in packaged form—either the ideological packages of our memory groups or the narrative packages of histories—it is easy to forget that, in reality, all past moments and the persons and events that occupied them are "timeless and discontinuous," a simple succession without inherent value. But neither living memories nor history books function as strict historical chronicles. As noted above, each form of recollection attempts to incorporate the discrete moments of the past into broader patterns, and in the process each distorts and reshapes the strictly mathematical flow of time (Lowenthal 1985:220). The most basic, yet perhaps most significant, means of manipulating the past involves the insertion of breaks into the natural sequence of events, "watershed" moments that divide the past into distinct periods and eras.

Eviatar Zerubavel, who has discussed this phenomenon extensively, notes that watersheds are significant because "they are collectively perceived as having involved significant identity transformations," moments when the life of the individual or group began to move in a new direction. This is the case because watersheds parallel the mental boundaries between the categories in a group's ideological system and function alongside those boundaries. Specifically, watersheds arise as the mental gaps between categories of concepts are superimposed onto the flow of time, projecting the group's overall way of thinking backward into the past. As such, "the temporal breaks we envision between supposedly distinct historical 'periods' help articulate the mental discontinuities between supposedly distinct cultural, political, and moral identities" (E. Zerubavel 2003:84–85; see also Y. Zerubavel 1995:8). For example, Westerners typically see 1789, the opening year of the French Revolution, as a major turning point in world history, and treat that event as a watershed moment dividing two distinct eras. This mental move is possible because Westerners believe that the culture and values of postrevolution France are irreconcilable with those of the monarchy, so that the France of 1788 and the France of 1790 cannot fit into the same mental category. "It is specifically as a form of classification that periodizing helps articulate distinct identities," in the sense that the division of the past into periods always reflects current group values and labels (E. Zerubavel 2003:85).

But while living memories and history books both divide the past into distinct periods that reflect an ideological perspective, they do so for different reasons and to a different degree. As Halbwachs notes, collective memory is a "continuous current of thought" whose boundaries grow and change across time and generations (Halbwachs 1980:80–81). The historical periods marked out by social memory, and the watersheds that divide those periods, gradually shift as the image of the past evolves to reflect new social values and categories. But when memory is committed to writing, these divisions of time become fixed and absolute—the periodization of the past in a history book obviously cannot be negotiated in the interaction between text and reader and can only change over time with revisions of the text (i.e., by destoying old copies of the book and producing new ones). While living memory can gradually (or suddenly) readjust the boundaries of temporal periods to reflect evolving values and perspectives, the history book sits on the shelf forever, proposing a specific division of time to every subsequent reader in every generation, even when its view of the past is radically obsolete from the perspective of current values. Books cannot forget.

The periodization of the past in history books thus differs radically from the periodization of the past in memory at two key points. First, the written past is "definitively closed." Because the contents of history books are permanent, their images of the past can only be changed by conscious acts of destruction (i.e., banning or burning the documents; Connerton: 75). For this very reason, although history books cannot prevent the ongoing evolution of the past in collective memory, they can and sometimes do subvert that evolution by preserving images of the past that are inconsistent with the latest version of the memory. In this sense historians are often "the guardians of awkward facts, the skeletons in the cupboard of the social memory," presenting information that challenges current views of reality because it was not forged in the context of today's perspectives (Burke: 110).

Second, while both history books and memories introduce artificial watersheds and periods in order to outline and manage the past, history books, unlike memories, can themselves function as watersheds in the group's history. The "prehistoric" or "aboriginal" era of any society's history refers to every facet of its existence before the moment when members of that society began to document and manage the past through writing. Eviatar Zerubavel has even suggested that the notion of historical periodization is enhanced by the technology of writing. "Indeed, it is our ability to envision the historical equivalents of the blank spaces we conventionally leave between the different chapters of a book or at the beginning of a new paragraph that enhances the perceived separateness of such [historical] 'periods'" (2003:87–88). Of course, ancient books such as the Gospel of John did not feature chapters, page numbering, or other modern publication techniques. But the very act of writing a Gospel marks John's attempt to locate the past in a physical space (the space of the written text) different from those public community spaces in which the Johannine Christians were accustomed to remembering and discussing Jesus.

Finally, the rhetorical impact of written texts may be magnified through a phenomenon that David Lowenthal calls "the virtues of vagueness and ignorance." The past often provides a more effective foundation for group solidarity when less is known about it, and vague allusions to a general past that is accepted as true but rarely investigated carry no less weight on radio talk-shows than quotations of academic tomes. Lowenthal notes as an example that Americans regularly appeal to the U.S. Constitution when discussing their rights and national identity even though many have never read that document and most do not know what it says (1996:134–36). This phenomenon is especially striking when the actual contents of the text in question are generally misunderstood, as in the belief held by most Americans that the U.S. Constitution calls for a strict "separation of church and state." In debates where the majority hold this view, the fact that such a phrase never appears in the document in question does not diminish the rhetorical force of arguments that appeal to it.

As the brief survey above has indicated, living memories and history books conceptualize and present the past in different ways. These natural differences can be exploited by those who wish to use the past to protect or promote their own interests and values. The following section will apply this principle to the specific case of the Gospel of John. Certain rhetorical moves were inherent in the production of the FG, and the predictable affects of these moves in an oral culture offer the best answer to the question, Why did John write a book about Jesus?

WHY JOHN WROTE A GOSPEL

The preceding discussions of John's view of memory and of the natural differences between living memories and written history books offer a new approach to the question, Why did John write a Gospel? If writing is viewed primarily as an archive, the FG was produced as an aid to memory, a storage bin for John's Jesus tradition. From this perspective, the FG would serve as an extension of tradition, preserving the community's witness to Jesus for posterity, and its contents would be synonymous with the contents of that witness. Under this model, John did not conceptualize an essential difference between his oral preaching and public readings from his book. But while the Gospel of John has certainly functioned as an archive of Johannine tradition in the history of the church, the author's peculiar view of Christian memory makes it unlikely that this was his primary motive for writing a Gospel. Because John envisioned the memory of Jesus as a dynamic, charismatic entity, it is difficult to explain why he would have felt the urgent need to write, and then recite from, a book about Jesus rather than simply speaking about Jesus with other "anointed" Christians (1 John 2:18–27). How could such a text improve on the work of the Spirit of Truth (John 16:13)? Instead, it appears that John wished to capitalize on the rhetorical value of writing by converting the fluid, charismatic memory of Jesus to a fixed history book, a move that would at once preserve his unique vision of Jesus, freeze that vision in a perpetually nonnegotiable medium, and assert the special authority of that vision against competing perspectives. As such, the FG is not only a record of John's response to his situation but also an aspect of John's response to his situation, an aspect that would transcend the value of the actual contents of the document.

At least five related facets of the shift from living group memory to history book would have made the production of the FG especially suitable to John's rhetorical purposes.

1. Jesus in Public

As noted above, memory treats the past as private experiences while history books treat the past as public events. The former phenomenon would be especially true in the Johannine context, where the memory of Jesus was seen as a work of the Holy Spirit. Every person who possesses the Spirit is a remembrancer, able to recall Jesus and guided by the Paraclete in her interpretations of that memory. The author of 1 John could appeal to this principle *ad hominem* to posture the Spirit/tradition as a special "anointing" that protects true Christians from heretical teachings (1 John 2:20–27). Yet John's charismatic approach to memory would also make it ultimately impossible to refute competing theological views, such as the views of Diotrephes or the "Antichrists" mentioned in 1–2–3 John (see 1 John 2:18–19; 2 John 7–11; 3 John 9–10). As private spiritual experience, the antichrists' countermemory of Jesus would not be subject to historical inquiry and would not demand the objectivity that makes it possible for historians to proclaim their versions of the past "true." John's history book, however, would posture Jesus as a public figure, making claims about his activity that are potentially subject to investigation. John points this out himself in John 19:35 and 21:24, apparently assuming that competing memories of Jesus cannot be supported by similar information.

By moving Jesus into the public past, John creates an image that claims to transcend private faith experience.

Of course, this does not imply that John sought to eradicate the influence of the Spirit in debates over the tradition. Were John thoroughly anticharismatic, passages such as John 14:26 and 16:13 would not appear in his Gospel. It seems more likely that John wished to balance and supplement the orthodox "anointing" with a written text that could complement that ongoing spiritual experience. Believers could now refer to the text of the FG as a touchstone for pneumatic memory in the same way that they could "test the spirits" by appealing to the community's established Christological creeds (see 1 John 4:1–6). As such, text and memory would work together to affirm John's witness to Jesus.

2. Frozen Frameworks, Trapped Time

Social memory is a plastic entity. Because memory's image of the past is always shaped by the group's present ideological categories, memories change as these categories change. In the process, new watersheds rise and are eventually replaced to continually break the flow of time into manageable periods, periods that in turn characterize the events and individuals who inhabit them. By producing a written Gospel, however, John could freeze one particular image of Jesus in the plot of a historical narrative and on the physical surface of the inscribed page. The written text, and its organizational scheme, would endure over time, making it more difficult for John's opponents to reconfigure the elements of memory and preventing the suppression and conflation of information stored within each category and period. Regardless of the Paraclete's ongoing influence, within the text of the FG every moment of Jesus' life— every saying and sign—is forever distinct and discrete, shaped to fit the events that preceded it and those that will follow. These recorded events and sayings would remain valuable for teaching and meditative reflection, but would always derive their default value from the literary context rather than from private spiritual experience.

3. A Shallow Data Pool

As noted above, a written Gospel freezes the image of Jesus in precise narrative boundaries. For this reason, while the Jews, the Antichrists, and other perceived opponents might challenge John's written memory of Jesus and might ban his Gospel from their synagogues and churches, they could never change or renegotiate the image of Christ encoded in that text. Nor could they expand or contract the database from which that image was built. Once the Gospel of John was written, any quest for further facts about Jesus would be pointless: all history books imply that what has been omitted from their database is irrelevant, a maxim that John states explicitly. Much to the dismay of modern scholars, John 20:30 and 21:25 both note that much more information could have been included in the story. John, however, has sorted through this bulk of data and has preserved everything necessary to produce and maintain genuine faith in Jesus, obviating the need for new revelations or further historical investigation. In this sense, the FG represents an early attempt to canonize a particular corpus of Christian material as uniquely authoritative in theological discussion.

4. The Gospel Watershed

History books create the illusion of a fixed database and a fixed flow of time. Historians choose some events from the mass of the past and ignore others; shape those they have selected to fit tight narrative frameworks with delineated temporal periods; and remove this activity from the realm of negotiation by committing the results of their labor to writing.

But as the past becomes more remote, later generations will have access to it only through these highly contrived texts, a fact that makes it possible to think of history books as themselves watershed moments in group development. This is especially the case for the first documents in any culture, whose appearance marks the dramatic transition from "the prehistoric period." In view of this fact, John may have wished not only to preserve one particular vision of how the past should be periodized, but also to create a document that would itself function as a watershed in his group's history. Within John's oral culture, the publication of a written memory of Jesus could be used to draw a bold line between the former period of debate over what *Jesus said* and the new period of debate over what *the text says*. After this critical moment, John and his allies could point to the FG and say, "We are no longer talking about whether Jesus did X or Y; we are talking about the meaning of what can be documented."

5. Faith without Reading

Obviously, even the most rudimentary inquiry into the veracity of a history book's claims requires a minimal familiarity with the specific contents of that text, yet most people in John's culture could not read. For this reason, John and his allies could exploit the "virtues of vagueness" when using their written Gospel to counter opposing claims about Jesus. The rhetorical force of vagueness would be obvious to any ancient Jew due to the pervasive presence and influence of the Torah, a document that Jews viewed as essential to their identity and heritage but that most of them could not read (see Thatcher 1998). In a similar way, John must have been aware that most of his Christian contemporaries and, indeed, the vast majority of the human race, were not sufficiently literate to read a document such as the FG (see Harris: 11–22). The fact that most Christians could not read would, however, make the contents of the FG even less negotiable, as few would be in a position to peruse the text and challenge its vision. Vague references to the contents of the FG would place John in an even stronger position when debating his opponents.

Whether or not John was conscious of these features of written history books or appealed to them only intuitively, all five would affect the reception of the FG in its original setting. It seems most likely, then, that John wrote a Gospel not to preserve the living memory of Jesus but to replace it with something more permanent and less negotiable (see Fentress and Wickham: 10). If "general history starts only when tradition ends and the social memory is fading or breaking up," it may be said that John wrote a Gospel to break his tradition (Halbwachs 1980:78).

THE STORY OF "THE WOMAN WHO ANOINTED JESUS" AS SOCIAL MEMORY: A METHODOLOGICAL PROPOSAL FOR THE STUDY OF TRADITION AS MEMORY

Holly Hearon

Social memory "comprises that body of reusable texts, images, and rituals specific to each society in each epoch, whose 'cultivation' serves to stabilize and convey that society's self image" (J. Assmann 1995b:132). The Second Testament, as a collection of texts that preserves "the store of knowledge from which a group derives an awareness of its unity and peculiarity" may be said to function as social memory for Christian communities (J. Assmann 1995b:130, 132; Olick and Robbins: 111). It constitutes a "fixed point," a record of Christian origins, which forms the basis for community identity (J. Assmann 1995b:129). According to Assmann, such texts represent "potentiality" which achieve "actuality" when a contemporary community brings the texts to bear on the life situation of the community by refracting the texts through the lens of its own perspective and experience (1995b:130; Fentress and Wickham: 24; Zelizer: 228). In moving the texts from "potentiality" to "actuality" the community engages in a search for meaning, seeking in the texts evidence of and insight into its identity (Fentress and Wickham: 73; Burke: 106; Coser: 26).

For many scholars, however, the texts of the Second Testament do not represent a "point of origin" so much as a step along the way in the formation of social memory. The Gospels, in particular, may be described as "actualizations" of "potentiality" residing in stories which circulated orally or in written form among early Christians but remained dormant until they were actualized through performance. In performance, these narratives would have been reinterpreted as they were "given a meaning appropriate to the context, or to the genre, in which [they were] articulated" (Fentress and Wickham: 85). The results, crystallized in the Gospel narratives, are differing, sometimes conflicting, "actualities" driven by the search for meaning in particular contexts (J. Assmann 1995b:130; Fentress and Wickham: 85).[1]

It is one thing to characterize the Gospels in terms of social memory; it is another to analyze narratives in the Gospels in relation to social memory theory. Fentress and Wickham suggest that in order to understand how a particular narrative functions as social memory, it would be necessary "to ask how far back in time events are remembered, how much their recounting owes to formal narrative structures (whether oral or written) ... how much these histories are local ... and how much non-local" (103) and, in addition, to examine the different images of the past at different strata in a given society as recorded in monuments, paintings, diaries, plaques, graffiti, as well as literary remains (103; see also Schwartz 1982:379; Burke: 89; Schudson 1989:107–8). If one wants to peer behind the Gospel texts, the challenges are obvious. As Schudson observes, there is only so much material from the past available to work with, and that material is neither infinite nor comprehensive (1989:107). These limitations mount exponentially the farther back we go. The Gospels add their own particular challenges because we have direct access only to the internal, narrative world of each text; the external contexts that gave shape to the narratives are largely hidden from us. Nonetheless, I want to use this opportunity to explore how social memory theory can assist us in reflecting on the texts of the Second Testament as "actualities," or expressions of the search for meaning in early Christian communities.

Of the many stories recorded in the Gospels, the story of the woman who anoints Jesus fairly begs for scrutiny as social memory. The phrase "what she has done will be told in memory of her," which concludes the versions recorded in Mark (14:3–9) and Matthew (26:6–13), makes it clear that, in these two instances, the narrators are attempting to establish the story as a part of the social memory of their audiences—all the more so, since these words are placed in the mouth of Jesus. Although this phrase does not appear in the versions recorded in Luke (7:36–50) and John (12:1–8), the presence of the story in all four canonical Gospels, a rare occurrence, suggests that the story was part of the social memory of the

---

1. Whether the Gospels represent a moment of transition from communicative memory (i.e., memories which are "socially mediated in specific groups" and characterized by non-specialization, thematic instability, disorganization [J. Assmann 1995: 127]) to cultural memory (i.e., memories that are formalized through ceremony and given into the safe keeping of designated "bearers of tradition" [J. Assmann 1995: 131]) is less clear. Assmann asserts that the "distinction between the communicative memory and the cultural memory is not identical with the distinction between oral and written language" (131).

emerging church. Social memory is selective and changes over time so that only those memories considered most important for the life of the community are preserved (Burke: 107; Olick and Robbins: 110, 128; Halbwachs 1992:182; Schudson 1989:108). Thus the presence of this story in all four Gospels is notable. If the story of "the woman who anointed Jesus" does not have to be told "in memory of her" it apparently does have to be told when remembering Jesus. Yet it does not have to be told in the same way, nor, by implication, to the same end. Nonetheless the story exhibits a certain stability as social memory, as will be shown: each of the extant versions gives shape to a particular understanding of the person and purpose of Jesus.

In order to align the discussion as closely as possible with social memory theory, I will organize my analysis of the story of the woman who anoints Jesus around the questions posed by Fentress and Wickham, cited above. My intent is both to demonstrate ways in which I believe social memory theory can be helpful for gaining insight into the nature of the Gospel narratives as social memory, and to point out where the biblical material imposes limitations on our capacity to engage social memory theory.

Uncertain History and Contested Memory

It is uncertain how far back in memory the story of "the woman who anointed Jesus" extends. Although social memory theory recognizes a degree of continuity between history and memory (Schwartz 1990:82), the historical origins of the narrative are ambiguous at best. A few scholars view the version recorded in Mark as a plausible account of an actual event (see Jeremias). Others find historical traces in the versions recorded in Luke or John, where the woman anoints Jesus' feet (see Daube; Holst; Coakley), while Mack (1988:200–201) and Corley (1993:104) trace the story more specifically to an encounter between Jesus and a prostitute (see also Derrett; Schweizer: 288).[2] Yet from the perspective of social memory theory, such endeavors to locate historical origins on the basis of the narratives alone are problematic. Fentress and Wickham observe, "There is nothing in the remembered image itself that informs us whether or not it refers to something real or something imaginary"

---

2. Sabbe challenges the view that the woman was originally a prostitute since the characterization of the woman as a sinner is a "typically Lukan trait" (1992:2070, 2080 n. 69). Corley, in contrast, thinks it unlikely that Luke would "take a story devoid of erotic overtones in Mark and deliberately transform it into a scandalous story about a streetwalker who comes in and caresses Jesus' feet unless some (undeniable) written tradition suggested it" (2002:91).

(48; Zelizer: 217). We can speculate, but we cannot be certain. Perhaps more to the point, the force and function of social memory does not rest, ultimately, in "what really happened" but in the capacity of the memory to construct a bridge between our remembered "origins" and our present context. This does not preclude investigation into "what really happened," but it points out some of the difficulties inherent in such a task: "We have no way of knowing, *a priori*, where, in oral tradition, historical facts are likely to lie.... All that can be said is that this sifting reveals the lowest common denominator of the versions" (Fentress and Wickham: 81; see larger discussion in 75–81).

A different approach to the question of origins is proposed by Sawicki. She traces the origins of the story not to an encounter between Jesus and a woman, but to a conversation among elite Hellenized Jewish women in Jerusalem who, in the process of grieving over the death of Jesus, came to believe that Jesus embraced his fate freely and expressed this vision in the form of a dramatic presentation during which Jesus "pledges his fidelity [to his fate] by allowing the *myron pistikon* to be poured over his head" (153; see 150–54). Sawicki identifies the underlying objection to the anointing as a protest against the idea that the Messiah should have to die (152, n. 5). This idea is eventually displaced as other objections are raised. When the women move their dramatic presentation from the *gynaikōn* to the *symposium*, objections are raised specifically against the role of the woman. This, in turn, gives rise to the present narrative structure and the various versions that find their way into the Gospels. Whatever the limitations of Sawicki's reconstruction (and there are several) she launches the story in the sphere of social memory and draws our attention to the interaction between the past and present experience in the construction of meaning.[3] Mack, also, is clearly cognizant of the rhetorical force of the story and views it as a construction of social memory by the author of Mark. However, unlike Sawicki, he sees Mark's elaboration of an early chreia as a disjunction from the past (i.e., covering over an embarrassing situation in which Jesus has an encounter with a prostitute) rather than an attempt to bridge past and present (200; Mack and Robbins 199–224, 309–12).[4]

---

3. Among the difficulties I have with Sawicki's proposal is the assumption that *symposia*, more than any other context, represents the most plausible setting for the formulation of Jesus' traditions. This assumption overlooks and, perhaps, underestimates the power of rumor and the less formal context of storytelling.

4. Others similarly see the story of the anointing as a reaction to an embarrassing situation which they identify as a tradition that Jesus was buried like a common criminal, without being anointed (Daube; Elliott: 106).

Attempts to construct an "original version of the story" founder on the same rocks as those who trace the story to a historical event. Mack, as Fentress and Wickham predict, reduces the story to the "lowest common denominator" with an added note about the character of the woman: "When Jesus was at table, a disreputable woman entered and poured out a jar of perfumed oil upon him. He said, 'That was good'" (Mack and Robbins 200). Others engage, effectively, in the construction of social memory based on the elements they include and those they leave out (Zelizer: 217). Elliott, for example, identifies the core of the story as an account of Jesus' consecration as king in association with his triumphal entry into Jerusalem (106). Bultmann isolates the original story in Mark 14:3–7 (1968:36–37, 263) in which a woman anoints Jesus on the head, and Jesus pronounces her action "good," while Holst suggests that the original story told of a woman who anointed Jesus feet with the nard and her tears, while those reclining at table objected that the nard could have been sold and the money given to the poor (439).[5] Like efforts to locate a historical event embedded in the story, each of these represents an attempt to locate a "starting point" against which we can measure the "social memory" that emerges in each of the versions recorded in the Gospels. Yet these efforts result in little more than speculation.

While the question of origins remains elusive, some scholars (myself included) are persuaded that a version, or more likely versions, of the story was in circulation during the pre-Gospel period. In arguing that a pre-Gospel tradition exists behind Mark 14:3–9, scholars observe that these verses can be removed from Mark 14 without disrupting the flow of the text (Brown 1966–70:1.452; Bultmann 1968:263; Schweizer: 290). Once removed from its literary context, the story is able to stand on its own as an independent narrative.[6] The genitive absolute in 14:3 (ὄντος αὐτοῦ) becomes the tenuous thread by which the story is woven into the larger fabric of the Gospel narrative (Wagner: 438). Yet as part of the Gospel narrative, the story of the anointing stands in tension with 16:1, where the narrator reports that the women go to the tomb to anoint Jesus (a tension Matthew apparently recognized since the evangelist alters Mark's text, stating that the women came to the tomb to "see" it—not to anoint Jesus).

While the version in Matthew is almost certainly copied directly from Mark, it is by no means certain that Luke and John are dependent on

---

5. For other attempts to reconstruct the origins of the story, see Coakley 1988; Daube 1950; Holst 1976; and Munro 1979.

6. Bultmann views vv. 8–9 as an addition to the story in order to link it with the passion (1968:36–37, 263; so also Schweizer: 289). Brown finds no evidence that the version in Mark ever circulated without a reference to Jesus' burial (1966:454).

Mark's text for their versions of the story.[7] The table below outlines major points of contact (highlighted in bold type) as well as differences between the versions recorded in Mark, Luke and John. What becomes readily apparent is that Luke shares little more than the broad strokes of Mark's version, while John represents a peculiar blend of the versions recorded in Mark and Luke. How one sorts out the relationship between the versions will, to a certain degree, be determined by how one understands the relationship between John and the Synoptics.[8] Sabbe, for example, asserts that John's version can best be explained in terms of literary dependence on Mark and Luke (1992:2052–54, 2064, 2081; 1982:299; so also Munro: 127–28), while Dodd is persuaded that the three versions arose in oral transmission, each evangelist using a separate strand of the tradition (Dodd: 162–72; see also Corley 1993:123; Fitzmyer: 686; Holst; Sawicki: 152; Schaberg: 373; Schnackenberg: 371; Schweizer: 288). Still others find Luke's version so different from that found in Mark that they believe it arose from a different source altogether (Brown 1966–70:1.450–52; Cranfield: 414; Dormeyer: 177; Johnson 1991:128; Legault: 140).

	Mark	Luke	John
Woman	anonymous	sinner	Mary
Anoints Jesus'	head with **alabaster jar of nard very costly:** πιστικῆς	**feet** with **alabaster jar of nard** **wipes with hair**	**feet** with nard **very costly:** πιστικῆς **wipes with hair**
Setting	**Bethany** **house** **meal:** κατάκειμαι	Galilee **house** **meal:** κατακλίθη	**Bethany** **house** **meal:** δεῖπνον
Householder	**Simon** leper	**Simon** Pharisee	Lazarus one who was dead
Time	two days before Passover after entry into Jerusalem	ministry in Galilee	six days before Passover before entry into Jerusalem

---

7. Lindars cautions that "in all cases of verbal agreement we must seriously reckon with the possibility of assimilation *after* the Gospels were written, in the process of transcription" (1981:413). Brown notes that John 12:8 agrees with Matthew rather than Mark, suggesting that it was a later scribal addition copied from Matthew (Brown 1966:449; see also Dodd: 165–66). Dodd poses the faint possibility that the description of the nard as "very costly" (πιστικῆς) may have been original to the text of John, to which the text of Mark was later assimilated (163).

8. This statement is something of an over-simplification. There are other possibilities that could be considered, but these are, in the end, simply variations on the theme.

Objector	"some"	Simon	Judas
Complaint	"For this ointment [τοῦτο τὸ μύρον] might have been sold [πραθῆναι] for more than 300 denarii and given to the poor [δοθῆναι τοῖς πτωχοῖς]."	"If this man were a prophet, he would have known who and what sort of woman this is who is touching him, for she is a sinner."	"Why was this ointment [τοῦτο τὸ μύρον] not sold [ἐπράθη] for 300 denarii and given to the poor [ἐδόθη πτωχοῖς]?"
Rebuttal	"Leave her," "For you always have the poor with you ... but you will not always have me."	Parable of debtors You showed no hospitality; she has shown love.	"Leave her," "The poor you always have with you, but you do not always have me."
	"She has anointed my body beforehand for burial."	Her sins have been forgiven	"that she might keep it for the day of my burial"
Reaction		Can Jesus forgive sins?	
Response	What she has done will be remembered	"Your faith has saved you—go in peace."	

To sort through the evidence in support of each version requires more space than is available here. The more important question for this study is: What difference does it make? In one sense, it makes no difference at all. We know so little about the pre-Gospel period that we have nothing against which to compare the narratives, no sure way to place them in a trajectory of thought, no means of locating them in relation to a community. In another sense, it does make a difference. If we were to conclude that Mark created the story, then we would have a situation in which an author is attempting to establish a previously unknown narrative as part of the social memory of a particular community. We have experiences of this today when the government establishes a new holiday, or an advertising campaign invites us to "remember when. . . ." It is not that such a thing is unimaginable, but that it raises questions about power, authority, and access in relation to the formation of social memory (Zelizer: 214). Who is creating the memory, for whom, and to what end? Once Mark becomes part of the canon, of course, the story is established as social memory for Christians in all times and places, but how might it be received in Damascus during the latter part of the first century? Can we assume that the author of Mark is in a position of sufficient influence that his created narrative would be viewed as persuasive? Or, since the Gospel itself does not bear the name of its author, does this influence reside with those who are circulating it?

If, on the other hand, the story is taken over by Mark from versions circulating in a pre-Gospel setting, it is probable that the story is already functioning as social memory for early Christians and that by incorporating the story, even slightly altered, into the Gospel narrative, Mark is drawing on the persuasive power of the community to lend authority to his narrative. As Fentress and Wickham observe:

> Individual narrators may expand or embellish the story in whatever way they wish; they will still tend to adhere to the plot as the group recognizes it. For the narrator's community, this stabilized version is 'the story,' and they may refuse to accept any major variant.... It is thus the remembering community which decides which version is acceptable and which is not. (74)

While shifting the locus of power from the evangelist to the community does not yield different results in terms of the narratives before us, it does alter the way we respond to the questions: Who is shaping the memory, for whom, and to what end? The story, already established as social memory, "comprises recollections of the past that are determined and shaped by the group. By definition, collective memory thereby presumes activities of sharing, discussion, negotiation, and often, contestation" (Zelizer: 214). The story represents a "field of contest" where members have met to "connect, clarify, and interpret events," in order to create meaning for the life of the community (Fentress and Wickham: 50–51; Zelizer: 217; J. Assmann 1995b:132).

EXAMINING GOSPEL NARRATIVES AS SOCIAL MEMORY: A METHODOLOGICAL PROPOSAL

The versions of the story preserved in the Gospels suggest that the story of "the woman who anointed Jesus" was fertile ground for contest. In the absence of "strata" (clear evidence of the shape and form of earlier versions which allow us to examine how these versions changed over time), it is necessary to adopt a different strategy for gaining insight into how the extant versions functioned as social memory. Fentress and Wickham observe that social memory "is not stable as information; it is stable, rather, at the level of shared meanings and remembered images" (59). This suggests an approach that focuses not on historical origins or "original versions" but, rather, on stable and unstable elements in the shared memory. In line with this approach, I propose a three-fold method for analyzing extant narratives as social memory: 1) identification of elements that appear to be stable with respect to the memory; 2) identification of elements that appear to be unstable and which may indicate points at which the memory is subject to contest and reinterpretation; 3) an examination of how those elements that are unstable reorient the memory in each version in terms of the image it projects (J. Assmann 1995b:132).

A review of the table on pages 104–5 reveals that the three versions are stable with respect to basic structure:[9] A woman anoints Jesus with nard (μύρου); an objection is raised by persons present; Jesus responds with a rebuttal. According to Mack these elements correspond to the form of the chreia, which consists of a scene, a challenge, and a response (1989:90). Mack proposes that the woman's action not only sets the scene, but, because it may be viewed as enigmatic, also poses the challenge (1989:91). He notes that there are other examples of chreiai in Hellenistic literature where it is an action, rather than a statement, that initiates the challenge and that it is not uncommon in such a case for a third party to articulate the challenge (1989:91).[10] The scene which sets up the challenge is dependent upon the response for its interpretation; in turn, the response is dependent upon the scene: the two go together and cannot be separated from one another (Mack 1989:106). The three versions of the story recorded in the Gospels, therefore, all conform to the same formal narrative structure (Fentress and Wickham: 103). While the form may be borrowed from a larger social context, it is, nonetheless, a "local" story, to the degree that it is a story for those already familiar with the person of Jesus and is further localized by the way individual narrators fill the unstable elements (Fentress and Wickham: 103).[11] The formalized structure suggests that there are a limited number of ways in which the story of "the woman who anointed Jesus" can be told, even across communities. Form also may be an indication of congruency in function. Chreiai, with their focus on argumentation, function to establish character (Mack and Robbins: 43–44). However, as will be shown, the character it establishes and how it is established is determined less by form and more by

---

9. Space prohibits a discussion of the version recorded in Matthew. Despite the close relationship to the version in Mark, it should not be assumed that Matthew shapes the narrative to the same end.

10. Mack, following Bultmann, observes that it is the action that sets the scene with the result that the sayings are predicated on the scene; that is, the sayings have not produced the scene (Mack 1989:91; Bultmann 1968:21, 56).

11. Those unfamiliar with Jesus might recognize it as a type of story that they were familiar with and would, perhaps, recognize some of the imagery. However, the stories are also full of imagery that would make sense only to those who know other parts of the Jesus story.

points of instability in the memory since it is at these points that the particular orientation of the narrative is revealed.

In addition to being stable with respect to form, the three versions are stable with respect to general setting. In each, this setting is described as a meal in the home of a person who is named.[12] At this point, stability ends.

The points at which the three versions suggest that the memory is "unstable" and, therefore, open to reinterpretation are as follows:

- ◆ the identity of the householder [Simon or Lazarus?]
- ◆ the description of the householder [Leper or Pharisee or One who was dead?]
- ◆ the location of the house [Bethany or Galilee?]
- ◆ the identity of the woman who anoints Jesus [anonymous or sinner or Mary?]
- ◆ the part of the body that is anointed [head or feet?]
- ◆ the timing of the anointing [two or six days before Passover or ministry in Galilee?]
- ◆ who challenges the action by the woman [some householder or Judas?]
- ◆ nature of the complaint [waste or character of woman?]
- ◆ defense of action by Jesus [for burial or demonstration of love?]
- ◆ defense of woman [told in memory of her or her sins are forgiven?]

There are, of course, other differences between the versions—in vocabulary and in expansions or deletions—but it is the configuration of these elements that gives shape to the narratives as social memory by evoking images within the shared memory of the audience and using them to encourage the audience to interpret the story in a particular way (Fentress and Wickham: 50–51).

Unstable Elements and the Shape of Memory

While many of the elements are drawn from settings and images within the Jesus narratives, the image of anointing belongs to a larger sphere. I begin my analysis, therefore, with an overview of the words employed to describe the anointing in order to establish the variety of images that might be evoked by any one word. Following this brief excursus I will examine how the "anointing" is given definition within the individual narratives.

---

12. Matthew, which is not under consideration in this essay, omits the reference to the meal.

In each narrative the woman uses nard (μύρον) to anoint Jesus, a substance which could evoke a variety of contexts. In the LXX, it is described as a sacred oil used to anoint the tent of meeting and the implements associated with it as well as the priests who serve in it (Exod 30:25). It is, in addition, used in preparing bodies for burial (2 Chr 16:14; T. Ab. 20:11; Apoc. Mos. 40:1), as a sign of celebration (Ps 133:2; Prov 27:9; Isa 25:6; Wis 2:7), and to make oneself desirable (Song 1:3; Jdt 10:3).

The action which forms the basis of each narrative is "anointing." In the versions recorded in Mark and Matthew, the woman anoints (καταχέω) Jesus' head. This verb is found only here in the Second Testament; in the LXX it is never used in relation to anointing, although a related verb is (ἐπεχέω). In three texts, where ἐπεχέω occurs also with the verb χρίω (but the word for "oil" is ἔλαιον), the verb is used specifically to describe "anointing the head": Exod 29:7, where Aaron is anointed as priest over Israel; 1 Kgdms 10:1, where Samuel anoints Saul king over Israel; and in 4 Kgdms 9:3, 6, where one of the sons of the prophets, instructed by Elisha, anoints Jehu king over Israel. The close relationship between the verbs is indicated by a parallel passage in Josephus (Ant. 9.108) where the verb καταχέω is employed to describe the anointing of Jehu. In other instances, the head is anointed with oil as a sign of joy or celebration (Eccl 9:7–8; Isa 25:7 [χρίω]), or hospitality (Luke 7:46 [ἀλείφω]), and is associated with banqueting or luxury (Amos 6:6 [χρίω]; Wis 2:7; Josephus Ant. 19.238–39 [χρίω]).

In the versions recorded in Luke and John, the woman anoints (ἀλείφω) Jesus' feet. Ἀλείφω can describe anointing in a variety of contexts: the anointing of priests (Exod 40:15; Num 3:3); to make oneself desirable (Ruth 3:3), or presentable (2 Kgdms 12:20; Esth 2:12; cf. 2 Kgdms 14:2; Dan 10:3); to express hospitality (Luke 7:46); or for the purposes of healing (Mark 6:13; Jas 5:14). Coakley cites a number of passages which describe feet, specifically, being anointed with oil (247–48): in Homer (Od. 19. 503–7) Odysseus' feet are washed and anointed by a female slave.[13] A similar story in which a female servant washes the feet of her master with oil is recorded in Sipre on Deut 33:24. In Aristophanes Vesp. 606–9 a daughter washes and anoints (ἀλείφω) the feet of her father, but in the hope of getting something out of him. Athenaeus (in Deipn. 12.553) notes that elite Athenians, who could afford to live in luxury, had a custom of anointing (ἐναλείφω) their feet with perfumes, a practice also noted among Roman elite by Pliny (Nat. 13:22). Šabb. 3:16 instructs readers to put oil on their foot before placing it in a shoe or sandal, suggesting that

---

13. D. MacDonald proposes that the works of Homer directly influence Mark's rendition of the anointing of Jesus (111–19).

the nonelite, too, may anoint their feet, but perhaps in a different context. In Petronius (*Satyricon* 70) anointing the feet is associated with prostitutes, here "long-haired boys."

A third word for anointing, which does not occur in the story of "the woman who anointed Jesus," is χρίω. In the LXX, this word is used most frequently to designate someone (priest, ruler, prophet, servant) or something (altar, tabernacle, tent of meeting) as set apart by God for a particular purpose (e.g. Exod 28:41; 29:36; 30:26; 40:9; Lev 8:10, 12; 1 Kgdms 9:16; 15:1; 16:12–13; 2 Kgdms 12:7; Isa 61:1). This is its exclusive use in the Second Testament (Luke 4:18; Acts 4:27; 10:38; Heb 1:9) although it is not used exclusively of Jesus (cf. 2 Cor 1:21). As noted above, it also occurs with the verb ἐπεχέω in the LXX (Exod 29:7; 1 Kgdms 10:1; 4 Kgdms 9:6). However, this is not the only context in which it occurs. Judith anoints herself (χρίω) in order to make herself desirable (Jdt 10:3), and the elite anoint themselves (χρίω) at banquets, a sign of their extravagance (Amos 6:6).

The intent of this overview of anointing is to demonstrate the variety of words that could be employed to describe the anointing as well as the variety of images that any one word might evoke. Because of this variety, what ultimately leads us to view the anointing in a particular way is not simply the act of anointing itself, but the other images that are evoked in the same moment as the anointing. They cannot be understood apart from one another, which is to say, it matters when and where the anointing occurs and who it is that is doing the anointing. The variability of these elements shifts the focus utterly.

In the Gospel of Mark, the setting provides the "clue" as to how the narrator wants us to view the anointing. The narrator has already designated a host for the meal, Simon (14:3), making it unlikely that the anointing should be interpreted as an act of hospitality. Since the host is identified as a leper (is he healed?—nothing leads us to assume so), the setting also is unlikely to be one of luxury. Were it so, the objection raised by those present would be undercut.[14] If we allow the larger narrative setting to influence our reading (the story, although it might circulate independently of Mark's text, would likely be told in conjunction with other stories which would have an impact on how the story was heard), we would have already heard mention of death, and so are prepared to view the anointing in conjunction with burial (14:1–2, 8; Corley 1993:105). The death motif is reinforced by the location of Simon's home in Bethany

---

14. Sawicki asserts that the vocabulary in Mark locates the anointing in the elite context of a *symposium*: e.g. κατακειμένου, πιστικῆς, ἀγανακτοῦντες, καλόν ἔργον, ἐποίησεν, μνημόσυνον, λαληθήσεται (152).

(which serves as a refuge from the dangers present in Jerusalem [10:32–34; 11:1–11; 14:3]) and the reference to Passover, which evokes images of both sacrifice and deliverance. However, a disjunction occurs at the moment of the anointing itself. The woman anoints Jesus on the head. As a symbolic act, this might do for burial (particularly since anointing for burial was an activity associated with women), but so might the feet. This invites us to examine more closely the choice the narrator has made at this point.

In the LXX, anointing the head is associated most often with setting someone apart for the service of God as priest, king or prophet. This image is evoked specifically by the use of the verb ἐπεχέω (καταχέω) in conjunction with χρίω (Exod 29:7; 1 Kgdms 10:1; 4 Kgdms 9:6; Ant. 9.108).[15] It is possible that, in Mark, the narrator is deliberately inviting us to see Jesus as God's anointed at the same moment that we are invited to see him as the one who is about to die (anointed beforehand for burial).[16] A similar juxtaposition is found in chapter 8 where Peter correctly identifies Jesus as "the Messiah" ("the anointed" [8:29]), an image which is immediately associated with Jesus' impending death (8:31–32)—and an image Peter denounces.[17] In chapter 14, we find a counterpoint to Peter in the anonymous woman, who identifies Jesus as God's anointed specifically in the context of death.[18] It is, in fact, her anonymity that allows her to function best in this way by locating her identity in her action rather than in her status.[19] The objection raised, then, is not against her person or her gender, but against her action, which is deemed a waste by an anonymous few.[20] Jesus' rebuttal, aligning her action with burial, is not a

---

15. Sabbe argues that the absence of χρίω militates against reading this as a royal or messianic anointing (1992:2059–60 [see especially n. 16], 2080; so also Cranfield: 415). However, this does not take into account the variety of ways in which various words for anointing are employed. The near absence of χρίω in the Second Testament suggests that this language was not central to descriptions of Jesus as the Christ. Elliott thinks Mark draws attention away from Jesus' anointing as Messiah by emphasizing the woman's devotion and renaming the anointing for burial (106).

16. Schaberg views the description of the woman's act as an anointing for burial as a correction that "depoliticizes the claim to royalty (which was probably the point of the earliest account), by means of the prediction of suffering" (374).

17. Lindars rejects the idea that the anointing stories in any of the Gospels are "intended as an acknowledgement of Jesus' messianic status" (1981:414; see also Sabbe, 1992:2071), contra Munro who thinks the original point of the story was messianic (130).

18. Sawicki comes to a similar conclusion, but by an utterly different route (150, 164, 170).

19. Tolbert observes that the woman who anoints Jesus illustrates Mark's assertion that the "first shall be last" and "slave of all" (358).

20. Mack states that Jesus' response to the objection redefines the issue in terms of intentionality: i.e. why does the woman anoint him? Her intention is to anoint him for burial (1989:96). I think this may be too large a claim. Jesus' response aligns the woman's action

diversion,[21] but a confirmation of his identity as the Messiah who must suffer and die (Tolbert: 358).[22] In this, the woman's twofold identity as prophet is revealed: as the prophet who anoints Jesus—just as the prophets anointed priests and rulers in Israel's memory (J. Dewey 1994: 501); and as the one who anticipates Jesus' death (Schweizer: 290–91; Beavis: 7; Sabbe 1992:2081). Jesus' closing words, "wherever the gospel is preached in the whole world, what she has done will be told in memory of her," both confirm the importance of the woman's prophetic action and commit to our memory the identity of Jesus that is revealed in her action (Mack: 311–12; Delorme: 123).[23] The narrative thus establishes a norm for the community in terms of its understanding of who Jesus is.

The versions recorded in Luke and John shape the narrative around a woman who anoints Jesus' feet. This action evokes a quite different set of images from those in Mark. As noted above, the verb $\dot{\alpha}\lambda\epsilon\dot{\iota}\phi\omega$ can refer to anointing in a variety of contexts. When used to describe the anointing of feet, this set of images is narrowed: it evokes a slave, anointing her master's feet to welcome him home; a daughter seeking favor with her father; the elite, indulging in luxury (as an interlocutor observes, how could the scent "be noticed or give any pleasure from that part of the body?" [Pliny, *Nat.* 13:22]); or consorting with a prostitute. To understand how the image of anointing functions in each narrative, it is necessary to examine how the narrator gives it shape through interaction with other "unstable" elements.

In Luke the anointing is understood in relation to a series of contrasts that drive the narrative (Tannehill: 116). It is persons, rather than location (which is somewhere in Galilee), that provide the context for the story.[24]

---

with his burial; whether it is intended to define her intentions is less clear. It seems to me that the force of the anointing is lost if it is not experienced in tension with the idea of death and burial.

21. Mack views the elaboration in Mark as an attempt to shift attention away from an embarrassing situation: i.e., a historical encounter between Jesus and a woman of disrepute (1989:94; so also Corley 1993:105; Schweizer: 288).

22. Numerous scholars have noted the narrator's use of a rabbinic argument at this point: i.e., anointing is superior to almsgiving (*Pe'ah* 4:19; *Sukkah* 49b) (Jeremias; Daube; Barrett; Mack and Robbins).

23. Mack views Mark's version as a response to what he calls the "Christ cult," that is, those who focus on the power of the risen Christ. To "preach the gospel" is not, according to Mack, to proclaim the kerygma (which he associates with the Christ cult), but to make the stories about Jesus memorable (311–12).

24. In Luke, the cross is not a means of effecting forgiveness for sinners; rather it is a sign of the need for forgiveness since, in putting Jesus to death, humankind has rejected God's innocent messenger. It makes sense, then, for Luke to place this story in the context of Jesus' ministry rather than in relation to his death and burial.

The setting is established by reference to the status of the householder who is described as a Pharisee, a fact mentioned twice in the first verse (7:36). The woman, in contrast, is identified as "a sinner" in the city.[25] The absence of names for these two characters at this point in the narrative keeps attention focused on their status. The woman takes her stand behind Jesus, washes his feet with her tears, wipes them with her hair, kisses them and, finally, anoints them (7:37–38). This series of actions is punctuated by the threefold repetition of καί, so that each action builds on the one that precedes, emphasis of final place being given to the anointing. The Pharisee, still unnamed, challenges not the actions of the woman, but the character of the woman as a "sinner" and, by association, the character of Jesus who, a reputed prophet, should have known "who and what sort of" woman she is (7:39). It is, in fact, this characterization of the woman which gives definition to the anointing at this point in the narrative. Framed by these references to the woman as a "sinner" (7:37, 39), the anointing cannot be that of a slave (a member of the Pharisee's household), nor of a relative since the woman is from the outside, in "the city." As a Pharisee, the host is unlikely to be consorting with a prostitute and it is his reaction to the woman that causes us to view the woman in precisely this way (Fitzmyer: 689).[26]

As the narrative continues, however, the anointing is reinterpreted. Jesus responds to the Pharisee's challenge (which the Pharisee has spoken only to himself, thus revealing that Jesus is indeed a prophet [Resseguie: 143; Mack 1989:103])[27] with a parable. It is only at this point

---

25. Many scholars read the description of the woman as one "known in the city" as an indication that she is a prostitute (Corley 1993:124; Green: 309; Seim: 90–91; Schottroff: 150). In contrast, Fitzmyer maintains that although the Pharisee implies that the woman is a harlot, it is nowhere stated explicitly in the text (689; so also Reid: 114).

26. Hornsby employs reader-response criticism to explore ways in which the story, within the context of Luke, leads us to view the woman as a prostitute. The reference to the woman's unbound hair is often understood as one of the marks of her characterization as a prostitute (e.g., Sawicki: 163). However, in view of how her actions will be reinterpreted by Jesus as an extravagant gesture of love, it is not clear to me that we should assume this to be the case. I understand Luke to be deliberately describing the actions of the woman in an ambiguous way so that the audience can be persuaded to move from one interpretation to the other. The hair, perforce, must be open to interpretation in more than one way. Reid suggests that since no one reacts to the woman loosening her hair, it is not a source of offense within the narrative (115). She also notes that there are other ways to interpret the unbound hair: for example, it could be associated with the flowing hair of the beloved in Song 4:1 and 6:5 (115). Schaberg similarly notes that while unbound hair may be the mark of a "loose woman," it is also associated with women prophesying in 1 Cor 11:56 (374).

27. Schaberg notes that while the woman is depicted as a prophet in Mark, in Luke this identity is transferred to Jesus (375).

in the narrative that we learn the Pharisee's name: Simon. Although the woman will remain anonymous, the parable and its interpretation that follows gives name to her actions, which stand in stark contrast to those of Simon. Her actions, again, are punctuated by the threefold repetition of καί, with final emphasis given to the anointing. Here, however, the anointing is defined in contrast to Simon's lack of hospitality.[28] Simon, as host, should have offered Jesus oil with which to anoint his head. In contrast, the woman willingly assumes the status of a slave, and anoints Jesus' feet. Her action underscores the shallowness of Simon's character, which has already been revealed in his callous misinterpretation of the woman's character and action.[29] Jesus goes on to pronounce that the woman's sins have been forgiven because she has loved much.[30] Thus the woman's actions are shown to extend beyond mere hospitality. They are a response to the person of Jesus and the message he represents: the visitation of God (19:44), and a manifestation of God's grace (5:32; 15:7; 19:10; 24:47; Johnson 1991:129; Kilgallen: 678–79; Green 1995).[31] This grace is underscored by the protracted conclusion to the story: Jesus tells Simon that the woman's sins are forgiven (v. 47), then announces to the woman that her sins are forgiven (v. 48), which prompts those gathered to ask, "Who is this who even forgives sins?" (v. 49; Elliott: 107; Holst: 438; Thibeaux: 152; Mack 1989:102; Johnson 1991:129; Green 1997:306). The woman models for us how we, as sinners, should respond to Jesus and by this action calls to memory who Jesus is.

For John, in contrast to Luke, the location of the story is essential. It is described in reference to three settings: temporal (six days before Passover), geographic (Bethany, already established in the minds of the audience as the village of Mary and Martha [11:1]), and persons (Lazarus,

---

28. Resseguie suggests that the narrator deliberately withholds the reference to Simon's lack of hospitality until this point in the narrative so that the audience is lured into thinking positively of Simon as the narrative begins, thus making his fall the greater (145–46).

29. Thibeaux sees this story as a reflection of conflict within the Lukan community over issues of inclusion: e.g., table fellowship with sinners (Thibeaux: 157).

30. The use of the perfect tense (ἀφέωνται) indicates that the woman's sins have been forgiven at some point prior to the present; her actions therefore do not result in forgiveness, but are shown to be in response to her experience of forgiveness (Thibeaux: 152).

31. Corley identifies several links between the story of the woman who anoints Jesus and the crucifixion (1993:127–28), as does Reid (117): e.g., the woman's tears mirror the women who weep in 23:27 (so Corley) and her kisses contrast with the kiss of Judas (so Reid). While several images may be compared and contrasted between these two narratives, I sense in this a desire to make the story of the woman who anoints Jesus conform to the versions found in the other Gospels. The Christological focus of the story of the woman who anoints Jesus causes me to think that the narrator deliberately separates the anointing from Jesus' death and burial (see n. 26).

whom Jesus raised from the dead). These are complex images. Passover signifies not only the festival during which Jesus' death occurs, but the essential nature of Jesus' sacrifice which, like the Passover lamb, marks those who shall receive life (1:36; 3:16; 10:15; 13:1; 13:31). Bethany, as in Mark, is a place of refuge, but it is also a place where Jesus' identity as "the resurrection and the life ... the Messiah, the son of God, the one coming into the world" (11:25, 27) has been revealed. Lazarus gives body and breath to Jesus' claim that he is the resurrection and the life. In John, then, the story of the "woman who anointed Jesus" is told in the moments between resurrection (Lazarus) and Jesus' life-giving death (Passover), and takes place among those who are "Jesus' own" (10:14): Lazarus, Martha, and Mary, all of whom Jesus loves (11:5). The story is to be heard and understood in reference to all three.

The woman who anoints Jesus is identified as Mary, the sister of Martha and Lazarus. She is not anonymous, a sinner, or an outsider to this gathering. She is a member of the family whose intimate relationship with Jesus has already been established in the minds of the audience (11:1–44). This fundamentally alters the way we experience the anointing. It becomes descriptive of the relationship between Jesus and Mary and cannot be understood apart from this relationship. Like the woman in Luke, Mary anoints Jesus' feet, but there are no tears, no kisses. There is no need here for extravagant contrast. She simply anoints his feet and wipes them with her hair. This action more nearly resembles the example from *Sipre* on Deut 33:24 where a female slave washes her master's feet in oil, yet the intimacy of Jesus and Mary's relationship suggests something more. One possibility is that the narrator is evoking images from the Song of Songs (see Winsor). Two phrases, in particular, resonate with the scene described in John: In Song 1:12, the king (a title of affection for the beloved) is said to be reclining on his couch, while the woman's nard gives forth its fragrance (12:2–3), and in Song 7:5b–c, the king says of the woman, "the curls of your hair are like purple, the king is bound in your tresses" (12:3a; see Winsor: 21–22). "King" is among the images John uses for Jesus (1:49; 12:13, 15; 18:33–19:22; cf. 6:15) while Mary is described as one whom Jesus loves. In evoking these images from the Song of Songs, the narrator describes Mary's intimate relationship with Jesus, her beloved, who, like the king in the Song of Songs, is caught in her tresses. The erotic overtones signal the depth of this relationship between the lover and the beloved.[32] This intimacy, in turn, reflects both the love that

---

32. Lindars identifies the point of the story as Mary's personal devotion to Jesus (1981:414). However, this does not take into account Jesus' own description of his relationship with his followers in John (17:21–23). Several scholars view the woman's action as

followers of Jesus are urged to bear toward one another (13:34–35) and describes the relationship of Jesus with his followers, as well as both his and their relationship with God (15:9–12; 16:27; 17:21–23, 26).

It makes sense, in this context, for Judas to be the person who objects to Mary's action, describing it as a waste. Of all the people present in the scene, Judas is the one who does not belong. He is the outsider, the one who is about to betray Jesus and who steals from the community (12:4–6). His objection is a diversion, motivated by greed and the hope of self-gain (12:6). In Mark, where the objectors are an "anonymous few," their comments merely reflect lack of insight into the true nature of the woman's action. Jesus' response is anticipated by the narrator's aside that Judas is about to betray Jesus—to send him to his death: the nard (not the anointing) is for the day of his burial.[33] In Mark, the narrator specifies that the woman, in anointing Jesus, has prepared him for burial (14:8). In John, a distinction is made: the nard becomes a sign of Jesus' anticipated burial, but the anointing remains a symbol of the relationship between Jesus and Mary now. It represents the intimate relationship between the believer and Jesus—between the lover and the beloved—by which we come to know and experience Jesus as the resurrection and the life.[34] Although it

---

prophetic, anticipating Jesus' death (Lindars: 414; Reinhartz: 583; O'Day: 388), but this view is rooted in the problematic τηρέω (see next note) and, it seems to me, reflects an effort to harmonize the version in John with that in Mark.

33. There is some dispute concerning how to best translate v. 7, and in particular, τηρήσῃ. The most straightforward translation would be "let her keep it for the day of my burial" (so the RSV), which renders the ἵνα clause as an indirect imperative (BDF 287.3; Schnackenburg: 369). However, this translation disturbs some scholars because it creates a tension with ch. 19 where Jesus' body is anointed, but by Nicodemus and Joseph of Arimathea. Daube proposes that τηρέω be translated "to keep in one's memory" (a meaning found in Luke 2:19, 51 and Gen 37:11), so that the phrase would read "let her remember" (191), but, as Barrett points out, τηρέω never means "remember" in John while it frequently means "keep" (414). Barrett suggests that a third alternative presents itself if we understand the αὐτό to refer to the anointing rather than the nard (414). Since it is possible to render τηρέω, "observe," the phrase then becomes "let her observe the last rite now with a view to my burial" (Barrett: 414). The difficulty with this proposal is that the antecedent of αὐτό is the nard, not the burial. In view of the difficulties, some translators render the phrase in some way that brings John into conformity with Mark (so the NRSV; this is what Brown prefers [1966–70:1.449]). However, such a translation cannot be borne by the Greek.

34. Some scholars have suggested that the anointing is tied to Jesus' identity as a king in John's Gospel, since it occurs just prior to his entry into Jerusalem (Elliott: 107; C. Koester: 114). This reading is possible if understood in connection with the Song of Songs imagery. Yet if this is the case, it signals that Jesus' role as king is understood in terms that are quite different from the Gospel of Mark (where it is possible that Jesus is anointed as a prophet rather than king). Others, because it is Jesus' feet that are anointed, are skeptical of any association between the anointing and royal imagery (Coakley: 243; Brown 1966–70:1.454).

is disputed whether v. 8 belongs to the text,[35] it underlines the fragility of the moment and intensifies the intimacy of the encounter between Mary and Jesus. In John, Mary's anointing of Jesus evokes in us the memory of Jesus as the one who lives in us and in whom we experience life, both now and in the resurrection.

CONCLUSION

This examination of the story of "the woman who anoints Jesus" in relation to social memory theory has resulted in both insights and challenges. No method has yet provided the key for uncovering all we would like to know about the pre-Gospel period and social memory theory calls attention to weaknesses inherent in some of our efforts. Specifically, it reveals that attempts to identify the historical origins of an event or the original form of a narrative when our only sources are the narratives themselves are problematic and likely to yield little more than the lowest common denominator among extant versions. At the same time, social memory theory challenges us to reframe our questions in ways that once again open up the text for study. For example, examining the various versions of the story in terms of stable and unstable elements draws attention to the christological focus of these texts. In particular, attention to the stable formal structure reveals how important it is to examine the role of the anointing in relation to the response. By failing to recognize how these elements work together, commentators have overlooked the role of the woman in establishing the identity of Jesus within the narrative.[36] Close attention to how the unstable elements work together reveals both the particularity of the christological images described by each version, and demonstrates how it is the configuration of these elements that gives shape to each image.[37] The three resulting Christologies suggest that, although the story of the woman who anointed Jesus has become a stable element in the narrative of Jesus, it is not yet stable in terms of its

---

35. Brown notes that John 12:8 agrees with Matthew rather than Mark, suggesting that it was a later scribal addition copied from Matthew (1966–70:1.449; see also Dodd: 165–66).

36. Particularly aggravating are commentators who assume that the woman performs the anointing unconsciously, with no knowledge of what she does (Brown 1966–70:1.454; Gundry: 804; Lindars 1981:419; Schnackenburg: 370). They, presumably, mean that the woman's purpose did not correspond with the interpretation given to her action by Jesus. However, their comments are presumptuous and re-enforce the role of the woman as a subject for men to debate rather than an actor whose role is central to the narrative.

37. Interpreters have tended to interpret the stories in view of one another—the disrepute of Luke's woman is heard in the other stories, or Luke's story is heard in relation to Jesus' death (see notes 36 and 38).

christological focus. Rather, it reflects the variety of Christologies that are emerging within and in response to the life situations of local communities.[38] This conclusion places the story within the context of competing responses to the question, "Who is Jesus," and invites us to reflect on how the story goes beyond a "simple act of recall" to become a reflection of "identity formation, power and authority, cultural norms and social interaction" (Zelizer: 214). In this paper, I have been able to do no more than demonstrate how the different versions point in this direction, but it is, I hope, enough to suggest the potential that resides in examining stories in the Gospels through the lens of social memory theory. Indeed, it is in their function as social memory that the power of these stories resides (Schudson 1989:109).

---

38. Mack, similarly, envisions the story evolving over the course of time in response to "practical and theological issues facing those communities" (1989:89; see also 91–92).

THE LOCUS FOR DEATH:
SOCIAL MEMORY AND THE PASSION NARRATIVES

Arthur J. Dewey

During the last twenty years or so a critical momentum has been growing. Scholars from a variety of disciplines have begun to explore the rich yield coming from investigation of social memory (e.g., Fentress and Wickham; Middleton and Edwards). The threshold recognition that memory is neither a simple individual affair nor a static holding pattern, but rather a creative social construction, has presented the critical conversation with a staggering challenge. The fundamental ways in which we have come to understand the past have to be reimagined. The simple acts and residues of historical memory need a second look.

This paper begins to explore what has been largely overlooked in the recent debate over the historicity of the passion narratives in the Gospels. What I touch on concerns not only what we would read as historical evidence, but also how we imagine or see the evidence. Indeed, my concern is to ask whether the construction of social memory can be understood from within the ancient mindset. In order to do so I shall enlist the recent insights of Mary Carruthers, who brings a nuanced perspective on ancient memory to the discussion (Carruthers 1998). Moreover, I shall attempt to provide a surprising example of Carruthers' theory of ancient memory. Despite its mute witness, Trajan's Column may well give the modern investigator a clue to the notion of memory location. From these considerations we shall return to the passion traditions in order to see what might be some of the probable consequences of this investigation. We may then begin to detect the memory craft of the Gospel writers.

---

* The original version of this paper was presented under the title "The Memory of a Death or the Birth/Death of Memory?" at the Annual Meeting of the International Society of Biblical Literature, Cambridge University, 24 July 2003.

THE RECENT DEBATE OVER THE HISTORICITY
OF THE PASSION NARRATIVE

If one were to chart the ways in which the passion narratives are read critically today, the apt distinction coined by John Dominic Crossan delivers the two ends of the critical spectrum: history remembered versus prophecy historicized (Crossan 1995:1–38). Are the Gospel writers delivering what happened to their listeners, or have the writers woven a tale from earlier prophetic lines? Are the passion stories fact or fiction? Of course, the critical response has not been so stark. Most scholars would conclude that there is a mixture of report and editorial revision. Yet the battle lines are very much formed. Was not a "kernel" of the passion narrative there from the beginning (see Brown 1993)? Or hasn't Mark spun an imposing fiction (see Mack)?

I do not intend to resolve this dilemma but to deepen the way in which we see the evidence in front of us. What is the texture of the evidence? But even more, how did the ancient writers weave narratives from their material? Does the way in which they handle their sources have something to say to our presuppositions about the evidence? Do the recent reflections of the social character of memory have anything to say to these questions?

THE PASSION NARRATIVE TRADITION:
RECENT OBSERVATIONS AND INTIMATIONS OF MEMORY

Recent scholarship has confirmed that the traditions of the death of Jesus are anything but simple. A complex layering of the historical evidence is a requisite first step in beginning to come to terms with the developing passion traditions.

Before I continue, I shall recall certain points about the passion narrative tradition, as I briefly indicate some of the complexity of this continuing investigation. Then I shall try to elicit possibilities of reading this evidence through the prism of social memory. Of course, all that follows, while subject to immense debate, can serve as the occasion for my investigation and proposal. Moreover, we may discern that our modern perspective may well condition the debate (both *in toto* and *in parte*) over the question of the historicity of the passion narratives more than we realize.

(1) If we take the presence of the Sayings Gospel Q seriously, we have to take into account that Q does not have a passion narrative. The death of Jesus becomes absorbed into the tradition of prophets' deaths (cf. Luke 11:49–51). There is nothing beyond an allusion to his death. The *Gospel of Thomas* evidently continues in this tradition. There is no mention at all of the death of Jesus in *Thomas*.

(2) Paul already knows a tradition that speaks of the death of Jesus. We can say briefly two things. First, the death of Jesus was understood as a heroic death, a martyr's sacrifice (Rom 3:21–26). Second, the Jewish sacred writings were invoked and applied in some fashion in speaking of his fate (1 Cor 15:3–5).

(3) The Markan passion narrative displays the elements of the Tale of the Persecution and Vindication of the Innocent One, as has been noted for some time (see Nickelsburg; Mack).

(4) More recently, Crossan and A. Dewey have independently argued for an earlier version of the *Gospel of Peter*. Dewey has shown that the entire first layer of *Peter* can be located on the template of the Tale of the Persecution and Vindication of the Innocent One (Crossan 1998; Dewey 1998).

(5) The Synoptic followers of Mark have apparently utilized the Markan base, adding further material, while typically reworking and eliminating other pieces.

(6) The Gospel of John shows a remarkable reworking of the passion narrative. If the writer of John knew of Mark, or an earlier version of the passion narrative, he, in his singularly creative way, has revised the passion narrative into a highly dramatic version.

With these observations in mind, it is important to point out that the long-standing assumption that there must have been some primitive passion narrative at the very outset of the Jesus movement becomes hard-pressed when faced with the evidence in the Sayings Gospel. Neither does Paul help sustain that assumption. Rather, it would seem that the evidence for a passion narrative comes somewhat later, with either an early version of the *Gospel of Peter* (55–65 C.E.) or the Gospel of Mark (70+ C.E.). With Paul there is evidence of the use of scriptural citations to touch on Jesus' fate. But there is no evidence for any interest in a narrative unfolding of his death. The *Gospel of Thomas* argues for at least some of the tradition progressing without any concern over such a narrative.

A second point comes from my own recent work on the passion narrative in John (Dewey 2001b). I have argued that in the Fourth Gospel "history" is not what we moderns would want it to be. The account of the final hours of Jesus is actually a creative invention that allows the listener the chance to participate, to "see" the meaning in the death scene of Jesus (cf. John 19:35–37). This recognition of the creative "memory" of the writer of the Fourth Gospel has led me to rethink a number of presuppositions regarding the critical apprehension of the death stories of Jesus.

A further note comes from the acoustic world of the first century. We are dealing with an oral culture. The worth and workings of memory are crucial, for without some scheme—some memory device—there is no survival of the meaning. First-century orality and memory raise the question: Do the Synoptic passion narratives display any clues to some sort of memory scheme? Indeed, in contemplating the use of a memory scheme, we must further wonder about the "invention" of that scheme. As we shall see shortly, the rhetorical *inventio* entails a construction of meaning. As recent work on social memory has shown, a simple recollection of "the facts" is no longer the issue.

There is a further observation to be made. When the various traditions are considered, can we begin to see that imaginative acts were underway to give some sort of "location" to the fate of Jesus? The Q material apparently locates the death of Jesus within the familiar pattern of the deaths of Jewish prophets (Luke 11:49–51). On the other hand, the Pauline material can be read as going in a number of directions. One can argue that a pre-Pauline understanding of the death of Jesus locates the fate of Jesus within the orbit of heroic Jewish martyrs. Yet noting that in 1 Cor 15:3–5 Jewish sacred writings are used to interpret Jesus' death does not help us very much, except to indicate the connection of Jesus' fate to a written tradition. There is also the further issue of how Paul transformed what he heard about the death of Jesus. Does he, for instance, in Gal 3:10–14 introduce the notion of shame—as well as blessing and curse—to the death of Jesus (that he has "graphically portrayed") to locate the fate of Jesus within the current debate over Gentile acceptability?

The matter of location becomes explicit when we reach the first evidence of extended passion narratives. It is either in the first layer of *Peter* or in Mark that we have the first extended narrative of the death of Jesus. Here we see that the story is, in fact, structured along the lines of the Tale of the Persecution and Vindication of the Innocent One. The meticulous analysis of Nickelsburg has demonstrated not only the presence of such a pattern in Hellenistic Jewish texts, but also that the constituent elements of that story pattern are present within the passion narrative of Mark. It should be noted that, unlike Mack, who follows Nickelsburg, Nickelsburg himself thinks that a pre-Markan passion narrative existed.

I have argued elsewhere that the earliest layer of *Peter* provides this pre-Markan source (A. Dewey 1990). But this is not the place to defend that thesis. What I would underline is the emergence of the pattern of the Tale of the Persecution and Vindication of the Innocent One. I would contend that with this pattern we have evidence of a social memory scheme.[1] What does this memory scheme suggest? It indicates that, for the author

---

1. For those who would dispute the priority of an early level of the Gospel of Peter and see Mark as issuing the earliest passion narrative, the point still stands. The scheme of the Innocent Sufferer has surfaced in the Jesus tradition.

of the earliest level of the *Gospel of Peter* to remember, he had to find a "place" or schema to locate memory; he had to re-member by going back to the imaginative repertoires of his time. Of course, George Nickelsburg has shown this repertoire of memory to be the widespread tradition of the Tale of the Persecution and Vindication of the Innocent One. I would further contend that this scheme has been the memory bed for Matthew and Luke and, perhaps, for John.

AN INTERLUDE: TRAJAN'S COLUMN AND THE CRAFT OF MEMORY.

Ancient stones, like ancient texts, stand mute. I would like to introduce at this juncture a magnificent example of such silence: Trajan's Column. I do this because the column's construction seems to demand some sort of reading. The column was begun after Trajan's successful campaigns in Dacia (see Coarelli).[2] Standing over 120 feet high and centered between two libraries (no longer extant) in Trajan's new forum complex, the column presents detailed, spiraling episodes of the two Dacian Wars. The scenes cover the entire range of Roman military life, from the campsite to the battlefield. So specific are the scenes that it has often been suggested that they were modeled from Trajan's own war commentaries. Originally a statue of Trajan topped the construction. The base of the column was intended as a tomb for the ashes of the Emperor. In effect, the column not only celebrated the triumphant Emperor, but also anticipated his divine honors upon his death.

On returning to the rather dizzying sight of the unfolding series of scenes running chronologically from the base to the very top, we can see that the entire column functions as an unwinding scroll.[3] The readers catch an eyeful as they move from scene to scene. While there has been some dispute over this characterization of the spiral frieze, Josef Strzygowski's original proposal (an "illustrated volumen") still holds sway (Coarelli: 11).

There are no words beyond the base, nor are there any obvious clues for the modern reader. But one can discern a variety of scene breaks, where a wall or some other building brackets a scene. The particular scenes are full of energy and would compel the reader to stay attentive. Nevertheless, I have often asked myself, What is the scheme according to which this column should be "read"?

---

2. This volume has plates for each of the scenes on the column.

3. The creative solution of decorating the column as an illustrated volumen may well have had its precursors in the long-standing "triumph painting," which provided a series of victorious vignettes (see Coarelli: 11).

It is here that the work of Mary Carruthers becomes helpful. In her two books, Carruthers has pointed the way to understanding ancient memory as an active craft (1990; 1998). Carruthers has made a major advance in the understanding of ancient memory. While she is appreciative of the contributions of Frances Yates to the study of memory (see Yates), Carruthers differs with Yates's assessment of memory. For Yates, the art of memory was to repeat previously stored material. There is a static quality to memory despite its fascinating, if not preposterous, constructions. Carruthers counters by arguing:

> The goal of rhetorical mnemotechnical craft was not to give students a prodigious memory for all the information they might be asked to repeat in an examination, but to give an orator the means and wherewithal to invent his material, both beforehand and—crucially—on the spot. Memoria is most usefully thought of as a compositional art. (1998:9)

Carruthers places the creative act of memory within the domain of ancient rhetoric, not psychology. In effect, memory for Carruthers is implicitly social, embedded in the discourse of the day. The act of memory starts with rhetorical *inventio*. Memory thus is not what we moderns usually consider it to be. It is not a reiteration or a re-presentation. Instead, it is a crafting of images, as well as a construction of a place for the images to inhabit. *Inventio* means both the construction of something new (the memory-store) and the storage of what is remembered (Carruthers 1998:11). For Carruthers, then, *memoria* is a locational memory. Further, "*the shape or foundation of a composition must be thought of as a place-where-one-invents*" (1998:21, emphasis mine).

In borrowing from the ancients, she speaks of memory as a "machine" (Carruthers 1998:22). Now this is not what we would first think. She is not talking about some sort of artificial intelligence. On the contrary, she uses the term *machina* as the ancients would—namely, a device of builders. It helps lift and move things. And what does the machine of memory build? Memory is the way in which the ancients think. Thinking is like constructing a building or a column. The act of memory is the work of invention. The person who would tell a story first invents—that is, he or she creates a structure and thereby provides a place for the inventory of images and things about which he or she would talk.

The clue to reading Trajan's Column was staring me right in the face. The column provides the space for the unwinding scroll, which contains the enormous number of running scenes. The stone scroll provides the space for re-membering. It wants to be memorized. It presents a public location and structure for viewers to take these scenes to heart and to keep the momentum going until they reach the imperial figure on top.[4] It is not only Trajan's success story; it becomes the locus, the place where others can begin to learn to re-member and thus retell the story. As the story spirals higher and higher, one climbs with it. The machine of memory lifts the images. The apotheosis of Trajan authorizes (in the root sense of the word) the reader to come along for this transcendent experience of victory and honor.[5]

Many scholars would simply write off this column as an exercise in myth making. But that would miss a wonderful clue to the ancient art of memory. Like much of Roman art, ancient memory is locational. It is about invention and inventory, about finding a place to put things. But it is not about repetition or re-presentation. Instead, it is essentially a craft of construction. The teller of stories discovers those structures which can accommodate what he has to say. The writer devises those patterns which can provide a superstructure.

There is also the matter of forgetting. Carruthers quite clearly has argued that forgetting is not erasure. Rather, forgetting is essentially a displacement (1998:57). Within the oral competition of the ancient world, there was a struggle for space. This also included memory space, especially the location of public memories. When forgetting occurs, it comes about through a displacement or translation of images.

A better pattern has been invented to locate and order the images. Certainly Trajan could have been honored with something less monumental. A number of scenes around an altar might have pleased Augustus's taste. But the intention was different with Trajan's column. The very structure delivers a lasting message that is located within the unfolding of the column scroll. The dizzying spiral would help place the reader on the royal road to the star—Trajan! At the same time, one identifies with each advance of the Legions over the Dacians. The story literally

---

4. It has often been pointed out that, given the location of the column, there was no true opportunity for the viewer to walk around the column and see every scene in order. Although one could have seen portions of the column from the flanking libraries, it does not seem that, until the modern age, the column could be viewed in its entirety. But the attempt to gain a "literal" reading of the column may well miss the rhetorical effect intended. Viewers would have been impressed with the unrolling campaigns. The column would have "authorized" the viewers' own recollection of the recent events. In sum, the initial impression would invite the viewer to become caught up in the momentum of victory.

5. It should also be noted that a spiral stairway inside the column led to a viewing platform. With skylight pouring in from the few windows, the climber would experience a turning, dizzying ascent, punctuated by rectangles of light. On reaching the top, one would emerge into the full light of day on the platform to enjoy a dominating view of the new and old fora.

unrolls in front of you. As readers move around the column they exercise their memories. Carruthers put it nicely: "remembering is a task of finding and of getting from one place to another" (1998:23). Thus the readers find themselves in one scene and then move on to the next, with the overall scroll providing the superstructure or memory location.

This superstructure or memory location can be called by another name: a commonplace. I use this term because it alludes to those things that are shared. It also can mean a public memory. The Vietnam Memorial in Washington, D.C., is a recent example of the construction of a "commonplace" where memories can be located and where future memory construction is "authorized" by the location itself. Jewish midrash is another example of creating a commonplace. One can construct a tale in which to locate and re-member various scriptural lines.

Finally, in contrast to the modern assumptions about ancient memory, it should be noted that ancient memory was heuristic, not simply mimetic. The work of memory was not to re-present, not to reduplicate, but to construct, to deliver a place for images. Of course, the notion of memory as construction contrasts greatly with the assumptions of many modern biblical scholars. They would look at the passion narratives as documents, recording what were essentially "the facts." While most would distinguish between the editorial hand and the original report or witness, there would be, nevertheless, the assumption that the nature of the text is that of a document. Indeed, one can certainly note that the modern familiarity with both the photograph and the phonograph has contributed to this sense that the evidence has a documentary nature to it.

The modern distinction between fact and fiction, between memory as reiteration and an unreal imagination was just not that crucial to the ancients. The very texture of the evidence, I would submit, points in a rather different direction. Carruthers puts it this way:

> The Biblical notion of remembering has tended to be dismissed, until quite recently, as "re-created memory," scarcely different from outright lying, and of no interest in the philosophy of mind at all. Instead, a "storehouse" model of memory, and the idea that memory is "of the past," has been emphasized to such a degree that memory has been accorded only a reiterative, reduplicative role—all else is "unreal" and thus "untruthful." Western ideas of memory have been concerned at least since the Enlightenment with what the philosopher Mary Warnock calls "the crucial distinction, with which we are all familiar in real life, between memory and the imagination (close though these may often be to one another). . . . [w]hat distinguishes memory from imagination is not some particular feature of the [mental] image but the fact that memory is, while imagination is not, concerned with the real. (1998:68)

Problematizing the Passion Narratives

From what has been presented it becomes possible to re-envision the growth and dynamics of the traditions about the death of Jesus. First, one can say that it is not simply a matter of recalling the death of Jesus; rather, it was the effort to find, first of all, a location in which one can perform the craft of memory. The basic task was to "invent" a *locus* for his death. It was not a matter of simply relating the facts. Instead it was a matter of invention and inventory. Specifically, one should not look immediately for "the facts," for a simple representation of what happened. One should look, rather, for how the memory has been crafted and structured. One can then see what has been enfolded in that memory structure. It would only be after this assessment that one could begin to determine—indirectly at best—what are the "facts of the case."

Let us go back to my earlier observations about the Sayings Gospel's version of the fate of Jesus. The writer of the Sayings Gospel has placed the death of Jesus within the typological structure of the deaths of Jewish prophets (Luke 11:49–51). Yet this fact does not necessarily lend itself to an extensive elaboration. Indeed, the focus of the Sayings Gospel lies elsewhere. The teachings and sayings of Jesus seem to carry the tradition forward.

The pre-Pauline material also seems to be located within the commonplace of the Hellenistic Jewish martyrs. Paul seems to be dislodging this memory pattern by translating the fate of Jesus into a more imperial location. Yet for Paul the story of the vindication of Jesus does not focus upon the extended story pattern found in the Tale of the Suffering Innocent One.

It is, indeed, the choice of the overarching story pattern of the Suffering Innocent One that carries the day for the social crafting of the memory of the death of Jesus. The earlier version of *Peter* may well have been the first attempt at locating the various scriptural conjunctions within the overarching Tale, but it is Mark that provides the authorizing locus and commonplace. The explicit use of citation formulae indicate that the writer can comfortably place the citations tradition within the pattern of the Suffering Innocent One. Moreover, this structure authorizes—that is, it gives the basis for further retelling and elaboration—as the story pattern gets filled in and revised. Matthew and Luke recognized the valuable structure provided by Mark. Their revisions are proof that the memory gamble worked. Whether by Peter or Mark, an imaginative commonplace has been constructed, in which the memory work on the death of Jesus can continue. The story pattern of the Suffering Innocent One is true, not because of the particulars of its content (mimetic memory), but because its form can allow the one remembering to find things out—because it can cue "new" memories. Matthew and Luke engage in translating other material into this story pattern. Whether they created this other material or it existed prior to their application, these writers have essentially taken the Suffering Innocent Tale as the template for crafting their memories. Thus, for example, the notorious "blood curse" passage in Matt 27:24–25 has been inserted into the scene already constructed by Mark 15:6–15. Matthew is not adding a new fact, thereby correcting or updating the historical record. Rather, he is elaborating upon one of the elements of the Tale of the Suffering Innocent One, as well as directing his gaze at his contemporary fellow Jews at the end of the first century. Such an insertion into the memory structure of Mark points up the "*intentio*" of Matthew.

Such an understanding of the memory craft of the Gospel writers also helps us to understand why certain elements are found in the narratives, while other more interesting (perhaps to us) tidbits are never mentioned. Precisely because of the nature of the elements of the Suffering Innocent Tale there are certain parts that would be present. However, some more salient facts or notes have never made it into the memory inventory. Because the death traditions of Jesus already featured the use of scriptural citations, these would become part of what would be included. This material, then, could also be "worked on." As I have pointed out elsewhere, the writer of the Fourth Gospel uses such scriptural pieces to great creative effect (A. Dewey 2001b). Further, one can also begin to see how the Sayings Gospel "disappears." What has happened is that it actually got displaced by being absorbed into the larger structures of Matthew and Luke. It is forgotten because it has fallen in competition to memory structures that work better in continuing the task of inventing.

If we return to the two ends of the spectrum regarding the nature of the passion narratives (history remembered versus prophecy historicized), we can see that the question has been framed very much from a modern documentary perspective. It does not even begin to touch on how ancient memory worked. Crossan, in arguing for prophecy historicized, has indirectly moved to the notion of a memory pattern that locates earlier traditions. He does not see fully what crafters of Gospel memories were consciously about. Nevertheless, his contribution forces subsequent investigators to consider well what the writers thought they were doing. I would submit that they were not intent on telling us what happened, or in replicating the historical situation of the fate of Jesus. Rather, they were interested in crafting a memory structure that could incorporate earlier imaginings. At the same time, this structure that was hit upon precluded other directions. It displaced other versions of the fate of Jesus. In sum, a locus for remembering the death of Jesus had been successfully invented and handed down. The subsequent history of the death of Jesus tradition is eloquent testimony to the success of this "authorized version."

CHRISTIAN COLLECTIVE MEMORY
AND PAUL'S KNOWLEDGE OF JESUS

Georgia Masters Keightley

INTRODUCTION

This study explores ritual as a site of memory in the early Jesus communities. More specifically, it has to do with the matter of Paul's knowledge of Jesus Christ. How is it that Paul, whom tradition holds did not know Christ "after the flesh," was one of the first disciples (if not the first!) to offer a thoroughly personal, intimate understanding of Christ's person and mission, an understanding that quickly came to be normative for the early Christian community?

Scholars have long debated the matter of Paul's familiarity with the earliest Jesus traditions. Gregory Jenks, a Westar Institute fellow, poses the problematic this way: "Was Paul drawing upon a primitive Jesus tradition inherited from the first disciples in Jerusalem, or was he contributing to the formation of an emerging Jesus legend that would later find literary expression in the gospel" (Jenks: 4–5).

That Paul had minimal information about Jesus is a conclusion some scholars draw from the apostle's insistence in Gal 1:11–12 that both his gospel and his apostolic call were entirely of divine origin (Bornkamm: 20). Support for this view is further marshaled from the argument from silence, that is, the dearth of references to the specifics of Jesus' life or teaching found in the authentic Pauline letters.

On the other hand, one argument that Paul must have known more about Jesus than his letters reveal is based on his claim to have persecuted Jesus' followers. F. Vouga holds that "Paul does not know Jesus through Christian tradition (Gal. 1:22–24) but through the tradition of Pharisaic, anti-Christian polemic" (Vouga: 100). Jerome Murphy-O'Connor concurs, saying that it was actually the existence of Christians that drew Paul's attention to Jesus in the first place, that "it is inconceivable that he should have persecuted Christians without learning something about the founder of the movement" (Murphy-O'Connor: 75). Other positions posit that Paul could have acquired additional details about Jesus' life and ministry on at least three other occasions: (1) as part of his preparation for baptism

(Hengel: 44–45); (2) during the three years he spent with the Damascus community (Murphy-O'Connor: 91); and (3) during his visit with Peter in Jerusalem (Murphy-O'Connor: 90–91; Dunn: 138–39).

It is to be observed, however, that this debate about Paul's knowledge of Jesus has focused narrowly on one particular kind of knowledge. That is, biblical scholars have sought to establish the individual facts of Jesus' personal history, his acts and utterances. Frank Gorman notes that scholars have tended to favor narrative texts and disregard other types of material for this reason. He attributes this to the Enlightenment concerns that have shaped modern biblical scholarship (Gorman: 18–20).

But that the New Testament literature gives access to another mode of knowing Jesus was proposed long ago by the Pauline scholar John Knox in a series of books and lectures published during the 1940s and 1950s.[1] From his close reading of the texts, but especially from his work with the Pauline letters, Knox discerned the existence of a common memory of Jesus, a memory of "Jesus as he was" that has been borne through the centuries by the Christian community "in, around, and underneath the Gospel materials" (Knox: 53). He described this shared memory as an affective one, that is, as "preserving something of the concrete quality, the felt meaning of the man himself" (42). He equates this with what Papias (ca. 150 C.E.) referred to as "the living and abiding voice."

In describing memory's content, Knox noted that the Christian community's impression of "the personal moral stature of Jesus" simply escapes, exceeds words. In evidence he points to the inability of the many "quests" to capture fully Jesus' personal qualities as these were known and apprehended by those closest to him. He goes on to say that the New Testament itself is read, even corrected, "under the influence of this prior [corporate] impression" of Jesus. Indeed, he reminds skeptics that it was the memory of Jesus that underlay and gave rise to the Gospel narratives in the first place, that without the community's memory/ies of Jesus the New Testament simply would not exist (49).

A second element of this felt memory "that does not rest solely on what the Gospels say" pertains to "the relation in which [Jesus] stood to his disciples and friends, and they to him." This relation was remembered as being

---

1. *The Man Christ Jesus* (1941), *Christ the Lord: The Meaning of Jesus in the Early Church* (1945), and *On the Meaning of Christ* (1947) originally took the form of a series of lectures Knox was invited to give. They were later republished as a trilogy entitled *Jesus: Lord and Christ* (1958). This material was given an important summation in *The Church and The Reality of Christ*, published in 1962.

one of love, that same kind or quality of love (agape) which the Church now knew as the bond of unity within its own life. It not only knew this love as a present continuing reality within the fellowship of the Church, but it also *remembered* it as already manifested in Jesus. (55)

Once again Knox proposes that what the Christian community (which is both the context and site where the Gospel materials can be read with full meaning) knows/understands about Jesus' relationship to his disciples, its character and quality both then and now, exceeds all efforts to abstract and transpose it to writing. In this instance, too, the Gospel narratives give us both more and less than memory. While the texts give *more* in terms of facts, they also give us *less* than what memory holds. "The Gospels performed the immense service of putting into written form the words of Jesus and the stories about him with which the earliest shared memories of Jesus were associated" (55). Despite the fact that absent factual data the remembrance of Jesus would be poorer, it is not to be concluded that memory is merely an aggregate of scattered oral traditions. To the contrary, memory conveys how the community felt about Jesus, how it experienced him. It is a knowing of Jesus that goes beyond the picture of him that derives from documentary sources. According to Knox, memory has to do with the apprehension of the quality and character of Jesus' person, the quality and character of his relation to his friends and followers.

Given that scholars generally agree that Paul knew far less about Jesus than is evidenced in the Gospels, it is striking to hear Knox claim that in some places Paul's letters actually convey a surer, more "authentic remembrance of Jesus" (53)! For instance, Knox indicates that the felt meaning of Jesus' words, "This is my commandment, that you love one another as I have loved you" (John 15:12), is "first reflected in the Epistles." That is, "when Paul speaks of 'the love of Christ' he is 'remembering' the love of Jesus for his disciples as well as recognizing the gracious presence of the risen Lord" (56). Without developing his insight further, Knox concludes that Christian worship practices are a likely means by which the collective memory of Jesus has been mediated throughout the generations. The regular reading of the New Testament and the celebration of the Lord's Supper have had the effect of "emphasizing within the life of the Church the importance of its memory of Jesus and of confirming the memory itself—this is so obvious as to need no discussion!" (47).

Today, developments in the social sciences/social theory support Knox's contention (1) that human communities not only share but are indeed constituted by bodies of shared memories and (2) that collective memory does have an affective side/dimension. Additionally, work in the new discipline of ritual studies confirms Knox's insight on ritual's role, namely, that collective memory is literally embodied in human bodies and is preserved, mediated in and through ritual performance. This essay's purpose is to show that a broader, more interdisciplinary approach to study of the New Testament presents the possibility of rich new understandings of this material. On the question of Paul's knowledge of Jesus, this methodology opens the way to new epistemologies, new perceptions of the complex reality that is Jesus of Nazareth.

Certainly contemporary social theory provides the conceptual tools for exploring Knox's belief that Paul's letters do in fact mediate an affective knowing of Jesus Christ. These categories are a means to exploring the thesis that because of Paul's exposure to the church's shared memory the apostle was able to recognize the heavenly personage who appeared to him (Hengel 1997:104)—that indeed the entirety of Paul's knowledge of Christ was rooted in the collective experience of the nascent church. His was a knowing of Jesus that exceeds the confines of mere abstract historical detail, and it this type of knowing that permeates the apostle's thinking and writing and that shines through his epistles.

My project here will be to consider Knox's thesis that Paul's sure knowledge of Christ came to him by way of Christian collective memory and to determine how this could be so by reviewing some points of collective memory theory, especially positions developed by the French sociologist Maurice Halbwachs. But I also want to attend to Knox's suggestion that one of the ways this memory/knowledge was mediated to Paul was by means of his ongoing participation in Christian ritual—that it was this experiential, affective knowing of Christ as apprehended in and through ritual that proved to be foundational for his theologizing. In this way I hope to recast and move the debate about Paul's knowledge of Jesus in a new direction.

Before moving on to consideration of this, a brief word must be said about approaching Paul by way of ritual theory. In the introductory essay to a volume of *Semeia* devoted to the treatment of ritual in biblical studies, Mark McVann noted that "a deeply ingrained suspicion of ritual is a hallmark of classical Protestantism" (7). He refers here to the traditional Protestant bias toward word over sacrament, a bias that scholars acknowledge has long worked to shape modern biblical studies. It should be noted too that it was John Knox's seeming willingness to give the church and its life priority over the biblical word that led his fellow scholars to dismiss his claims on behalf of ecclesial memory so quickly! For these reasons, then, it certainly seems no little irony to conduct an examination of the influence of ritual practice on Paul, the one whose work has been so central to the Reformation challenge to the Catholic view of the church and its life!

On the other hand, social theory demands that one not overlook the fact that, while Paul was the founder of churches, he was at the same time a functioning member of the same. It would be unrealistic to presume that the apostle did not regularly participate in the community's eucharistic meal or that he did not occasionally preside at such services. Given the evidence of the letters, it is impossible to ignore that frequent participation in community worship and prayer was integral to his life as a follower of Jesus Christ. What will be attended to and examined here is one aspect of Paul's own social location: not just that of founder but as active participant and fellow member of the body of Christ.

COLLECTIVE MEMORY THEORY

Perhaps the best known account of human memory is that provided by Augustine of Hippo in his *Confessions*. There the learned bishop describes memory as the conscious retrieval of some remnant of the past from the storehouse of one's mind (10.8:214–215).

In contrast to the notion that memory is either a matter of individual psychology or an act of interiority, the social theory perspective of Maurice Halbwachs presupposes that personal memory is possible only because of the prior existence of an external corporate memory. According to the sociology of knowledge, we are only able to apprehend our experience by means of the language and concepts society provides us to name, interpret and understand it (Halbwachs 1992:53). Our emotional perception of persons and events is likewise made possible and structured by what society has taught us (65). Because these hermeneutical tools originate within the community, it is understandable that society's own perspective on reality would necessarily become ours. This also explains why adoption of the group's standpoint is indispensable to the work of memory.

Per Halbwachs, memory requires that individuals look outside themselves and lay hold of the socially created frameworks into whose schemes their particular bits of reminiscence correctly fit. Although each of us belongs to many groups, it is normally the primary ones of family, nation and/or religion that supply the interpretive categories that define our personal identity and self-understanding. The coordinates of time and space furnish the parameters of collective memory's framework, and each is defined in accord with specific group needs and purposes. While we situate our personal reminiscences within what appears to be the conceptual/abstract past, the truth is this past always has as its reference the actual material space(s) the group occupies. In *La topographie legendaire des evangiles en Terre Sainte: Étude de memoire collective,* for example, Halbwachs showed how Christian memory has its roots in the terrain and contours of what were formerly Jewish holy places. In respect to time, personal reminiscence too must be fitted to the group's schema. For the Christian, time is appropriated on the basis of the yearly celebration of those events leading up to—and subsequent to—Holy Week. Thus, as Halbwachs argues, memory is not just the simple recall of facts; to the contrary, it involves the construction of an appropriate narrative scheme in which to locate our personal data (Connerton: 26).

In truth, memory's framework provides the community's overarching view of reality; it sets forth reality's fundamental order, character, and significance. Because individual memories tend to be well-defined, self-contained units belonging, as they do, to the various social milieux we inhabit, they possess a certain facticity (Halbwachs 1997:88–89). This enables us to grasp and then locate our recollections in their appropriate social setting. We do this by recalling two types of contexts. We can either situate an individual's experience by placing it in her life history, or we can locate that behavior in the history of social settings to which she belongs. Considered in this way, the individual's life narrative is shown to be part of an interconnecting set of narratives out of which personal meaning is woven (Connerton: 21). Halbwachs observes that while our memories seem uniquely our own, they are in reality but one limited point of view on the collective experience. Furthermore, these points of view change as we change social locations or shift social locations within the different groups to which we belong. In this way, forgetting may be understood as having less to do with physical or mental deficiency than it does with the fact that over time we lose touch with the group to whom certain memories belong and for whom such remembrances matter (Halbwachs 1997:93–94).

Finally, Halbwachs argues that memory is constitutive of community. Groups come into existence precisely because their members hold shared experiences. Because certain of these are deemed significant, they are held to be both formative and normative and give rise to a unique set of meanings and values. In other words, communities originate through people's living and struggling together through remarkable happenings. Communities are built up and sustained in the subsequent telling and retelling of what has transpired in the process of their coming-to-be (Irwin-Zarecka: 57). At memory's core are those narrative recollections of circumstances pertaining to the community's founding/origins. Important here too are the stories of its heroes—those individuals whose lives and actions are expressive of what the group values, and who figure into those events that exemplify what the community is and what it wants to be. For this reason, collective memory serves a variety of useful functions. More important perhaps, memory is a source of group identity, and in the constant retelling and celebration of its past, memory serves the community's cohesion by strengthening the bonds between its members. As we shall see, via ritual commemoration, memory also plays an indispensable pedagogical role.

Memory and History

The historical value of the Gospel accounts of the life, death and resurrection of Jesus of Nazareth has been a matter of long-standing scholarly debate. Knox's suggestion that the memory and the history of Jesus are two quite different things, however, serves to place the lack of detail about Jesus in Paul's letters in a new light. Does this suggest that for Paul, too, the church's memory proved to be far more illuminating, more valuable than fact? I now want to review how this possibility is supported and explained by the distinction social theorists make between memory and history.

In *The Social Frameworks of Memory*, Halbwachs asserts that all social frameworks are made up of both concrete and abstract representations—that is, the personal and the rational (Halbwachs 1992:174). Abstract and concrete are not two distinct entities, but are instead two different vantage points from which society can contemplate the same object. Religions too have this same double character: "Every religious representation is both general and particular, abstract and concrete, logical and historical"(178). At the same time, then, that Christianity may be regarded as a system of belief, it can also be construed as a concrete recollection of images, persons, and events belonging to a definite space and time, even incorporating those sentiments and feelings that coalesce around them. Halbwachs warns that if belief strays too far and/or becomes disconnected from its experiential base, it simply cannot survive. Belief acquires stability and permanence only by being rooted in the material, that is, in the places, persons, things of the social milieu. Thus, for example, that we can visit the very place (and places) in Jerusalem where the events of Jesus' saving work occurred—and even have some sense of what the first disciples themselves must have felt—provides strong warrant for believing the Passion Narratives to be true.

Iwona Irwin-Zarecka distinguishes memory and history in terms of their being two different ways of framing, and interpreting, the past. From its side, academic history attempts a rational, abstract view of what has gone before. Its purpose is to present an objective account of what has happened in a community's life, and to do this it relies on the conceptual and interpretive tools developed by the guild of historians for just such purposes. Scholars gather the material traces of the past, establish their authenticity, and then go on to make a critical evaluation of the product of their research. In the interests of instituting comparisons so as to identify and track change, the historian resorts to the periodization of time.

While this may meet the standards of her discipline and assist the analyses of she and her colleagues, such divisions are nonetheless arbitrary,
externally imposed and unknown to those who were the actual sub-
ject/agents of this history (19).

Memory, on the other hand, regards the community as it is from the
inside. While its recollection of the past is also selective, it draws on
those things that have relevance for conduct of the community's daily
affairs. Memory's focus is what the ancestors actually said and did, how
they engaged and were able to negotiate their times. Memory is concerned with making sense of the past as opposed to merely establishing
the basics of what happened. Memory is about meaning and the process
of evaluating how something measures up and fits into "the great
scheme of things."

Based on her study of Holocaust survivors, Irwin-Zarecka concurs
with Halbwachs that collective memory has an affective, visceral dimension that manifests a group's moral and emotional involvement with its
past (60). Visceral memory has to do with why *this* event, *this* person
means so much to us and proves to be determinative for our corporate
existence. She notes that a visit to a particular place can immediately call
up the strong feelings and emotions the individual/group associates with
it. Halbwachs, too, agrees that because collective memory unfolds across
the material/physical world, the affective states of feelings and intuitions
associated with particular bits of memory will come to be embedded
there (1997:89). In contrast to historical accounts which ask us to learn
and understand, Irwin-Zarecka asserts that memory calls us to "attention,
action and feeling"(151).

When viewed in terms of the distinction these two theorists make
between memory and history, Knox's claim that the church bears in its
substance a memory of Jesus which exceeds what is reported by the
Gospels can be seen to have merit.

COLLECTIVE MEMORY AS SEDIMENTED IN RITUAL

Memory has to do with knowing the past and, because remembrance
must be socially located and constructed, memory is a collective activity.
Review of some basic points of theory suggests that in the same way as
other communities, the Christian church too is constituted by a body of
shared memories. I have indicated that the church's memory of Jesus, as
memory, is a type of knowledge distinct from history, and that memory
continues to be a significant way the community knows Jesus. I now
want to go on to determine how the memory of Jesus is mediated to
church members by means of ritual practices. In this way I can begin to
lay out the case that it was via his participation in early Christian rituals

that Paul came to know and understand Jesus' person and purpose—that indeed it was his experience in ritual that underlies the understanding of Christ presented in the epistles.

In *How Societies Remember*, Paul Connerton observes that most studies of collective memory say little about its transfer from one generation of the community to the next. If they do, there is a tendency to focus on only one form of transfer. That is, scholars look to the inscribed remains of the past, such as are found in documents and texts and/or what is written in such material/physical forms as buildings, monuments, pottery, and household and personal goods. His book addresses another means of conveying the past, namely, its transfer by way of social-habit memory in commemorative ceremonies and in what he calls bodily practices. He begins by identifying three types of memory claims (22–23). Of interest here is what Connerton calls habit memory—that is, that instinctive ability to reproduce certain performances like riding a bicycle, or reading a book. It is an acquired knowledge of "how to do," but being able to do so without prior self-conscious reflection.

Connerton develops the thesis that societies also operate and depend upon habit memory. He notes that social worlds are generated by operations intersubjectively agreed upon and that taken-for-granted conventions must be acted upon for society to work. He argues that habit memory "is an essential ingredient in the successful and convincing performance of [social] codes and rules" (36). But habit memory is also indispensable to sustaining and conveying the social order from one generation to the next. Social habit memory, however, has been little studied and to get at its role in transmitting the past he examines commemorative rituals and bodily practices. Both are ways human societies preserve what has gone before and, for both, the body plays a crucial instrumental role.

Commemorative rituals are storehouses of the past in that they are deliberately backward looking and intend to call up the prototypical events and persons of the past. Because of their significance and meaning, performance of such rituals becomes a corporate habit. Making use of an economy of words and physical moves, the liturgy of the eucharist regularly re-presents and re-enacts the last public coming together of Jesus and his disciples. Connerton notes that in this verbal and physical doing, Christians not only realize the saving benefits of the paschal mystery— they become both cognitively and habitually proficient at what it means to be a member of the Body of Christ. Because of the centrality of eucharist to each Sunday Mass, Catholic Christians become skilled at performing the rite itself.

He observes that most studies of ritual fail to attend to ritual's form, its actual doing, focusing instead on the meanings conveyed in ritual performance. But such studies overlook a basic reason why communities turn to ritual to conserve their treasured meanings and values. Connerton notes the potential for invariance that is built into rites because of the way liturgical language and action work. While individuals can recite a myth without necessarily believing it, rite does not permit such latitude. To perform a rite is "to specify the relationship that obtains between the performers of the ritual and what it is that they are performing" (54). The stylized and stereotyped language of rite, its invariant sequences of speech acts, and "the limited resources of ritual posture, gesture and movement" all serve to strip communication clean of the broad range of nuance that everyday language permits. One either signs oneself with the cross or one does not; one either confesses "Jesus is Lord" or one does not.

This serves to highlight ritual's performative character. The language of rite—verbal as well as body—is neither an explanation nor a commentary on what is being done. To the contrary, rite intends to bring a state of affairs into being and it does so through a deliberate saying and doing. Connerton observes that by using the words "we" and "us" when the community is gathered for prayer, a collective personality is instantly created. "Performative utterances are as it were the place in which the community is constituted and recalls to itself the fact of its constitution" (59). Ritual curses, blessings, and oaths presuppose certain attitudes (e.g., trust, veneration, contrition, gratitude), and in the moment of their saying, these attitudes immediately come into play. And while such acts occur in and through the speaking, such attitudes fill the body and can be seen to exert a physiological effect on it. Additionally, performatives are encoded in rite's set postures, gestures and movements; these too are effective in that they are unequivocal, materially substantial and because they accomplish what they set out to do. To advance further his argument that habit is a form of memory, Connerton proceeds to examine some of the ritual-like bodily practices that are also a type of social memory. Although he does not take the time to explore his claim that ritual behavior has a carry-over effect permeating subsequent behavior and mentality (even to the point of becoming habitual!), Connerton considers a second type of activity which preserves the past, but which does so "without explicitly re-presenting it in words and images" (72). In this way he directs attention to the body's role in the formation of habit.

He begins by distinguishing between inscribing and incorporating social practices. Translating human sounds into the alphabet is an example of an inscribing practice. Incorporating practices, on the other hand, involve physical movements that convey messages to others; such transmission, however, requires that bodies be present and immediate to one another so that an exchange can occur.

Connerton identifies three types of incorporating practices. Certain gestures he classes as *techniques of the body;* these are movements which serve to illustrate what is being expressed verbally (79–81). He cites here the proclivity of ethnic New Yorkers to "talk with their hands." *Properties of the body* are a more formal type of incorporating practice. An example here is etiquette at table (82). The decorum one displays while eating is not only a sign of one's self-mastery; it is also an important social marker.

Ceremonies of the body refers to a whole system of behavior such as that created in eighteenth-century French society to allow display of privilege, and social status. While originally noble status pertained to blood kinship and family lineage, over time it came to be understood as a quality that inheres in a person. But to make this concrete and visible, a whole order of social practices had to be created.

Of these, what Connerton calls *ceremonies of privilege* were learned ways for behaving properly at court. One's style of dress reflected one's status, as did the physical location of one's seat in *parliamente;* status determined one's right to wear a sword, and be the first to speak. More to the point, one's rank permitted regular access to the bodily presence of the king (86–87). *Ceremonies of avocation* had to do with the overall conduct of everyday life. One leisurely spent one's time acquiring such competencies as fishing, gardening, or knowledge of the hunt. It took time and patience to develop these proficiencies, possession of which were understood to display the high breeding of the possessor. It was the naturalness and finesse with which one performed these endeavors that witnessed to the level of one's gentility; this in turn could be achieved only through repeated and consistent practice by the body.

Connerton classifies both commemorative ceremonies and bodily practices as habits which he defines as predispositions "formed through frequent repetition of a number of specific acts" which become an intimate part of the self. Habits are so powerful "because they are so intimately a part of ourselves." What is key, however, is that in the process of becoming habit, the physical moves of repetitive acts come to be inscribed in the body.

> By exercise the body comes to coordinate an increasing range of muscular activities in an increasingly automatic way, until awareness retreats, the movements flow "involuntarily," and there occurs a firm and practiced sequence of acts which take their fluent course.... Habit is a knowledge and remembering in the hands and in the body; and in the cultivation of habit it is our body which understands. (Connerton: 94–95)

In this nontextual and noncognitive way, memory is transmitted. Connerton emphasizes that habits of affection and behavior are not learned merely through the application of principle, but are only to be acquired in the actual practice, in community with those who behave in such a way. Habit becomes a way of life—it is the "propensity to go on doing the same kind of thing" (31). In this way then, the significant/ meaningful past is constantly practiced, performed and recapitulated in everyday life. Because habits are inscribed "deeply into the bone" and borne through the body, incorporating practices of social habit memory prove to be a most effective system of mnemonics.

Collective Memory and Ritual Theory as Applied to Paul

Paul wrote at a time when Christian memory of Jesus was in its formative stage. Because the memory of Jesus continued to be fresh and vital and could be easily verified, there was little urgency to preserve or collect individual remembrances. Halbwachs remarks that at this time Christian memory was widely distributed—that is, it lived and functioned within the entire group of believers (1997:54). Spatially separated subgroups (local churches) held individual pieces of memories related to Christianity's founding events. Study of the early literature confirms that variety—even disparity!—of belief was not yet a central issue, whereas diligence in converting others to the gospel most assuredly was (Halbwachs 1992:94)!

It is in the area of Christian ritual practice that one begins to see the most striking contrasts and redefinitions. Certainly it is here that differences between the new sect and its Jewish parent appear most obvious. Most strikingly, Christian prayer addresses and invokes God and Jesus together (Hurtado: 74-75)! Membership in the people of God now comes with baptism, not the rite of circumcision. In a dramatic shift, women too undergo this initiatory rite. And as reported in Acts, incipient Christian teaching and practice challenged Jewish ritual law concerning what foods could be consumed and with whom one could eat. Liturgy scholar Paul Bradshaw observes that, just as was true of Christian belief, the early church's worship practices exhibited considerable differences over quite fundamental elements (Bradshaw: 8). He proposes that each New Testament book "needs to be examined for what it may have to reveal about the worship of the particular Christian community from which it *emerges* as well as for remnants of even earlier liturgical traditions which it may have preserved" (53).

Martin Hengel has argued that Paul's Christology and soteriology—certainly the main lines of it—were almost completely developed prior to the composition of the epistles. He attributes this to the unknown thirteen to sixteen years between Paul's conversion and the end of the Syrian-Antiochene period—that it was this time "which must be regarded as the decisive era in which Paul gained that towering missionary (and theological) profile which we meet in the same way in his letters during the missionary work around the Aegean" (Hengel and Swemer: 12). He agrees with historian A. D. Nock that it was on the occasion of this interval—spent on mission in Syria and Cilicia—that Paul had both the need and opportunity to develop his personal theology, as well as his technique of preaching and argument. For proof, Hengel cites Paul's "unambiguously clear" position on the central question of "justification by faith alone," which he was obliged to defend at the Apostolic Council at Jerusalem.

If Hengel is correct that Paul's basic insights about Jesus Christ were formed early on, Margaret MacDonald finds their source in Paul's participation in Christian worship. She argues that "the Pauline correspondence itself grows out of and is rooted in, what is experienced in the midst of ritual" (237; also Hurtado: 42). Ritual was so crucial for the first Christians, she says, because it was here "that individuals discovered for the first time, or renewed their acceptance of, the authority that transformed their experience" (237). In other words, it was preeminently during ritual performance that Pauline Christians met firsthand—and came to know personally, existentially—the veritable meaning of the lordship of Christ. In a recent book, Luke Timothy Johnson argues that biblical scholars have virtually ignored the rich but complex language of religious experience so expressive of this kind of encounter that permeates the New Testament. He attributes this to "complex causes within scholarship," including "the lack of an epistemology specifically calibrated to the religious dimensions of human existence" (1998:4).

Is it possible that by positing his regular participation in early Christian rites, the solution to Paul's knowledge of Jesus Christ is ultimately to be found? More to the point, was it the vivid collective memory that had come to be embedded in the nascent Christian rites that brought the apostle to know Jesus Christ so personally and so well, an appreciation and understanding of whom becomes so transparent in the letters? If so, we must presume the major influence of those ritual forms associated with the life of the communities with which the apostle was connected during what Hengel calls his "dark period" (1997:11).[2] While there is

---

2. Hengel places Paul during this time in the geographical area "bounded in the south by Palestine and Arabia, i.e. the Nabataean empire, in the east by the client kingdom of Commagene and the frontier of the empire on the Euphrates, in the north by the Taurus and Cappadocia, in the north–west by 'Rough Cilicia', and in the west by the Mediterranean and Cyprus" (22–23). It would have been the ritual practices of the communities of this area that would have been of especial importance.

precious little information available about Paul or his work during this rather long time, 1 Corinthians nonetheless presents an important resource for the reasons that (1) it was written fairly early (ca. 54 C.E.); and (2) it makes reference to some key Christian ritual practices.[3] Paul takes great pains at different points in this letter to assure the Corinthians that what he has conveyed to them is nothing other than the traditions which he himself received (e.g., 11:2, 23; 15:3). He makes clear that what he has to say about the practices of baptism and eucharist were not original with him either.

To explore the instrumental role of ritual as this applies to Paul, the above review of select points of social theory presents four important considerations. First of all, ritual theory establishes that memory—here collective memory—pertains to action, to performance. Secondly, theory shows collective memory to have two dimensions: on the one hand, there is cognitive memory—those reminiscences of specific persons or events; on the other, there is affective, visceral memory that has to with the feelings and emotional commitments identified with these persons or events. Thirdly, memory—in contrast to history, whose primary interest is fact— is concerned with the significant, the meaningfulness of experience. On this basis, one can conclude that the objective meanings abstracted, reconstructed from experience and associated with cognitive memory can be distinguished from those deeply felt, visceral, subjective meanings expressive of the subject's moral and emotional involvement with the past associated with affective memory. A final point has to do with the claim that collective memory comes to be embedded in certain bodily practices that become habits. The question is, is there any evidence in 1 Corinthians to support these points of theory? On the basis of what Paul tells us, can one distinguish here between cognitive memory and affective memory? Cognitive meaning and affective meaning? And is there anything here relating to habit memory that takes the form of incorporating bodily practices? If such can be identified, this could go far in explaining how his early experience of Christian memory in the context of ritual made possible Paul's unique appropriation of the message and meaning of the Lord Jesus Christ.

A place to start is with Paul's remarks concerning the commemorative rites of baptism and eucharist, and to try to identify and separate out the two types of memory and their related forms of meaning, which the theory proposes are there to be found.

---

3. An important source here is Meeks, *The First Urban Christians: The Social World of the Apostle Paul* (New Haven: Yale University Press, 1983), 140–63.

Baptism

A review of baptism must begin with its performance. While scholars are agreed that initially baptismal practices varied from community to community, based on what we find in 1 Cor 6:11 as performed in this Pauline church the rite included: (1) some form of a washing with water; (2) done in the name of Jesus (see also 1:12–15); and (3) an anointing of the Spirit. While the letter does not make clear the extent to which some instruction about Jesus and his mission was a preliminary to baptism, Paul does insist that through his preaching God has acted to bring the Corinthians to faith (2:1–5; 3:1–9; 15:1–2). And about this, Paul exclaims in 2:2: "I decided to know nothing among you except Jesus Christ, and him crucified."

(1) *Cognitive memory:* According to earliest Syrian tradition, which per Hengel likely informed Paul's initial liturgical experiences, the baptismal rite is a *mimesis* of what happened to Jesus at the Jordan. At that moment, and with the coming of the Spirit, Jesus was believed to be invested as Messiah and to enter his eschatological kingship (Bradshaw: 149–50). It is interesting that in this letter there is no clear association of baptism with the dying and rising with Christ that figures so prominently in other epistles.

(2) *Cognitive meaning:* Baptism is the rite of entry into the Christian community, the body of Christ (12:13). This assembly, called into existence by God (1:9), constitutes itself as *ekklesia*/church as its members gather and invoke the name of Jesus (1:2; see Hurtado: 80). By its confession "Jesus is Lord," the community acknowledges itself to be subject to Jesus' authority and efficacy. In this way members "ritually constitute their worship circle as offering that submission" that is both "an anticipatory expression" as well as an already, locally defined realization of God's ultimate purposes (Hurtado: 53).

In baptism individuals are "washed," "sanctified," "justified" (6:11). Just as the Spirit empowered Jesus via his washing in the Jordan, so too by this ritual act human beings are reborn as children of God and given access to the fruits of Jesus' messiahship (e.g. 12:1–13) and life in the kingdom (15:12–58). The book of 1 Corinthians, especially chapters 12–14, presents a description of the divine power, the gifts, services, operations (12:4–6) now at work within the community where Christ exercises his lordship. As one of its effects, the baptismal washing eradicates such socially defined differences as gender and nationality and so creates out of individuals a new community whose principle of union is a sharing in the memory of Jesus and the saving power of the Spirit.

(3) *Affective/body memory:* Marking the body with water sets one apart, and by the visible, physical move of putting oneself forward for

baptism, one acknowledges Jesus' authority over one's person and life. Likewise, articulation of Jesus' name over the baptized most likely represented "a ritual means of bringing to bear upon the baptized the power of the exalted Jesus" and served to mark the person as the property of Jesus (e.g., 1 Cor 1:12; 3:23; Hurtado: 82). Baptism also brings individuals into a whole new set of material relationships. As a tangible sign of this new, higher bond that replaces blood kinship, one gathers regularly with this new family for prayer, instruction and the Lord's Supper; at such gatherings one experiences, in solidarity with one's brothers and sisters in Christ, the presence of Christ and the Spirit. As a sign of the degree of intimacy and familiarity baptism brings, Christians exchange the "holy kiss" when they come together for worship. In these gatherings too—in confessing "Jesus is Lord" (1:2)—the community itself becomes the temple of God, the material place/space of his dwelling.

As 1 Corinthians makes very clear, the Spirit's presence is manifested in quite visible ways via the body, both the social body gathered, and also the embodied individual. It is in and through the power of the Spirit that one can speak in tongues, prophesy, and give expression to the other gifts that evidence the Spirit's active agency. Paul's own testimony throughout 1 Corinthians indicates that in and through the rite of baptism, the body—social as well as individual—is impacted in a very significant, very physical way.

(4) *Affective/felt meaning:* According to Paul's report, to undergo the rite of baptism is to feel personally enriched. It is to experience inner transformation and change. It is a matter of apprehending oneself as called, chosen, and graced by God (1:17; 4:15; 9:1; 15:8–10). But again, this empowerment is something that is known uniquely by and in the body. A primary example here is glossolalia. This form of ecstatic utterance, which is the verbal expression of a strong emotional state, is indicative that one's being has been taken over by the power of God; it is a somatic expression of an invasion of God's own energy (Johnson 1998:124). The Spirit's presence effects distinct, recognized physiological change.

EUCHARIST

As is true for baptism, the earliest eucharistic meals most likely varied in form as well as theological understanding (Bradshaw: 70). According to what Paul supplies in 1 Corinthians, the ritual action took place at table in the context of a meal. In remembrance of Jesus, they took bread and wine, blessed, and shared them. Paul recounts what Jesus is reported to have said and done during the last meal he ate with his disciples. Per 11:23–24, over the bread Jesus said, "This is my body that is for you. Do this in remembrance of me." Over the cup he said, "This cup is the new covenant in my blood. Do this, as often as you drink it, in remembrance of me."

(1) *Cognitive memory:* Paul shares with the Corinthians a memory tradition of the meal Jesus had with his disciples before his death on the cross (11:23–25). As remembered, this meal was more than just an occasion for sharing food and companionship. Jesus is reported to have infused it with special significance by blessing, breaking, and sharing bread, by blessing and sharing the wine cup. He then directed his disciples to repeat these actions "in remembrance of me." Early on, memory linked the bread and wine with Jesus' redemptive death (11:24–25), which was in fact made constitutive of "the new covenant" (11:25; Hurtado: 85).

(2) *Cognitive meaning:* Sharing a meal became the centerpiece of Christian worship practice. Paul describes it as "the Lord's supper" (11:20), "the table of the Lord" (10:21), and in this presents Jesus as "the living power who owns the meal and presides at it and with whom believers have fellowship" (Hurtado: 85). This is not unlike the understanding of the cult-meals of the time held in honor of pagan deities.

The meal had rich significance, some of which is already in evidence in 1 Corinthians. First of all, it is a commemoration of Jesus' sacrifice of self for others. In 15:3 Paul reiterates the tradition that Jesus "died for our sins." Eating together is both a means of remembering as well as a vicarious participation in Jesus' suffering, death, and resurrection (10:16).

This meal in his name also celebrates Jesus' continuing presence with them as the risen Lord and as dynamic Spirit. At the same time, the ritual meal looks forward to and anticipates the Lord's final return in glory; the gathering anticipates the heavenly eschatological banquet and the fulfillment of Jesus' messiahship. Says Paul: "For as often as you eat this bread and drink the cup, you proclaim the Lord's death until he comes" (11:25–26).

Finally, the meal is the setting for experiencing (and renewing) the fellowship created between Christ and believers, believers with each other. As Knox argued, the early community was convinced that the quality of its life together replicated the *koinonia* that existed between Jesus and the disciples. Certainly it was recognized that because of Jesus an entirely new set of relational patterns had come into being. One now has table fellowship with women, slaves and Gentiles, and the poor. Paul also makes clear that Jesus' presence to the community has direct consequences for personal behavior, both in terms of conduct at table (11:17–34) and the conduct of the Christian's everyday life. One must live out one's life in a manner worthy of those called to the table of the Lord (5:8, 11).

(3) *Affective/body memory of event:* Christians physically gather in a place, at table, to eat together. Speaking, postures and gestures give rise

to an attitude of praise and prayer, a feeling of thanksgiving and joy. Whenever Christ in the Spirit is present, as is always true when the community comes together for eucharist, this has a visible, powerful effect on the body. One can be in close proximity to women, slaves and Gentiles without any feelings of discomfort or impropriety. Postures and gestures are other ways of expressing one's subjection to Christ's authority, confirmed in the verbalization "Jesus is Lord." And of course, while being together in the presence of Christ and the Spirit is the source of incredible joy, it can also be a source of excess and disorderly behavior!

(4) *Affective meaning:* The meaning of the Christ event is fully incorporated by the body. While eating and drinking is necessary to preserve physical health, this ritual action is known as instituting real union with Christ, as well as a sharing with others in the Spirit. This presence of the Lord is experienced as transcendent power in which all participate; this reveals itself in many ways, but especially as personal wisdom, illumination, insight, and discernment. Sharing food and a meal with others in close proximity creates feelings of unity, cohesiveness, and a sense of belonging to something larger than oneself. It creates a feeling of being part of a great energy field which "marks off the time and space devoted to such meals as distinctive, thus heightening the sense of boundaries around the group" (Johnson 1998:165). Experience of Christ's presence manifests itself in joy, ecstatic expression in word and body. One feels changed, created anew. This confirms the sense that the body has been called to—and has even begun—a new level of existence. But this in turn requires disciplining one's body and behaving in an appropriate way.

The foregoing analysis directs attention to some of the ritual elements in 1 Corinthians so as to highlight the relations that obtain between collective memory, bodily performance and felt meaning, and in this way to establish a clear link between Paul, ritual and the church's memory.

We have examined the proposal, based on memory theory, that vivid memories of Jesus (both cognitive and affective) came to be embedded in the commemorative rituals of baptism and eucharist. In the very physical acts of washing, eating, drinking and sharing food, coming together to make community out of those once strangers, memories of some of the significant things Jesus said and did were dramatically brought to consciousness. But in the course of these physical enactments, the meaning and implication of Jesus Christ was also something perceived and felt within the body, corporate and individual. In some instances meaning was a matter of being physically filled/flushed with a sense of joy and gratitude for God's mercy and forgiveness, something made possible by Jesus and the cross. In other cases, meaning pertained to a new-found internal capacity for discernment and understanding—of being impelled to reach out to others in a spirit of charity and love like Jesus' own. The point here is that participation in Christian ritual is a vehicle for coming to know, both with one's mind and with one's body, what is it to be "in Christ." Doing, experiencing the behaviors that are linked to Jesus via collective memory becomes a means to knowing "Jesus as he was."

Consequently, as a member of the *ekklesia* and a regular participant in its worship, would not Paul have had similar experiences? Whether as participant and/or observer at the baptismal ceremonies of others, would not this have served to reinforce the mystery of his own call to continue Jesus' work of the gospel? And what would have been the felt impact when, in company with his fellow Christians, he partook of the bread and heard the words, "This is my body that is for you"? As 1 Corinthians suggests, in the same way as other members of the community, Paul was often compelled to ecstatic utterance in an effort to express his acute awareness of all that God's power was effecting in him. As member and active participant in Christian corporate life this was, for Paul, to become ever more aware of the profound mystery that is Jesus Christ.

According to our theory, too, repeated performance of these memorial rites served to deepen and renew the memory of Christ and all that this meant—not just in believers' hearts. In and through the habit of ritual, memory and meaning came to be inscribed into their very sinew and bone. Would it not then be appropriate to conclude that in 1 Corinthians Paul is speaking out of his own rich, ecclesial experience—here I refer to the cumulative experience that accrues from being a witnessing, worshipping member of the Christian church?

I agree with Johnson that there is need for adequate language and categories to open up for analysis what the body experiences of the early Christians must have been in the performance of the church's earliest rites. However, by relying on Paul's own words in 1 Corinthians about what was remembered, what was likely performed, and what was felt, we are afforded important clues as to the indispensable role early Christian ritual must have played in bringing Paul himself to the profound, intimate experience of Jesus Christ, such as is reflected in 1 Corinthians.

BODILY PRACTICES

A final point of theory has to do with the thesis that collective memory is sedimented and conveyed in what Connerton calls bodily practices. While he indicates that habits are created in and as a result of regular participation in such commemorative rites as Christian baptism and eucharist, he does not explicitly link these to his treatment of those incorporating bodily practices that "preserve the past deliberately without explicitly re-presenting it in words and images" (72). He does note, however, that such practices always intend to convey a message, and consequently have some cognitive reference. Careful review of 1 Corinthians strongly implicates the linkage between commemorative rites and bodily practices. In truth, formation of Christian habits is precisely what Paul intends for members of the Corinthian church. Why would he otherwise devote so much of the letter to instructing his hearers in the particulars of the new mode of living into which baptism into Christ has plunged them? He sees a direct connection between everyday lifestyle and all forms of participation in the community's life. Evident too is his recognition that Christian behavior has the person of Jesus Christ, both as remembered and now present, as its referent: "Be imitators of me as I am of Christ" (11:1).

In a seminal article written in 1982, Theodore Jennings drew attention to ritual's noetic function. At the same time, his examination also provides insight as to how ritual is a means of coming to know. He begins by noting that in ritual performance, individuals are given the opportunity to discover and explore new ways of being and acting in the world. This may occur in the first-time experience of a ritual; on the other hand, it may be a repeat performance "within the already known repertoire of ritual action," where allowances for differences in cultural and individual personal appropriation of a rite are made. Jennings highlights the body's explicit role in this coming-to-know. In performance, what is known is achieved through "a bodily action which alters the world or the place of the ritual participant in the world" (114). This action is not to be construed as a case where the mind becomes embodied in ritual; rather, the body "minds itself," attends to itself in ritual action. In other words, knowing is a product of the doing of ritual. What is known emerges from the subject's direct engagement and interaction with what is there to be known. Jennings makes the point that this is precisely the intention of the Catholic doctrine of transubstantiation. It attends to the fact that human engagement, in the form of ritual action over the bread and wine, serves to transform/make their elements known as something else.

But in addition to allowing participants to try out, and even practice, new behaviors, Jennings says ritual offers these behaviors as prescribed models of conduct. More exactly, ritual performance fosters experience of "an ontological or cosmogonic praxis" (117). To perform a ritual is to learn how the world acts, how it comes to be; it is to step into reality's own rhythm. For our interests, ritual's repetitive character invites imitation of itself; it invokes a response. Ritual performance encourages the observer "to participate responsively in the ritual action"; this may mean completing it, continuing it, or perfecting it, but whatever way is chosen, ritual incites one to action. To put it another way, commemorative rites stimulate the imitation and repristination of their recommended behaviors outside of ritual space.

What bodily practices then do the commemorative rituals of baptism and eucharist thus generate?

What Connerton calls *techniques of the body* are those gestures that are manual words designating associations and/or relationships. Here one could class Paul's admonition, "Greet one another with a holy kiss" (16:20). Such practice expresses the regard one must have for one's brothers and sisters in Christ. But such a gesture, constantly repeated, would over time work to shape one's disposition and attitude toward others in a positive way, becoming a silent but remarkable witness to the love Christ bears all. Conversely, Paul's admonition to shun the sexually immoral by banishing them from the common table (5:11) is a dramatic, concrete way of demonstrating the rupture that sin creates within the community's life.

As we have seen, *properties of the body* pertain to maxims of conduct intended to control bodily appetites, and so form individual sensibilities in socially defined ways. Paul spends a considerable portion of the letter advising the Corinthians about the need to exercise mastery over the body and its impulses. In chapters 5–8 Paul names those behaviors unworthy of those who bear the name of Christ. He cites sexual immorality, idolatry, greed, drunkenness, and the subjection of fellow believers to the judgement of non-Christians; the marriage/remarriage of virgins and widows and the consumption of food offered to idols are also potentially deficient. Note how these instructions directly implicate the body. What Paul counsels here is the reversal of worldly practice for the reason that even in their bodies, those baptized into Christ have been transformed and made capable of the life of the kingdom. The detailed instruction that Paul gives as to the proper conduct of the Christian body underscores that what the body does is rife with significance and meaning.

In general, *ceremonies of the body* have to do with lifestyle, the overall pattern of one's daily affairs. Of these, *ceremonies of privilege* pertain to Paul's outline of what constitutes proper conduct in the Christian assembly. They spell out the proper way to give expression to the many gifts the Spirit has bestowed, and do so in such a way that will preserve order and even encourage interested onlookers to baptism. What Connerton calls *ceremonies of avocation* are essentially summed up by Paul in 1 Cor 13. For the Christian, the greatest spiritual gift—"a still more excellent way"—is the way of love. As 13:4f. indicates, love must become a daily practice, even to the point that it becomes the unthinking, second nature response of habit.

While other examples of bodily practices can be found in 1 Corinthians, my interest has been limited to a few that illustrate the direct connection that obtains between the memory of Christ that is sedimented in ritual, the habitual bodily practices which the rites inspire and ways in which these bodily habits are in their own way bearers of the memory of Christ. As Connerton notes, such practices intend to convey a message, one that is "a knowing and remembering in the hands and in the body" (95)—a message that only the body can fully understand or appreciate.

What is striking about 1 Corinthians is Paul's seeming recognition of this, as evidenced by his anxious concern for the body and its everyday behaviors. It gives new meaning to his assertion: "You were bought with a price. Therefore glorify God in your body" (6:20). This is clearly something that Paul himself seems to understand well—that it is in and through the body that one truly becomes Christian; that it is only in and through the body that one can fully experience and know the power of salvation in Christ. But, in the final analysis, he also seems to know well that it is only by way of the church's rites, and the bodily practices they inspire and give rise to, that the imitation of Christ becomes fully possible. Only when the church's memory of this comes to be inscribed deep into the Christian's very bone can one truly be said to be capable of putting on the mind and heart of Christ.

CONCLUSION

To the end of his life, John Knox continued to express dismay that his biblical scholar colleagues were unable to see what his careful scrutiny of the New Testament literature brought him to see so clearly: that the Christian community bears at its heart a living and abiding memory of Jesus the Christ. In retrospect, Knox's inability here can be attributed to the lack of theoretical tools he had at his disposal to explain how or why the Christian community has the power of memory—how memory comes to be transmitted through the generations. Thanks to developments in the disciplines of social theory, especially Halbwachs' seminal contribution, and work being done in the emerging discipline of ritual studies, it is now possible for a new generation of biblical scholars to appropriate, with much appreciation and gratitude, John Knox's remarkable and prescient insight. At the same time—and as this essay has tried to show—this new methodology opens exciting new possibilities for knowing, apprehending the Christ that Paul knew so intimately and so well!

COLLECTIVE MEMORY AND HEBREWS 11:
OUTLINING A NEW INVESTIGATIVE FRAMEWORK

Philip F. Esler

Hebrews 11 brings into remembrance a catalogue of figures known from Israelite tradition, some named and some unnamed, and insists that in various respects, especially their faith, they are exemplary for the audience of Christ-followers to whom the document was directed some time in the first century C.E. Here, then, we have a text that seems ripe with promise for an investigation tied to the connections between social memory and Christian origins that are explored in this volume. This expectation will be abundantly verified as this investigation advances.

Since social memory represents a fairly new framework for interpreting biblical texts, I will begin with an account of the theoretical resources that seem necessary for the task. First of all, there is the oral context in which Hebrews was written, since this setting gave a distinct character to the practices of memory carried on within it. Secondly, there is social memory itself. Thirdly, there is the desirability of linking ideas concerning social memory with various aspects of social identity, especially the relation of time and its passage to group identity and group beliefs. I will illustrate the distinct character of the approach that results from the integration of these three perspectives by contrast with avowedly "intertextual" approaches, such as that represented in Pamela Eisenbaum's important, yet (I will submit) somewhat misdirected treatment of Heb 11, *The Jewish Heroes of Christian History: Hebrews 11 in Literary Context*, published in 1997.

The aim of Pamela Eisenbaum's contribution is to bring out the distinctiveness of what she calls the "Jewish heroes" of Heb 11 within their setting in the Bible, which she calls their "literary context." She employs two explicitly articulated theoretical perspectives. First is rhetoric. Second, there is the interpretative/hermeneutic role played by the author of Hebrews. She is interested in the way the author reworks "the biblical text, tradition, or history." She imagines a collection of texts in existence called "the Bible" and the author continually interacting with those particular texts and involving the audience in that interaction. But she is also interested in some extrabiblical texts. She focuses upon Neh 9:6–38, Ps 105, Sir 44–50, 1 Macc 2:51–60, Wisdom 10, 4 Macc 16:16–23, the Covenant of Damascus 2–3, and 4 Ezra 7:105–111. The Hebrews author, in her view, is immersed in *textual interpretation*. She argues that Heb 11 is "one of the earliest examples of a truly Christian retelling of biblical history" and represents "the nexus between one Christian's perception of the past and his vision of the future. In that one hermeneutical moment," she writes, "the author transformed the present and initiated a new future—taking one small step toward a kind of Christian identity that did not also imply Jewish identity" (14). One of the resources she uses in relation to hermeneutics is the notion of "intertextuality," referring to the notion that discourses are in dialogue with previous discourse or cultural codes, so that every text "is made up of marked and unmarked inclusions of previous texts" (122). This concept has been taken up in biblical research by Richard Hays, Daniel Boyarin, and many others (see Aichele and Phillips). "Thus intertextuality," writes Eisenbaum, "is an accurate designation for the use of the biblical text in the retellings, because it encompasses conscious and unconscious weaving of previous texts and textual traditions into one's own voice" (122–23).

In the present essay, while availing myself of many of Eisenbaum's perceptive views, I part company from her in rejecting "intertextuality" as a useful way of describing the relationship of Heb 11 to Israelite tradition in what was a largely oral society, and in postulating the need for a specific interpretative model that fuses collective memory with social identity in such an oral context.

The Oral Character of the Context of Hebrews

In 1990, Paul Achtemeier argued that biblical critics should take far more seriously the oral character of the environment in which the New Testament appeared. Following Walter Ong, he described this culture as one of "high residual orality," meaning one characterized by "habits of thought and expression ... derived from the dominance of the oral as a medium in a given culture" (Ong 1971:27–28), which nevertheless engaged significantly in communication by means of literary creations. Achtemeier then accurately observed:

> Such a predominantly oral environment presented a situation almost totally different from that within which we currently operate, even though they had written documents as do we. The apparent similarity has led modern scholars to overlook almost entirely how such an oral overlay would affect the way communication was carried on by means of written media (3).

After considering how written documents were created and read in the Hellenistic period (with stress on the centrality of reading aloud at all stages and the physical characteristics of document production, including the lack of divisions between words and sections; see Achtemeier: 9–19), Achtemeier briefly explored some consequences of these phenomena for interpreting the New Testament, on the basis that it must be understood as speech. He was concerned with the way in which texts contained special verbal clues to aid in communication. In relation to the Gospels, this approach would focus on aural cues designed to separate parts of the narrative. As for speeches, it was necessary to see how they were organized by aural devices—for example, through anaphora (= repetition). Some of these devices were also to be found in the letters, with anaphora being common, but also parallelism, *inclusio,* and alliteration (Achtemeier: 19–25). I have recently outlined the rich variety of such features present in Rom 12:9–21 and proposed that they were explicable on the basis that this section of the letter contained a fragment of Paul's oral proclamation (2003a:316–33).

The importance of orality in the study of Heb 11 had been recognized by Michael Cosby, two years before the appearance of Achtemeier's article. Cosby was particularly interested in how the sound of Heb 11, when read aloud as any ancient text was, would have affected the message it communicated. He rightly called attention to the importance of aural effects in ancient rhetoric (4–8). In his detailed examination of Heb 11 he frequently mentioned such sound effects—for example the prominent anaphora, πίστεί "by faith" (41–55). These aspects of Heb 11 are similar to those mentioned by Achtemeier. It is, nevertheless, difficult to accept the view of Pamela Eisenbaum, that "the orality of Hebrews 11 has been thoroughly studied by Michael Cosby" (136). The significance of orality goes far beyond the investigation of aural effects of this type, something Achtemeier himself made clear in 1990 (although she does not cite him in her book).

In the last section of his essay, Achtemeier indicated in general terms that the question of orality is much larger than the recognition of aural effects in New Testament writings and their correlation with rhetorically shaped patterns of meaning. He noted, for example, that if an ancient reader was using a scroll it would have been extraordinarily difficult to locate a given passage; apart from having to roll and reroll, there would have been no visible indication of where various parts of the composition began or ended. Nor, in the absence of a system of internal divisions, was there any way of referring others to a passage except by using the words themselves. These technological limitations meant that "references were therefore much more likely to be quoted from memory than to be copied from a source," a conclusion that led Achtemeier to two implications of fundamental importance. First, the assumption that a New Testament author (he cites Paul, but the point applies to all of them) "is laboriously quoting from a source he has in front of him is overwhelmingly likely to be false." As a result, any attempt to determine which textual version an author is using will tend to be an exercise in futility. Secondly, we must completely reassess our assumptions of the way that these authors used sources and, in particular, we must not demand of them the same standards we apply in relation to accuracy in quoting sources (27).

Achtemeier concluded his essay by asserting, with complete justification, that in "these and other matters, one suspects, scholarly suppositions have prevailed that are simply anachronistic when applied to the actual environment in which documents were written and read." It was necessary to challenge these suppositions "if we are to form a clear and probable picture of the way the New Testament documents were produced and the way they functioned, within the oral environment of late Western antiquity" (27). Achtemeier did not proceed to investigate what these issues might mean in relation to the investigation of any particular New Testament works and that task, in relation to Heb 11, will occupy us later in this essay. Yet even Achtemeier did not fully appreciate the radical consequences of his proposal. Since he wrote his essay, moreover, two works have appeared that provide solid evidence for the high levels of illiteracy among both Greco-Roman and Judean populations. (For my argument that "Judean" be substituted for "Jew" or "Jewish" in relation to the first century C.E., see Esler 2003a).

In 1989, William Harris argued for low literacy rates in the Greco-Roman world. Catherine Hezser has suggested that his figure of 10 to 15 percent for fourth-century B.C.E. Greece would probably have applied in the Roman period as well. In her own substantial monograph, Hezser argues that in spite of the common view that literacy rates were higher among Israelites because of their use of written texts in prayer and worship, in fact their literacy rate must have been lower than elsewhere, especially because of the high percentage of the population living in rural areas in Palestine. The rate was possibly as low as 3 percent (496). Harry Y. Gamble has recently estimated that literacy levels among Christ-followers were probably similar to those in the population at large—about 10 to 15 percent (5, 10). The general accuracy of these well-argued estimates is assumed in what follows.

Clearly these works heighten the urgency with which the matters raised by Achtemeier need to be taken seriously. They also make Richard Hays's description of Israel (admittedly published before the works by Harris or Hezser had appeared) as "a reading community," in relation to an intertextual approach to Paul's letters, appear wide of the mark (21).

Yet, in addition to this demonstration of high levels of illiteracy in all relevant publics in the first century Mediterranean world, there are two further factors that suggest the need for a more thoroughgoing development of the general issues raised by Achtemeier toward the conclusion of his 1990 essay. These are the role of collective memory, and the mechanisms for its maintenance and manipulation, in the life of groups in an oral context, and the extent to which this phenomenon impacts upon group identity. I am dispensed from a fuller discussion of social memory and social identity because Alan Kirk and Tom Thatcher discuss the former in this volume, and because I have considered both areas at length in other places recently (2003a; 2005). We will now briefly consider these factors before proceeding to an interpretation of Heb 11 that takes all three issues into account.

Not only is Eisenbaum wrong in thinking that the oral dimensions of Hebrews had already been assessed by Cosby, but she has moved in the opposite direction by actively taking up the notion of "intertextuality." This word, apparently coined by Julia Kristeva (1969), refers to the notion that discourses are in dialogue with previous discourse or cultural codes, so that every text "is made up of marked and unmarked inclusions of previous texts" (122; Kristeva; Culler: 100–18). Intertextuality has been employed in biblical research by Richard Hays and Daniel Boyarin. Eisenbaum finds intertextuality useful as it brings out the "dialogical" aspects of a text, meaning the extent to which the text is "a dialogue between text and interpreter," whether the "dialogical" format is evident or not. Sometimes an author's use of previous texts will be conscious and sometimes unconscious. "Thus," writes Eisenbaum, "intertextuality is an accurate designation for the use of the biblical text in the retellings, because it encompasses conscious and unconscious weaving of previous texts and textual traditions into one's own voice" (122–23). We will have cause to doubt this view in relation to Heb 11 later in this essay.

COLLECTIVE MEMORY AND GROUP IDENTITY

Maurice Halbwachs (1877–1945), under the influence of his teacher in sociology, the great Emile Durkheim (1858–1917), regarded memory as the production of human beings living together in society. "(I)t is in society," he wrote, "that people normally acquire their memories. It is also in society that they recall, recognize and localize their memories" (1992:38). His thesis was that memory was socially determined. Yet, perhaps because Halbwachs had worked with the individualistic philosopher Henri Bergson (1859–1941) prior to his exposure to Durkheim, he was able to resist some of the extremes of Durkheimian social determinism. It is probably for this reason that Halbwachs interested himself in groups within society, rather than just with the larger reality of society itself (1980:33). "Let us remark in passing," Lewis Coser observes, "that almost everywhere that Durkheim speaks of 'Society' with a capital S, Halbwachs speaks of 'groups'—a more cautious usage"(Coser 1992:22). Collective memory relates to groups, not society at large. Halbwachs was also sensitive to the role of individuals: "While the collective memory endures and draws strength from its base in a coherent body of people, it is individuals as group members who remember" (1980:48).

Halbwachs differentiated between "autobiographical memory," a memory of some person or event of which the subject had had personal experience, and "historical memory," which was a memory of events or persons known to him not through personal experience, but from the memory of others or through written records or commemorations, including those of phenomena before a person was born. Such a memory "remains a borrowed memory, not my own" (1980:51). Yet Halbwachs insisted that it was wrong to overemphasize the distinction between autobiographical and historical memories, for in fact they interpenetrated one another (55–59). The reality of that interpenetration was "collective memory," which represented the zone of interaction between individual and personal remembrances and reference points from the memories of others or from historical records (59).

Halbwachs was especially concerned with the activity of a group reconstructing its memories in the present. Although theorists such as Barry Schwartz have argued that Halbwachs went too far down this road, thus imperiling the continuity within which a group stands in relation to its past, he was certainly correct in asserting the capacity of groups to reconstruct the past, typically by the invention of tradition or the capture of traditions generated by other groups. More problematic was Halbwachs' neglect, as Paul Connerton has shown, of the manner in which collective memories are passed on—communicated—from one generation to another. Connerton rightly insists that "to study the social formation of memory is to study those acts of transfer that make remembering in common possible" (39).

We are able to distinguish social memory from the activity of historical reconstruction. The latter involves systematic and dispassionate investigation into human activities in the past from the traces that have been left behind, whether there is a living memory of those activities or not (Connerton: 13–16). Human beings seem driven to compose narratives of the past as a way of retaining significant memory.

Yet narratives of the past can be the cause and site of conflicts within and between groups. "Memory contestation," write Olick and Robbins, "takes place from above and below, from both center and periphery" (126). The notion of "countermemory" has been used in relation to Michel

Foucault's notion of written texts that serve to challenge dominant discourses, including living memories (see Bouchard). Yet a form of
countermemory more relevant to residually oral cultures may be seen in
the way in which members of an ethnic group that have experienced a
rupture in the taken-for-granted reality of their identity develop new
ways to construe their past and thus make sense of their present (Cornell:
45–46). Often they generate narratives that can be repeated (and revised)
by word of mouth as well as in written form. Here we have a counter or
contested memory of wider application than that present in Foucault's
writings. The phenomenon of contested memory brings us face-to-face
with our third and last theoretical issue—group identity.

"When we remember," Fentress and Wickham accurately suggest,
"we represent ourselves to ourselves and to those around us. To the
extent that our 'nature'—that which we truly are—can be revealed in
articulation, we are what we remember." From this observation they
deduce that "a study of the way we remember—the way we present ourselves in our memories, the way we define our personal and collective
identities through our memories, the way we order and structure our
ideas in our memories, and the way we transmit these memories to
others—is a study of the way we are" (7).

This relationship between memory and identity, taken together with
Halbwachs's focus upon the location of collective memories in groups,
allows us to propose the social identity theory developed by Henri Tajfel
(a social psychologist at Bristol University, England in the 1970s and
early 1980s) as a helpful body of ideas for augmenting the collective
memory model. According to Tajfel (who died in 1982), "social identity"
is that part of an individual's identity that comes from belonging to a
particular group. It embraces a cognitive dimension (the sheer fact of
belonging to a group like this), an emotional dimension (how it feels to
belong) and an evaluative dimension (how members rate their groups in
relation to others). Because the members of groups often tell themselves
who they are in contrast with out-groups—who they are not—intergroup
phenomena feature prominently in social identity theory (see Tajfel;
Hogg and Abrams).

Although social identity theorists initially tended to analyze groups
from the perspective, as it were, of a snapshot taken at a single point in a
group's existence, more recent work by Susan Condor and Marco Cinnirella has emphasized the importance of duration over time in group
identity. The very fact that we possess identities depends on our capacity
for relating fragmentary experiences across temporal boundaries. Condor
stresses the extent to which social life is a temporal trajectory rather than
a static set of positions, where social agents take up identities, ideas and
practices and hand them on to others. Cinnirella is concerned to develop

the theory of social identity so that it may be able to address past social identities and address the ways in which groups reconstitute past, present and future to create meaningful "stories" at the level of the group and the individuals that comprise it. He has introduced to the discussion the notion of "possible selves," the beliefs held by individuals ("personal selves") or groups ("social selves") as to what they were like in the past and what they may become in the future. Particularly significant is Cinirella's emphasis on the way in which a group that has an orientation to the past will proffer figures from the past (historical or imagined) as prototypical of group identity and that such figures will influence the possible social selves the group generates for the members. In this process the group mobilizes existing collective memories or invents new ones to tell itself who it is in the present.

Having set out these ideas and perspectives relating to the residually oral culture of the first century C.E.—collective memory and group identity sensitized in the area of chronological duration—I will now discuss how, in general terms, they shed light on Heb 11, and then consider their usefulness in relation to a sample of features of the text.

ORALITY, MEMORY AND GROUP IDENTITY IN RELATION TO HEBREWS 11

The oral nature of the context within which Hebrews was published sets the initial bearings for this investigation. The majority of the initial audience (somewhere from 85 to 95 percent) were illiterate. They would have first encountered the document by hearing it read aloud to them. Thereafter their access to it would have been either from their recollection of its contents or from hearing it read aloud on later occasions. It is most unlikely that they would have had a copy of the text (except perhaps a few literate members with the financial resources to commission one to be made) and most of them would not have been able to read it if they did have copy. These same considerations apply to their position vis-à-vis the range of Israelite literature that would have been the ultimate sources for the account of figures from Israelite history laid out in Heb 11. They would not have owned these expensive texts and would not have been able to read them, or find their way around them, if they did. Although some of these texts may have been held in local synagogues, it is impossible to assess whether even the few literate members of the Hebrews audience would have been in a position (typically because they were Judeans or God-fearing non-Judeans) to gain access to such Israelite writings.

The author of the work knew all these things when he (and it is probably a "he") was dictating the work to a scribe. He knew that the only way his message would install itself in the hearts and minds of those he intended and expected would hear it was through the processes of memory (unless, perchance, the document was read to them again). He knew that they would hear his message, remember some of it and then by conversation among themselves thereafter bring features of it back into recollection. To revert to the Halbwachs formulation, the author was envisaging a communal setting in which they would acquire, recall, recognize, and localize these memories. In short, the author was propagating a supply of collective memories for that segment of the first-century Christ-movement whom he anticipated would hear his message. He was creating a stock of memory that would come to have a close association with this particular group. It is self-evident that the author was using writing to achieve this effect. Nevertheless, as Fentress and Wickham point out, it is usually the case in an oral society, or in one that is only partly literate (as here), that writing is "still envisioned as an adjunct to memory" (9, 11). In a society like this it is hard to envisage how knowledge can be widely preserved, except by living memory.

Clearly, the people described and the events recounted in Heb 11 lived or occurred centuries or even millennia before the lifetimes of the original recipients of the discourse. Yet, as we have seen, memory does not just arise from personal experience (= "autobiographical memory"), but can be generated from other sources, such as the memory of others or written records of phenomena occurring before a person was born. These memories ("borrowed" or "historical") interact with personal memories to form collective memories.

As far as Hebrews is concerned, at least some of its audience had personally experienced the hardships described in Heb 10:32–34 while being urged to retain their confidence in the future (Heb 10:35). People such as this would have found it comparatively easy to integrate memories of these events with the cognate experiences and future hope attributed to the figures from Israel's past in Heb 11. The previous sufferings of the audience of Hebrews constituted a fertile ground for bringing personalities and events from the history of Israel into living connection with them.

According to Halbwachs, the remembrances we hold are in very large measure *reconstructions* of the past. While it is possible for us to remember certain things accurately, he was concerned with how our memories are reconstructions of the past generated in collective contexts such as families, school classes and religious groups. In this context it is noteworthy that the author of Hebrews has been very selective in those figures from, and features of, Israelite history he chooses to mention in Heb 11. For example, he omits God's giving of the law to Moses on Sinai, does not name anyone after David, and ignores the destruction of Jerusalem in 587/6 B.C.E. and the Babylonian captivity. He also highlights certain aspects of that history and introduces conspicuous new features (such as Abraham's belief in resurrection [11:19] and Joseph's foretelling of the exodus [11:22]). Clearly these devices represent reconstructions of Israel's past that the author has adjudged appropriate to the group of Christ-followers whom he was addressing. It is not easy to determine how many of these reconstructions were the result of the conscious choice of the author, as opposed to his reproduction of views he himself remembered from elsewhere. Nevertheless, it is undeniable that those of his audience who encountered his version of Israelite history and assimilated it as memory would have come to hold a remembrance of the past that was pervasively reconstructed. It is of little moment whether the events thus taken into the collective memory of the group from Israelite tradition had happened or not. What matters is that they comprised a past that had become alive and significant for the audience.

Fentress and Wickham correctly summarize Halbwachs as having asserted that "social groups construct their own images of the world by establishing an agreed version of the past" and that "these versions are established by communication, not by private remembrance" (x). This summary also seems accurately to capture the strategy of the author of Hebrews in composing this document to be communicated to other Christ-followers of his time.

We have seen that Halbwachs has been criticized for devoting insufficient attention to the reality of groups existing for a considerable duration—certainly beyond the lifetime of any of their members. Anthropologist Fredrik Barth's proposal for the tendency of ethnic groups to persist over long periods by continually modifying the cultural indicia whereby they express their distinctiveness—and thus the boundaries separating themselves from out-groups—represents a phenomenon of the sort in question. Israel itself maintained a separate identity by reinventing itself after crises, as can be seen in its reestablishment on the land after exile in Babylon, as I have argued elsewhere (2003b). But despite these objections to his theory, that Halbwachs was correct in relation to some groups emerges precisely in relation to Heb 11. For here we have a group of people who, although new, and actually the successors of an earlier (Israelite/Judean) group (which continued to exist), present themselves as its continuation, and thus as old and ancestral. In this case—as with others like it, such as the strategy in Luke-Acts of presenting the Christ movement as ancestral and embedded in Israelite tradition (Esler 1987:215–29)—a (fairly) newly formed group has colonized the past through the active appropriation and reconstruction of certain elements and the creation of memory. It is true, however, that Halbwachs (believing that memories are always socially constructed in the present) failed to give adequate thought to how collective memories are passed on within the group from one generation to another. This issue is obviously central to the thought of the author of Heb 11. His whole interest lies in creating a rival version of the collective memory of Israel and then transmitting it to members of the group. The author is engaged in an act of communication that makes this transmission possible.

The precise reason that the author of Hebrews interacted so frequently with Israelite tradition throughout the course of the document and produced his version of Israelite history in chapter 11 constitutes one of the biggest mysteries of research into the document. While this phenomenon reflects in general terms the origin of the Christ movement among Judeans in Palestine, attempts to produce more specific explanations based, most typically, upon hypotheses concerning the balance of Judeans and non-Judeans in the audience addressed by the author are not very persuasive. To step back a little and seek an explanation at a higher level of social explanation, however, allows us to give due prominence to Connerton's view—formulated in relation to the elements of recollection in a phenomenon as radically new as the French Revolution—that "all beginnings contain an element of recollection" (6). In Heb 11 we have a very strong element of recollection, since the author is having his audience receive memories that go back as far as Cain and Abel. That is quite a recollection! Israelite memory and tradition were obviously a central part of the old order that the new movement was encountering. It was necessary for its members to be able to suppress—that is, to forget— aspects of that memory and tradition that were not capable of reconciliation with the new order. These plainly included the Sinai covenant and the history of the people in the land, especially the exile and return. Elements such as these are simply eliminated in the narrative crafted by the author of Heb 11.

The fact that the Hebrews author has chosen a narrative form to tell, in his highly selective fashion, the history of Israel is testament to the widespread use of narrative by human groups to encapsulate the story of their origins and identity. Fentress and Wickham point out that there is more to stories than just the recording of events. They suggest that stories provide people with a set of stock explanations that underlie their predispositions to interpret reality in various ways that extend back into the past and forward into the future: "memory is not merely retrospective; it is prospective as well. Memory provides a perspective for interpreting experiences in the present and for foreseeing those that lie ahead" (51).

COLLECTIVE MEMORY, SOCIAL IDENTITY, AND TIME

Ultimately we are dealing with the identity of the Christ movement, whom the author of Hebrews was addressing in this document. By retelling the story of Israel's past, he was able to say important things about who they were. The identity of the group is installed in the selves of individual members as social identity. This is not to deny that there are other aspects of their selves which are personal—that is, idiosyncratic to themselves—but as we know absolutely nothing about individuals in the audience to which Hebrews was directed, the point is entirely academic.

The immediate context of chapter 11 in Hebrews begins at Heb 10:19 and extends to the conclusion of the letter. Up to Heb 10:18 the author has mainly been dealing with Jesus Christ. The characteristic of the long section of the text beginning at 10:19, however, is that the author begins an exploration of the status, obligations and destiny of those who have faith in Christ. In short, he expatiates upon their identity, their sense of who they are that they derive from belonging to a group such as this, with its cognitive, emotional and evaluative dimensions.

The recent work on social identity by Condor finds abundant responsive data in the text. Condor emphasizes the extent to which the members of groups exist in a state of temporal continuity: aware of the past and the future, of their predecessors in the group and those who will proceed them, a sense of continuity marked by memory and anticipation (which Condor actually terms retroactive and proactive memory). Beginning at Heb 10:19, the author articulates a chronological framework for the group that embraces past, present, and future. The past includes fairly recent events represented by the "blood of Jesus" and his opening the curtain (10:19–20)—that is, his passion and death—and continues with the period afterwards, when some of the author's addressees converted and then endured various forms of hardship (10:32–34). In Heb 11 we will learn that the past of the group also extends back to encompass figures as long ago as Abel, Enoch, and Noah, as well as people from Israelite history beginning with Abraham. The present is a time for holding fast to their confession (ὁμολογία) in faith and hope, and for meeting and encouraging one another (10:22–25, 36–39). Finally, there is a pronounced future dimension. This encompasses the coming judgment for those who sin after receiving knowledge of the truth (10:26–31), and Mount Zion and the heavenly Jerusalem in store for those who endure—the firstborn enrolled in heaven and the spirits of the just made perfect (12:22–24). This comprehensive chronological picture accords closely with the proposal of social identity theorists that our possession of identities is dependent on our ability to relate experiences across temporal boundaries—past, present, and future.

Hebrews 11 begins with the statement: "Faith (πίστις) is the assurance of things hoped for, the conviction of things not seen" (11:1). This verse summarizes what the author has been saying in 10:19–39, with v. 39 stating, "We are not of those who shrink back and are destroyed, but of those who have faith (πίστις) and keep their souls." But Heb 11:1 turns out to be programmatic for the whole chapter, as indicated as early as 11:2 when the author continues, "By this [i.e., faith] the elders [οἱ πρεσβύτεροι] were attested." There then follows a long succession of statements, largely concerning these elders, beginning with the assertion "by faith" (πίστει).

From the perspective on the temporal dimension of social identity proposed by Cinnirella, the narrative of figures from the past in Heb 11 represents an exposition of possible social selves for the Christ-followers for whom the text was composed. They are real or imagined figures in the past, now boldly enrolled as members of the group, who are proto-typical of its identity and whose memory can be reactivated for the purpose of identity construction in the present. The author's colonization of these figures on behalf of his group, by including them within its col-lective memory, has already been mentioned. We are now able to situate this daring enterprise within the further perspective of the creation and maintenance of the group's identity.

The efforts taken to enlist these figures into membership of the group are worth noting. The most remarkable expression of this effort comes at the end of Heb 11: "And all these, though attested by faith, did not receive the promise, since God had foreseen something better for us, lest apart from us (χωρὶς ἡμῶν) they should be perfected" (11:39–40). Here the author, according to Koester, "links previous generations to the Christian community of his own time," as an example of the emphasis that Hebrews places on "the unity of God's people over the generations" (2001:520). Koester's basic observation is accurate, yet he overlooks the remarkable reconstruction of Israelite memories involved in taking this step. The notion that the perfection of the great figures from Israel's past—and indeed from earlier in the human record known from the book of Gene-sis—could not take place apart from the perfection of those who believed in Christ would have struck Judeans who were not members of the Christ movement as blasphemous effrontery. This observation raises the ques-tion of contested memory in Heb 11, which is covered below.

Yet the sentiment of Heb 11:40 is not the only example of the author's including the people mentioned in Heb 11 in the new group. They are also the great cloud of witnesses mentioned in Heb 12:1. Here they are likened to those looking on at an athletics stadium (and, proba-bly, as having previously run the race) while the group members directly addressed by the author take to the track. This image binds the old and current athletes closely together. Similarly, since we learn in Heb 11:16 that "God has prepared for them (i.e. the elders) a city," it is difficult to conceive that they are not to be found in the "city of the living God," as included among "the assembly of the firstborn who are enrolled in heaven" (Heb 12:23)—together with Christ-followers, presumably—and as numbered among the "spirits of the just men made perfect" of Heb 12:23. Thus they are joined with Christ-followers in the future, as well as in the present.

We now consider the data in Hebrews concerning the next aspect of the model set out above: the extent to which collective memories are contested, especially in an oral culture. Here we see very clearly the necessity of moving from a text-based framework of understanding to one based on the processes of memory. In any context in which there exists both a traditional stock of memory—especially one of such variegated richness as characterized by Israelite tradition—and a range of groups struggling to survive and prosper, it is inevitable that the social memories of that setting will be the subject of lively contestation. Hebrews provides evidence of this (the whole document, not just in chapter 11) in the extreme lengths to which its author goes to *detextualize* the main body of tradition with which he is interacting—namely, those Israelite works which later came to be regarded as the canonical Hebrew Bible.

In many other New Testament writings it is clear that their authors have in mind *written* Israelite texts. Thus quotations from, or references to, those works are frequently prefixed with the word γέγραπται, "it is written," where the perfect tense conveys the meaning of something written in the past, the significance of which extends into the present (a nuance well-captured in the translation "it stands written"). This usage appears nine times in Matthew (2:5; 4:4, 6, 7, 10; 11:10; 21:13; 26:24, 31), four times in Mark (1:2; 7:6; 11:17; 14:27), and eight times in Luke (2:23; 3:4; 4:4, 8, 10; 7:27; 10:26; 19:46). As far as Paul is concerned, the same usage is extremely common in Romans and Galatians, and also appears in 1 and 2 Corinthians. Secondly, in the other New Testament writings it is often expressly stated that Jesus fulfilled things that were written about him in Israelite Scripture (for example, Luke 22:37; 24:44; John 5:46; 12:16; 15:25). Thirdly, there are frequent references to the γραφή or the γραφαί—the "writing" or the "writings"—which contain the passages mentioned in this way. At Rom 1:2, indeed, Paul uses the expression "the sacred writings" (γραφαῖς ἁγίαις) of Israelite Scripture, thus indicating that by the mid first century C.E. there was already a sense of a collection of Israelite writings that were especially revered—no doubt meaning the law, prophets and the writings that were eventually to be regarded by Jews as canonical, a view also evident in Josephus (C. Ap. 1. 8).

In Hebrews, on the other hand, this textual dimension has almost completely disappeared. Eisenbaum has noticed data relevant to this issue but misses their significance. Thus, she claims that its author never uses the expression "it is written" (γέγραπται) "in any form in connection with biblical material" (97). This observation is important but not quite accurate. The word γέγραπται is found in relation to Israelite Scripture once in Hebrews, at 10:7. Yet this occurrence may be regarded as an exceptional case, for the word appears in a quotation from Ps 39:7 (LXX), not in the author's own words, but within a statement made by Christ: "Then I said, 'Lo, I have come to do your will, O God,' as it stands written of me in the roll of the book." Eisenbaum correctly observes that the author never uses the word "Scripture" (γραφή) and never names a biblical book (98). On one occasion (Heb 2:6), we might add, the author says, in a remarkably blasé fashion, "Someone has testified somewhere saying [διεμαρτύρατο δέ πού τις λέγων]," before quoting no less a source than Ps 8:4–6! Often, indeed, the author breaks into what *we* know is a quotation from Israelite Scripture, but without any indication that he is doing so. Nor, one might further add, does the author say that anything he asserts in regard to Christ or his impact on the world explicitly represents the fulfillment of Scripture (although Christ's words at Heb 10:7 come close to this).

Instead, when the author is introducing a quotation from Israelite Scripture, he relies, as Eisenbaum notes, upon verbs of "saying," to the complete exclusion of expressions such as "it is written":

> Although the use of saying verbs to introduce an OT citation is common among many other ancient exegetes besides the writers of the NT, especially in Qumran and the Mishnah, no other author uses them to the complete exclusion of writing verbs or references to Scripture qua Scripture, i.e. as written text. (97)

These instances constitute what she has helpfully described as the "oracular" mode, where the author recycles biblical quotations as "dynamic proclamations directed immediately at his audience" (112).

Eisenbaum comes agonizingly close to appreciating the significance of her valuable observations. At one point she even says that there "is no doubt that the oral and immediate character of Scripture is what is most stressed in Hebrews ... For him (i.e., the author), these divine words flow directly from the mouth of God to the listener" (99). Nor does she link this phenomenon with her proposal that the work promotes the "denationalization" of Israel's "heroes," their severing from the leadership of Israel, which she observes in Heb 11.

The inevitable conclusion, once one treats the oral context with due seriousness, is that *the lengths taken by the author to detextualize the primary source of Israelite tradition that he is employing necessitate jettisoning textual interpretation, let alone intertextuality, as an explanatory framework for his aims or achievement.* This conclusion does not imply that the author is not aware of texts from Israelite Scripture—although he may have

retained them in his memory and need not have had physical access to
any of the texts from which come the passages he cites (as Heb 2:6
strongly suggests). Rather, the point is that, with the exception of Heb
10:7, he obliterates all reference to the textual form in which these
Israelite traditions were embodied. Someone in the original audience of
Hebrews hearing it read who was not already familiar with Israelite
Scripture would have had virtually no idea that the author, in numer-
ous places throughout his composition, was drawing on its resources!
Anyone, Judean or non-Judean, who already had some familiarity with
Israelite Scripture, typically through attendance at synagogue on the
Sabbath, could not help but have been struck by the extent to which the
sources of the passages cited had been suppressed.

Now that I have demonstrated the general applicability of the perspectives on orality, memory and identity to Heb 11, the time has come to
investigate in more detail a sample selection of the figures in Heb 11. To
keep this essay within manageable limits I will restrict myself to three of
them—Abel, Enoch and Noah.

THE PRESENTATION OF ABEL, ENOCH AND NOAH IN HEBREWS 11

Abel

Abel is the first elder mentioned in Heb 11. As far as Israelite Scripture is concerned, Abel appears in Gen 4. Cain is born to Adam and Eve
(4:1), and then Abel. Abel becomes a keeper of sheep and Cain a tiller of
the ground (4:2). For a reason not stated in the text, God prefers Abel's
offering to Cain's (4:3–5). Cain is angry (4:6) and, although rebuked by
God (4:7), murders Abel (4:8). God calls Cain to account, saying, *inter
alia*, "The voice of your brother's blood is crying to me from the
ground" (4:9–10). Then Cain receives his punishment (4:11–12). The
way Abel is presented in Heb 11 illustrates virtually all of the issues
raised above *in nuce*:

> By faith [πίστει] Abel offered to God a greater sacrifice than Cain, on
> account of which he was attested as righteous [δίκαιος], God testifying in
> relation to his gifts, and through which, although he died, he still speaks.
> (11:4)

The first point to note is that neither the faith of Abel nor his being
righteous occur in the "biblical" texts Eisenbaum considers in relation
to him—neither in those that came to be canonical Hebrew Scripture,
nor in the Apocrypha, not even in 4 Macc 16 and 18. For these aspects,
she is forced to resort to "extra-biblical traditions about Abel,"

although only in relation to righteousness, since Abel "bears no reputation as faithful" (148–49). This immediately forces us to ask, however,
why we are using the word "biblical" at all in this context. Why not
simply say that we dealing with Israelite tradition? We may grant that
what came to be included in the Hebrew Bible had a special authority,
while also insisting that this was just one of a number of texts that
reflected and, perhaps, enriched the Israelite understanding of this
figure. In fact, there are other texts that do refer to Abel's being righteous. Extant examples include *1 En.* 22:7, the *Mart. Ascen. Isa.* 9:8 and
28, Matt 23:35 and 1 John 3:12. There may well have been others that
are now lost. But rather than assume that the author of Hebrews was
using any particular text or texts, the nature of the oral environment in
which he was writing suggests, following Paul Achtemeier's lead, that
we approach the problem from a different direction altogether. We
should drop our natural, but entirely unwarranted, supposition that
the author was working with written texts and reimagine him as operating on the basis of what he had stored in his memory, and the
memories he could assume were held by his audience. This impels us
to conceive of Abel as a focus of a number of different traditions held
in memory, as a memory site.

On this approach, the Hebrews author draws upon the information
(or possibly passages) concerning Abel he has memorized from whatever
source and comes up with a description that stresses Abel's faith and
righteousness. We really have no idea what texts, if any, he had in mind.
If, however, he had had any exposure previously to the practice of reading Israelite writings (either in Judean synagogues or the house
congregations of the Christ movement), he and his audience were probably more familiar with the Gen 4 picture of Abel than others, because
even in the first century C.E., the Pentateuch (along with the Prophets and
the Writings) seems to have received greater prominence than other
Israelite writings. In an oral culture—where people learn by heart large
amounts of text and where finding a reference in a written manuscript is
a formidably difficult exercise—the author's reliance on his own memory,
fortified from whatever written or oral source, is exactly what we would
expect. Probably, if asked, he himself would have been unable to nomi-
nate all the sources for the composite picture of Abel stowed away in his
memory. In a setting such as this, after all, we must reckon with the fact
that people talked about important figures in Israelite tradition like Abel,
so the author's familiarity with him need not have been derived solely
from written texts.

Rather than assuming the Hebrews author engaged in the interpretation of texts, or (still more improbably) was adept at "intertextuality," we
must regard him as being involved in the maintenance or manipulation

of Israelite memory. While there can be no doubt that he was utilizing collective memories of Israel in relation to Abel, it is impossible for us to know the extent to which he was relying on oral sources of information in addition to whatever texts he may have had physically at his disposal (not many, one suspects) or have heard read aloud and, in various degrees, memorized in the past.

Further, it is indisputable that the author is *contesting* memories derived from Israelite tradition. This maneuver is most apparent in his innovative attribution of faith to Abel as the motivation for his offering a better sacrifice. Within the Christ movement of the first century C.E., faith had become a distinguishing feature. While this emphasis on faith is most clearly seen in Paul's letters, in Hebrews faith is also a prominent aspect of what the author is trying to communicate, as many scholars have observed (see, for example, Grässer; Hamm; Lindars 1991:108–12; C. Koester 2001:125–27), even though it does not have the same specialized meaning as for Paul. The assertion that "by faith" Abel offered a better sacrifice would have struck most Judeans of the time as unjustified—even outlandish—but for the in-group of Christ-followers it was an essential feature, not just of their attitudes and beliefs, but of their *identity* in the sense set out above.

The modification of memory for in-group purposes is also evident in the description of Abel as righteous. This point emerges more later in the description of Abraham (Heb 11:17–18) that notably omits any reference to the righteousness of Abraham, even though this must have been well-known in Judean circles from synagogal readings of Gen 15:6 (where Abraham's faith was reckoned to him as righteousness) and Gen 18:23–33 (where Abraham's negotiation with God over saving Sodom if the town contains a certain number of righteous people assumes that he, Abraham, is himself righteous). In Genesis the only person depicted as righteous before Abraham is Noah (Gen 6:9, 7:1). The strategy of the Hebrews author, accordingly, is to ignore the righteousness of Abraham, the father of Israel, and retroject it back onto Abel. While Abel himself had no progeny, the fact that he was righteous reveals that righteousness was a possibility in the world long before Abraham. This reading pulls the rug out from any claim Judeans might make that they were exclusively righteous by virtue of their descent from righteous Abraham. Here we see an example of what Eisenbaum persuasively describes as the author's attempt to render inconsequential the "ethnic particularity" of Israelite history (3), although she has overlooked this point in relation to Abel. One might seek to counter this conclusion with the argument that perhaps at 11:4 δίκαιοι just means "innocent," but this view falters on the strong sense of group belonging that characterizes the use of this word and δικαιοσύνη elsewhere in Hebrews (1:9; 5:13; 7:2; 10:38; 11:7, 33; 12:11, 23).

In sum, these attributions of faith and righteousness to Abel represent the creation and communication of what has been called a "counter-memory" (see above) to designate a memory that differs from, and challenges, dominant memory and discourse.

Enoch

Enoch is the next figure to appear (Heb 11:5). According to Eisenbaum, what "the author says of Enoch closely follows the rendering in the LXX (Gen 5:24)" (150, 152). Does it? The LXX runs as follows:

Καὶ εὐηρέστησεν Ενωχ τῷ θεῷ καὶ οὐχ ηὑρίσκετο ὅτι μετέθηκεν αὐτὸν ὁ θεός.

Compare this with Heb 11:5, where I have underlined the sections that do seem dependent in some way upon the Genesis account:

Πίστει Ἐνὼχ μετετέθη τοῦ μὴ ἰδεῖν θάνατον, καὶ οὐχ ηὑρίσκετο διότι μετέθηκεν αὐτὸν ὁ θεός. πρὸ γὰρ τῆς μεταθέσεως μεμαρτύρηται εὐαρεστηκέναι τῷ θεῷ.

The comparison hardly supports Eisenbaum's view. While most of the language of the LXX does appear in Heb 11:5, the order of the two main elements is inverted, there are several smaller differences, and the author of Hebrews adds a number of new elements.

The biggest change is the insertion of Πίστει at the beginning of the verse as the explanation for his being taken by God. While this revision is in line with the repeated anaphora of "faith" in Heb 11, we have just seen how, in relation to Abel, it contests Israelite memory by attaching a central feature of the identity of the Christ movement to this important figure from Israelite tradition. In fact, as Attridge (318) and Koester (2001:151)—both following Braun (349)—note, the description of Enoch as faithful was not unknown among Israelites, but it was very rare. Yet for the Hebrews author to bring the story of Enoch under its rubric gives faith a striking prominence. He is reworking the collective memory of the group for whom he composed the work in the interests of its ongoing identity in the present.

In addition, Hebrews adds the result of Enoch's being "taken," a point on which ancient Israelite/Judean opinion was split. Some considered that Enoch had been taken by death (*Tg. Onq.* on Gen 4:4; *Gen. Rab.* 25:1). But most assumed he had been assumed directly into heaven (see *1 En.* 12:2; *2 En.* 3:1–3; *Jub.* 4:23). This latter reading had particular significance for the manner in which Hebrews appealed to members of the Christ movement, since it represented another example of the fact that it is faith that leads to "the preservation of the soul" (περιποίησιν ψυχῆς), as claimed in Heb 10:39. This promise of preservation was clearly the appeal the figure of Enoch held for the author.

Noah

The colonization of Israelite memory and tradition in the interests of the Christ movement continues with Noah (Heb 11:7). Again, a summary of the account in Genesis (6–9) is prefixed by the word πίστει. Yet more important is the statement that "he became an heir of the righteousness that comes by faith" (τῆς κατὰ πίστιν δικαιοσύνης ἐγένετο κληρονόμος). Whereas the author has previously brought Abel and Enoch within the realm of faith, he now takes a more daring step to assimilate these primeval figures to the Christ movement. Commentators frequently miss this point. It is not enough to say, with Attridge, that this "odd notion apparently refers to the fact that Noah is next in sequence of those like Abel who, because of their faith, were attested to be righteous" (320), and to point to the connection between righteousness and faith from Hab 2:4 in Heb 10:38. Nor is it sufficient to argue, as does Koester, that the author can use this connection to propose that Noah, well-known for his right- eousness (mentioned in Gen 6:9 and 7:1), must have had faith and that he serves as an example encouraging the Hebrews audience to persevere in the hope of righteousness (2001:477, 483). Eisenbaum more helpfully notes that Noah "has become a member of the elect people who are set apart from the rest of the world" (153). Yet she does not go quite far enough.

The author of Hebrews is, in fact, retrospectively enlisting Noah into the Christ movement. For "the righteousness that comes by faith" does not refer to some general form of righteousness and faith, but to that now available as a result of Christ's salvific action—"the new and living way which he opened for us" (Heb 10:20). This particular faith and this partic- ular righteousness are what one attains by membership in the in-group that has gathered with Christ at its heart. Noah became a member of this group potentially. This is the meaning of the statement that he became an *heir* of the righteousness that comes through faith: he had the entitlement to this privileged identity in the past and, inevitably, now that Christ has come and by his offering "has perfected for all time those who are sancti- fied" (Heb 10:14), Noah has entered into his inheritance. By this means Hebrews establishes—for the Christ-followers who constitute the audi- ence of the document—Noah as an eminent predecessor in their identity from the primordial period of human life on earth. Noah thus becomes, in the language of social identity theory, prototypical of the Christ-following in-group. He becomes a possible self for its members. Hebrews reworks the remembrance of Noah to create a collective memory that helps to tell the audience who they are in the present. The author achieves this rhetorical effect by emphasizing the readers' superiority over any Judean call on their attention in relation to Noah as a result of his location within Israelite tradition by demonstrating how his "true" identity was as an early member of the Christ-following in-group. Noah's membership was potential (he was an "heir") until the coming of Christ, and now it has, by necessary implication, become actual.

Eisenbaum has pointed out another respect in which the author of Hebrews alters the Genesis picture of Noah to accord with his communicative strategy. She notes that in Gen 6:9 Noah is described as "being perfect in his generation" (τέλειος ὢν ἐν τῇ γενεᾷ αὐτοῦ). Perfection is certainly one aspect of the Genesis picture of Noah that may have found its way into Israelite memory, especially as it was reinforced by the fact that only Noah and his family escaped destruction in the flood. Yet in Hebrews, where perfection is an important theme (as D. Peterson has shown), the emphasis falls on the way in which Christ is the model (Heb 2:10; 5:9; 7:28) and agent of perfection (10:14). Related to this christological theme is the notion that these (admittedly great) figures before Christ "should not be made perfect apart from us" (11:40). There is no suggestion in Hebrews that Noah was perfect. Eisenbaum reasonably proposes that in 11:7 "the author consciously avoids making reference to Noah's perfection because perfection cannot be achieved apart from Christ" (153). Thus the Hebrews author modulates the memory of Noah found in Israelite tradition by suppressing one of its prominent features.

CONCLUSION

This investigation reveals how the author of Hebrews has sought to create in chapter 11 a panoply of memories for his audience by contesting central aspects of the collective memory of Israel. He is intent on effecting a communicative act that will make remembering in common possible. He pervasively reconstructs the Israelite past in order to establish and maintain a particular identity for the Christ movement in the present that also possesses a trajectory trailing into the future. The processes by which this result is achieved are explicable within the constraints and opportunities of a residually oral culture characterized by high levels of illiteracy. Alternative construals based on the notion of intertextuality, even the exegetically accomplished study of Eisenbaum, are not well adapted to the demands of such a context. The extent to which this "cloud of witnesses" (Heb 12:1) has become a permanent feature of Christian imagination is proof of just how successful was this exercise in identity construction. For these reasons, Heb 11 represents a particularly rich example of the relationship between Christian origins and social memory.

EARLY JEWISH BIRTH PROPHECY STORIES AND WOMEN'S SOCIAL MEMORY

Antoinette Clark Wire

Elijah, a Tishbite from the land of the Arabs
of the tribe of Aaron
living in Gilead because Tishbi was a gift to the priests.
When he was about to be born
his mother Sochaba saw bright shining men were greeting him
and they were wrapping him in bands of fire
and were giving him flames of fire to eat.
And his father Asom came and reported in Jerusalem
and the oracle said to him
"Don't be afraid
for his dwelling will be light
and his word a verdict
and he will judge Israel with sword and with fire."
This is Elijah
who brought fire down from heaven three times
and held rain in his own tongue
and raised the dead
and was taken up into heaven in a whirlwind of fire.

(Lives of the Prophets 21)

I want to put myself at the confluence of three recent methods of study to see if their interaction can help me understand the meaning of twenty-six early Jewish birth prophecy stories like the one above.[1] I will draw on

---

1. I have translated and discussed these stories in *Holy Lives, Holy Deaths: A Close Hearing of Early Jewish Storytellers*, 25–101. See its introduction and notes on my textual and translation decisions. Because my attention is on oral stories at the turn into the common era rather than on their writing, I include stories about births of late Second Temple figures not recorded until somewhat later, as well as stories like this one about Hebrew Bible figures first recorded in late Second Temple times. The stories are drawn from various Pseudepigrapha (11), the New Testament (10), Josephus (2), the Babylonian Talmud (1), Midrashim (1) and Targums (1). I would appreciate hearing about other Jewish birth prophecy stories stemming from the Maccabean to Bar Kokhba times.

aspects of narrative inquiry from research in education, oral tradition analysis from folklore studies, and social memory theory from sociology and anthropology. My aim is to determine what these stories can tell about the social world of Jewish women in the early Roman Empire.

Narrative inquiry was developed in Canada to overcome the reductionism of quantitative analysis in the study of school education. D. Jean Clandinin and F. Michael Connelly write up their research as a detailed narrative of intensive teaching experiences in intercultural urban contexts. Here multiple approaches are attempted, some with ambiguous results, and colleagues' and students' participation is enlisted throughout. Rather than providing impersonal conclusions supported by statistically significant data, they give access to questions that arise within complex situations. Narrative inquiry recognizes that the frameworks which scholars bring to their study are determining factors that shape what can be seen and require attention and critique. Therefore these researchers tell how their own study began, developed and ended, putting their social setting and the research process, methods and human interactions at the center of the story.

To begin this paper as a narrative inquiry—although I cannot do the approach justice here—I recognize that I am a triple outsider in the methods I will use, being trained on the coasts of the U.S. in literary and historical study of early Christian texts—not in education, folklore or anthropology. Even within literary and historical fields I transgress in that I did not specialize in Second Temple Judaism, but I found my texts in large part embedded there. Nor in my day were we trained in Women's Studies, but I found my texts in large parts built by men from women's stories. From this position out on more than one limb, I became practical and reached for whatever methods might work.

Folklore studies provided me the initial approach to analyze the 129 Early Jewish stories which I translated in *Holy Lives, Holy Deaths*. Its subtitle, *A Close Hearing of Early Jewish Storytellers*, shows that my ear was tuned for the way these stories were essentially speech. Their literary settings provided a kind of vestigial performance context in which the writing storyteller could be heard, though without sound or sight. At the same time each story pointed to a range of more complete performance contexts, perceptible on the one hand in the story's sequence and primary themes (which I call text) and, on the other, in its speech characteristics such as syntax, diction, rhythm, and direct discourse (which I call texture). This identification of a story's text and texture as pointers to its storytelling contexts, which I adapted from an early article by Alan Dundes (Wire: 8–11; see Dundes), is close to the distinction made by social memory theorists James Fentress and Chris Wickham between the semantic and sensory ways in which a society remembers its traditions

(28–36). They note that sequences and configurations can be encoded in writing as semantic memory (text), but at the most basic level human identity is shaped by the sounds and sights of sensory memory (texture), especially the patterns that are repeated in story, song and ritual.

I had been collecting early Jewish stories to learn who had told them and why they did so, with particular interest in possible access to women's voices and purposes. I found signs that each kind of story I gathered had been told by several different groups with their own distinct aims. There seemed to be four general reasons for storytelling: assertion of what is not commonly known; celebration of something everyone acknowledges; confirmation of what is contested; and legitimation of what is disparaged. These functions not only showed the speaker's stance, but also the kind of context that provoked the story: listeners are expected to be informed or taken aback at an assertion; willing or even eager for a celebration; doubtful, if not opposed, at a confirmation; and somehow dissociated from institutions and practices being legitimated. The birth prophecy stories had no single function, but showed traces of transmission from three groups—most clearly writers who used them largely for confirmation and/or legitimation, groups including women who turned them to celebration in pilgrimage or festival songs, and women giving birth or assisting in birth who prophesied life against death.

The major weaknesses of this study—to pick up the narrative of my research—were, for one, my relative isolation from others studying oral traditions in these texts, though reading could orient me to past study and several experts gave feedback in translation. Also significant was my steep learning curve in the classical and Jewish sources, not to mention how two thousand years have sifted our sources down to a few tailings and put the live performances altogether beyond reach.

What turns me toward social memory theory at this point—in addition to the chance to work with others in a group reading cross-culturally—is the growing awareness that stories do not carry the culture alone. Were the stories even one of two, three or ten repositories of tradition, what I learn from the stories could simply be tossed in with other people's findings from monuments or rituals to get the whole cultural stew. But the stories are integral to the whole of the remembered past and cannot be understood at all without, for example, the times and places they are told, which involve certain physical arrangements and human roles that are the clues to what matters and who counts. Even beyond the performance context of its stories, the daily life and recurrent events of a community reflect long-standing practices and values. No part of this cultural whole can be understood in isolation, no matter how intangible this kind of life-encompassing context remains.

I am attracted to social memory studies because it takes on the task of understanding how societies shape and reshape the whole picture they have of who they are and what they are about—their complex cultural scripts and grand narratives. You who practice this method call it "social memory," apparently because you expect that the present is conceived in terms of a somehow remembered past—itself a question here in twenty-first-century California. But under Fentress and Wickham's stipulation that "memory is not merely retrospective; it is prospective as well" (51), social memory study may be the right conversation in which to inquire how a practice of telling birth prophecy stories about future liberators functioned for their tellers and hearers. Specifically, I will ask how readers of Scripture and leaders of communities took part in this process, what village and temple singers contributed, and how new mothers, midwives and family members at birth had cultivated a genre for this.

I see my potential contribution to social memory studies to be of two kinds. First, by applying its insights to a very specific group of stories from one broad culture, I can test what the general theory contributes to more focused research. Second, I will ask if these birth prophecy stories limit us to speaking strictly of their separate functions for distinct social groups, or if such telling can be said to have mobilized a general confidence in past liberations prophesied at birth, which could raise the society's expectations of liberators to come. Granted that, as Halbwachs said, individual perceptions always appear in a configuration of the whole (1992:49–53), is the configuration distinct for each group that tells these stories or does it merge into a common tradition at certain times and places? Were there factors here that elevated personal or family memories into social memories which helped to sustain a culture against alien forces and generate new life forms within it? In terms of narrative inquiry, my challenge will be to take this early Jewish "oikotype" (Ben Amos, 1982; Fentress and Wickham: 74)—this way of speaking called birth prophecy stories which I have identified using a folklore analysis—and risk bringing it into conversation with people studying social memory in other settings. I do this in order to propose some functions of these stories within the framework of Jewish social memory at that time—without obscuring the fact that this is also a project within the shifting framework of a Christian woman's social memory today.

We must begin by reaching back, recognizing that early Jewish birth prophecies cultivate an ancient Israelite genre preserved in celebrations of its progenitors' struggles to survive and thrive in a harsh land by God's help. So Gen 5:29 says that Lamech names his son Noah ("rest" or "relief"): "Out of the ground that the Lord has cursed, this one will bring relief from our work and from the toil of our hands." Emblematic of all such prophecies in Scripture is the angel's message to Abraham, who has been promised offspring in old age as the stars of the sky and the sand of the sea: "Your wife Sarah shall bear you a son, and you shall call his name Isaac ("he laughs"). I will establish my covenant with him as an everlasting covenant" (Gen 17:19). But these brief etymologies of the ancestors' names play a minor role in the corpus of Israel's epic story and diminish markedly after the Genesis narratives.

It is in the period of the late Second Temple, extending from the Maccabees as far as Bar Kokhba—the time called early Judaism because the rabbis were cultivating the oral Torah that became Judaism's access to the written Torah—that the birth prophecy genre apparently came into flower. Elijah, who first appears in Scripture at the moment he speaks God's message to King Ahab (1 Kgs 17:1), is now given the birth story above that tells his mother's fiery vision of glowing figures that wrap him in fire and feed him flames. This account not only encapsulates in its final sentence his scriptural life story from fiery Mt. Carmel to fiery chariot, but it presents the angel's words that he will be Israel's light and judgment and manifests them in the vision of fire (Wire: 66–73).

This birth story of Elijah from *The Lives of the Prophets,* a perhaps first-century Jewish listing of the prophets' origins and burial sites, is followed by an account of Elisha's birth, at which the golden calf in Gilgal bellowed so loudly that it was heard in Jerusalem, signifying the end of Israel's molten gods. These nonscriptural stories about Scripture's two great miracle-working prophets make no distinction between biblical text and interpretation, suggesting that Scripture and story are both known orally. It is the prophets themselves, rather than the Bible, that are considered authoritative, and the storytellers who carry their traditions reach back to the prophets' births for visions appropriate to prefigure such deeds. The birth prophecy genre not only dramatizes the stories, but locates these prophets within the grand narrative of God's providence that ensures leaders will be born to fit every need of Israel for protection and discipline.

Where tradition already provided the storyteller a birth narrative, as for Moses, new prophecy stories came to be added:

The spirit of God fell on Miriam at night.
And she saw a dream
and she recounted it to her parents that morning saying
"I saw [a dream] this night
and look! a man was standing there in linen clothing!
And he said to me
'Go and say to your parents
"Look! What is born from you will be thrown out in the water.
In the same way water will be dried up through him.
And I will do signs by him

and I will save my people
and he himself holds leadership always." ' "
And when Miriam recounted her dream
her parents did not believe her.
(L.A.B. 9.10; Wire: 46)

Here a quote inside a quote inside a quote causes no confusion when the storyteller speaks first as the girl telling her vision, then as the man appearing to her, and finally as God addressing her parents through them both. If the prophecy of Elijah comes in fire, Moses' prophecy comes in water, from the bulrushes to the reed sea. Were there more time for storytelling, no doubt the speaker would fit in an account of water at the well for Zipporah, water in the Nile turned to blood, or water in the desert from the rock.

Stories are created about yet earlier prophecies given by Abraham's great grandmother and Noah's great grandfather and on back to Cain's mother Eve, who is visited by the angel Michael (L.A.B. 4.11; 1 En. 106. 1–18; L.A.E. 21; Wire: 27–30, 38–39). In each case the child's role is signified and the future is shown to proceed according to God's provision for Israel.

But not only patriarchal and antediluvian times inspire stories. They are also told about first century C.E. figures:

At this time Helena Queen of the Adiabenes and her son Izates changed their life to take on the customs of the Jews for this reason. Monobazus King of Adiabene who had the name Bazaeus, succumbing to desire for his sister Helena, was carried away by the relation into marriage and made her pregnant. And once when he was lying with her and resting his hand on his wife's stomach when she had fallen asleep, he thought he heard some voice commanding him to take his hand from her womb and not to constrict the baby in it, who by God's providence would experience both a fortunate beginning and a like ending. Shaken by the voice, he immediately woke up his wife and told her these things, and he named the son Izates (genius).... (Ant. 20.17–21; Wire: 74–76)

The story can still be heard through Josephus's prolix style, and he goes on to tell, in many more pages, how Izates and his mother become Jewish proselytes and patrons. In spite of Izates's circumcision, his people accept him as king at his father's death, perhaps with help from his mother's story of the God of Israel speaking in a Gentile bed. Not only kings but contemporary prophets were being celebrated through stories of their births—John the Baptist, whose father Zechariah was struck dumb in the temple for doubting Gabriel's prophecy, and Jesus of Nazareth, whose mother Mary praised God for her news from Gabriel (Luke 1:5–36).

But why did early Jewish storytellers turn their skills to birth prophecy accounts? It cannot be explained simply by the popularity of birth prodigies in the Greco-Roman world, since Jewish stories do not have the usual prodigy motifs of the god or snake mating with the mother, followed by signs in the heavens among the birds, clouds and planets (with the exception of Matthew's star of Bethlehem). It is the political events being prophesied that best indicate why the early Jewish birth stories are told. In the story of Miriam above, God says through the angel, "I will do signs by him and I will save my people, and he himself holds leadership always" (*L.A.B.* 9.10). In another story God speaks to Moses' father in a dream: "He will free the Hebrew people from the oppression of the Egyptians, and he will be remembered as long as the universe lasts, not only by the Hebrew people but also by foreigners" (*Ant.* 2.216; Wire: 47). The angel says to Samson's mother Eluma, "As [God] himself said, he will free Israel from the hand of the Philistines" (*L.A.B.* 42.3; Wire: 55). Hannah says in her praise to God:

> Drip, my breasts, and tell your testimony,
> because it is ordained for you to nurse.
> For he who is nursed by you will be established
> and the people will be illuminated by his words
> and he will make known to the nations their limits
> and his horn will be greatly exalted.
> (*L.A.B.* 51.3; Wire: 60).

Simeon holds the infant Jesus of Nazareth and prays:

> Now, master, release your servant in peace according to your word
> for my eyes have seen your deliverance
> which you have prepared before the face of all the people,
> a light for revelation of the Gentiles
> and the glory of your people Israel.
> (Luke 2:29–32; Wire: 87)

The consistent message of these prophecies is that God will deliver Israel from its enemies through the newborn child, and will reestablish among the nations the glory of Israel and the praise of God. Many predictions end with the promise that this new rule will last from age to age. The social context is unmistakably Roman imperial occupation of Israel and the exploitation of its people under what must have seemed an endless series of violent Herodian and Roman rulers. Whether the Jewish stories tell past birth prophesies that God fulfilled when they escaped from Egypt and took possession of the land, or they tell recent prophecies about to be fulfilled, they celebrate that God has provided liberators and assert that God will continue to provide. They prophesy not just a moment of respite, but a prophet who "will be a light to this nation for a long time," or a patriarch whose offspring "will be multiplied forever" (*L.A.B.* 51.7; 4:9; Wire: 61, 39). God's deliverance is described in traditional images of military victories and kings enthroned so that the exact hopes of the present are not specified, yet there are no signs that apocalypse is anticipated. The newborn child is expected somehow to lead Israel out of foreign occupation and into a time of independence and dignity.

In other accounts the focus is less on overcoming foreign powers than on cleansing the earth, as suits Noah's story:

> And this child that was born will be left to survive
> and his three children will be saved when those on earth have died.
> And he will wean the earth of the corruption that is in it.
> (*1 En.* 106.16–18; Wire: 30)

Or the child will be the one who judges and purifies Israel. Of Elijah it is said, "He will judge Israel with sword and with fire." (*Liv. Pro.* 21). And at Melchizedek's birth God is quoted as saying:

> He will be to me a priest of priests forever—Melchizedek.
> And I will sanctify [him]
> and I will make him into a great people serving me.
> (*2 En.* 71; Wire: 36)

And the angel says to Joseph of Bethlehem:

> Joseph, son of David, do not be afraid to take Mary as your wife
> since what is born in her is from the holy spirit.
> And she will bear a son
> and you will call his name Jesus
> because he will save his people from their sins.
> (Matt 1:20–21; Wire: 86)

The specific benefit to Israel is only suggested in Elijah's giving a verdict, Melchizedek's restoring the priesthood and Jesus' saving Israel from its sins. But in any case this child or his progeny is expected to overcome the corruption in which Israel is held and usher in a time of justice and peace.

So when we ask who told these stories and in what contexts, and how broad their impact was in early Jewish social memory, we can begin with the writers we read and the circles they came from. Because the stories they told are only loosely connected to Scripture, they betray the writer's scribal interest in interpreting written texts when a story is used to explain the Torah or Prophets. Matthew says that the birth of Jesus occurred in order to fulfill Isaiah's prophecy of a son named Emmanuel (Matt 1:22–23; Isa 7:14; Wire: 86). The rabbis tell a birth prophecy story to explain why Scripture says that Miriam watched over her brother Moses in the basket and why she danced with her tambourine when Pharoah's chariots and horsemen were drowned in the sea—namely, to confirm that her prophecy had been fulfilled:

And Miriam the woman prophet, the sister of Aaron
took [a tambourine in her hand. . . .][2]
The sister of Aaron and not the sister of Moses?
Rabbi Amram said Rab said
but some said that Rabbi Nachman said Rab said
"It teaches that she prophesied
when she was [only] the sister of Aaron
and she said
'It is destined for my mother to bear a son
who will be the savior of Israel.'

And on the day that she bore Moses
the whole house was filled with light.
Her father stood up
and he kissed her on her head.
He said to her
'My daughter, your prophecy is established!'

And on the day they threw him into the river
her father stood up
and he slapped her on her head.
He said to her
'My daughter, where is your prophecy?'"

It is this that is written
And his sister placed herself at a distance
to know what would be done with him
to know what would be the outcome of her prophecy.
(*Sotah* 12b–13a; Exod 15:20; 2:4; Wire: 50–51)

Here the Scripture that calls Miriam a woman prophet and Aaron's sister when she dances at the sea is explained by bringing in a story of her

---

2. Phrases from the Hebrew Scripture are italicized for purposes of comparison, and in this case extended a few words to show the context referred to.

prophesying salvation before her younger brother's birth. Another Scripture confirms the story by explaining how, in spite of her father's
unbelief, she stands watch over the exposed child to know her prophecy
is fulfilled. So the scriptural narrative is traced from fulfillment at the sea
back to prophecy at birth, and from this prophecy forward through the
bulrushes toward fulfillment, linking past and future in an iconic Scriptural frame. The celebration at the sea becomes an assertion that God has,
does, and will fulfill women's birth prophecies.

In addition to these stories that interpret words of Scripture, birth
prophecy stories with multiple functions are found in the apocalyptic text
of *1 Enoch,* the priestly text of *Jubilees,* the historian Josephus, the retellers
of Scripture writing in *Biblical Antiquities,* as well as in a popular list of
prophets' burial places, in sectarian Gospels and in Targums, the Talmud
and Midrashim. Though not dominating any kind of text, or even frequent anywhere, the spread of attestation is significant. It says that
writers across Palestinian Judaism knew such stories and occasionally
found reason to include one or two in a text. Yet although many kinds of
early Jewish writers knew birth prophecy stories, this is not sufficient
witness that these stories had a widespread place in early Jewish social
memory because the literate were at that time only a small fraction of the
population—likely not more than five percent in the Roman East and virtually all male (see Harris).

But a second setting of early Jewish birth prophecy storytelling
points beyond this circle and suggests that the literate were hearing these
stories from the wider population. One-fourth of the stories I could locate
refer explicitly to song or include what appear to be praises sung to God
after the child's birth, a fact that suggests some musical transmission of
these stories. The account above of Miriam singing at the Red Sea to celebrate the fulfillment of her prophecy does not include the song she sings.
Rather it explains her reason for singing one of the oldest and best-known
songs in Scripture:

> Sing to the Lord for he has triumphed gloriously!
> The horse and his rider he has thrown into the sea!
> (Exod 15:20–21, cf. 1–18)

Mary's Magnificat and the prayer of Simeon celebrate Jesus' birth
and predict his work (Luke 1:46–55; 2:29–32; Wire: 84, 87). Though Luke
is not explicit that these were sung, their rhythm, parallelism and themes
of praise suggest it. The same applies to Zechariah's blessing of God for
his son John after he regains his voice and is filled with the Holy Spirit
(Luke 1:67–79; Wire: 79), and probably also applies to Elizabeth's blessing
of Mary (Luke 1:42–45; Wire: 83). The practice of birth prophecy songs of

praise could help explain why Luke's Gospel—which seems to begin as a musical—does not sustain the genre.

Best known among Scriptural birth prophecy praises, the song of Hannah is rendered in two very different early Jewish stories. In *Biblical Antiquities*, the woman who was once silenced by taunts and insults bursts out in pages of challenge and prophecy:

> "Speak, speak, Hannah, and refuse to be silent!
> Sing praises, daughter of Batuel, for your miracles that God has done with you.
>
> Who is Hannah that a prophet comes from her?
> And who is Batuel's daughter that she has borne a light for the peoples? . . .
>
> Look! the word has been fulfilled
> and the prophecy has come to be!"

The text ends with the pilgrimage setting of the song:

> *And they departed* from there
> and they gained ground with delight
> rejoicing and exulting in heart
> at all the glory God had done with them.
> And the people went down in unison to Shiloh
> with tympanies and dances
> lutes and lyres
> and they came to Eli the priest, offering him Samuel.
> (*L.A.B.* 51:6–7; 1 Sam 2:11 LXX; Wire: 60–61)

Yet more striking is the song of Hannah in *Targum Jonathan of the Former Prophets.* The three passages, in which this targum departs significantly from the Hebrew text it is translating, are all hymns that must have been so well known it was impious to omit them: the song of Deborah, the song of Hannah, and the song of David (*Tg. Neb.* Judg 5; 1 Sam 2:1–10; 2 Sam 22:2–23:7).[3] After Hannah predicts release from the Philistines in the time of her son Samuel, she foresees her fourteen great-great-grandsons singing and playing harps as Levites in the sanctuary. She goes on to predict, in detail, God's revenge against Assyria, Babylon, and Greece and ends by extending her prophecies into the speaker's recent past and even the future:

> Concerning the sons of Haman she prophesied and said

---

3. Harrington and Saldarini note the unusually innovative nature of these three songs in the Aramaic text but make no proposal about possible reasons for this.

"Those who were satiated with bread and were swelling in plenty and were spreading out in wealth have become poor.
They went back to hiring themselves out for bread—food for the hole.
Mordecai and Esther who were thin became rich and forgot their poverty.
They went back to being free people.
So Jerusalem who was like a sterile wife
is destined to be filled with her people of exile.
And Rome which was filled with great numbers of people—
its military camps will be gone and it will be captured and it will be burned."
(*Tg. Neb.* 1 Sam 2:5)

The singing of birth prophecies—whether in village settings, on pilgrimages to Jerusalem, or this one possibly in the temple by Levites—attests that birth prophecy stories were known in much broader circles than the literate. Their function was clearly celebrative, and unless Hannah's story was adapted by the Levites, such singing would have been informal and, we would assume, include women's voices. Yet because mixed male and female song is not widely attested in traditional societies, a gender-specific genre should be considered. In this collection of stories, other than Luke's attribution of birth celebration songs to Zechariah and Simeon—perhaps to balance male and female stories of annunciation and of blessing—all the songs are sung by women—in Luke by Mary and Elizabeth, in *Biblical Antiquities* and the *Targum of the Former Prophets* by Hannah, and in the *Babylonian Talmud* by Miriam. This fact points toward a setting in early Jewish community life parallel to the funerary setting of the lament and the return-from-war setting of the victory song—that is, in a specific context where women's singing had developed a distinct genre. This context could be the announcement of birth to the men of a family, or the presentation of a child at circumcision, or the journey to the sanctuary for offerings, as suggested in Mary and Joseph's temple visit in Luke or in Hannah's song from *Biblical Antiquities* above ("they gained ground with delight, rejoicing and exulting"). These songs would be heard by literate people and reflected in their written celebrations.

Beyond public celebrations in writing and song, a third location where these birth prophecy stories give signs of being at home is among women, and specifically women in the setting of giving birth. Although some scholars have proposed that Luke adapted the birth canticles about John the Baptist and Jesus directly from the Septuagint song of Hannah, the wide variety and distribution of early Jewish birth prophecy stories makes simple literary dependence unlikely. Writers may go back to Hannah's story, but because no two ways of telling it are alike—whether about Hannah or other mothers of the people—the storytelling has apparently left the page and come to life in those who are engaging each other's hopes and fears with new tellings.

The particular ways in which women appear in these stories point to them as the active storytellers. In the first place, most of the stories I was able to locate either tell the mother's prophecy, dream or vision, or that of a female relative (Wire: passim). Several stories tell of a father's or a male relative's experience, but in three of these cases he wakes up his wife immediately to make it a common problem, or she is the one who receives the power to conceive, or she is the one who praises God (Wire: 28–30, 33–37, 42–44, 47, 74, 76–79, 86). The strong focus on the woman's role does not exclude male tellers who want to dramatize a birth, but then one might expect the role of the prophet would shift to men in the family, and in fact this shift can be seen occurring in different accounts of a birth or in the manuscript traditions of some stories (Wire: 41, 42 n. 18, 72, 87).

Second, many of the details in the narratives are drawn from the physical experience of women for whom birth is their most life-threatening and life-giving event. To speak this way would not be an easy imaginative leap for male storytellers in a society where men are excluded from the birth process. The inability to get pregnant is a crisis that Eluma blames on her husband. A child leaping inside Elizabeth's womb begins the prophecy of John the Baptist. The long delay of Cain's birth is a trauma broken only when Eve receives the angel Michael. The gentle labor of Jochabele that "did her no violence" confirms faith in the prophecy about Moses. And the dripping breasts of Hannah are her witnesses that God has answered her prayer (Wire: 54, 83, 27, 47, 60). Each step in the mother's physical experience of birth is given meaning from prophecy.

Third, though a few stories dramatize the birth crisis as a father's problem—Lamech, Nir and Joseph are each sure that the child is not his (Wire: 28–30, 33–37, 86)—most stories are absorbed in women's social problems. Barrenness is especially highlighted, but also abuse, pregnancy before marriage, difficulty in birth and threats to the child. Women not only survive to tell the tale, but they exhibit remarkable persistence against the disbelief of parents, husbands and priests (Wire: 46, 51, 54–56, 58). The woman is the protagonist, even the heroine, whether the story ends with her buried "in bright and splendid garments" or leading a procession of people "with tympanies and dances, lutes and lyres" (2 En. 71; L.A.B. 51:7; Wire: 35, 61).

Finally, the stories as a whole may point to women tellers in the exorbitant delight in the newborn child. Whether the child appears as an angel or as a boy dressed from birth in priestly garments, he is all that could be dreamed of in perfection (Wire: 90–92, 35). Of Noah it is said:

when the child was born
the body was whiter than snow
and redder than a rose,
the hair all white, as white as wool
and woolly thick and glorious.
And when he opened his eyes
the house lit up like the sun!
And he stood up from the midwife's hands
and he opened his mouth and praised the Lord.
(1 En. 106.2–3)

The story of the birth of Rabbi Ishmael, the high priest and martyr, shows that lavish praise of the child is not curbed by any concern about offending the father:

They said about Rabbi Ishmael the high priest
that he was one of the seven most beautiful people
who were in the world
and his face was the image of an angel of the Lord of Hosts.
When most of the days of Rabbi Yose his father were spent
his wife had said to him
"My lord, my man
what is this that I see?
Many people succeed in their progeny
but we have not succeeded in having children
since we have no heir, son or daughter."
Rabbi Yose said
"This happens for them because they guard themselves
[this ought to say: their wives (guard themselves)]
when they leave the bathhouse.
If something should meet them that is not fitting
they go back to the bath
and they bathe a second time
and because of this they succeed in their progeny."
And she said to him
"If this is the thing that obstructs
look! I will take on being strict in these very things."

And when she went to the bath
and she left the bath house
a single dog met her.
She went back and bathed a second time.
[A camel] met her.
She went back and bathed
until (she went back and bathed) eighty times.
The Holy One Blessed Be He said to Gabriel

"The righteous woman takes great pains.
Go and appear to her in the image of her husband."
Immediately Gabriel left
and he went and sat at the entrance of the bath house
and he appeared to her in the image of Rabbi Yose her husband
and he grasped her and carried her to her house.
And the same night she became pregnant with Rabbi Ishmael.
And he was made beautiful in countenance
and beautiful in appearance
in the image of Gabriel.
(*Midrash on the Ten Martyrs;* Wire: 90–92)

From these indications of early Jewish women storytellers, extending through the Second Temple period and beyond, I propose a practice of women telling each other birth prophecy stories in the days before and after birth. Social memory theory identifies such a circle of people in a specific context as a "framework of memory." The framework in this case is shaped by people who stand at the culminating point of their social impact and physical danger. As they wait for hours and days until the child's arrival, they recall for each other births which were turning points in their people's history. The message is not only that the mother and child survived the ordeal, a boon in itself, but that a prophecy or vision revealed the promise of this child to save the people—a promise proven true in well-known subsequent events.

Whether these stories of the past are being repeated from previous tellings or are being generated out of pieces in Scripture or legend, they will reflect in some way the setting in which they are being told—such as the plight of the mother, the family or the people—in order to give encouragement and a challenge to see beyond the crisis. Something said by the mother or grandmother before, during or after the birth may become the seed of a prophecy connected to this child, so that a new story begins to take shape. It asserts this live birth in a time of many deaths, and it projects the significance of this birth for the people's future. The child is forseen as the one who will save his people, in Rabbi Ishmael's case through his martyrdom, which will atone for Joseph's brothers selling Joseph into Egypt. In this way, women of a community name their children as Israel's hope for liberation from alien peoples and values. When such prophecies are realized in subsequent events—not a common thing!—the stories become threads for weaving the framework of memory, commemorations that are available to help people survive in hard times and to encourage a vision from the next mother who waits for a child.

But to what extent do the birth prophecy stories rise above the way specific groups use them for their common purposes of assertion, celebration, confirmation or legitimation and become a culturally unifying social memory that speaks for a people? I have shown how, as we trace the stories back from their writers' purposes to their use in song, and their apparent place in birth settings, that the circle of tellers widens, ending in a group—women present at birth—that over time may encompass half of Israel's population. We see here the three major modes of commemorative activity traced by social memory theory: the transmission of oral texts, commemorative ritual, and writing. Through the women's storytelling, their birth announcement or pilgrimage songs, and the writers' many kinds of texts, the circle of those who know these stories in some form ripples wider and wider.

Once they know the story, they can adapt it for whatever purposes they choose, and we see women asserting life against death, women joined by others celebrating hope in song, and writers confirming their faith in God and legitimating their communities. Have the stories, then, no social function that can bind together the distinct frameworks of memory where they are cultivated? Most of the story is flexible, but the nature of the prophecies is such that the child is always proclaimed to be the good fortune of the people. This emphasis does not change. While specific contexts and tellings differ, the stories are taken by everyone as the people's history, asserting its hopes. This broad application means that the stories make their claim beyond any one group's purpose. It may be immaterial whether this aspect of the story arises from the fact that Jewish birth stories are always positive, or from the fact that the situation of Israel under Roman occupation was always negative. One could say that it is the long-standing oppression of Israel by succeeding empires that keeps these prophecies focused on reclaiming the people's freedom and integrity, making the stories not just one writer's tirade, or even women's history, but the social memory of Israel. Or one could say that, whatever the social context, a birth is new life, and its story draws everyone in to join this family's joy. In any case, each telling involves a memory of a past joyful promise, and a persistent waiting in the present sadness for the people's future rebirth.

At this point I am faced with the question of whether I can hear these stories as history, or whether they are mythology. Are they fact or fiction? Some social memory theorists, beginning with Halbwachs, are called "presentists" because they stress that present needs shape a culture's memories, while others remind them that it is nonetheless the past that is remembered (Halbwachs 1992:49–53; cf. Burke; Schudson 1989; Coser; Kirk's introductory essay to this volume). My very act of collecting stories of one kind may seem to line me up in the presentist camp, since the stories are treated as a type that might reproduce itself in appropriate settings, regardless of events. And miraculous elements in many stories further compromise their credibility to the modern ear.

But the claim of the prophets, and of Paul of Tarsus, to have been chosen "from my mother's womb," is witness to some practice in Israel of mothers making predictions about God's purposes with their newborn children (Isa 49:1, 5; Jer 1:5; Gal 1:15). Since such a prophecy or account of a vision cannot readily be falsified, I suggest that it is best respected as a family tradition, in which accuracy in detail is not as much the point as credibility of the speaker, and of the God in whose name the prediction is spoken. Most important, the prophecies that have survived matter because they have been fulfilled in real time, or are expected to be fulfilled so as to change the life of a violated people. In order to understand these stories we have to hear them as they are told, not as fables for teaching or as fantasies for entertainment, but as legends in the technical sense—that is, as accounts of past events with lasting significance for a people: as social memory.

THE MEMORY OF VIOLENCE
AND THE DEATH OF JESUS IN Q

Alan Kirk

Jesus' death frequently is treated in scholarship as a theological reification. Because Q seems to feature comparatively little theological reflection on Jesus' death, it is often suggested that allusions to Jesus' death in Q have a secondary status in the materials and that Jesus' death played a marginal role in the worldview of the so-called Q community. We will attempt to overcome the limits of this perspective by recovering the nature of Jesus' crucifixion as fundamentally an act of ritualized violence that had a formative rippling effect upon the memory of the group that had aligned itself with him, an effect that ultimately issued in the emergence of Q itself as a commemorative artifact.[1]

VIOLENCE AND MEMORY

Violent events become engraved in the collective memory of the group affected. Roy Rosenzweig and David Thelen report the frequency of the visits of Oglala Sioux to "such places as the Wounded Knee massacre site, Crazy Horse Mountain ... " (164–65). The experience of violence is "an injury, a wound, or an assault on social life as it is known and understood" (Neal: 4). It brings about a social disruption, a rupture with what has gone before so significant that it leads to commemorative activities crucial for a group's subsequent identity formation and moral repristination (Malkki: 58–59; Farmer: 119; Wagner-Pacifici: 301–9). As such it takes on archetypal significance within the collective memory with enormous capacity to shape group perceptions (Neal: 6–7). The Wounded Knee massacre, for example, "is a shaping force in the lives of

---

1. As described programmatically in the introductory essay to this volume, memory theory assesses the semantic interaction between a community's sacralized pasts and present social realities in contexts of commemoration. Readers should refer to the introductory essay to place the present essay in its methodological context.

almost all the Sioux residents of Pine Ridge reservation" (Rosenzweig and Thelen: 172).

Liisa Malkki draws attention to the "social imagination of violence ... both in the perpetration and in the telling" (293), referring to cases in which violence is a symbolically encoded, sociopolitical act. Torturous deaths—such as crucifixion was—can be highly symbolized forms of violence, with the disfiguring, distending, dismembering, smashing, and perforation of the human body routinized and choreographed to display and enact publicly the socially degraded status of the victim. Malkki states with regard to the 1972 genocide of Hutu in Burundi:

> Hearing scores of accounts of cumbersome, difficult mutilation and killing, the listener eventually begins to become numb to their horror and to ask grimly practical questions. For instance: Would the process of killing tens or hundreds of thousands of Hutu not have been more efficiently pursued with guns and bullets? ... "This death, they [the Tutsi] said, is not designated for the Hutu." The meaning of an "honorable" or "normal" death was brought up by many, and it was generally believed that the Tutsi considered Hutu unworthy of bullets. (96)

Hutu were frequently murdered with sharpened bamboo poles thrust from anus to head or vagina to head. "In the case of both men and women, the narratives suggest, a systematic connection was made between the vagina or anus and the head through the penetration of bamboo poles.... such connections did not appear haphazard or accidental. Rather, they seem to have operated through certain routinized symbolic schemes of nightmarish cruelty" (92). It hardly needs to be spelled out how crucifixion was an exhibitionist act of political violence of precisely this sort.

Violent acts freighted with symbolism of this kind are taken up and find their *symbolic inversion* in the "social imagination"—the memory—of the group affected. To return to Malkki's analysis of the operations of memory in Hutu refugee camps:

> The accounts of the atrocity, remembered and retold, themselves become acutely meaningful themes in the mythico-history [Malkki's term for commemorative narrative].... they had been incorporated into the overarching moral order expressed in the mythico-history. The stories of atrocity thus stand as ordering stories at an extraordinary level.... acts of atrocity are not only enacted and perpetrated symbolically; they are also, after the fact, stylized or narratively constituted symbolically. (95)

In this way the traumatic experience of violence comes to inscribe itself upon the collective memory in the form of what George Bonnano refers to as a "nuclear script"—that is, a cognitive schema that fundamentally

organizes memory, supplies group orientation, and exerts a determinative effect upon perception and interpretation of subsequent experience
(179–82). To use Michael Schudson's terminology, it takes on the dimensions of a "'pre-emptive metaphor,' a past, traumatic experience so
compelling that it forces itself as the frame for understanding new experiences" (1989:167; see also Schwartz 2000:225).

The experience of violence is *commemorated*, and in this way it is
etched into the social memory. Tel Aviv "commemorated Rabin by
changing the name of the square ... to Rabin Square and erecting a monument on the spot where he was killed" (Peri: 121). Commemoration of
the S.S. massacre in the French village Oradour-sur-Glane "entailed
establishing monuments and commemorative rituals in the interest of
shaping memory for the long term" (Farmer: 60). Violence poses a particularly difficult challenge to the hermeneutical impulse that drives all
commemoration, because of the massively disruptive and disorienting
effect of violence upon the affected community. It generates a sense of
fragmentation, of the disintegration of a moral and social order previously experienced as stable and routine (Neal: 4–22). In this crisis
context, commemorative activities represent the exertion of strenuous
effort to restore moral coherence and social continuity by working out
the *meaning* of violence suffered, "the desperately needed understanding
of what had occurred" (Yerushalmi 1982:38). In the face-to-face discourse of the group affected (Malkki: 105; Namer 1987:154) the events at
stake are forged into a "master commemorative narrative" (Y. Zerubavel
1995:7), a memorial artifact in its own right, or to revert to Malkki's term,
"mythico-historical reconstruction" (244). The commemorative narrative
thus fashioned becomes a "set piece" in the group's memory. "The facts
of the atrocity [at Oradour-sur-Glane] ... form the heart of the commemorative narrative ... the story of the horrific events of 10 June was
recounted to visitors to the ruins and to French children at school.... It
became a set piece.... the complexity of the historical context ... over
time, was pared away to produce a simple tale of French innocence violated by Nazi barbarism" (Farmer: 29). Engraved in the social memory, it
acts as a cognitive script definitive for the group's self-understanding,
for interpretation of its perceptions of reality, and for defining itself as a
moral community: "The mythico-history of the Hutu past in Burundi
serve[s] as a paradigmatic model and interpretive device for giving
meaning to and acting upon the socio-political present of the refugee
camp" (Malkki: 105; see also Neal: 22).

The *martyrdom* script lies ready at hand as a kind of conceptual
master narrative for interpreting, and hence mastering, acts of violence
inflicted with encoded social and political meanings. The massacre at
Oradour-sur-Glane gained the status of an "archetypal atrocity" (Farmer:

58), and the town "became France's *village martyr* (martyred village), a testament to French suffering.... stand[ing] for the ultimate victimization of innocent French people" (Farmer: 1–2). Jews that perished in the Rhineland during the first Crusade for refusal to convert, along with victims of later pogroms, were commemorated in martyrologies (*Memorbücher*) for "the catastrophe simply could not be explained by the stock notion of punishment for sin, for the Ashkenazic communities of the Rhineland were holy communities, as their own response to the crisis had demonstrated" (Yerushalmi 1982:38–39, 46).

The invoking of an existing cultural script—for example, martyrdom—to fix the meaning of, and give narrative coherence to, the specific experience of violence brings us into touch with the central dynamic of social memory: its interpretive "keying" (Schwartz 2000:225–32), or "analogic mapping" (Malkki: 121), of the experiences of the present with salient events of the past that exist as semantically dense *Erinnerungsfiguren* (J. Assmann 1992:52), or "frame images" (Schwartz 1998a), and occupy secure niches in the cultural memory. This memorializing activity (*Erinnerungsarbeit*) becomes particularly pronounced—it "spikes"—in the face of crisis and calamity, as the community urgently ransacks the archetypal past for images that might explain and give meaning to the tragic, or otherwise deeply troubling, present (Schwartz 1998a:7–8; 1996a; J. Assmann 1992:254; see also Yerushalmi 1982:38; Prager: 219; Peri: 113). Keying to cultural memory images and scripts renders such experiences intelligible, and so counters the threat of moral and social anomie, by associating them with established normative patterns and sacred narratives. Yerushalmi states that "there is a pronounced tendency [in medieval Jewish chronicles] to subsume even major new events to familiar archetypes, for even the most terrible events are somehow less terrifying when viewed within old patterns rather than in their bewildering specificity" (1982:36).

A few examples will suffice to illustrate the "keying" work of memory. On 11 November 1945, De Gaulle brought into Paris coffins of fifteen people who had perished "in the most recent conflict" and had them "solemnly transported ... to the Arc de Triomphe, and soldiers laid them around the Tomb of the Unknown Soldier [from WWI]" (Farmer: 6–7). "Moments after President John F. Kennedy was buried in Arlington National Cemetery, a black limousine pulled up to the Lincoln Memorial. The two people inside sat silently for ten minutes, gazing at the memorial and thinking about the image inside. Scanning the past for images to make sense of their grief, Bobby and Jackie Kennedy had found Abraham Lincoln" (Schwartz 2000:ix). A poster from World War II connects two images: Lincoln writing his letter of consolation to Mrs. Bixby in the early 1860s, and soldiers dying in the early 1940s. "So conceived, Lincoln is not so much a historical object as a historical symbol under which the calamities of the present are subsumed and interpreted" (Schwartz 1998a:7). As these examples indicate, keying is hermeneutical activity in which denominators common to the present event in question and the image from the salient past are perceived, and accordingly come to illuminate one another (Peri: 113). Some connected Rabin's assassination with Kennedy's and thereby "expressed the feeling that this was the assassination of a hero who embodied the hope for a new future," while the political left compared it with "the 1933 assassination of the leader of the Labor Party, Haim Arlozorov," a keying which "served the left in its claim that political murders are the province of the [political] right in Israel" (Peri: 114)—hermeneutical maneuvers, moreover, that illustrate social memory's entanglement in political struggles and social conflict. Keying as a semantic transaction masters a distressing event; it gives it intelligibility, coherence, meaning, and narrative integration with the sacred past. Just as critically, it engineers that event's consolidation into structured memory—its metamorphosis in its own right into an evocative memory image (Schwartz 2000:231; see also Prager: 4; Fentress and Wickham: 73–74; Neal: 6–7, 22).[2]

KILLED PROPHETS AND MARTYRS IN Q

We now turn to apply this analytical approach to Q, with our initial point of entry the passage in 11:47–51:

> [47]Woe to you, for you build the tombs of the prophets, but your forefathers killed them. [48]Thus you witness against yourselves that you are the sons of your forefathers. [49]Therefore also Wisdom said, I will send them prophets and sages, and some of them they will kill and persecute [50]so that a settling of accounts for the blood of all the prophets poured out from the founding of the world may be required of this generation, [51]from the blood of Abel to the blood of Zechariah, murdered between

---

2. Part of the problem with the Holocaust, by contrast, lies in the lack of precedents in the cultural memory of Jewish suffering that might bestow meaning upon it. Memory is a process of linking to cultural narratives to give meaning to events. In the case of the Holocaust, no such memory scripts are available, and memorialization falters. Vera Schwarz states, "The Creator is always testing the Jewish people, testing Abraham, testing Isaac and, finally, testing Job. . . . But in the death camps, the possibility of dialogue vanished. There can be no 'test' of the Holocaust. What lingers after Auschwitz is simply the shock–effect of a brutal, experienced reality, the throbbing trace of an event. . . . It leaves in its wake nothing but stammering speech and a wounded imagination. . . . [Primo] Levi reaffirmed the power of memory words. Returning to the language of Genesis, he described the madness of the war years as *tohu–vavohu* (unformed and void)" (80–81).

the sacrificial altar and the House. Yes, I tell you, an accounting will be required from this generation![3]

The passage bristles with interpretive difficulties. We will focus upon analysis of commemorative keying as a formative feature of the excerpt.

Killed Prophets

This oracle is the climax of the catena of Woes that began with 11:39. In the Woes, a prophetic-speech genre (accusation), Jesus accuses those addressed of injustice, impurity, and venality. In 11:47–48, the accusation shifts suddenly to the topic of killing prophets. This culminating woe in turn shifts to the prophetic oracle of judgment in 11:49–51, which thrice makes reference to the killing of the prophets and the righteous. What accounts for the sequence at this point shifting from the classic prophetic impurity and immorality charges to the insinuated association of the addressees with killing of prophets, and in fact, to the grave pronouncement that an accounting for the blood of all the prophets is to be required of "this generation"? Scholarship on Q, notorious for its lack of consensus on many other matters, tends to converge in the view that the oracle is in some manner making retrospective reference to Jesus' own violent death. The passage may be read on three intersecting planes. First, the scraps of narrative detail in the Q 11 materials leading up to and culminating in the woe and oracle—materials characterized by aggressive challenges to Jesus' prophetic credentials issuing from hostile interlocutors—establish a setting contemporary with Jesus. At the level of its dramatic presentation of Jesus' own speech, therefore, the oracle projects a premonition of mortal danger. Second, Q, brought together after Jesus' activities and demise, inevitably adopts a perspective on that career and death. Thus these verses refract their "living" subject through the prism of the convictions Q displays with respect to his life and death. That Jesus' own death is encompassed by the oracle is corroborated by the introduction of Abel and Zechariah, who likewise suffered violent deaths, for this coheres with the practice in the preceding sections of Q of associating Jesus with exemplary figures of Israelite epic. Finally, the passage reflects the identity of the successor community, that is, its own self-understanding of likewise being threatened by, if not actually subjected to, the experience of violent persecution.[4] This sense of imminent threat is confirmed by the

---

3. From *The Critical Edition of Q* (eds. James M. Robinson; Paul Hoffmann; John S. Kloppenborg; Minneapolis: Fortress, 2000).

4. An interpretive problem is whether Wisdom's oracle is wholly retrospective—that is, looks back over an epic history of sending and rejection, a history culminating in "this

immediately adjoining "martyr-paraenesis" of Q 12:2–12 (Schröter 1997:355–58; see also Kirk: 203–14).[5]

The oracle displays the hallmark operations of commemorative keying. The prophets, and the violent deaths of the prophets, held a secure place as *Erinnerungsfiguren* in the cultural memory of ancient Judaism. A memory script, that is, an iterative sacred narrative, incorporated this deaths-of-the-prophets motif, namely, the pattern according to which Israel chronically rejects the prophets God sends to call her to repentance. The oracle maps an analogy between Jesus' violent death and the deaths of the prophets, and accordingly appropriates the deuteronomistic cultural script of sending and rejection for comprehending and interpreting this event.[6] This conflation of the present, or recent past, with the epic past to form a unified picture, is one of the most characteristic operations of social memory: "In the cultural memory of a group, these two planes of the past are pushed together in a seamless manner" (J. Assmann 1992:49–50; see also Lowenthal 1985:250; Fentress and Wickham: 115; Schwartz 1998a). "The present [Hutu refugee camp context] was incorporated quite continuously and cumulatively into the mythico-historical discourse describing the past in Burundi—just as the past was, in a sense, inserted into the present. Thus, significant contemporary events of daily life in the camp were transformed into mythico-historical events" (Malkki: 106). Q 11:47–51 does not merely establish the death of the righteous messengers as a term of comparison for Jesus' death; rather, it integrates the death of Jesus into the sweep of that sacred narrative, in fact as its climactic episode.[7]

---

generation" and, presumably, its rejection of Jesus—or whether the successor community numbers itself in the line of those prophets and sages, inclusive of Jesus, commissioned by Wisdom and subjected to rejection and death. These two possibilities likely are not mutually exclusive: the boundary between the killing of Jesus and then, in a sequel, his followers, is in this case blurred. We might say that the violence, perceived or real, hanging over the affiliated community is the rippling aftershock from the killing of Jesus. Both are signs of condemnation of "this generation."

5. We see that martyr-paraenesis (12:2–12) follows directly upon the introduction of the martyr motif in reference to Jesus' death (11:47–51). This is a wholly intelligible macro-sequence that can only be put down to Q composition.

6. A contemporary example is Zionist commemoration of Joseph Trumpeldor, an early settler who died defending the Tel Hai settlement: "The oral and written literature about Trumpeldor often created a link between him and the famous Jewish heroes of Antiquity" (Y. Zerubavel 1994:109).

7. In a similar manner, the "frame image" described by Schwartz—a World War II poster "depicting contemporary soldiers parading before George Washington's bedraggled troops at Valley Forge (the low point of the Revolution)"—"gave meaning to current military difficulties by defining them as momentary episodes in a longer narrative" (Schwartz

In the face of the disruptive event of Jesus' violent death at the hands of political elites, the affiliated group looks to the past, that is, to ancient Judaism's cultural memory of the violent fate of the prophets, to find its bearings. By this means the disturbing experience of violence is given meaning, and thereby an important step is taken toward mastering it. This commemorative operation, semantically nourished by the rich streams of ancient Jewish memory, simultaneously subjects Jesus' death to metamorphosis into memory, that is, it gives it coherence, shape, and elevated status as a durable, semantically dense *Erinnerungsfigur* in its own right in the memory of the commemorating group. Its integration as an episode in the sacred narrative of the sending and rejection of the prophets, the already-existing cultural memory script, or, as Valensi would put it, its being "harmonized with the great tradition" (289), is also crucial to its anchoring in memory, whence it can exert ongoing effects upon the life and identity of the commemorating group. Commemorative keying weaves Jesus' violent death—if left uncommemorated like countless other Roman crucifixions a passing, unmarked event—into the long tapestry of memory (see Simondon: 98).

Formatively at work in this project commemorating violent death is the agonistic *politics* of memory, a contest over the memory of Jesus taking place within an ongoing situation of at least latently violent social conflict (see Scott: 385–88). Corresponding to its torturous, degrading disfigurement of the human body, crucifixion was a form of symbolically weighted imperial violence that attempted, if not to subject to oblivion, at least to degrade and dishonor publicly the memory and status of its victims, if remembered at all remembered as discarded social deviants. That Jesus died at the hands of Romans, whereas the epic connection with Zechariah in particular evokes intra-Israel conflict, has little bearing.

1998:13–14). Y. Zerubavel states that "the pilgrimage [to Masada] introduces a *mythical temporal framework* [emphasis added] that fuses into a single representation the Hasmoneans' revolt, the defense of Masada, and the modern Zionist's struggle for liberation" (1995:126). Namer has a fascinating description of this phenomenon shaping 1945 commemorations in France, as the French sought to come to terms with the troubling events of World War II by integrating them into the grand narrative of national memory: "On the morning of April 2, the French army was fêted, and then the journey along the parade route began, setting out from the *Invalides* (Louis XIV, Napoléon). It passed by l'Etoile, then stopped before the statue of Clémenceau. The itinerary of the procession functioned to link these commemorative sites together into a unity. It symbolized the entire history of France and at the same time the continuity of the war from 1914 to 1944. *The route actualized successive commemorative sites in quite the same way as a verbal recitation moves from word to word [L'itinéraire actualise des lieux de commémoration successifs tout comme le dire d'un récit va de mot en mot]*" (1987:204–5, emphasis original).

Native elites were incorporated, if ambiguously, into the imperial system. Q 11:47–51 contests the memory of Jesus. It integrates him, precisely in virtue of his violent death, into the epic memory tapestry of Israel. With the same commemorative maneuver the group passes a moral judgment on Jesus' death, and, accordingly, aggressively attacks the moral legitimacy of its opponents, the Romans and their local elite clients who were responsible for executing Jesus. Far from the latter being guardians of the sacred social and moral order, in a breathtaking status reversal they are analogically mapped to those elites in Israel's sacred narrative who killed God's messengers, the prophets.

Martyr

Q 11:47–51 depicts Jesus' death as the rejection of a prophet, but also, keying to a cognate script in ancient Judaism's cultural memory, as the killing of a righteous man. The latter ascription, no less than the former, is an aggressive commemorative strategy responding to Jesus' degradation and death. Abel, who was not a prophet, and Zechariah epitomize the righteous who are unjustly killed. Kloppenborg points out that "what is common to the two figures is the fact that innocent blood was shed" (145).[8] The killing of Zechariah is recounted in 2 Chr 24 and then finds midrashic development in rabbinic sources, where it is fitted into a sequence with other martyrs viewed as prophets (Halpern Amaru: 169). The pragmatic effect of the story in rabbinic sources was to offer assurance that the violent deaths of rabbis, successors of the prophets and priests, would not go unavenged (Halpern Amaru: 178–79; Blank: 341). Accordingly, in rabbinic usage the appearance of the story marks a commemorative response to painful deaths and tragedies of calamitous proportions. A genealogical, though not direct, relationship between the Q and rabbinic versions of the Zechariah story is likely—both specify the innermost court as the location of the killing—but cannot be demonstrated. Nevertheless the rabbinic and Q versions function homologously in as much as they are brought to bear upon catastrophically violent events.

The appearance of martyr motifs is a reliable indicator that a commemorative response to violence is underway; they are a memorializing reverberation of traumatic events that have shaken a community. The keying of Jesus to archetypal martyrs in the cultural memory is evidence

---

8. Wisdom of Solomon 10:3b depicts Abel as a murder victim, not an early envoy of Wisdom. Zechariah was a prophet, but the 2 Chr 24 narrative, as well as rabbinic retellings, concentrate on his murder.

of a concern to transform the horrific public stigma attaching to the exe-cuted person, and by extension to the identity of the affiliated group. Moreover, like the "death of the prophets" motif, it constitutes an indictment: those who sit in judgment—tyrants who break the bodies and spill the blood of the innocent—are themselves judged guilty. The martyr claim promulgated by evocation of Abel and Zechariah reverses guilt ascriptions in a manner that renders the dominant order itself guilty.[9] If asserted publicly it constitutes a frontal attack on the authori-ties, opening a new chapter in a struggle over social and moral legitimacy.

Jesus' Death and Moral Exhortation in Q

With the appearance of martyr scripts applied to Jesus we enter into *normative memory;* that is, we observe the essential connection between commemoration and moral exhortation. Group-constitutive norms are immanent in memories of foundational persons and events (Halbwachs 1992:59; Schwartz 1998a:8–9; J. Assmann 1992:16–17; 2000:127–28; Malkki: 53–54). It is by virtue of its normativity that the past makes program-matic, urgent moral claims upon a community (J. Assmann 1992:76–80; Schwartz 2000:xi, 304). Deaths of significant persons summon forth com-memorative activities focused upon the virtues these individuals embodied in life and in their death. Martyrs, by definition heroic persons killed because of steadfast commitment to a set of emblematic virtues, attract intense cults of commemoration. A violent death, commemorated as a martyr's death, itself is instrumental in establishing the urgent nor-mative claims of the virtues the person embodied and died exemplifying, and in mobilizing a social movement cohering around those norms (Y. Zerubavel 1995:148–54). Commemorative narratives coalescing out of the experience of violence aspire to be far more than mere records of events for posterity. Rather, bound up in the transfor-mation into commemorative narrative is the indelible infusion of constituent events and personae with categorical moral meanings. Thereby such narratives, raised to culture-constitutive status, become "moral ordering stories on a cosmological level" (Malkki: 244); they are "most centrally concerned with the reconstitution of a *moral order* of the world" (56). This is to say that they comprehensively organize reality in moral terms and constitute the commemorating community as a

---

9. Likewise a formative feature of the adjoining "martyr–paraenesis" Q 12:2–12 (see Kirk: 203–14).

"moral community" (53–55, 73). This operation is particularly crucial in the wake of violence, for violence seems to shatter the moral order of the world.

Commemoration of salient persons and events therefore entails inculcation of emblematic norms. The Greek funeral speech contained paraenetic elements: "The anonymous and collective homage of the *logos épitaphios* unfolded in accordance with precise roles of composition: exordium, encomium (ἐπαίνεσις), exhortation (παραίνεσις), and consolation (παραμυθία)" (Simondon: 101). The same is true of funerary epigrams: "It is this [paraenetic] dimension of collective memory that gives to funerary epigrams their commemorative value, even when it's a matter of private inscriptions that celebrate merits other than martial ἀρετή, for example, the justice and the wisdom (δικαιοσύνη and σωφροσύνη) of Sosinos of Gortyne ... or again, the σοφία of a physician" (Simondon: 100). It is through inculcation of its distinctive norms that a community incorporates its members and subjects them to moral formation (J. Assmann 2000:17; Y. Zerubavel 1994:111; 1995:28, 44; Ben Yehuda: 238–39). The normative dimension of social memory is, accordingly, brought to bear in a community's various educational *Sitze im Leben*, distilled into various commemorative artifacts—the instructional, paraenetic genres and media appropriate to the socialization goals of those settings (Schwartz 2000:249; Y. Zerubavel 1995:138–42; J. Assmann 1992:141–42; 2000:127). One may, then, speak of a synergistic connection that exists between *commemorative* and *instructional* activities. A community's ritualized activities commemorating martyrs, accordingly, become opportunities not just for narrative recitations of the martyr's life and death, but also for instructional artifacts and activities aimed at inculcating and securing commitment to those emblematic norms (Y. Zerubavel 1995:28–29, 41, 91, 108, 148; Malkki: 53–54; Connerton: 43).

Recitational and instructional impulses that converge around cults of collective commemoration find expression in respectively differentiated genres. Jan Assmann captures this aptly with his rubric *Formative* and *Normative Texte*. *Formative Texte* refer to narrative genres, that is, foundational histories and myths, whose retellings integrate the community into the sweep of a sacred narrative, and *Normative Texte* refer to instructional genres calibrated to inculcate the cognate norms. "Normative texts codify the norms of social behavior; here belongs everything from individual proverbs, to Wisdom literature, to the Shulhan Aruch [a medieval Talmud epitome]," while to formative texts "belongs everything from tribal myths, to sagas of origins, to Homer and Virgil" (J. Assmann 2000:127). These are not mutually exclusive generic categories; in a given text one will predominate, thus positioning it toward either the narrative or instructional pole, but elements of the other will likely be found to some degree (J. Assmann 2000:127; see also 1992:16–17, 141–42).[10]

Assmann's model has implications for our understanding of Q and the location we assign it in emergent Christianity. In terms of its determinative genre profile, Q is an instructional text, which is to say its definitive components are Jesus' ethos-defining teachings (see Kloppenborg; Kirk).[11] Q's *commemorative* focus on Jesus' violent death in 11:47–51 coheres with its overall pragmatic focus upon *moral exhortation* covering multiple topoi, for we have seen the necessary, even generative connection that exists between the two. The joint appearance of these elements in Q should no longer perplex us, and positing social-history, redaction-history shifts to account for it hardly seems necessary. We also are in a position, invoking Assmann's rubric of *Formative* and *Normative* texts, to assess the meagerness of narrative elements in Q compared to its richness in various genres of moral exhortation. We recall that commemorative ritual, narrative recitation, and moral formation through paraenesis are constellated activities, various dimensions of the group-constitutive enterprise (see Halbwachs 1992:223–24; Y. Zerubavel 1995:94, 138–40; Ben Yehuda: 135–36, 152; Malkki: 53–54). This range of commemorative activities requires respectively differentiated genres, clustering around the *Formative* and *Normative* poles. Q is positioned toward the *Normative* end of the spectrum. Narrative recedes in Q because of its genre-specific commitment to the social task of moral formation, of inculcating norms; nevertheless we have seen that Q coalesces around the memory of Jesus' violent death, commemorating it in an idiom appropriate to its genre and pragmatic task.

An illuminating comparison is the symbiotic relationship that exists between sacred narrative (*Geschichte*) and Law (*Gesetz*) in the commemorative tradition of the Hebrew Bible:

> The imperative, "Remember!" has reference to two realms, each of which are equally binding: the laws of the Covenant, which are to be observed in all circumstances and in all their details, and the history, which founded and grounded these laws. The laws receive their meaning on account of the history [of deliverance from Egypt]. Only the person who does not forget the flight from Egypt knows that the Law

---

10. "Knowledge of the sort that defines social identity encompasses two quite different complexes, that can be comprehended under the categories 'Wisdom' and 'Myth'"(J. Assmann 1992:141).

11. Others also come to this conclusion. Horsley and Draper argue that Q is, as regards genre, a prophetic text, but acknowledge the significant presence therein of "covenant instruction" (206–7, 233–35).

signifies freedom, and is able to follow it. In fact, all communities live within the bounds of foundational stories, from which they draw the ordering and direction of their actions. (J. Assmann 1992:296)

We have seen that commemorative narratives, particularly those arising out of the experience of violence, are "concerned with *order* in a fundamental, cosmological sense.... with the ordering and reordering of social and political categories, with the defining of self in distinction to other, with good and evil.... [with] the reconstitution of a *moral order* of the world" (Malkki: 56). Helmut Koester recognizes that the emergence of early Christianity's foundational story, grounded "in the actual suffering and death of the historical Jesus of Nazareth" and commemorated in eucharistic ritual, simultaneously brings into existence a new social and moral order that entails "new legislation." "As Augustus [in establishing his new order] had made recourse to the legislation of Caesar, the new community reached back to the words of Jesus as part of this legislation, especially the commandment of love, in which all the law and the prophets are summarized" (Koester: 349). Koester makes no reference to Q in this connection, but Q sets out in a series of instructions, reinforced with prophetic exhortations, the contours of a comprehensive moral and social order that, moreover, is anchored in its inaugural, programmatic "Love Your Enemies" paraenesis (6:27–35) and, as we have seen, is grounded in the memorializing, in Q 11, of Jesus' violent death.

It is therefore quite impossible to sustain the view that Q is representative of a distinct community, "the Q community," with little interest in Jesus' life and death, defined by its focused reverence for Jesus as a "sage," or, correspondingly, that Q, by virtue of its genre characteristics, bears witness to a distinct theological and social formation and accompanying trajectory in primitive Christianity. Q's low ratio of narrative to moral exhortation is largely a function of genre constraints, the functional role it plays in helping carry the moral-exhortation load at some site of early Christian commemoration (see Fentress and Wickham: 162; Yerushalmi 1982:14–15, 31–32, 45–46). These observations should not be construed as a denial of diversity in primitive Christianity's reconstructions of its salient past, as suggesting that Q's view of Jesus can be easily collapsed into the images emerging in other streams of early Christian tradition, or as suggesting that Q is a supplement to a Passion Narrative like that found in Mark. Comparative reconstruction of Q's commemoration of Jesus must, however, proceed on methodological grounds other than the questionable ones that more often than not have undergirded claims for Q's radical uniqueness in the context of early Christianity.

Q AS COMMEMORATIVE ARTIFACT

That Q aligns Jesus' death with the death of the prophets and coordinates it with the martyr framework is hardly an indicator that Q ascribes comparatively less importance to Jesus' death—a widespread view that seems to take the extensive space allotted the passion narrative in the Gospels as its dubious evaluative norm. On the contrary, the appearance of these motifs attests to the tremendous problem Jesus' violent death posed to the community that identified itself with him, as is evidenced by its invoking hermeneutical frameworks from Israel's epic past—Israel's cultural memory—to give meaning to and master it. Moreover, these frameworks are indicators of a political and social conflict, a struggle for control of the memory of Jesus' death, for this frameworking strategy is, in effect, an attempt to reverse the moral and social signification of Jesus' status-degrading death and to attribute culpability to that thin though powerful stratum of local elites, incorporated into the Roman order, responsible for his condemnation and execution.

Frame-imaging is the definitive feature of social memory, and we have found this dynamic operating within Q. Our analysis has largely concentrated on how Q keys Jesus' death to potent archetypal images existing in the cultural memory of ancient Judaism. The effect of this activity is to shape and transform Jesus' violent death into a durable *Erinnerungsfigur* in its own right, symbolically and hermeneutically potent, with a leading position in the emergent cultural memory of early Christianity. We see a group urgently at work retrieving and constructing its own salient past, and hence its distinct identity, within the flux of its Jewish cultural identity—an identity initially as unstable as the contested memory of Jesus himself (see Halbwachs 1992:202). We see Christian cultural memory in formation, "the quest for durability and identity within the flow and depth of time" (Assmann and Assmann 1988:34). As a group-constitutive *Erinnerungsfigur*, the death of Jesus comes available to act as a symbolic and moral resource for organizing and interpreting the community's new experiences, and for mobilizing the community to face fresh crises. Conversely, the present experiences of the community, harassed and facing at least the threat of violence (Q 12:2–12), act heuristically and reciprocally upon the resources its salient past makes available to it.

Might it be possible, therefore, to understand Q, taken as an integrated body of tradition, as an artifact of the formative effects of cultural memory? Assmann argues that the "crisis in collective remembering" that arises in the wake of a "breakdown in tradition" (*Traditionsbruch*) leads to articulation of memory in durable cultural artifacts and practices through, among other strategies, textual inscription (J. Assmann

1992:218–22; 2000:87–88; see the introductory essay to this volume). "*Traditionsbruch*" refers to the point of serious breakdown of "communicative memory"—in the case of emergent groups usually at the forty-year threshold—or, analogously, to any disruption or transformation on a scale to bring about the collapse of the usual communal supports for memory and, consequently, that suddenly problematize the group's immanent connections to its past, as well as the smooth functioning of usual forms of transmission. In such cases a community is confronted with loss of intimate connection to memory, and so, if it is not itself to dissolve along with its memory, it turns more intensively to writing as a means of stabilizing memory, of reworking connections to the past and of appropriating that past in a manner that responds to circumstances that may be drastically altered (J. Assmann 2000:87–88; 1992:165, 294).[12]

Accordingly, one way to account for Q in its documentary form is to locate its emergence at the point of breakdown of "communicative memory," that is, of the face-to-face, oral forms of transmission, that begins to occur at approximately the forty-year threshold, a breakdown that may well have been exacerbated by other forms of crisis. We can easily understand the need for codification of the community's constitutive norms in such circumstances, a codification that not only looks to the past, but reconstitutes the group in response to the exigencies of its contemporary situation.

We must not overlook, however, that for the social life of the group identified with him the violent death of Jesus itself would have constituted a massive rupture on the scale that Assmann associates with the appearance of concentrated cultural memory activities. Death taken by itself has this effect: Assmann notes that "the most original form, so to speak the primal experience of that break between Yesterday and Today, in which the decision between disappearance or preservation forces itself as an issue, is death. Only with its end, with its radical discontinuousness, does a life obtain that form of pastness upon which a culture of remembrance can be built" (J. Assmann 1992:33). The dimension of violence magnifies the sense of rupture, of an absolute separation from the past, of the sort that leads to the commemorative activities crucial to a

---

12. Assmann invokes deportation and exile to illustrate this problem: "Deportation signified in the world of that time the end of collective identity. With the loss of the homeland all the necessary frameworks of collective remembering collapsed, the connective structures of the culture tore apart, and the deported community disappeared without a trace into its new surroundings" (1992:294). This crisis leads to the production of Torah as a written artifact.

community's reconstitution and moral repristination. For the Hutu the violence they experienced in Burundi:

> represented an end or a culmination in the mythico-history insofar as "the past" that lived in Burundi stopped at the moment of flight. In a strictly chronological sense, of course, the refugees' years of exile in Tanzania ... were also "the past," but for them, these years lay on the opposite side of a great historical divide from the premassacre years.... the flight from the homeland marked a moment of fundamental transition, a crossing of multiple borders—spatial, social, and symbolic. (Malkki: 58–59; see also Farmer: 119; Neal: 61)

The death of Jesus, through political violence, would bring about the sort of radically altered situation, dissolution of previous group frameworks, and discontinuity from all that had gone before such that if the community were to survive it would need to reconstitute its memory, and with the same stroke the coherence of its own social and moral identity, in the context of intense commemorative activities. We have seen that a crucial element of this project is supplying the violent events themselves with moral intelligibility and integrating them into the community's story. In this scenario the community takes up Jesus' ethical teachings, places them in the new framework of the postdeath situation, aligns them with the reality of Jesus' violent death, gives them fresh, stabilizing connections with Israel's cultural memory, and thereby reconstitutes itself as a moral community centered on commemoration of Jesus, a commemoration that becomes the *"Mythomotorik"* driving its historical development.

It is hardly necessary to choose between the first (later shift from communicative to cultural memory) and the second (coalescing of commemoratively focused traditions of moral exhortation hard upon Jesus' death) scenarios. In both cases cultural memory dynamics are at work. It is possible with the latter scenario to posit the emergence of Q as a coherent body of oral tradition, with the factors associated with the former scenario contributing to its ultimate emergence as written artifact. Taking this view allows us to account for Q's investment in the past—its manifest nucleation around commemoration of Jesus' death—but also for the fact that it represents a living tradition of moral exhortation with ongoing vitality in the historical development of early Christian communities.

READING THE *GOSPEL OF THOMAS* AS A REPOSITORY
OF EARLY CHRISTIAN COMMUNAL MEMORY

April D. DeConick

In cultures where literacy is minimal and an oral consciousness dominates, the dominant power of the mind is memory (Ong 1982:36). This memory includes not only individual memory, but also social or communal memory, as I prefer to call it. Communal memory is "the shared dimension of remembering" (Zelizer: 214), the group's "remembered history" (Lewis: 11–12). As such, it transcends the individual or personal sphere to include a community's literature, art, sanctuaries, ruins, place-names, holidays, relics, rituals, and so on (Schwartz 2000:9). It is literally the "repository of tradition" (Halbwachs 1980:78).

The nature of communal memory—its characteristics and tendencies—is particularly important for scholars of early Christianity to consider when reading and interpreting the literature produced by these ancient people. Most prominent is the tendency of communal memory *to depend on shared frames of references within a culture as it thrives on remaking the past into a history with contemporaneous meaning* (Zelizer: 228). Communal memory does not simply retrieve, recall, or preserve past traditions and historical experiences. Nor does it invent new traditions or history out of thin air, or offer completely distorted fabrications of it (Appadurai: 20). Rather, communal memory tends to reconfigure the past—its traditions and historical experiences—to make it conform to the present experiences and future expectations of the group (Hutton 1988:314).

These retrospective reconstructions of the past are largely achieved by adapting old traditions and historical facts to the beliefs and spiritual needs of the contemporary group (Halbwachs 1992:199). Remembrances are "pieced together like a mosaic" (Zelizer: 224), representing not the sum total of what actually happened, but fragments of the past that have been

---

* I wish to thank Illinois Wesleyan University for supporting the completion of this article with a generous grant. The ideas presented here are discussed and developed more fully in my book, *Recovering the Original Gospel of Thomas: A History of the Gospel and Its Growth* (London: T&T Clark, 2005), especially chapters 1, 6, 7 and 9.

rearranged and reconnected into a new interpretative framework, resulting in an "original" picture that aligns the contemporary community with its past experiences and its future expectations. For the historian of early Christian history and literature, therefore, issues such as historical accuracy and authenticity are best set aside. Replacing them are other issues like communal identity, membership, authority, experience, interaction, and so forth. The issue for the scholar shifts from investigating how accurately a text depicts what actually happened to why a particular group of Christians constructed its memories in a particular way at a particular time (Zelizer: 217; Thelen: 1125).

Although the process of re-creating the past is ongoing for a community, *the process is particularly responsive to societal, political, cultural, and religious pressures exerted on a group* (Bodnar 1989:1201–21). The community's experiences of pressure cause memories of its past to "confront each other, intermingle, fuse, or erase each other" (Wachtel: 216–17). In such cases a "memory crisis" has ensued, threatening the present's connection with its past (Terdiman: 3). In response, the community generally will transform or shift its traditions (Shils: 213). This response is mitigative in that it is intended to relieve the pressure originally exerted on the group while maintaining its connection with the past. The shifting of a community's traditions is the consequence of the fact that its memory is grounded in the past, present, and future simultaneously. Memory formations are not static but dynamic, and tied into the everchanging present. To remember is not to re-collect, but to reconstruct, to conform constantly the presentation of the past to shifts in social morphology and situation, to pressures exerted on a group (Namer 1987:53; Halbwachs 1992: 40). As internal and external factors change, communal memory—the repository of a group's traditions—is continually subjected to renovation in both gradual and sudden ways (J. Assmann 1992: 41–42).

Study of the *Gospel of Thomas*, it seems to me, would particularly benefit from an analysis informed by theories of social memory, since so much of previous scholarship on this text has been tied to using it to recover the historical words and message of Jesus.[1] Since the sayings of

---

1. J. Schröter is the only other scholar of whom I am aware that has applied social memory studies to the *Gospel of Thomas* (see 1997). He limited his application to the foundational work of Aleida and Jan Assmann. Schröter proposed that Mark, Quelle, and *Thomas* should be understood as "remembrance phenomena." The Jesus traditions within these texts, he says, represent early Christian reflection on the past, rather than the transmission of authentic historical Jesus material. He argues that Mark, Quelle, and *Thomas* reflect three ways of remembering Jesus, ways that steered the process of selection and interpretation of the traditions. *Thomas*'s "remembrance" of Jesus is identified by Schröter as occurring in the post-synoptic phase of early Christianity and as most similar to the remembrance of the

Thomas, according to these scholars, present us with a picture of a proverbial Jesus uninterested in issues of eschatology, like cosmic destruction, God's judgment, and the establishment of a new world, some scholars questing after the historical Jesus have discovered in *Thomas* a Jesus who is a philosophical humanist, a sage for all ages.[2] Although some of these scholars have regarded a few of the more esoteric sayings as later, perhaps representing protognostic or gnostic traditions, they generally have viewed the *Gospel of Thomas* as an early Christian text which has not been tampered with by proponents of cross theology or apocalyptic destruction, since the *Gospel of Thomas* is silent when it comes to cross theology and apocalyptic Son of Man sayings (see especially Cameron 1994; 1996; 1999).

If communal memory, however, operates as studies have shown, this perspective on *Thomas* is wholly at fault. It would *not* mean that the sayings in *Thomas* represent the words or perspective of the historical Jesus, sayings largely unadulterated by later Christian doctrines. To the contrary, it would mean that *they represent an accumulation and reinterpretation of remembrances of Jesus' words which have been accommodated to the present experiences of an early Christian community.* In this case, *Thomas* would be read as a repository of communal memory, containing not only early and later traditions, but also the reformulations of these traditions based on the contemporary experience of the community. Therefore, *a reconstruction of the community and its memory can be distilled if we first examine the*

Jesus tradition found in John, although much more ascetic and clearly on the path to Gnosticism. He thinks it essential methodologically to describe the place of the composition of *Thomas* through a comparative analysis with other early Christian texts while setting aside tradition-historical questions (1997:462–81). Because he has made this methodological move, separating comparative analysis from tradition-historical questions, he has not recognized either the lengthy evolution that this Gospel underwent or the early Jesus traditions within it—early traditions that have been overlaid with newer traditions or reinterpreted in response to shifting communal experiences and reformulations of communal memory.

2. Proponents of this view rely heavily on the work of Robinson and H. Koester in their pioneering volume, *Trajectories through Early Christianity.* This view is most dominant in American scholarship, particularly among those scholars who belong to the Jesus Seminar. For examples of this position, see Davies: 13–17; Crossan 1991:227–302; Cameron 1991; Patterson: 94–112; Funk: 121–39. J. W. Marshall has provided a "moderate" critique of this position in his article, "The Gospel of Thomas and the Cynic Jesus" (37–60). From his form-critical analysis of the "binary *logia*" and the kingdom sayings, he concludes that, although "the apocalyptic eschatology of Q2 and the Synoptics" is lacking in *Thomas,* some sayings reveal a redaction of "a future orientation and the theme of reversal" in the interest of a theology of unification (53). Although his analysis of *Thomas* reveals serious flaws in the picture that some scholars have painted of the Cynic Jesus, he offers no comprehensive explanation for how, when, or why this redactional shift was taken in *Thomas,* nor does he show awareness in his article of the extent of this shift.

issues raised in Thomas's *sayings, and then reflect on their use and reuse of traditional ideas and materials.* This approach is markedly different from the common one which first assumes a community for *Thomas*—whether it be gnostic, encratite, Jewish-Christian, sapiential, or otherwise—and then works to interpret *Thomas* and reconstruct its tradition or traditions on this basis.

If *Thomas* were read as a repository of communal memory, what would this reading tell us about early Christianity, and the Thomasine Christians in particular? Could we recover the pressures and experiences this community faced? Could we come to understand how this community reconfigured its past and transformed the earlier traditions that it had inherited? This rereading of *Thomas* is an enormous task and can not be fully addressed in the present format.[3] But a focused investigation into *Thomas*'s connection with apocalypticism seems to me to be an excellent place to concentrate because so many of the question and dialogue units in *Thomas* appear to be concerned with apocalyptic issues.

Why are these question and answer units so significant? Because the voice of the community is most audible in the secondary questions and introductory clauses posed by the disciples to Jesus. Far from representing historical dialogues that Jesus held with his disciples, these units are reconfigurations of older traditional sayings. By elaborating these older sayings into question-and-answer units and dialogues, the Christians enriched the meaning of the traditions for their present communities, aligning them with their contemporary memory. They provided these older traditional sayings with new contexts and interpretations. In this way, perplexing questions facing a community could be answered directly by Jesus in their Gospel. Polemic for opposing views could be supported by Jesus' words. Instruction about emerging ideas and practices could be addressed with Jesus' voice. The old traditions were made contemporary and, in the process, sanctified by Jesus.

As we will see, the results of such a rereading of *Thomas* challenges the current opinions expressed by many scholars that *Thomas* provides us with either an example of an early nonapocalyptic form of Christianity, a "wisdom" Christianity more true to the teachings of a proverbial Jesus, or an example of a later gnostic one, a form of Christianity that deviates from the teachings of Jesus. When we examine *Thomas* from this new perspective, we will discover that the sayings material in *Thomas*, which has been secondarily developed, has been reworked to

---

3. I undertake this task fully in my monograph, *Recovering the Original Gospel of Thomas: A History of the Gospel and Its Growth* (London: T&T Clark, 2005).

reformulate older apocalyptic traditions, shifting the ideology of the traditions away from an earlier eschatological emphasis to a mystical one. Although the focus of the present article is too narrow to discuss this process at length, the present analysis is accordant with my previous work on *Thomas*, suggesting that the reformulation of apocalyptic traditions appears to be the result of the Thomasine community reconfiguring an earlier form of their Gospel, the "kernel" *Thomas*, an old speech Gospel from Jerusalem much concerned about the imminent Eschaton and its demands (see DeConick 2002).

1. An Apocalyptic Memory Crisis

In the *Gospel of Thomas*, the community poses the following questions on the apocalyptic front:

> Tell us how our end will be. (18.1)
> Tell us what the kingdom of heaven is like. (20.1)
> Shall we then, as children, enter the kingdom? (22.3)
> When will you become revealed to us and when shall we see you? (37.1)
> When will the rest of the dead happen, and when will the new world come? (51.1)
> When will the kingdom come? (113.1)

These questions reveal substantial information about the Thomasine community. They are not simply rhetorical flourishes used to introduce some of Jesus' sayings in a collection, nor are they questions of curiosity on the part of the Thomasine Christians. They are serious mitigative questions raised by the community to confront some eschatological problem that faced the Thomasine Christians. In their Gospel, they have posed a series of questions in order to bring forward the community's resolution through Jesus' responses. What will the end be like? When is the kingdom going to come? What do we have to do to enter the kingdom? When will we see Jesus? When will the dead achieve their final rest? When will the new world, the kingdom of God, be established?

Why would a community of Christians pose these questions in their Gospel and not others? What do their questions reveal about the problems facing their community? Undoubtedly, the eschatological expectations originally held by community members had been seriously challenged. From their questions, it appears that the contemporary community members were wondering when and how God would fulfil his eschatological promises, a problem not unfamiliar to other early Christian communities in the mid-to-late first century. The Thomasine Christians were concerned that the end of the world, the establishment of the kingdom or the new world, the final rest of the dead, and the return of Jesus had not yet happened! They were a community in the middle of a memory crisis. Their traditional expectations were threatened by the reality of their present experience, the experience of the non-Event, when the kingdom did not come.

2. A Reconfiguration of Apocalyptic Expectations

The fact that these mitigative questions and their answers actually have accrued in their Gospel, however, indicates that enough time had passed in the community's memory without the fulfillment of their original expectations for the older traditions to be reconfigured and aligned with the community's new expectations. They had weathered the crisis by shifting their apocalyptic expectations. What transformation did their traditions undergo in the process? The answers they provide to the very questions they had posed in their Gospel is a logical place to start this inquiry:

Have you discovered, then, the beginning that you look for the end? For where the beginning is, there the end will be. Blessed is he who will stand in the beginning. He will know the end and will not taste death. (18.2–3)

It is like a mustard seed, the smallest of all seeds. But when it falls on tilled soil, it produces a great plant and becomes a shelter for birds of the air. (20.2–4)

When you make the two one, and when you make the inside like the outside and the outside like the inside, and the above like the below, and when you make the male and female one and the same, so that the male not be male nor the female female; and when you fashion eyes in place of an eye, and a hand in place of a hand, and a foot in place of a foot, and an image in place of an image, then you will enter [the kingdom]. (22.4–7)

When you disrobe without being ashamed and take up your garments and place them under your feet like little children and tread on them, then [you will see] the Son of the Living One, and you will not be afraid. (37.2–3)

What you look forward to has already come, but you do not recognize it. (51.2)

It will not come by waiting for it. It will not be a matter of saying, 'Here it is,' or 'There it is.' Rather, the kingdom of the Father is spread out upon the earth, and men do not see it. (113.2–4)

It is clear from this handful of mitigative responses that the community appears to have reacted to the disconfirmation in the three typical ways predicted by social psychologists for close-knit groups holding certain strong beliefs (see Festinger, Riecken, and Schachter; Hardyck and Braden). Disconfirmation will often lead groups to new hermeneutical levels since they develop explanatory schemes to rationalize the disconfirmation. The hermeneutic consists of demonstrating that "the disconfirming event was not disconfirmation but actually confirmation of their expectations" (Carroll: 126). The disconfirmation had only arisen in the first place, the group may conclude, because the group had not interpreted its traditions or Scripture properly. In fact, it is a normative move for a community to say that the group did not correctly understand the original tradition, text, or prediction.

This normative move is present in the Thomasine Gospel, where we can see the development of explanatory schemas to rationalize the disconfirmation, along with arguments that the disconfirmation really was not disconfirmation but misinterpretation on the part of the community. For instance, they insist that the end of the world had not come as they had expected. The members of the early community merely had misunderstood Jesus by "waiting" for the end to come or "looking forward" to a future event (*Gos. Thom.* 51, 113).

New explanatory schemes often give rise to new hermeneutics that the community designs to change its original cognitive holdings. The disconfirming experience can cause the group to reinterpret their baseline traditions or, conversely, their understanding of the contemporary events (Carroll: 110). This new hermeneutic determines how the tradition will be understood or the text read from then on.

In the case of *Thomas*, we can see a new apocalyptic hermeneutic replacing an older one. The community members maintained in their *responses* to the questions which they had posed that, indeed, their expectations had not actually been disconfirmed, but had been confirmed when the now "correct" hermeneutic was applied to the old traditions. So, in the responses to the questions, they posited that the kingdom had already been established on earth but no one had noticed its coming (*Gos. Thom.* 20, 51, 113). Did not their Gospel tell them that Jesus, in his lifetime, had taught that the kingdom already had begun to break into the world? It was like a tiny seed that had fallen unnoticed on tilled soil and now had grown into a large plant (*Gos. Thom.* 20). They concluded that the kingdom had continued to grow since Jesus' death. Now, at the present time—just as Jesus had predicted!—it had fully arrived on earth. The anticipated "rest" of the dead and the "new world" had "already come" (*Gos. Thom.* 51, 113). Since the kingdom was now spread out among them on the earth (*Gos. Thom.* 113), Jesus would be revealed to them immediately and directly (*Gos. Thom.* 37).

Such was the new apocalyptic hermeneutic that replaced the previous one. The community members, however, did not perceive this hermeneutic to be new; rather, they pereceived it as the correct hermeneutic through which Jesus' words should have been understood in the first place. The community members just had not previously recognized this fact (*Gos. Thom.* 51). This is a function of communal memory, to make the past relevant to the present experience of the group in a seamless way.

A community faced with disconfirming evidence may try to avoid references to it in the future, especially when the belief impinges on reality in a severe way. The community may attempt to create an environment or ideology that avoids the subject completely (Carroll: 93–94). Or the community may identify current events with past predictions or traditions, collapsing the expectations as it demonstrates their fulfillment in the present (114).

Such is the situation in the *Gospel of Thomas.* The community attempted to avoid further problems associated with future disconfirmation by collapsing its expectations in these question-and-answer units and dialogues, demonstrating the fulfillment of its expectations *in the present.* In this process, its hermeneutic shifted away from an eschatological interpretation of Jesus' sayings to a mystical one (DeConick 1996). The kingdom—the new world—was not a future event at all, but was realized in their community as the re-creation of the beginning of time before the fall of Adam. It was actualized by individual community members as they tried to transform their bodies into the utopian Adamic state of being through encratic performance—the immediate, rather than future, transformation of the human self into the image of God, the androgynous primordial Adam (*Gos. Thom.* 18, 22, 37). In such a paradisiacal community, visions of Jesus could be anticipated (*Gos. Thom.* 37).

Thus their interpretative revision shifted the apocalypse from an imminent cosmic event to an immanent personal mystical experience. As the new introduction to the old Gospel (*Gos. Thom.* 1) aptly states, "The person who finds the interpretation (*hermeneia*) of these sayings will not experience death." This hermeneutic was not some philosophical or intellectual explanation, but a mystical one. The believer was supposed to apprehend his or her divine Self and God by meditating on the sayings of Jesus in the Gospel and practicing the encratic ideal it honored.

This crisis in theology must have been very acute for the Thomasine Christians since the sayings tradition in *Thomas* appears to have been drastically reshaped in order to bring the sayings in line with the community's own experience of the non-Event and its shifting communal memories. In addition to this handful of mitigative question-and-answer units (*Gos. Thom.* 18, 20, 22, 37, 51, 113), we find a series of sayings that are best understood to be later accretions in the Gospel (DeConick 2002), serving similar mitigative functions. They directly address the problem of the delayed Eschaton by developing the concept of the *fully* present kingdom on earth (*Gos. Thom.* 3.1), speculating about the primordial Adam and the encratic ideal (*Gos. Thom.* 4, 11, 16, 19, 21, 23, 27.1, 49, 75, 85, 105, 110, 114), and shifting emphasis to the mystical dimension of apocalypticism, away from the eschatological dimension (*Gos. Thom.* 1, 3.4–5, 7, 19, 24, 28, 29, 38, 50, 56, 59,61, 67, 70, 77, 80, 83, 84, 85, 108, 111.3).

So their resolution appears to be a radical hemeneutic that revised the older eschatological traditions preserved in the kernel sayings 10, 11.1, 15, 16.1–3, 23.1, 35, 40, 57, 58, 60.1–5, 61.1, 64, 65, 68.1, 71, 74, 79, 81, 82, 98, 103, 107, 111.1. These older sayings appear to have been eschatological warnings about an impending cosmic destruction. In them, Jesus gives advice about how to prepare for the final day and God's judgment. The end times are described in these sayings as chaotic, a reversal of the status quo (11.1, 16.1–3, 35, 58, 60.1–5, 64, 65, 68.1, 71, 74, 79, 81, 82, 98, 103, 111.1). The only people to find relief will be the faithful few who are able to maintain their exclusive commitment to God and Jesus (10, 15, 23.1, 40, 57, 61.1, 82, 107). So imminent is the coming of God's kingdom that it is likened to a mustard seed which will soon become a big shrub (20.2–4) or a pinch of yeast which will soon leaven fine loaves (96). When these expectations of the community were threatened by the experience of the non-Event, these traditions underwent a hermeneutical shift within the communal memory, resulting in new material accruing in the Gospel—material that reinterpreted the old.

The accumulation of these sayings in the *Gospel of Thomas* suggests that the message of Jesus, which the community had retained over the years in their Gospel, experienced the type of incremental interpretative shift commonly occurring in traditions subjected to communal memory. As the eschatological coming of the kingdom of God came to be a non-Event, these Christians felt pressure to recast their original apocalyptic traditions. The future fulfillment of the eschatological promises of Jesus receded in favor of their present mystical reality. In other words, the temporal dimension of the apocalypticism of Jesus' message was collapsed, refocusing the community's apocalyptic hopes on the atemporal mystical dimension. The cumulative result of the remaking of the traditions was a shift away from understanding the apocalyptic traditions in eschatological terms.

3. A Hermeneutical Shift

The shift from eschatological to encratic and mystical is explicitly developed in the secondary question-and-answer unit (*Gos. Thom.* 37; see DeConick and Fossum). The question expresses concern, and perhaps even disappointment, that the imminent return of Jesus had not yet occurred. The community demands to know when this will happen:

> His disciples said, "When will you become revealed to us and when shall we see you?" Jesus said, "When you disrobe without being ashamed and take up your garments and place them under your feet like little children and tread on them, then [you will see] the Son of the Living One, and you will not be afraid."

The imagery in this secondary unit suggests that, at this time, the ideal conditions necessary to "see" Jesus were not perceived by the community to include the collapse of the world and the end of history. Rather the ideal condition is the state of each individual person. This ideal state is said to be that of a "child" who has renounced his body, returning to the prefall state of Adam when Adam was not afraid or ashamed to come into God's presence. Jesus will be revealed to the disciples when they, like children, remove their clothes and tread on them without shame or fear, an idea developing out of a certain exegesis of the Genesis story, particularly verses 2:25 and 3:7–10.

Here the community is describing a situation in which the eschatological vision of Jesus is now believed to be achievable in the present, particularly when the person renounces his or her body and becomes a "child" again in the Garden. This belief is an expression of an encratic ideal which also is expressed in the dialogue unit 22, and several other sayings that accrued in the Gospel (4.1, 16.4, 21.1–4, 23.2, 75, 114). In fact, in saying 37, achieving this ideal through the practice of celibacy is perceived to be a prerequisite to the vision of God. If a ritual practice is alluded to in this saying, it is likely from an analysis of the imagery that the community had anointing in mind, one of the initiatory rituals that the early Christians performed at baptism (see DeConick and Fossum). The community may have believed that the performance of the initiatory rituals combined with an encratic lifestyle prepared the human being for visionary experiences of God and his Son.

The mitigative response to the non-Event is quite pronounced in saying 38.2, where a rationalization of eschatological expectations is made:

> Jesus said, "Many times you have desired to hear these words which I am saying to you, and you have no one else to hear them from. *There will be days when you will look for me and will not find me.*" (38)

In this unit, the older saying of Jesus is appended with a startling *"new"* observation: "There will be days when you will look for me and will not find me!" This accretive clause serves to alleviate the disappointment of Jesus' nonappearance eschatologically, noting that Jesus had predicted this. Further, the clause alludes to the disappointment of failed mystical practices. The saying takes on a very practical problem that faces all mystics: there would be days that they sought direct experiences of God, desiring to hear his voice or gaze on his form, only to be faced with failure. In this way, the saying seems to appeal to the preceding saying (37), reminding the believer that even though Jesus did promise the encratite Christian a beatific vision of himself, this would not happen "on demand." The believers may desire this experience, just as they desire to hear Jesus' words. But as Jesus himself says, there will be times when it will not happen no matter how intense the believers' desire.

The quest for an ecstatic vision of God, a direct experience of the divine, is quite pronounced in saying 59, an accretion that clearly delineates the vision quest as a premortem experience—something that must be achieved during the believer's lifetime, rather than after death:

> Jesus said, "Look for the Living One while you are alive, lest you die and then seek to see him and you will be unable to see (him)." (59)

Wilhelm Bousset recognized this mystical distinction in his famous work, "Die Himmelsreise der Seele." He understood the ecstatic soul journey as one that occurs during the life of the performer, rather than after the body's death. He thought that such a mystic journey could anticipate the moment of death, but it had to be performed in the *present* if it was to bear the hallmark of mysticism (see Bousset). Saying 59 bears this very hallmark. Jesus commands his believers to seek visions of God before their own deaths. In fact, if the believers wait for postmortem visions, they will have waited too long and will suffer severe consequences. They will be denied the vision and its guarantee of immortality. This saying displays the telltale signs that this community has recast its original apocalyptic dream based on their present experience.

Add to these sayings the fragment of ascent lore found in saying 50, and the magnitude of the mystical shift that has occurred in the communal memory becomes even more pronounced:

> Jesus said, "If they say to you, 'Where did you come from?,'
> say to them, 'We came from the light,'
> (the place where the light came into being on its own accord and established [itself] and became manifest through their image).

If they say to you, 'Is it you?,'
say 'We are its children, and we are the elect of the living Father.'
If they ask you, 'What is the sign of your Father in you?,' say to them, 'It
is movement and rest.'" (50)

The context in which these questions and answers make the *most* sense is
that of the ascent of the soul through the heavenly spheres and the interrogation of the soul as it journeys to God (DeConick 1996:43–96). We find
such interrogations at death to be characteristic of Egyptian, Orphic, and
some gnostic traditions. Since Logion 50 gives us no indication that the
context is death, we can assume a premortem context based on the fact
that *Thomas* advocated mystical ascent before death in sayings 37 and 59.
For this idea, there is ample evidence in Jewish sources, where we discover that the mystic could expect the angelic guards to be hostile and
question his right and worthiness to be in heaven (cf. *Ascen. Isa.* 10.28–29;
3 En. 2, 4 and 5; *Apoc. Ab.* 13.6; *b. Ḥag.* 15b; *b. Šabb.* 88b–89a; *Shemot Rabbah*
42.4; *Pesiq. Rab.* 96b–98a; *Gedullat Mosheh* 273; *Hekhalot Fragments* lines
28–38; *Hist. Rech.* 5.1–2). Moreover, he could anticipate life-or-death tests
to be administered by the angels. He had to memorize passwords and
hymns in order to appease the guards of heaven and insure his safe passage to the foot of God's throne (*Apoc. Abr.* 17–18; *Hekhalot Rabbati* 1.1;
2.5–5.3; 16.4–25.6; *Hekhalot Zutt.* 413–415; *b. Ḥag.* 14b; *Ma'aseh Merkavah* 9,
11, 15).

Even though the language in these sayings describes the ecstatic
experience prominently in mythic terms of a heavenly journey and
vision of the Father and the glorious Jesus, the Son of the Living One
(24.1, 37, 38.2, 50, 59), the transformation itself was understood also to
be an interior psychic experience of the soul, as can be clearly seen with
the creation of a dialogue between Jesus and his disciples in saying 24.
A *newer question* (24.1) now introduces and recontextualizes an older
saying (24.2–3):

> His disciples said to him, "Show us the place where you are, since it is necessary
> for us to seek it." He said to them, "Whoever has ears, let him hear. There
> is light within a man of light and he lights up the whole world. If he
> does not shine, he is darkness."

The disciples' question represents the voice of the community. They
ask Jesus to show them where he lives since they must "seek" this "place"
in order to be redeemed. Here, the language of mystical journey to the
"place" where Jesus is has been connected to a psychic discussion about
the interior "man of light," the soul. Here, the ecstatic "journey" is an
internal one, resulting in an immediate transformation of the soul into its
original state of luminosity. The transformative effects of this journey are

the subject of several other sayings in *Thomas*, sayings which invoke both the Jewish story of the person's recovery, through mystical encounter, of the original image of God in which he or she was created (*Gos. Thom.* 19, 22, 70, 84, 106) and the Hermetic story of the return, through Self-knowledge, of the person's fallen soul (3.4–5, 56, 67, 80, 111.3).

All in all, these sayings represent the voice of a community whose members are no longer waiting for death or the eschaton in order to enter heaven and achieve immortality. Instead of waiting for heaven to come to them, they are invading Eden, believing the eschatological promises of God fulfilled in the present. Their apocalyptic expectations have collapsed, shifting their theology away from hopes of an imminent eschaton to achieving mystical premortem experiences of God. They developed an encratic theology and regime, working to transform their bodies into the prelapsarian Adam and Eve, and their church into paradise even while they lived on earth. In a community where Eden had been regained, mystical visions of Jesus and God were accessible to the practitioner. The believer could experience all the fruits of the new world now, living like an angel on earth, gazing on God like an angel in heaven.

4. Final Remarks

Reading the *Gospel of Thomas* as a repository of early Christian communal memory suggests that the Gospel contains traditions and references to hermeneutics that serve to reconfigure older traditions and hermeneutics no longer relevant to the experience of the community. Even this brief commentary on the traditions in *Thomas* reveals that the community's original eschatological expectations were disconfirmed by its contemporary experience of the non-Event. When the kingdom did not come, rather than discarding their Gospel and closing the door of their church, the Thomasine Christians responded by reinterpreting Jesus' sayings, believing themselves to have previously misunderstood Jesus' intent—to have applied the wrong hermeneutic to his words. So they aligned their old traditions with their present experience, rationalizing the non-Event, shifting their theology to the encratic and mystical, and creating a new hermeneutic through which the old traditions could be viewed. This response is visible in the way in which they revised their Gospel, adding question-and-answer units and dialogues that addressed the subject specifically, along with a series of new sayings that worked to instruct the believer in the new theology and guide him or her hermeneutically through the Gospel.

The community had become an advocate for a fully present kingdom—the new world of Eden—which they re-created among themselves. Their church was Paradise. They were Adam and Eve before the fall.

Through encratic performance and mystical practice, they believed that they had achieved the eschatological promises of God in the present, including the ultimate transformation of their bodies into the original luminous image of God. The non-Event became for them the fulfillment of the event. Jesus' promise of the imminent end had been actualized within the boundaries of their community!

This reading of the *Gospel of Thomas* suggests that the scholarly consensus that this Gospel exemplifies an early Christian, nonapocalyptic Gospel preserving the message of a philosophical Jesus is highly suspect. In fact, the opposite appears to be the case. The earliest version of the *Gospel of Thomas*, which I call the kernel *Thomas*, looks to have been an apocalyptic speech Gospel emphasizing the imminent eschaton and its demands. It is only in the face of a communal memory crisis, which also was experienced by other Christian communities in the mid-to-late first century, that the text's emphasis was shifted away from the eschatological interpretation of Jesus' sayings to the mystical. The person no longer waited for the end to arrive and Jesus to return. His or her transformation or immortalization was achieved immediately through imitative performance and direct mystical apprehension of God and his Son.

THE WORKS OF MEMORY: CHRISTIAN ORIGINS AS MNEMOHISTORY—A RESPONSE

Werner H. Kelber

Magna ista vis est memoriae, magna nimis, deus, penetrale amplum et infinitum. (Great is that power of memory, beyond all measure, O my God, a spacious and boundless mystery.)
—St. Augustine

Mnemosyne, said the Greeks, is the mother of the Muses; the history of the training of this most fundamental and elusive of human powers will plunge us into deep waters.
—Frances A. Yates

Memory is the matrix of all human temporal perception.
—Mary Carruthers

Memory is the way in which the ancients think.
—Arthur J. Dewey

PROLOGUE

The modern academic study of memory is generally acknowledged to have been initiated by the sociologist Maurice Halbwachs (1877–1945). Since the middle of the twentieth century, in part dependent on Halbwachs and in part quite separately, memory has steadily emerged as a pivotal concept in cultural studies and as principal topic of research in the humanities and social sciences. The significance of this memory boom is twofold. On the one hand, memory has provided wide-ranging explanatory powers and conceptual insights that have proven useful for viewing central issues such as representation and cognition, identity and imagination, tradition and ritual, communication and media, and many more, in new perspectives. Certain aspects of intellectual disciplines such as history, classical studies, ancient philosophy, medieval studies, and literary criticism, for example, have been significantly enriched as a result of memory work. Secondly, a continually growing body of interdisciplinary studies has developed around memory, exhibiting her as a vitally integrative force that allows us to discern different and even disparate cultural phenomena and academic disciplines within a larger intellectual framework. Aspects of literary and political theory, religious and art history, historiography and the cognitive sciences, for example, can plausibly be linked around the dynamics and communities of memory. Memory, in the words of Patrick Hutton, embodies "the quintessential interdisciplinary interest" (1993:xiii). In view of a veritable avalanche of books and articles on memory and remembering, mnemonics and memorial processes, memory images and memory places, the ethics of remembering and *damnatio memoriae*, commemoration and memory theater, one cannot escape the impression that memory has risen to a status of paradigmatic significance in the humanities and social sciences. Mnemosyne, it seems, is the topic of everyone, and no one has exclusive monopoly over her.

In this emergence of memory in the twentieth century we experience the revival of a *topos* that has played a major civilizing role throughout Western culture. Long before memory had been assigned a place as one of the five divisions in ancient (and medieval) rhetoric, and Quintilian had paid his respects to memory as "the treasure-house of eloquence" (*Inst.* 11.2.1, etc.), her virtues had been acknowledged by mythology. According to myth, Mnemosyne, at once the goddess of memory and of imagination, had born Zeus nine daughters, the Muses, who personified and presided over different modes of the arts and sciences. Unmistakably, this myth of Mnemosyne and her Muses articulates the centrality of memory in human culture. As mother of the Muses, Mnemosyne was the origin of all artistic and scientific labors and the wellspring of civilization. From the perspective of that myth, it was not scribality or literary exegesis, not logic or rhetoric even, that was perceived to be the central, civilizing agency, but memory.

Modernity's Commemoration of Memory

Three features define the strikingly original work on *mémoire sociale* by Halbwachs (see 1980; 1992), the student of Henri Bergson and Emile Durkheim. In the first place, memory is a social phenomenon, inextricably allied with group formation and identity. Thriving and enduring within sustaining social contexts, she is both a facilitator and result of the socialization of human culture. Remove the life-sustaining system of group identity and confirmation, and memories wither away. Secondly, the process of remembering does not work purely for the benefit of retaining the past as past. That is to say, remembering is not fed primarily by the needs for preservation of the past in its state of pristine authenticity. Rather, memory selects and modifies subjects and figures of the past in order to make them serviceable to the image the community (or individuals) wishes to cultivate of itself. Socialization and memory mutually condition each other, seeking in the last analysis preservation not of the past as such, but of present group identity. Thirdly, Halbwachs developed a theory concerning the antithetical relation of memory versus history. Viewing the matter from what today may be termed a positivistic view of historiography, he held that the past begins to assert itself as historical actuality only after social groups that were thriving on the cultivation of memories had departed from the scene. Only when the past was no longer claimed and inhabited by the collective remembering of social groups could history, uncontaminated by memory's distortions, have its true say. There is a sense, therefore, in which history has to wait for its debut until it has ceased to exist in and as memory.

It remains the significant intellectual accomplishment of Halbwachs to have (re)discovered the past as remembered past and to have defined it as a social construction that consolidates the symbolic and historic group identity within the social framework (*cadres sociaux*) of the present. It is this social concept of memory that in our generation Jan and Aleida Assmann have taken up, modified and developed—an endeavor which in turn has contributed to the renaissance of the thought of Halbwachs.

Pursuing an aspect of memory entirely different and independently from Halbwachs, Frances Yates, in *The Art of Memory*, traced an archival, mnemotechnical memory tradition from its ancient locus in Greek rhetoric through its medieval transformations up to the hermetic, esoteric forms it took in the Renaissance, and on to scientific modernity. In particular, she deserves credit for having brought to academic consciousness the phenomenon of interior visualization and the role image-making and visually based memory practices played in cognitive processes. The localization of "the place of the art of memory at the great nerve centres of the European tradition" (368) allowed Yates to construct links between such diverse features and persons as the anonymous Ad Herennium, ancient rhetoric, Augustine, Thomas Aquinas, memory theaters, Ramism, Protestantism, hermeticism, mysticism and the rise of the scientific method. Viewing cultural history largely from the perspective of mnemotechnics and spatially constructed concepts of memory, she traced the retentive, archival facilities of memory through Western history. A model of erudition and originality, *The Art of Memory* is a classic in twentieth-century literature on memory and, to my knowledge, the first book in modernity that has in effect reconstructed Western history as mnemohistory.

Mary Carruthers's two magisterial volumes, *The Book of Memory* and *The Craft of Thought*, have been on the forefront of a growing body of scholarly literature intent on enlarging and revising conventional concepts of the literary, documentary culture of the Middle Ages. Examining medieval practices of reading, writing and composing, prayer and meditation, pedagogy and visualization, the nature and habits of the medieval craft of thought, and above all the function of memory, memory training, and the neuropsychology of memory, she unfolded a religious, intellectual and ethical culture still rooted in theories and practices that were fundamentally memorial in nature. The layout and pictorial, decorative design of manuscripts, for example, often functioned in symbiotic relations with memorial needs, and the compositional structure of texts, citational habits, and certain institutional practices are well understood, she suggested, as arising from memorial activities. Given the fact that medieval manuscript culture interfaced with oral, rhetorical, memorial needs and activities, concepts such as text and textuality, logic and cognition, authorship and textual composition did not mean in medieval intellectual life what they came to mean in typographic modernity. At the same time, however, Carruthers discovered that issues raised by modernity's deconstructionism and psychoanalytic theory had been anticipated by, and sometimes lay at the heart of, the medieval tradition. In sum, she concluded that the culture of late antiquity and the Middle Ages must be viewed as a predominantly memorial, rather than a purely documentary and textual, one.

Perhaps the least known, yet philosophically and historically highly consequential work on memory and the reconstruction of the past is Janet Coleman's *Ancient and Medieval Memories*. Distinguished by a superior knowledge of ancient philosophy, medieval philosophy/theology, and the cognitive sciences, the book demonstrates an uncommonly profound and subtle grasp of the relations between language, logic (cognition) and reality throughout the ancient and medieval intellectual history of the West. Ranging from classical, monastic and Thomistic ideas all the way to Ockham's nominalist launching of the *via moderna*, and culminating in a study of modern psychological and neuropsychological theories of cognition (minus Halbwachs' sociological theory, however), Coleman has produced a hugely impressive Western intellectual history with a focus on theories and practices of (re)constructing the past.

In important ways, Coleman reasoned, ancient and medieval consciousness of the past was unlike modernity's understanding and uses of the past, so that the modern approach to the past must be viewed as representing both a recent and very particular development. Medieval theologians, philosophers and historians, far into the twelfth and thirteenth centuries, were not inclined to entertain interests in the pastness of the past. When discordant records or voices of the past manifested themselves, medieval thinkers were more inclined to harmonize them than to plumb them for historical veracity. The past was primarily elaborated and employed in the sense that "some moral, exemplary and universal aspect of that past could be interpreted for use in the present" (Coleman: 299). Deep into the high Middle Ages, she claims, there existed no conceptual consciousness of the issue increasingly accentuated in emergent modernity: whether we know the past in its particularity as past, or whether it was accessible only as it inhabited, or we made it inhabit, our present.

The watershed figure in the transition to a "modern" approach to the past was, according to Coleman, the British Franciscan friar William of Ockham (1285–1349?). Negatively, Ockham's objective was to challenge a deeply held philosophical realism that insisted that language, memory and sense perception collaborate in the interest of higher, universal ideas, values and knowledge. In this, his epistemology ran counter to the universalizing thrust of Platonic, Augustinian and much of scholastic philosophy. Affirmatively, Ockham's skepticism with regard to philosophical realism moved the particular, the experiential, and the contingent to the center of inquiry. His model of mind and language focused with unprecedented force upon the status and quality of distinctiveness, including the particularity of texts. Scripture, indeed all texts, were assumed to be operating according to something akin to an intrinsic linguistic economy, and the operations of the mind—everybody's mind— were such that they could access the internal textual logic via the *cognitio intuitiva*. Memory, far from being the treasure house of eloquence, or the metaphysical abode of trinitarian psychology, or the vehicle of conversion, came to play the role of the intellect's "power which strictly allows mind to refer to the past as past" (Coleman: 522). Much of what was to become characteristic of Renaissance and humanistic assumptions about an immediate and direct apprehension of Scripture—of any text—and of the accessibility to the past, was theoretically anticipated by Ockham.

Since the 1980s an interdisciplinary group of scholars under the guidance of Jan and Aleida Assmann has produced a steadily growing body of work dealing with what they termed "cultural memory." Deeply inspired by the pioneering work of Maurice Halbwachs, they viewed memory as being inextricably tied to group and group identity. One aspect, however, that distinguishes their work from Halbwachs is the latter's polarization of memory vis-à-vis history. Jan Assmann has coined the phrase "Der Mythos vom 'historischen Sinn,'" and expressed doubts whether a strictly historical meaning was a viable proposition at all (1992:66–68). Since the presence of the past is always the result of mediated transactions, the past is neither retrievable nor preservable as a historically fresh and memorially untouched reality. "Vergangenheit steht nicht urwüchsig an, sie ist eine kulturelle Schöpfung" (1992:48): the past does not present itself as an elementary force of nature, it is a cultural construction. Cultural memory, in Assmann's view, is therefore the more appropriate concept that captures all human dealings with the past. For this reason there cannot be a sharp conceptual distinction between history and memory, because the past as cultural construction is never immune to, and always dependent on, memorial participation and mediation.

Yet Assmann is careful to concede that there existed since Herodotus (484?–425 B.C.E.) something of a theoretical curiosity—an urge for knowledge irrespective of present identities ("identitätsabstrakt")—that should be acknowledged as an approach to the past different from cultural memory. Within the domain of memory studies, historiography that aims at identity neutrality would have to be assigned to the category of cold memory (1992:43 n. 24).

Entirely in Halbwachs's sense, cultural memory for Jan Assmann functions dynamically, and not in terms of storage or archive. It undertakes the work of remembering the past by reappropriating the latter in the interest of molding and/or reimaging and/or stabilizing group identity. Identity formation is a key term that is derived from the legacy of Halbwachs, even though he had used it only sparingly. Memory, according to this understanding, operates selectively, seizing upon, modifying and contextualizing figures and subjects of the past in order to feed the needs and define the aspirations of the group. Cultural memory, therefore, recognizes both a regressive gesture toward the past, seeking to retrieve as much of the past as seems appropriate, and an orientation toward the present (and future), preserving what is deemed to be useful in the present.

While both Assmanns have reflected on the interfacing of cultural memory with media dynamics (J. Assmann 1992:87–129; A. Assmann 1999:188–217), the principal representatives of the recent upsurge in orality/literacy studies (Lord 1960; 1991; Havelock 1963; 1978; Ong 1967; 1977; 1982; Goody 1968, 1977; Foley 1987; 1990; 1991; 2002) have as yet not seriously connected with the massive work in memory studies. At best, orality/literacy studies have examined the interrelations between mnemotechnics and the media, but they have not, to my knowledge, integrated the discourse worlds of Halbwachs, Yates, Carruthers, Coleman and others. Ong is exceptional in so far as he has written an essay on the role written and printed texts impose on readers, fictionalizing their identity as it were (1977:53–81)—an insight, we shall see below, that addresses aspects of memory studies. In view of the fact that memorial processes entail an intricate meshing of cognitive, linguistic and social dynamics—all features that are relevant to speech, scribality and their mutual interfacing—the dearth of reflection on memory in orality/literacy studies seems curious. Biblical scholarship no doubt can benefit not merely from orality/literacy studies and recent memory work, but from a constructive linking of the two.

Precisely what happens to the memorial apperception of the past in a shift from oral performance to scribal mediation is both complex and variable. But a crucial aspect in that shift pertains to the relation that exists between communicator and recipients and specifically the communicative dynamics transacted between the two. The medium of oral communication actualizes itself in face-to-face performance with live audiences. "For the speaker, the audience is in front of him" (Ong 1977:56), and it is by virtue of the speaker's accountability toward the audience and the latter's responsiveness to the speaker that communication is transacted. That is to say, communication operates within social and intellectual boundaries that are not merely dictated by the speaker, but delimited by audiences' needs and expectations as well. Moreover, faced both with the risks of forgetting and the task of recall, oral diction is in a special way pressured to attend to the needs of memory. More than that, operating apart from and/or in the absence of the materiality of the scribal medium, orality has no choice but to enter into a binding contract with a mnemonically structured language. For this reason, formulaically and rhythmically shaped diction, various kinds of repetition and parallelism dominate orally functioning communication. Memory devices are deeply etched into the structure of oral discourse and knowledge.

In the case of scribality, the communicative status of scroll or manuscript enters into relations with recipients that are quite different from oral discourse. "For the writer, the audience is simply further away, in time or space or both" (Ong 1977:56). One may delete the word "simply" because it is the very temporal and physical distance between producer and consumer of communication that marks a difference in the shift from oral to scribal communication. In all instances, the dictator, composer and scribe operate in the absence of a live audience. As a result, those in charge of scribal compositioning are deprived of or, as the case may be, released from face-to-face responsiveness. This crucial circumstance effects a lessening of direct accountability and a sense of emancipation from communal pressures. From the perspectives of memory, the agents in the production of scroll and manuscript are less bound by the strictures of mnemonic imperatives, because to some degree the handwritten objects assume archival functions. Needless to

say, scribally mediated communication in the ancient world is frequently rhetorically shaped so as to call on and effect hearers or readers.
But again, the temporal and physical distance facilitated by chirography
allows for a loosening of mnemonic strictures, a relaxation of social,
intellectual and linguistic boundaries, as well as for a broadening of the
range of recipients.

The consequences this altered state of the communicative dynamics
carry for the work of memory are far-reaching. Most importantly,
memorial processes transacted by scribal mediation are capable of exer-
cising greater freedom vis-à-vis the past and tradition. This release from
the immediacy of oral accountability empowers memory not merely to
appeal to and reinforce group identity, but to challenge and reshape it.
In the terms developed by Ong, there exists in literary history a tradition of fictionalizing audiences: "The historian, the scholar or scientist,
and the simple letter writer all fictionalize their audiences, casting them
in a made-up role and calling on them to play the role assigned"
(1977:74).

We need to be very clear on this matter: orality can, and often does,
challenge and recast individual and social identities as well. Much of the
Jesus tradition itself serves as a telling example. The point here is to
acquire a hermeneutically appropriate understanding of the potentials of
scribality that is in keeping with media studies. All too often the relation
between oral tradition and the written Gospel has been conceptualized in
terms of a steady or accelerating flow of tradition, intimating continuity—unbrokenness even—conceding only minimal compositional powers
to Gospel scribality, and casting the Gospel narrative into the role of cold
memory. More recently, studies that have exhibited greater sensitivity
toward oral/scribal dynamics (see Boomershine; Malbon; J. Dewey;
Shiner) have insisted that in "the Mediterranean world, writing was
largely understood as representing oral speech" (Shiner: 14) so that the
narrative Gospel was written not only to be oral performance, but written
in the manner it had been performed in oral tradition. Granted that
Mark's Gospel, as much of ancient literature, was intended to be recycled
in oral performance, was it truly oral traditional literature in the sense it
has been proposed by Lord (1978:33–91), namely, simply a variant of an
oral narrative tradition? In different words, is it conceivable that the
Gospel's chirographic production was entirely unaffected by the potentials of the scribal medium?

In view of scholarly models that espouse the unproblematic relation
between oral tradition and the written Gospel, it merits restating the
potential of scribality, including Gospel scribality, to disengage itself
from oral imperatives—to turn a deaf ear even to the needs and expectations of live audiences—so as to undertake a productive redescription of

tradition, to challenge social identities, and to recommemorate the past—in short, to generate hot memory.

Jan Assmann has astutely developed the concept of *Traditionsbruch*, associated with scribality, that may entail risks of forgetting not known to orality:

> Schriftlichkeit, darauf kommt es mir hier vor allem an, stellt an sich noch keine Kontinuität dar. Im Gegenteil, sie birgt Risiken des Vergessens und Verschwindens, die der mündlichen Überlieferung fremd sind, und bedeutet oft eher Bruch als Kontinuität. (1992:101; see also 99–103, 216, 294)

The scribalization of tradition is, therefore, by no means a guarantor of continuity and stability. Scribally transacted memory may appropriate the past, not necessarily in keeping with oral tradition, but in deviating from or even rupturing with it. To be sure, a scribally mediated memory, due to scribality's storage function, gives the impression of having solved the problem of forgetting. And yet, the media complexities of the scribal medium go far beyond its function as a means merely of stemming the tide of forgetfulness. Deeper sensitivity to media hermeneutics can alert us to the phenomenon of writers' scribally enforced distance from hearers, which may enhance both the desire and the ability to break with tradition, to canonize an alternate viewpoint, and thereby implement a form of forgetfulness.

MEMORY AND CHRISTIAN ORIGINS

The vibrant work of memory has found next to no response in New Testament scholarship. In spite of this impressively productive memory work in the human and social sciences, Mnemosyne is by and large not perceived to be a pressing issue in current biblical scholarship. Jens Schröter seems to be exceptional in having adopted Jan and Aleida Assmann's concept of cultural memory as a heuristic device in reading Mark, Q, and *Thomas* as different modalities of remembering Jesus (1997:462–86). For the most part, however, the exceedingly significant and influential memory work that is being carried out in the humanities and social sciences, and which has deeply informed the essays in this volume, has up until now left next to no discernible traces in the guild. This glaring disregard of memory studies is one more example of a growing isolation of biblical scholarship from the human and social sciences.

How is it possible that New Testament scholarship has been able to conduct its research without paying attention to the boom in memory work, disregarding the profoundly useful explanatory categories it has produced? In his introduction to this volume, Kirk reflects on this astounding "myopia ... a problem almost uniquely of New Testament scholarship" (1). He points to classical form criticism and its concept of tradition which had caused memory's marginalization or, as the case may be, amnesia. In their jointly written essay, Kirk and Thatcher expose the disappearance of memory as an analytical category from the work of Käsemann, Perrin, the Jesus Seminar, and above all from Bultmann's form criticism. Kirk and Thatcher's analysis of how memory fared in the work of key figures in the recent history of New Testament scholarship merits deep reflection. Because form criticism dominated many of our methods and assumptions over the longest part of the twentieth century, we shall extend Kirk and Thatcher's reflections on form criticism and its disconnect with memory studies.

One may single out three features that distracted classical form criticism from taking the workings and function of memory in late antiquity, and scholarly reflections on them, into serious account. First, from the outset Bultmann's form-critical project of isolating and examining orally imaginable units was premised on, and oriented toward, finding the original form: "The aim of form-criticism is to determine the original form of a piece of narrative, a dominical saying or a parable" (1963:6). This programmatic intent cast Bultmann's form critical project from its inception into a search for the origin, diverting attention away from exploring the memorial and mnemotechnical dynamics of oral tradition. Second, Bultmann's concept of the Synoptic tradition disallowed any serious consideration of memory as a dynamic, motivational force. To a considerable extent the Synoptic history was assumed to have been driven by what I have defined as the principle of "intrinsic causation" (Kelber 1983:2–8), whereby the transmission of Jesus materials was propelled by "the immanent urge to development which lay in the tradition" (Bultmann 1963:373). If tradition is empowered by its own evolutionary gravity, the forces of remembering in the process of traditioning would seem to be minimal at best, and irrelevant at most. Third, as is well known, it was, and to some extent still is, the form critical premise that Mark's Gospel composition merely brought to fruition what was already lodged in tradition so that "his whole enterprise is explicable only in terms of the importance which the tradition itself had" (Bultmann 1963:347). Once again, therefore, there is no place for memorial dynamics in tradition; the latter is rather mechanistically conceived as a unidirectional transmission of mostly oral materials. Nor is there a place for memorial dynamics on the level of Gospel compositioning because narrative creativity is limited to a channeling and fusion of forces and trends that were for the most part already inherent in tradition. Mark merely brought to fruition what had been well developed in tradition.

Significantly, these very features that steered form criticism away from memory's active participation, both in the work of tradition and in the Gospels' composition, are entirely untenable by widely shared standards of current Gospel scholarship. The notion of "the original form" is a phantom of the literary—not to say typographic—imagination and incompatible with oral hermeneutics. Oral tradition operates with a plurality of original speech acts, which suggests a principle entirely different from and indeed antithetical to that of the one, original form. The concept of "intrinsic causation," moreover, misconceives the nature of the Synoptic, oral tradition. Spoken words are not subject to a forward oriented directionality, and are in fact incomprehensible in any diagrammatic form or fashion. To be sure, spoken words are communicable from one person to another, but they do not travel in the sense of covering spatial distance from one observable point to another. And finally, as far as the Gospel compositions are concerned, form criticism's vast underrating of narrative productivity—indeed creativity—on the level of Gospel compositioning is widely recognized today. At this point, the exploration of the narrative poetics of the Gospels has progressed far enough to make us realize that each Gospel, far from being merely the product of dynamics in the tradition, is the result of a compositional volition, deliberately constructed plot causalities, and a distinctly focused rhetorical outreach. Our reflections on the astounding "myopia" in New Testament studies, therefore, suggest more than a failure on the part of form criticism to come to terms with memory. More, and indeed something more important, is at stake here than the absence of memory, a condition that could conceivably be remedied by integrating memorial dynamics into the work of form criticism. Put differently, the failure to make room for memory in Gospel studies is no mere oversight that could be corrected by adding the missing dimension. This scholarly "myopia" has to do with fundamental conceptual flaws inherent in form criticism, which have centrally affected the methods and assumptions of almost a century of scholarly approaches to the Gospels.

The one instance in which memory, conceived as key concept, has entered into the discourse world of New Testament scholarship was provided by Birger Gerhardsson. Aptly entitled *Memory and Manuscript,* his *magnum opus* will stand as a classic in twentieth-century biblical studies. Significantly, the very author who has shown a keen interest in memory is also deeply critical of the methods and assumptions of form criticism. Yet Gerhardsson has not benefited from the scholarship of Halbwachs and those working in his scholarly tradition, either. As is well known, the author of *Memory and Manuscript* has modeled his concept of tradition and memory on Pharisaic, rabbinic Judaism in the Tannaitic and Amoraic period, dated roughly from the calamity of 70 C.E. up to the fifth century.

Based on this analogy, Gerhardsson constructed a model of the early Jesus traditions in which memory assumed the role of principal facilitator of the transmissional processes. This particular affiliation of rabbinic mnemonic techniques with early Christian traditioning practices has been widely criticized. As a rule, however, critics have failed to give Gerhardsson credit for having insisted on the centrality of memory in the early Christian tradition. The observations by Kirk and Thatcher in their jointly authored essay are, therefore, all the more commendable: "Gerhardsson's proposal resonates with social memory theory in its recognition of the constitutive nature of memory for a community" (35). For Gerhardsson, tradition is inconceivable without memory, and vice versa.

This alignment between social memory theorists and Gerhardsson on the centrality of memory must not blur the differences that separate the concepts of memory expounded by Gerhardsson on one hand and the authors of these essays on the other. Gerhardsson envisioned a mechanical commitment of materials to memory and a passive transmission by way of continual repetition. Changes that did occur in the processing of traditional items remained confined to interpretive adaptations. On the whole, the work of memory as key arbiter of tradition was, therefore, characterized by fixity, stability and continuity, and the primary purpose of transmission was the deliberate act of communicating the legacy of Jesus for its own sake. No allowance is made, on this model, for memory's active participation in the operations of tradition.

It is worth observing that the first and virtually only time memory is introduced as a key concept in the modern study of Christian origins, it is presented as cold memory, highlighting its retentive function and reducing it to strictly preservative, reproductive purposes. As conceived by Gerhardsson, memory is the grand stabilizing agent in early Christian culture. Not one of the authors of the essays in this volume subscribes to this concept of cold memory. Whereas Gerhardsson opted for an early Christian memorial culture transacted as passive transmission under the aegis of cold memory, the present authors without exception advocate a notion of hot memory propelled by active remembering and socialization. As far as I can see, Kirk's statement in his introductory essay expresses a view to which all contributors seem to give their assent: "The activity of memory in articulating the past is dynamic, unceasing, *because it is wired into the ever-shifting present*" (10). On this view, all essayists appear to be agreed.

For two reasons Gerhardsson merits a place at the table of our memory discourse. As stated before, he is the one New Testament scholar who has assured memory its central place in the history of early Christian traditions. If we rightly lament the fact that "a sharp distinction between 'memory' and 'tradition' is fundamental for most contemporary models of the development of primitive Christian theology and the composition history of the Gospels" (Kirk and Thatcher: 25), we should likewise acknowledge that Gerhardsson is the scholar who has taken exception to this distinction. The specificity of his memory model aside, the author of *Memory and Manuscript* deserves credit for having insisted on the inalienable synergism of memory and tradition. On this point he was right, and the form critics on the wrong track.

In particular, Gerhardsson has displayed a keen perception of the mnemonic structuring of many of Jesus' sayings. One would have thought that it was to be the first order of the form critical project to examine the extraordinary degree to which Jesus sayings have kept faith with heavily patterned speech, and to explore features such as alliteration, appositional equivalence, proverbial and aphoristic diction, contrasts and antitheses, synonymous, antithetical and tautological parallelisms, rhythmic structures, and so forth—all earmarks of mnemonics which abound in the Jesus logia. But form criticism, as we have observed, instead of focusing on oral style and performance, preoccupied itself with oral tradition and above all tradition's origin, and rapidly conceived of itself as a tool in the quest for the proclamation of the historical Jesus. It is not normally acknowledged that Gerhardsson, more than the form critics, displayed informed sensitivity to the rhythmically and formulaically patterned diction of Jesus sayings. To be sure, the mnemonic usability and auditory feasibility of large parts of the Jesus tradition suggested to him memorization, literal consistency, and passive transmission. By way of rebuttal, we need to emphasize, along with the essayists of this volume, that already Jesus' own mnemonically structured speech as well as its continuing existence in the commemorative activities of his followers was subject to the constructive and reconstructive work of social memory. Still, in view of the widely practiced dissociation of tradition from memory, Gerhardsson deserves credit for having insisted on mnemonics at the heart of the formative stage of the Synoptic tradition.

Two, we should not dismiss Gerhardsson's basic insight from our memory work because it provides us with a much-needed opportunity to conduct scholarship in a broader, cultural context. At this early stage in our deliberations, let us not prematurely narrow down the range of possible memorial practices and the scope of memorial conceptualizations. The concepts of memory espoused by the essayists and by Gerhardsson respectively represent memory's repetitive and recollective side, and both deserve to be kept in mind because they constitute the two classic manifestations in the memory tradition. Repetition carries forward the legacy of the past, reconstituting the past in the present, while recollection reconstructs the benefits of the past in response to the needs of the present. Manifestly, Gerhardsson has captured memory's repetitive moment, and the authors of this volume have sided with her recollective activities. Let us be clear: on the whole, it will be difficult to subscribe to a memorially activated tradition that carries semantically inert pieces of information across time, the whirling wheel of change, and equally difficult to deny memory's incessantly constructive ambitions to reactivate the past in the interest of current affairs.

And yet, before we opt unilaterally for a constructionist model of memory, let us keep in mind that it was precisely the interplay of the repetitive and the recollective elements that bestowed upon Mnemosyne a sense of complexity—of ambiguity even. Ever so often, memory exists in the paradoxical tension between these two aspirations: to resurrect the images of the past so as to transport them into the present, and to reconstruct the images of the past so as to integrate them into the present context. It is one of the most impressive features of Kirk's introductory essay that, while principally subscribing to memory's inclination to bring the past into alignment with the present, it also recognizes, in agreement with Barry Schwartz, "how the depth of the past might inform, shape, support, not to say constrain the dispositions, interests, and actions of those situated in the sphere of the present" (13). If, therefore, we can acknowledge that in memory's work the past sets limits and defines the scope of what is to be remembered, while the present is inclined to reactivate the past, we have actually moved beyond a strictly constructionist model. On this view, what memory will bequeath to us is contingent on a balance of revisiting and reconstructing the past. This is by no means to challenge the explicit or implied objection the contributors have raised to a model of remembering the past for the past's sake alone. But it is to acknowledge that the past provides thematic, cognitive and linguistic patterns of what it is that is to be remembered. On this view, one may speak of memory's interplay between the past and the present, at times attributing greater force to the remembered past and at times to the remembering present.

Interestingly, Gerhardsson, in his *magnum opus,* made reference to the extensive work by Marcel Jousse on rhythm and bilateralism in the ancient Near East and specifically in the language of Jesus (see 1925; 1974; 1975; 1978). Indeed, to many of Jousse's readers it came as something of a shock to see him approach Jesus under anthropological and linguistic aspects as a Galilean rabbi teaching according to the oral style method of his time and milieu. It was a central idea of the work of Jousse that memory was not accidental or supplementary to cognition in antiquity— especially to the predominantly oral mindset of the ancient Mediterranean culture—but as elementary as gravity in the physical universe. Unfortunately, neither Gerhardsson nor the form critics ever availed themselves of

Jousse's extensive research on oral style. We are confronted with a chapter in New Testament scholarship that is fraught with irony and haunted by inexplicable absences. Shortly after Bultmann's first edition of *The History of the Synoptic Tradition*, Jousse published his seminal work on *Le Style oral rhythmique et mnémotechnique chez les verbo-moteurs*, which was subsequently followed by a series of important articles. Between 1924 and 1928 the book was the subject of considerable debate in Paris, and Milman Parry, who at that time studied at the Sorbonne, was deeply influenced by Jousse's work. And so it came that Jousse, the scholar who wrote extensively on the oral-style method of Jesus' language, provided essential analytical categories for the Parry-Lord theory that was to revolutionize our comprehension of the Homeric epics. For reasons next to impossible to fathom, Jousse has remained conspicuous by his absence from form critical work, past and present—the very work that was designed to explore orality in the early Christian tradition.

It is conceivable that the most significant thesis that social memory theory has articulated in the essays of this volume lies in the conceptualization of tradition. The deliberations of Kirk and Thatcher on tradition in their jointly authored piece deserve the most serious attention of the readers. Affirming the performance mode of tradition, they recognize close affinities between orality and social memory theory: "As such, 'oral tradition' and 'social memory' are closely related terms, and the connections between them should be explored by biblical scholars" (41). In his essay on collective memory and Heb 11, Esler has set high standards in demonstrating the methodological fruitfulness of approaching a biblical text with the combined insights provided by oral and memory theory. I shall take up the challenge and carry forward the discussion by connecting theories about tradition that have been developed in orality and in social memory studies respectively.

I shall use John Dominic Crossan's magisterial research on the historical Jesus as a test case because it is based on a remarkably developed methodology which seeks to display sensitivity to oral hermeneutics (see 1983; 1991).

In reconstructing the message of the historical Jesus, Crossan is entirely dependent on and committed to the form critical method. He shares the form critical premise that embedded in the Gospels lie orally identifiable units which can be isolated from their narrative contexts, examined and pruned of secondary accretions, and traced backwards through assumed compositional stages all the way to their genesis. A meticulously designed apparatus of methodological principles is devised to extrapolate, collect, evaluate and classify the available Jesus sayings and stories. Entirely in keeping with Bultmann's form-critical project, Crossan intends to "search back through those sedimented layers to find what Jesus actually said and did" (Crossan 1991:xxxi). In the form critical vein, tradition is here perceived as a movement away from oral simplicity and purity and as a process of accretion and sedimentation. As a corollary, by retracing the layers of tradition one can arrive at the objectified past—that is, "what Jesus actually said and did" (Crossan 1991:xxxi).

Crossan's methodology is a marvel of methodological sophistication. Words are isolated, categorized and systematically grouped by virtue of resemblances, frequency and chronological priority so as to make them serviceable to logical analysis. Based on the notion of thematic resemblance, aphorisms and stories are collected, juxtaposed and held up to comparative interrogation. The logic of quantification places a high value on the numerical strength of materials. Whether a saying occurs once or several times is perceived to make a difference as far as authenticity is concerned. Lastly, the principle of chronological priority is used to allocate data at a fixed time in history. The intent of this methodological apparatus is to allow scholars to weave their way through the accretions and layers of tradition back to those aphorisms and stories that exist with the highest frequency in the oldest stratum of tradition.

In the history of biblical scholarship, Crossan's methodological apparatus may be viewed as the fruit of a long-standing and intensive scholarly laboring with chirographically and typographically manufactured words. Its assumptions have been developed in sustained working relations with the handwritten and, above all, the print Bible, the first major mechanically constructed book in modernity. It is the chirographically and typographically constructed words that facilitate the possibility to break apart and analyze scripts, to make clinical interventions in texts, to differentiate between primary and secondary units, and, finally, to segregate a text into distinctly profiled layers.

To reacquaint ourselves with the oral hermeneutics of Jesus' proclamation is exceedingly difficult because it runs counter to the typographic habits and print sensitivities that have informed historical, critical research for more than four centuries.

Let us rethink the issue of the *ipsissimum verbum*—the so-called original words of Jesus—conventionally taken to be the starting point of the tradition, and almost without exception assumed to be an irrefutable fact of linguistic existence. The form critics, and many of the questers for the historical Jesus, have expended an inordinate amount of labor on the reconstruction of these so-called original words of Jesus. From the perspective of orality studies, this search for the *ipsissima verba* of Jesus has consistently disregarded the fact that the oral medium is characterized by a plurality of speech acts and not by one, original *logion*. When the charismatic speaker pronounced a saying at one place—and subsequently chose to deliver it, with audience adjustments, elsewhere—neither he nor his hearers would have understood this second rendition as a second-hand version of the first one. Neither he nor his audience would have thought of differentiating between the primary, original wording and its secondary, derivative version. Instead, each proclamation was perceived to be a, and indeed the, autonomous speech act. There exists, therefore, in the oral medium a multiplicity or, to use a Heideggerian term, an equiprimordiality of speech acts. This simultaneity of multiple originals suggests a principle entirely different from, and indeed contrary to, the notion of the one *ipsissimum verbum.*

In contrast to most questers, Crossan has exhibited sensitivity to the fact that the notion of the *ipsissimum verbum* is incompatible with the hermeneutics of oral performance. Instead of operating with the *ipsissimum verbum,* he seized upon the structural core or the *ipsissima structura* as the appropriate category for oral discourse. "Oral sensibility and ipsissima verba are ... contradictions in terms. Or, to put it otherwise, even if orality speaks of *ipsissima verba* it means *ipsissima structura*" (1983:38). Once a saying has been selected by virtue of its chronological priority and numerical superiority, the underlying mnemonically stable, generic structure is then extrapolated by comparison with all extant parallel versions. This is the *ipsissima structura* that is claimed to go back to Jesus himself. The specificity of meaning Jesus attached to or expressed via the structural core is subsequently determined by the reinstatement of the core in a reconstructed historical context.

Now, it is a commonplace that speakers in oral and predominantly oral cultures frequently operate with stable, formulaic diction. That was the key discovery of Jousse with regard to the Jesus sayings. But in contrast to specialists on orality, Crossan made core stability the carrier of the one, single sense, thereby defining oral proclamation in favor of stability. Or, to put it differently, he has dealt with *ipsissima structura* as biblical scholars traditionally have dealt with the *ipsissimum verbum.*

It is, of course, possible that the structural core of a saying, each time it is spoken afresh, entails the one single meaning. But it has to be said that theorists in oral discourse and tradition do not, as a rule, interpret structural stability in terms of single meaning. It is far more appropriate to imagine the aphoristic core as a kind of instrument on which the oral performer plays and from which (s)he elicits a variety of musical tunes. And the performance is most frequently carried out by variations on a given theme and even modulations of the structural core. Variability of core structures, and not reduction of the core to single meaning, is what characterizes oral performance.

In the last analysis, therefore, Crossan's quest for the *ipsissima structura* operates, not unlike the form critical search for the *ipsissimum verbum,* on a mode of reasoning which infers from multiple particulars to singularity, from multiformity to primal, oral purity, and from equiprimordiality to structural stability. It reveals what may be logic's (print logic's) deepest desire—namely, to arrest the flow of time and to secure a sense of permanence for orality. And yet, the words of the charismatic speaker do not allow themselves to be reduced to core structures with single meanings, if only because oral proclamation lives and feeds on the—for print's logic—disquieting currents of temporality. The hermeneutics and aesthetics of orality strongly suggest that Jesus' proclamation was multiform, polyvalent, and in all instances equiprimordial. That is to say, Jesus the oral proclaimer operated with a plurality of speech acts, representing similar or variable meanings, whereby every single proclamation was a freshly autonomous event. If, therefore, we imagine Jesus as the commencement of tradition, we should not think of it in terms of the *ipsissimum verbum* or the *ipsissima structura,* but rather as a plurality of similar and disparate words. The relationship between Jesus and tradition is not, therefore, imaginable in terms of stability versus change, as all questers employing form critical methods have assumed, because oral discourse itself, whether used by Jesus or in tradition, is characterized by multiple speech acts with similar and different meanings. In the Beginning were the Words.

It is precisely at this point that the hermeneutics of orality interface with theories of social memory. Neither one of them understands tradition as a movement from stability to development, or from originality toward hermeneutical variations, or from singularity to multiformity. Approach tradition with an exclusive interest in historical originality and you have misunderstood the operations of tradition altogether. Affirmatively, both oral hermeneutics and social memory theory view tradition as a dynamic process ceaselessly engaged in the activity of reorganization and self-constitution.

According to Kirk and Thatcher, social memory connotes a stream of commemorative activities—of continual rememorizations—so that what has been called tradition "is, in fact, the substance of 'memory'" (40). If we integrate media theory, one may say that tradition understood as remembering constitutes an interminable interplay of oral, chirographic, typographic and artistic negotiations between the past and the exigencies of the present—at times giving more weight to the past and at times to present circumstances, but always seeking to synchronize the past with the present. Once we realize the operating force of memory, we can no longer think of tradition as an assembly-line production carrying inert items of information to be collected and objectively preserved for posterity. Nor is the notion of tradition as a process of accretion and sedimentation very plausible, because it rests on a clearly imaginable, yet deeply unrealistic, developmental model. It is frequently possible to observe a text negotiating the memory of the past, but rarely ever in terms of placing layer upon layer, or shifting from simplicity to complexity, far more often in terms of creative redescription. Nor is the trajectory model of tradition introduced by Robinson and Koester fully satisfactory, because in seeking to reconstruct tradition along the line of intelligible directionalities it has made transmission per se—understood in the developmental mode—the sole key to tradition. Memory does not seem to have been assigned a role in the trajectory model. Yet transmission and transmissional directionality is not all there is to tradition. Orally transacted communication, for example, is nondirectional; it cannot be said to flow in this or that direction. Trajectories, moreover, as conceived by Koester and Robinson, are transmissional processes exclusively based on textual documentation. Solely focused on textuality, and marginalizing both oral and memorial operations, the trajectory model takes on the specter of an eerily abstract trafficking in intertextuality. With social memory, however, a grand motivating force is invoked which operates primarily in the interest of group formation and identity reinforcement by bridging the demands of the past with the needs of the present. The key function of mnemohistory—this memorially empowered tradition—is not transmission per se, but negotiation between what for the moment we shall call a constitutive past and the contingencies of an ever-shifting present.

If one envisions tradition as a continual process of commemorating activities, can we imagine the heart of tradition as a mediation between a stable past and an ever-shifting present, or is not what we tend to refer to as past always already caught up in rememorization? In different words, does the past have an existence as a permanently objectifiable entity outside of and apart from memory's desires and arbitrations? One may think of the past as a correlate to social identity, being in the process of negotiations, as part and parcel of a continuous stream of memorializing processes and practices, and as an inescapable component of Halbwachs' *cadres collectifs*. In dealing with the past we are, therefore, in the words of Kirk and Thatcher, dealing with what in effect is always already a "commemorated past" (32 n. 1). Indeed, mnemohistory traffics with commemorated pasts rather than with an objectively constituted past. Once again, social memory and oral/scribal hermeneutics converge in insisting that the past of Jesus' proclamation is not accessible as an unelaborated, empirical commodity, any more than "the original saying" exists apart from equiprimordiality. In the words of Kirk and Thatcher, "'tradition' and 'memory' are not elements ... that can be pried apart through application of particular criteria" (33). In sum, the perspectives of memory theory and media hermeneutics, along with narrative poetics, will increasingly cast doubt on the feasibility of extrapolating "original" and "originally historical" materials with clinical precision from their textually assigned locations.

It is insightful, from this perspective, to revisit Paul's mode of nurturing the memory of Jesus. The apostle is clearly misapprehended if the perceived absence of Jesus material in the Pauline epistles prompts desperate scholarly attempts in search of Pauline familiarity with the historical Jesus. As Keightley has persuasively demonstrated, Paul's memorial knowledge of Christ was mediated in the commemorative rituals of the eucharist and baptism. It was there that he "met the Lord," always fresh and alive. Keightley's reading is entirely in accord with Paul's oral disposition toward language and presence (Kelber 1983:140–51). The power of the gospel, the efficacious proclamation of redemption, and his experience of Christ are all rooted in profoundly oral, memorial hermeneutics.

A number of essayists have illuminated the significance of social memory for our understanding of the Gospels. Memory may well hold a vital key to the Gospels' deeper compositional and motivational forces. Ever since Heinrich J. Holtzman 140 years ago postulated the so-called Two-Source Hypothesis with its threefold assumption of Markan priority, autonomous Q source, and Matthean and Lukan dependencies on Mark and Q, Gospel studies have been locked in a tightly constructed scheme of a singularly textual, documentary rationality, a kind of "typographic captivity" (Kelber 2002:70–74). Recent work on the narrative poetics of the Gospels notwithstanding, our theoretical propositions, methodological premises and explanatory powers are firmly in the grip of the Two-Source Hypothesis and its predilection for literary relations and clean source-critical explanations.

Three considerations may alert us to the limited usefulness of the Two-Source Hypothesis. One, recent narrative criticism has made it abundantly clear that each of the three Synoptics (and John as well) are informed by compositional ambitions and a will to emplotment. Ostensively, more is involved in the Gospel compositions than the use of sources—more even than the creative use of sources. Two, the fact that each of the three Gospels (and John as well) is involved in plural issues and traditions, in multiple themes and conflicts, poses serious questions to the Two-Source Hypothesis and its singularly source-critical rationality. Three, each Synoptic narrative plot (and that of John as well) is designed not merely to retrieve the past, but also to address present issues and circumstances with a view toward the future. The notion of transmission of traditions does not, therefore, adequately conceptualize the Gospel compositions. Given the fact that we now can and must understand the Gospels as being driven, among other things, by multiple narrative causalities, can we in good conscience still cling to the strictly documentary Two-Source Hypothesis, the notion that the appropriation, revision and conflation of literary sources provides the single most persuasive rationale for the composition of the Synoptic Gospels?

These insights into the narrativity of the Gospels, and the resultant softening of the explanatory value of the Two-Source Hypothesis, might in turn incline us to shift attention toward social memory theory. Could we bring ourselves to think of the Gospels, or parts of the Gospels, ultimately as the work of memorial processes? Horsley's essay serves as a significant entrée to this subject. For some time now he has been developing the concept that both Q and Mark were grounded in early Israelite memories about Moses and Elijah-Elisha. In *Whoever Hears You Hears Me,* he elaborated the thesis that the Q discourses were shaped according to ancient Israelite covenant renewal structures. In *Hearing the Whole Story,* he further applied this notion to Mark, arguing that that Gospel's Jesus conducts himself both in words and actions that are designed to bring about the renewal of Israel (see especially 177–201). In keeping with these earlier studies, Horsley in his piece for this volume explicates Jesus' discourses in Mark 10 as a covenantal charter, and expounds the well-known double cycle of miracle stories (Mark 4:35–8:21) as reminiscences of Israel's popular tradition: Jesus' (Moses') crossing of the sea, Jesus' (Moses') feeding of the people, Jesus' (Moses') launching of the exodus, Jesus' (Elijah's and Elisha's) healings. Tapping into Israel's repertoire of Moses' covenant and Elijah/Elisha's renewal themes, Mark (and Q), according to Horsley, have thus constructed their respective pieces in ways that deeply resonate with the people's social memory.

There can be little doubt that the two sets of five Markan miracle stories, each consisting of a sea crossing, three healings, and a feeding, carry motifs taken from Exodus and the Elijah-Elisha cycle (Mack: 91–93, 215–24). We may, therefore, guided by Horsley, look upon them as residues or retrievals of the memory of ancient Israel. But what precisely are the operations of memory in this instance? Memory, we saw, invariably deals with already commemorated pasts because no past can assert itself in the raw. She is the mediating agency that makes the past accessible to us. To this we must now add that the commemoration of foundational personages is especially inclined to avail itself of mnemonic frames, symbolic patterns, or, in Halbwachs's terms, *les cadres collectifs.* Personages who do not seem fathomable within available categories and appear to exceed current models of comprehension make special demands on memory. Precisely in such cases, memory may fall back upon tradition-honored patterns and seize upon ancient mnemonic frames that are familiar to hearers. In different words, out-of-the ordinary personages are especially vulnerable or, if you will, receptive to mythicization. We are here at the intersection of social memory and myth. The covenant renewal patterns and the Elijah-Elisha motifs provide such "a fundamental framework of organization and interpretation in Mark and Q and the movements they addressed" (Horsley 2001:28). As Jesus is cast into categories that are constitutive of Israel's identity and her relations with God, he is turned into a widely accessible and memorable *Erinnerungsfigur* (J. Assmann 1992:200–202). As carrier of ancient values and virtues shared by the group, he can now function as a believable focus of identity.

It merits our attention that in this instance we are confronted with a special mode of mediating the past. Jesus' conversion into a memorially accessible figure is accomplished by recourse not to recent memories of, or about, Jesus, but to the distant memory of the group. We encounter here what may be called the archaeology of memory, which operates not merely selectively, with regard to Jesus and his subsequent tradition, but archaically, in using a venerable, deep past for present identification and mythicization.

Some essayists examined individual sayings and stories from the gospels or stories taken from larger biblical traditions in light of social memory theory. Hearon explored the story of the woman who anointed Jesus (Mark 14:3–9) as part of the social memory of the emerging church by studying the Markan, Lukan and Johannine versions with a focus toward stable and unstable elements. Wire identified an early Jewish and Christian tradition of birth prophecy stories that resulted from commemorative activities undertaken by and for women in critical times before and after birth. Since it was, and continues to be, the project of form criticism to illuminate the oral identity of stories and sayings extrapolated from larger textual bodies, the recreative tendencies of tradition and performance circumstances, and social contextuality—all features emphasized by the essayists—the challenge will be to define with great methodological clarity the difference between form criticism and social memory theory, or perhaps the advantage of one method over the other.

Apart from viewing certain segments of biblical texts as products of memory's desires, it seems eminently plausible to view the entire Gospel as paradigmatic of memorial drives. We are not thinking here of Mark's mnemonic disposition toward oral delivery (see Shiner), but rather of the Gospel's compositional intent as being motivated by the dynamics of social memory (Kelber 2002). Transmission for the sake of preservation and the arbitration of literary sources are not the only, and not necessarily the most important, dynamics of the Gospels' composition. A deeper, far more complex force driving the formation of the Gospels is the retrieval of the past for the benefit of the present. Remembering Jesus, and not the transmission of traditions or the juggling of literary sources, provided the deepest impulse for the Gospel compositions. What matters most in the literary, memorial composition of the Gospels is not the preservation of tradition or the negotiation of literary sources per se, but rather the reconstitution of the memories of Jesus in the interest of shaping group identity.

A significant aspect in any reflection on the memorial arbitration of Gospel compositions is Jan Assmann's notion of *Traditionsbruch*. Once again, we link up memory theory with media studies, but this time with scribal dynamics. Kirk (6 in this volume) has taken up Assmann's observation that after a period of some forty years communicative memory exhibits a tendency to enter into a critical stage. "40 Jahre sind ein Einschnitt, eine Krise in der kollektiven Erinnerung" (J. Assmann 1992:218). It is the point where, in the ancient experience, the generational memory ceases to function and a new group of memory carriers has to negotiate the crossing of a difficult memorial threshold. One of Assmann's prime examples is the book of Deuteronomy (1992:50–52, 215–22), fictionalized as Moses' farewell speech and addressed to the Israelites who, after some forty years of wandering in the wilderness (Deut 1:3), were encamped on the plains of Moab and poised to enter the promised land. What is of interest to Assmann is Deuteronomy's complex interfacing with Israel's social, cultic, and memorial history. As is well known, Deuteronomy is by a near scholarly consensus identified as "the book of the law" that was discovered in connection with King Josiah's restoration of the temple (2 Kgs 22:2–13), and used in the royal cultic reform. The primary objective of that reform was the centralization of the cult place, an undertaking that aimed at the termination of polytheism and syncretism, and the closing or destruction of non-Israelite cult places. Josiah's forced centralization amounted to a revolution of such unprecedented harshness and terror—comparable to Akhenaten–Amenophis IV's monotheistic revolution in the fourteenth century B.C.E.—that it was tantamount to a serious *Traditionsbruch* (J. Assmann 1992:216, also n. 44)—an event that cried out for explanation and guidance. There lies a deep memorial significance in the fact that Deuteronomy, framed as Moses' legacy of coping with Israel's *Traditionsbruch* and identity crisis following some forty years of wilderness existence, came to serve as a legitimating document for the cultic revolution in the seventh century. In linking up with the memory of Moses who, after forty years, was faced with a critical threshold experience, Josiah's revolution has turned him into an *Erinnerungsfigur* and Deuteronomy into a highly relevant book of remembrances. One regressed into the sacred past and "discovered" Moses' farewell speech that accounted for and provided guidance in the *Traditionsbruch* Israel suffered in 622 B.C.E. in the wake of the cultic revolution of Josiah.

As far as the concept of *Traditionsbruch* is concerned, is it too far-fetched to draw an analogy with the Gospel of Mark in defining and illuminating its historic location at a seminal juncture in early Christian history? As we saw above, the chirographic medium can engender the kind of distancing that is necessary to construct alternate visions in the face of traditional memories, loyalties and imperatives. If we date the Gospel some forty years after the death of the charismatic founding personality, and in all likelihood in the aftermath of the destruction of Jerusalem in 70 C.E., one could conceivably understand the document as a narrative mediation of a threefold crisis: the death of Jesus, the devastation of Jerusalem culminating in the conflagration of the temple, and the cessation of a generation of memories and memory carriers. Could we not be dealing here with an acute example of a *Traditionsbruch* that, following an initial trauma, was acutely compounded by a secondary dislocation some forty years later? Does not the Gospel make sense when we imagine its historical location at a point where present events severely challenged Jesus' commemorated past(s)? And could not the well-known "oddness" of Mark's Gospel be an index of its particular situation that called for a reformulation and reorientation of the collective memories of Jesus?

Ever since modernity has discovered Markan priority, interpreters have (frequently) been tempted to accommodate the Gospel's uncommonly puzzling features to what was assumed to be the Gospel's foundational identity. But to do full justice to the "oddness" of Mark, one may need to keep in mind that the Gospel, far from constituting primary foundationalism, constructs a secondary foundation not necessarily in reaffirmation of, but as corrective gesture vis-à-vis tradition—in short in response to a *Traditionsbruch*.

Mark's Gospel, we saw, is ill explained as the product of stable mnemonics or the repository of archivally transmitted memories, or, we venture, as oral traditional literature. Nor, we reiterate, is it simply the result of intra-Gospel processes or the arbitration of literary sources. Instead, we suggested, the Gospel's deepest compositional motivation was a regressive gesture into the past to recapture Jesus as an *Erinnerungsfigur* for the benefit of solidifying present group identity. At this point, we can reiterate and sharpen our earlier thesis of the Gospel composition. Granted that all remembering is a mediation of commemorated pasts with the present, the special case of Mark suggests that we have to do with a second order rememorization—that is, a redescription of the memories of Jesus in the wake of an excruciatingly painful *Traditionsbruch* that compounded the initial trauma.

Mark is not the only example of a reconfiguration of early memories in the canonical tradition. Esler, in his essay on collective memory and Heb 11, insightfully united oral and memory theory in interpreting the ancestral witnesses of faith in Heb 11 as a product of contested memories. Thatcher observed the redescriptive side in the compositional dynamics of the Gospel of John, and DeConick in those of the *Gospel of Thomas*. Operating on the premise of a recollective, rather than a repetitive, functioning of memory, these essayists postulate John and *Thomas* dealing with memory crises and facilitating memorial realignments with contemporary communal experiences. In the case of John, Thatcher envisioned a transition from the vicissitudes of oral memories toward a scribally secured permanence which necessarily entailed a distortion of orality's fluid memories. We add parenthetically that some twenty years ago, along similar lines, Bruce Woll had argued that John was responding to a deeply charismatic community that had, in a typical oral vein, blurred the lines between the earthly Jesus and the ascended and/or risen Lord. In the case of *Thomas*, DeConick, courageously challenging a virtual commonplace of *Thomas* studies in the U.S., espoused the Gospel's reformulation of prior apocalyptically rooted memories in the direction of mystical and encratic memories. In both instances, the interfacing of medium with memory lies at the heart of the work of the Gospels' memorial reconstructions. We reiterate J. Assmann's observation stated earlier and enunciated several times in this piece: scribality—in relation to oral drives and dependencies—is empowered to detach itself from memorial and communal identities and to reconceptualize commemorated pasts in the interest of present identities. In paraphrasing Assmann, we may say that scribality, especially when employed at points of memorial crises, may facilitate a degree of forgetfulness—distortion even—of prior memories, in the interest of retaining/constructing a particular version of them.

Perhaps no event in Christian origins has made greater demands on memory than Jesus' death. How is memory to deal with the massively disruptive trauma of the crucifixion? We shall not reflect here on the faith of resurrection, which is a modality of overcoming death more than remembering it. In the perspectives of the psychodynamics of remembering, distance is a prerequisite for facing up to the death of Jesus—the absence it spelled, the silence it brought, the horrors it entailed. Hence, the classic form critical premise that the passion narrative constituted one of the oldest coherent narrative pieces, and one constructed in close proximity to the historical events, risks a profound trivialization of the ordeal of remembering Jesus' death. Does not, in this case, historical criticism exhibit a sense of intellectual crudeness, failing to probe the deeper springs that motivate and nourish the story of death? The relative narrative coherence of the passion narrative, implicitly or explicitly given as indication of early compositioning, proves first and foremost narrative competence and not necessarily early production and/or closeness to the events narrated (Kelber 1983:184–99). Psycho-dynamically, the traumatic death of the Messiah is unlikely to have been the first event negotiated in coherent narrative. To the contrary, one has to stand apart from the trauma—temporally, mentally, emotionally—so as to be able to appropriate it as memorial history.

Our earlier observation that the past exists only as remembered past applies with special force to the events surrounding the crucifixion. No event in Christian origins is less likely to be transmitted in its factual rawness, and no experience is more in need of mnemonic frames and mediating patterns, than Jesus' death. The eucharistic ritual is, of course, one way of absorbing the shock effects of the execution and securing its ritual representation. The passion narrative is another way, designed to mediate the violence in narratologically accessible categories. It "was not a matter of simply relating the facts," Arthur Dewey rightly states (127), challenging conventional ignorance about the processes of remembering. To make the trauma of violence socially accessible, one had to tap into Israel's memorial repertoire, both recent and ancient, in search of memory places that were capable of localizing, as well as humanizing, the unrepresentable. In following Nickelsburg, A. Dewey suggested that the Tale of the Persecution and Vindication of the Innocent One served Mark—and Matthew and Luke via Mark's mediation—as a memory place on which Jesus' death was located. In all likelihood, this tale furnished the authorizing locus on which the trauma could be constructed. Yet another way of mediating the unspeakable was the well-known feature of tapping "a catena of ancient texts" (Kermode: 104)—Pss 22 and 69 in particular—for the composition of the passion narrative. There is a tendency among interpreters to explicate the passion narrative's compliance with ancient biblical texts in terms of the doctrinal schematization of promise and fulfilment. Even Kermode, literary critic par excellence, thinks of the Psalm passages as "a prophecy or promise . . . that will later be kept, though perhaps in unexpected ways" (106). But what if one were to approach the passion narrative from the perspective of the difficulties of remembering Jesus' death, and view the Psalm references as an "interpretive 'keying'" (Kirk: 194 in this volume, following Schwartz)—a memorial template as it were—that furnished narrative fragments for the violence so as to make it comprehensible and in a sense bearable within older patterns?

Even the hypothetical Q, traditionally assumed to have been silent on Jesus' death, engaged in commemorative maneuvers to mediate the passion. In invoking Israel's commonplace of the death-of-prophets (Luke 11:49–51)—an archetypical memory of violence—Q, by implication, has keyed Jesus' own death to the fate of prophetic personalities in Jewish history (see Kirk; A. Dewey: 120 in this volume). Without expounding

Jesus' crucifixion, Q has nonetheless summoned forth an ancient memory of Israel—a commemorative frame as it were—for referencing and orienting the primal violence that had traumatized the Jesus movement.

EPILOGUE

Biblical studies as an academic discipline is by and large the product of particular cultural developments that originated in the late Middle Ages, accelerated in Europe's premodern period, and acquired a historically identifiable profile in the seventeenth and eighteenth century Enlightenment period. Informed by nominalism's skepticism toward the transcendental signified (and a corresponding privileging of the literal sense), deeply impacted by the high tech of the fifteenth century, and spurred on by logic's (typography's logic!) imperial drive toward the formulation and implementation of method, the academic approach to the Bible increasingly came to understand itself as historical, critical scholarship.

Among the key features that typify the historical, critical approach to the Bible, the following may be cited: the exploration of the historical conditionedness of texts both in regard to their genesis and with a view toward authorial intentionality; reliance on the literal, that is, historical, sense (*sensus literalis sive historicus*); an almost single-minded focus on texts, intertextuality, literary sources and textual stratification theories; interest in the production of texts more than in their consumption; and a fascination with questions of origin.

In the centuries that saw the rise and flowering of historical, critical scholarship, memory has not fared well, nor has orality. The fact that a broad spectrum of issues related to memory and orality was entirely intrinsic to our ancient Jewish, Greco-Roman and Christian legacies and to ancient Mediterranean humanity at large, points up the patently culture-bound dimension of the historical paradigm. Do we dare say that in a fundamentally cultural sense the so-called historical criticism of the Bible has proven to be mnemohistory at least as much as historiography?

During the last century, the virtual absence of the works of memory from the historical paradigm was to a considerable extent correlated with form criticism. Because the methodological assumptions inherent in form criticism held sway over the longest part of biblical scholarship in the twentieth century, the critical analysis and gradual demise of the method—dramatically initiated by Güttgemanns and reinforced by growing insights both into oral, rhetorical culture and into the narrative nature of the Gospels—carries far-reaching implications for the discipline. What we are wrestling with are not merely the flaws of a particular method, but the inadequacy of a theory that was fundamental to our understanding of the verbal art in biblical studies.

Separately and interactively, orality/scribality studies, social memory (and narrative criticism, in the case of the Gospels), have the potential of exposing the flaws of the historical premises of form criticism, and its complicity with modernity's typographical mode of thought. Separately and interactively, orality/scribality, social memory and narrative criticism hold it within their powers to point in the direction of a reformulation of the historical paradigm. In the end, it may come down to an understanding of the intersections of oral, scribal, narrative, and memorial dynamics, or simply of the interfacing of memory with manuscript. But memory, we claim, may hold the key.

JESUS IN FIRST-CENTURY MEMORY—A RESPONSE

Barry Schwartz

Shortly after George Washington's death, the New Republic's leading men realized they were living in a nation without a past—that the great legacy they had acquired as Englishmen was gone and had to be replaced by a new past that could make up in intensity what it lacked in time and depth. The nation's writers and artists thus began the great task of monument making, poetry writing, ritual observance, painting, place naming, and hagiography. What made this activity so significant—so exuberant, so forced—was its timing. The growing commemoration of the New Republic coincided with a steady erosion of its unity, culminating in a devastating civil war.

The Christian communities of the first century, like the American nation of the early nineteenth, went through a similar commemorative era. Between a new, self-governing nation and a new religious minority disdained within its own society there is a big difference, but the two entities felt the same need to represent their newness and to anchor it to a framework of tradition. How does a people without a past of its own, whether living in 50 C.E. or 1800 C.E., satisfy this need for itself and its posterity?

The people of the Second Temple era lived in the throes of a legitimation crisis, a time when the world around them became everyday more oppressive. It was a season of revolution—as revolution was then understood (Horsley 1987; Crossan 1994): wise men, possessed by visions, saw God, exorcised demons, and performed miracles. Signs of the apocalypse and the end of the world abounded (Perrin and Duling: 95–126). The people sensed the time of the Messiah approaching. They yearned for him, and to so many Jesus seemed so right. Jesus condemned the elites as he fed the masses, forgave the outcast, broke bread with the unworthy, healed the poor, and comforted the oppressed. As Jesus' followers aligned his life to the Mosaic covenant and his Passover death to the exodus and to ancient prophecies of the Messiah's advent, he became a symbol of liberation, hope for a new and just world, and contempt for an establishment that served, rather than resisted, God's enemies.

MEMORY AS A CULTURAL SYSTEM

The social memory of Jesus was, like any form of understanding, "an act of recognition, a pairing in which an object (or an event, act, or emotion) is identified by placing it against the background of an appropriate symbol" (Geertz 1973:215). Jesus' life was an "object"; sacred history, an "appropriate symbol." "Keying" was the practice connecting object to symbol. Keying makes present scenes meaningful by articulating their relation to the past. Abraham's answering God's call to sacrifice his son, for example, is a symbolic event that defines the crucifixion's significance. Keying the crucifixion to Abraham's sacrifice, in turn, makes memory a cultural system because it matches present trauma to a publicly accessible—that is, cultural—frame of historical reference. Keying is communicative movement—talk, writing, and ritual that publicly connects otherwise separate realms of memory.

If this volume accomplishes its purpose, the reader will gain a sense of *what* and *how* first-century Christians thought about Jesus. Such insight cannot come from any single essay, for the memory of Jesus is too comprehensive to be grasped from the perspective of just one of our authors; yet each author reveals an aspect of memory invisible from the perspective of any other. Together, the essays constitute more than a collection of interesting insights; they comprise a wide and coherent vista on first-century Christian memory.

MEMORY-WORK

Jesus' contemporaries were not just conscious of his existence; they were conscious of his being something. To know Jesus they had to key his words and actions to the nourishing symbols of their tradition. The resulting match was messy but not muddled. Jesus' interpreters made him relevant by exaggeration, even invention, but they could not have ignored credulity's limits. Unrestrained by the authority of testimony or the force of evidence, the essence of their Messiah would have evaporated. Christians wishing to preserve Jesus' prestige therefore assumed three tasks: to propose an image of him resonant with the known facts, to overcome images that defied those facts, and to make their own images prevail. This volume's main achievement is to show how first-century writers and public men and women carried out these tasks and why they succeeded.

Jesus' admirers employed three kinds of memory-work to portray him. First, they keyed images of Jesus directly to the sacred history of Israel (*framing*). Second, they revised and conceived multiple versions of Jesus' life, without reference to Israel's history (*reproduction*). Third, they sustained a tension between authorial creativity and invented history, on the one hand, and, on the other, authorial discipline and authentic history (*dual representation*).

Memory-work genres are classifications based on similarities and differences in the way Jesus' contemporaries represented him. Making such distinctions involves sorting and combining representations and abstracting elements with a view to making the welter of Jesus images comprehensible. Genres, however, are not descriptions of reality; they are "ideal types" (Weber 1949:89–98), analytic concepts for comprehending activities by emphasis and simplification. No contemporary thought about Jesus simply by keying an episode in his life to an episode in sacred history, brooding over multiple versions of it, or wondering whether oral accounts were more likely to have been contrived than written ones. Memory work is a concept, not a historical, ethnographic, or biographical account. Memory work, like a lens, filters extraneous materials the better *for us* to see the kind of recollecting relevant to our purposes. Since memory work is a limiting concept against which real situations are scanned for cultural significance, the words and deeds we record, combine, and conceptualize today connect us to the first-century Christian's imagination of Jesus.

FRAMING: KEYING PRESENT TO PAST

Social memory's primary function—the keying of the recent to the ancient past—is cleanly addressed by Richard Horsley, Alan Kirk, Antoinette Wire, and Georgia Keightley. The point of Horsley's "Prominent Patterns in the Social Memory of Jesus and Friends" is apparent in its epigraph, which indicates that "the absolutely new is inconceivable." In "all modes of experience," Horsley adds, "we always base our particular experiences on a prior context to ensure that they are intelligible at all." If Jesus were as radical as the form critics and their admirers maintain, his contemporaries would have never understood him. Not only the content of the Jesus story but its stubborn continuity makes the strongest impression on Horsley.

No generation adds much to what it receives from the past, especially in a "postfigurative culture" (M. Mead: 1–24) whose members conceived their ancestors identical to themselves and found in their virtues the source of all moral authority. Crossan, however, believes that Jesus' way of thinking differed from his contemporaries' and claims that his database contains "totally new" statements that set Jesus' words apart. Horsley's finding these statements saturated with Judaic tradition conveys the kernel of his essay. Jesus' admirers keyed his sea crossings, exorcisms, healings, and wilderness feeding to comparable episodes in the drama of ancient Israel. Horsley's determination to transcend the perspective of the twenty-first century thus brings us into contact with the Jesus of the first century—not the originator of a new relation between humanity and God but the culmination of a long line of prophets sent by God to instruct Israel in God's ways. Bringing closure to three thousand years of history, nothing Jesus said or did could have struck his followers as novel. That the historical frame, not the verbal minutiae, of Jesus' life was transmitted across generations is the basis of Horsley's critique of the Jesus Seminar, whose "copy and save model" ignores the very world within which Jesus' reputation emerged. Jesus' followers never obsessed over his particular sayings; they embraced his life and the sacred history in which that life was embedded. "Of what story or stories do I find myself a part?" (MacIntyre: 201) is the question they asked in their effort to define the meaning of their own lives (see also Johnson 1999: 72–74).

That memory orients experience, including the experience of traumatic death, is the message of Alan Kirk's "The Memory of Violence and the Death of Jesus in Q." The story begins at a critical point of conflict: as Jesus condemns the Pharisees' and lawyers' moral corruption, he foresees and defines the meaning of his own fate:

> 'I will send them prophets and apostles, some of whom they will kill and persecute,' so that this generation may be charged with the blood of all the prophets shed since the foundation of the world, from the blood of Abel to the blood of Zechariah, who perished between the altar and the sanctuary. Yes, I tell you, it will be charged against this generation. (Luke 11:49–51; see also Matt 23:29–36)

The crucifixion stunned and humiliated the early Christians, but they found their bearing by integrating it into Israel's story, then by commemorating it, reversing its stigma, and assigning culpability to the Jewish elite and Roman oppressors. Remembering the crucifixion—and this is the significant point—was essential to overcoming its effects. Discussing it, working it over in their minds, locating it within a meaningful frame of historical reference, the little circle of Christians comprehended and so mastered it.

As Kirk explains why the crucifixion was unrepresentable in nonnarrative sources, like Q, he raises the most serious questions about Jesus being what Hopkins calls a "reconstructed sacred hero," especially when his reconstructed narrative is allegedly achieved, as Hopkins tells us, by "fitting him into a matrix which had already been formed in the Jewish Scriptures" (Hopkins: 299). Kirk's goal is to explain why Jesus' death was aligned to Scripture in the first place. What counts, in this regard, is not a particular reading of the crucifixion but its properties: the timing and symbolism—the sheer humiliation of it—that compel Christians to read it one way rather than another.

Antoinette Clark Wire, like Horsley and Kirk, sees first-century Christians making sense of Jesus' life by locating it under the canopy of tradition. In Wire's "Early Birth Prophecy Stories and Women's Social Memory," God's words to Mary recapitulate God's words to the mothers of Abraham, Elijah, Elisha, Moses, Samson, and John the Baptist. The practice of women telling each other birth prophecy stories—visions of their sons turning the world upside-down—was part of the era's messianic rage, and the topic hardly varied: God's newborn will deliver Israel from its enemies and reestablish the glory of God's people. Jesus appears as the latest—and last—of the men whom God has brought to the world to do his will. Many prophecies failed, but the few successes became "threads weaving the framework of memory." And what is a framework if not an instrument of sense-making? Christianity's early storytellers situated every episode of Jesus' life, from birth to death, in relation to its historical precedents, performing a literal identification of present and past, human and divine.

If the keying of present to past events can be reasonably stipulated, what about its transmission? Georgia Masters Keightley's "Christian Collective Memory and Paul's Knowledge of Jesus" asks how Paul managed to give such a moving account of Jesus' mission without having known him. Her premise is threefold: that (1) social memory "provides the community with its overarching view of reality," setting forth its "fundamental order, character, significance"; (2) the framework of memory is transmitted in ritual settings; and (3) since social order has a time frame "pertaining to the community's founding origins," tradition must be its sustaining mechanism. Yet, Keightley's merit is to show how ritual transforms as it institutionalizes. When baptism replaces circumcision and ancient food taboos disappear, the lines dividing men and women, Jew and Gentile, shift. Paul's rituals universalized Christianity while extending Jesus' own embracing of the outsider and the despised. Through ritual, Jesus denied invidious social distinctions within Judaism. Through ritual, Paul embraced the Gentile world and denied the privileged status of Judaism itself.

To be told that Paul learned about Jesus through ritual is no surprise, for most Christians learned about him in this way (Meeks: 140–63). Moreover, Keightley fails to show how rituals enabled Paul to understand Jesus as he did. We know from Emile Durkheim (1965) and Stefan Czarnowski (1975 [1919]) that ritual's power resides in its capacity to assemble and arouse its participants emotionally and morally. Keying mundane experience to a sacred past, ritual fuses Christianity's worldview to the moods and motivations its sacred symbols induce. In this light, Paul's love for Jesus may have stemmed less from the facts of Jesus' life than from emotions generated by its commemoration. Jesus was not commemorated because he was adored; rather he was, for most, adored because he was commemorated.

Keightley's illustration of Christian ritual keying the life of Jesus into the narrative of Jewish history is a telling example of framing, but if the continuity between the life of Jesus and its historical frame were perfect, he would be just another Jewish prophet. He claimed to be more, and for that claim to mean anything his life had to be distinguished from the heritage with which it had been identified. Philip F. Esler confronts this dilemma in "Collective Memory and Hebrews 11."

Hebrews' author was selective. He omitted Moses' Sinai covenant and David's kingdom, and he modernized history by making Abraham's belief in resurrection prophetic of Jesus' return. He portrayed Abel, Enoch, and Noah as possessors of "faith," a distinguishing feature of first-century Christianity, and so enlisted them retrospectively as "heirs" of salvation and by implication precursors of Christianity. Ancient Israelites had little to say about "faith," but their connection to Jesus became evident once the new Christians pointed it out. Clarifying the way early Christianity at once maintained and modified its link to ancient Israel, Esler's insight points to a variant of memory work's primary function: framing. He shows contemporaries identifying themselves to themselves by recasting, then embracing, their beginnings.

REPRODUCTION: MULTIPLICITY AND REVISION

Framing refers to the keying of one class of narratives—the stories of Jesus' life—onto another class—the stories of antiquity. To remember, in this light, is to subsume an exceptional event, like a virgin birth or crucifixion, under a more general class of events where a community traditionally finds its identity. Kirk, Horsley, and Wire discuss this process in its simplest form; Esler's account, wherein Jesus' life is keyed to historical events adjusted for better connection, is slightly more elaborate. Because events are understood in so many different ways, however, the concept of framing requires complements. Holly Hearon's and April DeConick's essays on multiple and revised versions of Jesus' life are so useful because they show redundancy as well as keying to be necessary to social memory's function. Edmund Leach's statement about the variants of myth clearly applies to reproductive memory-work:

> Let us imagine the situation of individual A who is trying to get a message to a friend B who is almost out of earshot, and let us suppose that communication is further hampered by various kinds of interference—noise from the wind, passing cars, and so on. What will A do? If he is sensible he will not be satisfied with shouting his message just once; he will shout it several times, and give a different wording to

the message each time, supplementing his words with visual signals.
(Leach: 63–64)

Reproductive memory-work refers to projects undertaken for different
reasons—to correct or deliberately color earlier versions of an event, or to
explain an event that disappoints or confuses—but the outcome is the
same: alternative versions of the life of Jesus.

Holly Hearon's account of the woman who anointed Jesus nicely
illustrates redundancy in the service of memory. Mark's anointer reveals
her prophetic gift and reconfirms Jesus' messianic mission by anointing
his head in anticipation of burial. John's anointer, acquainted with Jesus,
models an intimate relation between the sinners and the savior of the
world. Luke's version of the story sets the scene much earlier in the home
of a Galilean Pharisee. When an outcast woman washes Jesus' feet with
her tears and dries them with her hair, the Pharisee condemns her and
commands her to desist, but Jesus, moved by her love, bids her to continue and forgives her sins.

The anointing stories emerge in three different Christian communities and define Jesus in three different ways, but Hearon, the most
restrained of this volume's contributors, never tries to connect the content
of the stories to the social environments in which they were promulgated.
The basic question, "Who is creating the memory, for whom, and to what
end," might make the narrative "a fertile ground for contest," but Hearon
does not say what the contest is. Also, her fascinating remarks about
women's roles in establishing Jesus' identity are points casually dropped
rather than arguments developed. The essay tantalizes gender scholars
but is more immediately resonant with witness perception experiments
(see Loftus) showing different onlookers conveying the essence of a scene
redundantly by remembering different details.

As Holly Hearon analyzes variant versions of Jesus' anointing,
April DeConick's "Reading of the *Gospel of Thomas* as a Repository of
Communal Memory" confronts the ultimate problem of Christian
memory: Jesus' failure to return in judgement and save Israel. The first
century witnessed many people waiting eagerly for Jesus to return, but
the longer they waited the more doubtful seemed his messianic claim.
Thomas's author meets these doubts by replacing an apocalyptic
prophecy with a mystical one: many would look for the Messiah but
not find him. God's kingdom had already been established, and if so
few noticed it was because it happened so gradually—as a mustard
seed develops into a full plant. DeConick's contribution to *When
Prophecy Fails*, a venerable case study of faith becoming stronger after
disconfirmation, is to describe a prophecy succeeding by being modified to fit its outcome.

I use the term "modified" rather than "reconstructed" to emphasize DeConick's view of *Thomas*'s motive: to "correct," not "reinvent." There is something in tradition and memory, according to Edward Shils, which calls forth a striving "for 'better' truth, for greater clarity and coherence" (214). The very attachment to tradition requires the clarification of its ambiguities. Because *Thomas* was moved to illuminate rather than manipulate Jesus' words, DeConick's essay, more than any other in this collection, challenges the constructionist project. If the remembering of Jesus was an effort to resolve tensions facing church and community, then why, so many years after the second coming became problematic, did the Gospel writers attribute to Jesus the promise to return in the first place? Why did they "invent" a prophecy already in doubt? They could have surely concocted a more convenient story. Their felt obligation to record what they believed Jesus said (*because* Jesus said it) reflects the past's resistance to efforts to make it over, even when those efforts might resolve a great dilemma of faith.

If memory-work consisted solely of correction, however, it would have none of the significance that framing—the keying of present events to the sacred past—affords, and we would be incapable of answering questions about the meaning of Jesus' mission and the Christian community's ability to remember it. The problem for twenty-first century scholars is to realize not only that *Thomas*'s audience was more receptive than they, but also that it was not stupid. Given Jesus' failure to return in person, Christians must have believed in Jesus ambivalently; non-Christians must have felt vindicated in their doubts about his being the Messiah. This memory crisis widened the arena for both the play of imagination and efforts to restrain it.

DUAL REPRESENTATION: SPONTANEITY AND RESTRAINT

Between life and form, Georg Simmel declared, there is an irreconcilable opposition. "Form means limits, contrast against what is neighboring, cohesion of a boundary by way of a real or ideal center." Life means a continuous stream of impulse opposed to all fixed forms and limits (Simmel 1971:365). The fundamental character of human experience resides in the resolving of such opposition, and social memory is an aspect of this dynamic: at once endless flux, imaginative creation, variable, and open-ended, yet enclosed in its carriers and contents. Social memory's tendency to change is checked by its tendency to limit and make itself permanent. While reproductive memory-work refers to the safeguarding of Jesus' renown through variation and revision, dual representation refers to contrasting but interdependent depictions: casual, even playful, constructions of Jesus' life opposed by deliberate efforts to render that life unchangeable.

In "The Locus for Death: Social Memory and the Passion Narratives," Arthur Dewey represents one side of this dualism. First-century memory, he declares, was a "creative social construction." Antique historical writings carried no evidentiary weight; they were "inventions" allowing listeners to "see" the meaning of historical events. For example, the Passion Narrative, first appearing in the *Gospel of Peter* (55–65 C.E.) and Mark (ca. 60–70 C.E.), was structured along the lines of the "Tale of the Persecution and Vindication of the Innocent One"—a schema that had for centuries subsumed a variety of martyrological events. For Dewey, the memory bed of the Gospels consisted not of historical events but of the narrative schema that made them meaningful.

To appreciate Dewey's claim that "the act of memory is the work of invention," of "constructing" or "delivering a place for images," one may contemplate his excursus on Trajan's Column, a Roman shrine which "delivers a place for images" that "authorize" a particular reading of the past. Such sites of memory trump eye-witness testimony. "The modern distinction between fact and fiction, between ... reiteration and an unreal imagination was just not that crucial to the ancients." The passion, then, is merely one of many items drawn from a warehouse of materials to animate the Tale of the Persecution and Vindication of the Innocent One. That tale embodies commonplace, not truth, and allows the rememberer to "find things out" and to frame "new" memories.

For Tom Thatcher, new "historical" (written) memory pulverizes and replaces new "communicative" (oral) memory, constituting an inexorable movement toward objectification, formalization, and permanence. His essay demonstrates a major function of social memory: making the past at once permanent and mutable.

Since speakers restate their ideas in various ways, and different listeners bring their own interpretation to what they hear, dual representation is symptomatic of efforts to standardize memory by transforming oral into literate units. In "Why John Wrote a Gospel," Thatcher captures the formal (scriptural) aspect of the tension to which the concept of dual representation alludes. Written history does to oral history (whatever its truth value) what ice does to water: by freezing oral tradition, writing preserves it. To freeze, however, is also to alter: John wrote a Gospel not to preserve a particular moment in the *oral* memory of Jesus, but to replace it with a *written* version. Few doubt John's ends: to counter the influence of antichrists and to recruit, legitimate, and prove the superiority of his own brand of Christianity; but no one has asked why John took the trouble to pursue his goals through writing. Since he believed Jesus' memory could be forever preserved by the Holy Spirit alone, he must have written his story for tactical reasons: to enchant the unbeliever, and to outshout and outlast his opponents.

Thatcher's point—that writing performs the function of making a statement permanent and more authoritative—builds on a venerable theme. Belief in immortality through writing appeared in Homer, Virgil, and Ovid. Their contemporaries sensed a kind of magic in the written word, something that could preserve its creator and his words—a way of transcending death. In the Roman empire, the written word performed the added function of affirming legal rules, commands and instructions, and cementing hegemony. But Thatcher goes further, suggesting that written memory has a constructive edge of its own. Writing permanently restructures reality through distortions inherent in the writing process, including arbitrary beginning and ending points, and periodizations based on the demands of presentation and argument rather than on rules of validation. First-century revisions of sacred history were based not only on new facts and imaginings, but also on new forms of communication. Such was the contribution of Scripture to early Christian memory.

CONCLUSION

Maurice Halbwachs, Rudolph Bultmann, and their successors were serious constructionists. They analyzed the commemoration of Jesus by matching representations of his life to real social predicaments in such a way as to make it seem the former were derivatives of the latter. They educed but never explained the relationship, ignoring connections among social experience (of which memory itself is a constituent), the contents of oral and written history, and the commemorative rituals through which these contents were collectively realized. They never got beyond a simple correspondence theory of social memory. Concerned with the way early Christians molded the story of Jesus to their own preoccupations, they saw memory reflecting reality but never as a social force in its own right. Their analyses cast memory as a construction rather than a selectively moral and inspirational marking of history.

The essays in this collection explore many aspects of social memory that constructionism ignores, but important omissions should be mentioned. That two of these essays deal with the crucifixion, but none with the resurrection, is a major shortcoming, for the conviction that God raised Jesus is the foundation of belief in Jesus' divinity and messianic mission. A second shortcoming stems from the authors' conveying such a strong sense of Christianity's inevitability. Resurrection preserved belief in Jesus' claim to be the world's Messiah, but none of our authors attempt to explain why so precarious a claim could spread as rapidly and deeply as it did. Jesus' adversaries must have attributed his miracle stories either to fabrication or to magic and sorcery. Why, then, in light of his failure actually to reappear as the Messiah, was the story of his resurrection so convincing? Thirdly, doubt and conviction are basic properties of collective memory; yet, most contributors bracket the issue of historical veracity, refusing to worry—as did the Christians about whom they write—whether Jesus and his achievements might be a figment of the collective imagination rather than a real man doing real things. Reality, however, makes a difference. If we cannot at least estimate the authenticity of an event, we have no way of knowing whether different communities or different generations have distorted it. If we cannot estimate authenticity, we can reach no understanding of how commemoration selectively celebrates the historical record. Lacking historical benchmarks, we can only say that social memory varies; we can never know how much or in what direction.

Shortcomings, however, cannot define significance. As I see it—and my viewpoint is sociological, not historical—this volume has identified important dynamics of early Christian memory. I have tried to bring this achievement to mind by relating the realities of Christian memory to three concepts. The concept of framing refers to early Christian writers and speakers in ritual settings keying remembrances of Jesus (fragmentary and limited as they were) to traditional narratives, including Moses' covenant, the murder of the righteous, birth prophecies (Horsley, Kirk, Wire, Keightley), and the keying of the life of Jesus to past events after transforming the latter into prefigurations of the former (Esler). The reproduction concept refers to episodes in the Jesus story appearing in multiple versions or as prophecies transformed in order to accommodate their failure to materialize (Hearon, DeConick). Remembering, however, was more than a matter of keying and multiplication; some first-century authors tried to conjure stories from their own imagination (Dewey), but were opposed by others intent on perpetuating witnesses' memories through the written word (Thatcher). The concept of "dual representation" is an effort to capture this tension. Dual representation, like framing and reproduction, is not the deliberate strategy of any single speaker or writer; it is, to repeat, an investigator's construct, an effort to represent and link together two contrasting portrayals of Jesus, each dependent for its meaning on the other, long after they were produced. The overall picture is one of half-truths, contradictions, distortions and inventions. Beneath the messy surface, however, is a coherent pattern produced by primary keyings that leave details of Jesus' life open to infinite reinterpretation while securing its essence to history and tradition.

This tripartite memory-work typology is not limited to first-century Christianity. At a time when the Great Seal of the United States bore an image of Moses leading his people from slavery, the American people dubbed George Washington "The American Moses" and imagined him as their defender against the Great Pharaoh, George III. Intellectuals, steeped in classical as well as biblical history, keyed their hero to exemplars from Roman antiquity, including Cincinnatus. However, the views of Washington's enemies, as well as admirers, grasp the fuller complexity of his image, which the concept of reproductive memory-work seeks to capture. Envy and bitter resentment over one man being given credit for the nation's founding, so explicit in John Adams and Thomas Jefferson's correspondence, was part of the broader nineteenth-century perspective. Superimposed on these framing and reproductive processes were wondrous products of fantasy countered by steadfast assertions of fact—the stuff of the dual representation genre. Mason Locke Weems, the most famous fantasizer of all, published imaginative accounts of young Washington chopping down cherry trees while Jared Sparks, editor of *North American Review*, drew on original papers and letters to write what he hoped would be George Washington's last biography. The people of the first and nineteenth centuries, then, needed flexible memories to show where their great men fit in the scheme of things. These people were ready to entertain different ideas about the men who changed their lives, but they were unwilling to entertain no ideas at all, to shrug off and forget Jesus and Washington as men whose fate had no bearing on their own. To do so would be to leave the world to itself and to abandon efforts to understand it. Many alienated men and women of our day may be able to live contentedly without memory, but there were fewer such people in Washington's day and fewer still in Jesus'.

Initial scholarly efforts are bound to be wrong in many ways, but Alan Kirk, Tom Thatcher, and their colleagues have given the field of biblical studies its first systematic statement on social memory. They take memory not as a metaphor for myth and distortion, but a selection of events from the historical record (an imprecise record but nonetheless historical) for reflection and celebration. They have pulled back the curtain on the way Jesus was remembered by his own generation. Their contributions to this volume disagree with one another in many ways, but a dominant thread appears. We know now, even more certainly than before, that history and memory, so often seen as polar opposites, must be interdependent. Jesus' life has been to some extent distorted by conditions external to it, but there would be no memory to distort without a vague but obdurate reality warranting—indeed, demanding—preservation.

I have compared first-century Christianity with the new American republic because their similarities are more instructive than their differences. America, a land of Englishmen, had to establish a past similar to and different from England's. The new Christianity, like the New Republic, had to differentiate itself from a Jewish society of which its earliest members were a part. But if social memory is essential to a new moral community, what were the early Christian communities, especially the first-century ones, to do? How does a church without a past of its own create one? That the collective memory of early Christianity consisted almost entirely of stories transmitted orally in ritual settings, sparse and undecorated by iconography, monuments, shrines, and place names—in short, a symbolically impoverished environment—makes this achievement even more remarkable. In one generation—no longer than it took Americans to establish their unique past—Christianity's chronicles gave to Jews and Gentiles alike a narrative that would instruct, inspire, and provoke for centuries.

WORKS CONSULTED

Achtemeier, Paul J. 1990. Omne Verbum Sonat: The New Testament and the Oral Environment of Late Western Antiquity. *JBL* 109:3–27.

Aichele, George and Gary A. Phillips, eds. 1995. *Intertextuality and the Bible. Semeia* 69/70.

Alonso, Ana Maria. 1988. The Effects of Truth: Re-presentations of the Past and the Imagining of Community. *JHS* 1:33–57.

Appadurai, Arjun. 1981. The Past as a Scarce Resource. *Man* NS 16:201–19.

Assmann, Aleida. 1999. *Erinnerungsräume: Formen und Wandlungen des kulturellen Gedächtnisses.* Munich: Beck.

Assmann, Aleida, and Jan Assmann. 1983. Schrift und Gedächtnis. Pages 265–84 in Assmann, Assmann, and Hardmeier.

———. 1988. Schrift, Tradition und Kultur. Pages 25–49 in *Zwischen Festtag und Alltag: Zehn Beiträge zum Thema Mündlichkeit und Schriftlichkeit.* Edited by Paul Goetsch, Wolfgang Raible, and Hans-Robert Roemer. Tübingen: Narr.

Assmann, Aleida, Jan Assmann, and Christof Hardmeier, eds. 1983. *Schrift und Gedächtnis: Beiträge zur Archäologie der literarischen Kommunikation.* Munich: Fink.

Assmann, Jan. 1983. Schrift, Tod und Identität: Das Grab als Vorschule der Literatur im alten Ägypten. Pages 64–93 in Assmann, Assmann, and Hardmeier.

———. 1988. Égypte ancienne—la mémoire monumentale. Pages 47–56 in Gignoux.

———. 1992. *Das kulturelle Gedächtnis. Schrift, Erinnerung und politische Identität in frühen Hochkulturen.* Munich: Beck.

———. 1995a. Ancient Egyptian Antijudaism: A Case of Distorted Memory. Pages 365–76 in Schachter.

———. 1995b. Collective Memory and Cultural Identity. *New German Critique* 65:125–33.

———. 2000. *Religion und kulturelles Gedächtnis: Zehn Studien.* Munich: Beck.

Attridge, Harold W. 1989. *The Epistle to the Hebrews: A Commentary on the Epistle to the Hebrews.* Hermeneia. Philadelphia: Fortress.

Augustine. 1975. *Confessions.* Translated by R. S. Pine-Coffin. Baltimore: Penguin.

Baltzer, Klaus. 1971. *The Covenant Formulary.* Philadelphia: Fortress.

Barrett, Charles K. 1978. *The Gospel according to St. John.* 2nd ed. Philadelphia: Westminster.

Barth, Fredrik. 1969. Introduction. Pages 9–38 in *Ethnic Groups and Boundaries: The Social Organization of Culture Difference.* Edited by Fredrik Barth. London: George, Allen & Unwin.

Bartlett, Frederic C. 1964. *Remembering: A Study in Experimental and Social Psychology*. Cambridge: Cambridge University Press.

Barton, Stephen. 1991. Mark as Narrative: The Story of the Anointing Woman (Mk 14:3–9). *ExpTim* 102:230–34.

Baxandall, Michael. 1972. *Painting and Experience in Fifteenth-Century Italy*. New York: Oxford University Press.

Beavis, Mary Ann. 1988. Women as Models of Faith in Mark. *BTB* 18:3–9.

Becker, Carl. 1935. *Everyman His Own Historian: Essays on History and Politics*. New York: Crofts.

Bell, Catherine. 1992. *Ritual Theory, Ritual Practice*. New York: Oxford University Press.

———. 1997. *Ritual: Perspectives and Dimensions*. New York: Oxford University Press.

Bellah, Robert N., Richard Madsen, William M. Sullivan, Ann Swidler, and Steven M. Tipton. 1985. *Habits of the Heart*. Berkeley and Los Angeles: University of California Press.

Ben Amos, Dan. 1982a. Analytic Categories and Ethnic Genres. Pages 38–64 in *Folklore in Context: Essays*. New Delhi: South Asian Publishers.

———. 1982b. The Concept of Genre in Folklore. Pages 65–85 in *Folklore in Context: Essays*. New Delhi: South Asian Publishers.

Ben Yehuda, Nachman. 1995. *The Masada Myth: Collective Memory and Mythmaking in Israel*. Madison: University of Wisconsin Press.

Blank, Sheldon H. 1938. The Death of Zechariah in Rabbinic Literature. *HUCA* 12/13:327–46.

Blomberg, Craig. 1995. Where Do We Start Studying Jesus? Pages 17–50 in *Jesus under Fire*. Edited by Michael J. Wilkins and J. P. Moreland. Grand Rapids: Zondervan.

Bodnar, John. 1989. Power and Memory in Oral History: Workers and Managers at Studebaker. *JAH* 74:1201–21.

———. 1992. *Remaking America: Public Memory, Commemoration, and Patriotism in the Twentieth Century*. Princeton: Princeton University Press.

Bonanno, George A. 1990. Remembering and Psychotherapy. *Psychotherapy* 27:175–86.

Boomershine, Thomas E. 1988. *Story Journey: An Invitation to the Gospel as Storytelling*. Nashville: Abingdon.

Bornkamm, Gunther. 1971. *Paul*. Translated by D. M. G. Stalker. London: Harper & Row.

Bouchard, Donald F. 1977. Introduction. Pages 16–25 in Michel Foucault, *Language, Counter-Memory, Practice: Selected Essays and Interviews*. Edited and translated by Donald F. Bouchard and Sherry Simon. Ithaca, N.Y.: Cornell University Press.

Bousset, Wilhelm. 1901. Die Himmelsreise der Seele. *ARW* 4:136–69. Freiburg: Mohr Siebeck.

Boyarin, Daniel. 1990. *Intertextuality and the Reading of Midrash*. Indianapolis: Indiana University Press.

Boyarin, Jonathan, ed. 1994. *Remapping Memory: The Politics of Time and Space*. Minneapolis: University of Minnesota Press.

Bradshaw, Paul. 2002. *The Search for the Origins of Christian Worship: Sources and Methods for the Study of Early Liturgy.* New York: Oxford University Press.

Braun, Herbert. 1984. *An die Hebräer.* HNT 14. Tübingen: Mohr Siebeck.

Brown, Raymond. 1966–70. *The Gospel according to John.* 2 vols. AB 29–29A. Garden City, N.Y.: Doubleday.

———. 1993. *The Death of the Messiah.* New York: Doubleday.

Bruce, Frederick F. 1983. *The Gospel of John.* Grand Rapids: Eerdmans.

Bultmann, Rudolf. 1962. The Study of the Synoptic Gospels. Pages 7–78 in *Form Criticism: Two Essays on New Testament Research.* Translated by Frederick C. Grant. New York: Harper. [orig. 1934]

———. 1963. *The History of the Synoptic Tradition.* Translated by John Marsh. New York: Harper & Row. [orig. 1921]

———. 1968. *The History of the Synoptic Tradition.* Translated by John Marsh. Rev. ed. New York: Harper & Row.

———. 1971. *The Gospel of John: A Commentary.* Translated by G. R. Beasley-Murray, R. W. N. Hoare, and J. K. Riches. Philadelphia: Westminster.

Burke, Peter. 1989. History as Social Memory. Pages 97–113 in *Memory: History, Culture, and the Mind.* Edited by Thomas Butler. New York: Blackwell.

Burkert, Walter. 1985. *Greek Religion.* Translated by John Raffan. Oxford: Blackwell.

Cameron, Ron. 1991. The Gospel of Thomas and Christian Origins. Pages 381–92 in *The Future of Early Christianity: Essays in Honor of Helmut Koester.* Edited by B. Pearson. Minneapolis: Fortress.

———. 1994. Alternate Beginnings Different Ends: Eusebius, Thomas, and the Construction of Christian Origins. Pages 507–21 in *Religious Propaganda and Missionary Competition in the New Testament World: Essays Honoring Dieter Georgi.* Edited by L. Bormann, K. Del Tredici, and A. Standhartinger. NovTSup 74. Leiden: Brill.

———. 1996. Mythmaking and Intertextuality in Early Christianity. Pages 37–50 in *Reimagining Christian Origins.* Edited by E. Castelli and H. Taussig. Valley Forge, Pa.: Trinity Press International.

———. 1999. Ancient Myths and Modern Theories of the Gospel of Thomas and Christian Origins. *MTSR* 11:236–57.

Carroll, Robert P. 1979. *When Prophecy Failed: Cognitive Dissonance in the Prophetic Traditions of the Old Testament.* New York: Seabury.

Carruthers, Mary. 1990. *The Book of Memory: A Study in Medieval Culture.* Cambridge: Cambridge University Press.

———. 1998. *The Craft of Thought: Meditation, Rhetoric, and the Making of Images, 400–1200.* Cambridge: Cambridge University Press.

Carson, Donald A. 1991. *The Gospel according to John.* Pillar New Testament Commentary. Grand Rapids: Eerdmans.

Casey, Edward S. 1987. *Remembering: A Phenomenological Study.* Bloomington: Indiana University Press.

———. 2000. *Remembering: A Phenomenological Study.* 2nd ed. Bloomington: Indiana University Press.

Cinnirella, Marco. 1998. Exploring Temporal Aspects of Social Identity: The Concept of Possible Social Identities. *JSP* 28:227–48.

Clandinin, D. Jean, and F. Michael Connelly. 2002. *Narrative Inquiry: Experience and Story in Qualitative Research.* San Francisco: Jossey-Bass.

Coakley, J. F. 1988. The Anointing at Bethany and the Priority of John. *JBL* 107:241–56.

Coarelli, Filippo. 2000. *The Column of Trajan.* Translated by Cynthia Rockwell. Rome: Editore Colombo.

Cohen, David William. 1994. *The Combing of History.* Chicago: University of Chicago Press.

Coleman, Janet. 1992. *Ancient and Medieval Memories: Studies in Reconstruction of the Past.* Cambridge: Cambridge University Press.

Collins, Elizabeth. 1998. Reflections on Ritual and on Theorizing about Ritual. *JRS* 12:1–7.

Condor, Susan. 1996. Social Identity and Time. Pages 285–315 in *Social Groups and Identities: Developing the Legacy of Henri Tajfel.* Edited by Peter Robinson. Oxford: Heinemann.

Connerton, Paul. 1989. *How Societies Remember.* Themes in the Social Sciences. Cambridge: Cambridge University Press.

Cooley, Charles Horton. 1964. *Human Nature and the Social Order.* New York: Schocken. [orig. 1902]

Corley, Kathleen E. 1993. *Private Women, Public Meals: Social Conflict in the Synoptic Tradition.* Peabody, Mass.: Hendrickson.

———. 2002. *Women and the Historical Jesus: Feminist Myths of Christian Origins.* Santa Rosa, Calif.: Polebridge.

Cornell, Stephen. 2000. That's the Story of Our Life. Pages 41–53 in *We Are a People: Narrative and Multiplicity in Constructing Ethnic Identity.* Edited by Paul Spickard and W. Jeffrey Burroughs. Philadelphia: Temple University Press.

Cosby, Michael R. 1988. *The Rhetorical Composition and Function of Hebrews 11: In Light of Example Lists from Antiquity.* Macon, Ga.: Mercer University Press.

Coser, Lewis A. 1992. Introduction: Maurice Halbwachs. Pages 1–34 in Maurice Halbwachs, *On Collective Memory.* Edited and translated by Lewis A. Coser. Chicago: University of Chicago Press.

Cranfield, C. E. B. 1959. *The Gospel according to St. Mark.* Cambridge Greek Testament Commentary. Edited by C. F. D. Moule. Cambridge: Cambridge University Press.

Cressy, David. 1994. National Memory in Early Modern England. Pages 61–73 in *Commemorations: The Politics of National Identity.* Edited by John R. Gillis. Princeton: Princeton University Press.

Crossan, John Dominic. 1983. *In Fragments: The Aphorisms of Jesus.* San Francisco: Harper & Row.

———. 1988. *The Cross That Spoke: The Origins of the Passion and Resurrection Narratives.* San Francisco: Harper & Row.

———. 1991. *The Historical Jesus: The Life of a Mediterranean Jewish Peasant.* San Francisco: HarperSanFrancisco.

———. 1994. *Jesus: A Revolutionary Biography.* San Francisco: HarperSanFrancisco.

———. 1995. *Who Killed Jesus?* San Francisco: HarperSanFrancisco.

————. 1998. *The Birth of Christianity*. San Francisco: HarperSanFrancisco.

Culler, Jonathan. 1981. *The Pursuit of Signs*. Ithaca, N.Y.: Cornell University Press.

Culpepper, R. Alan. 1998. *The Gospel and Letters of John*. Interpreting Biblical Texts. Nashville: Abingdon.

Czarnowski, Stefan. 1975. *Le culte des héros et ses conditions sociales*. New York: Arno. [orig. 1919]

Daube, David. 1950. The Anointing at Bethany and Jesus' Burial. *AThR* 32:186–99.

Davies, Stevan L. 1983. *The Gospel of Thomas and Christian Wisdom*. New York: Seabury.

DeConick, April D. 1996. *Seek to See Him: Ascent and Vision Mysticism in the Gospel of Thomas*. VCSup 33. Leiden: Brill.

————. 2002. The Original Gospel of Thomas. *VC* 56:167–99.

DeConick, April D., and Jarl E. Fossum. 1991. Stripped Before God: A New Interpretation of Logion 37 in the Gospel of Thomas. *VC* 45:123–50.

Delorme, Jean. 1991. Parole, Évangile et mémoire (Marc 14, 3–9). Pages 113–25 in *La mémoire et le temps*. Edited by Daniel Marguerat and Jean Zumstein. Geneva: Labor et Fides.

Derrett, J. Duncan M. 1964. The Anointing at Bethany. *SE* 2 [TU 87]:174–82.

Dewey, Arthur J. 1990. Time to Murder and Create: Visions and Revisions in the Gospel of Peter. *Semeia* 49:101–27.

————. 1998. The Passion Narrative of the Gospel of Peter. *Forum* 1:53–69.

————. 2001a. Can We Let Jesus Die? Pages 135–59 in *The Once and Future Faith*. Santa Rosa, Calif.: Polebridge.

————. 2001b. The Eyewitness of History: Visionary Consciousness in the Fourth Gospel. Pages 59–70 in *Jesus in Johannine Tradition*. Edited by Robert T. Fortna and Tom Thatcher. Louisville: Westminster John Knox.

Dewey, Joanna. 1989. Oral Methods of Structuring Narrative in Mark. *Int* 43:32–44.

————. 1994. The Gospel of Mark. Pages 470–509 in *Searching the Scriptures: A Feminist Commentary*. Edited by Elisabeth Schüssler Fiorenza. New York: Crossroad.

Dodd, Charles H. 1963. *Historical Tradition in the Fourth Gospel*. Cambridge: Cambridge University Press.

Dormeyer, Detlev. 1998. *The New Testament among the Writings of Antiquity*. Sheffield: Sheffield Academic Press.

Duchesne-Guillemin, Jacques. 1988. La commémoration: Temps retrouvé temps aboli. Pages 13–20 in Gignoux.

Dundes, Alan. 1965. Text, Texture and Context. *Southern Folklore Quarterly* 20:251–61. Repr. as pages 20–32 in *Interpreting Folklore*. Bloomington: Indiana University Press, 1980.

Dunn, J. D. G. 1985. Once More—Gal 1:18 *historesai Kephan*; In Reply to Otfried Hofius. *ZNW* 76:138–39.

————. 2003. *Jesus Remembered*. Grand Rapids: Eerdmans.

Durkheim, Emile. 1961. *The Elementary Forms of the Religious Life*. New York: Collier. [orig. 1912]

————. 1965. *The Elementary Forms of the Religious Life*. New York: Free Press.

————. 1982. *The Rules of Sociological Method and Selected Texts on Sociology and Its Method*. London: Macmillan. [orig. 1895]

————. 1984. *The Division of Labour in Society*. London: Macmillan. [orig. 1893]

————. 1989. *Suicide: A Study in Sociology*. London: Routledge. [orig. 1897]

Eisenbaum, Pamela M. 1997. *The Jewish Heroes of Christian History: Hebrews 11 in Literary Context*. SBLDS 156. Atlanta: Scholars.

Elliott, J. Keith. 1974. The Anointing of Jesus. *ExpTim* 85:105–7.

Esler, Philip F. 1987. *Community and Gospel in Luke-Acts: The Social and Political Motivations of Lucan Theology*. SNTSMS 57. Cambridge: Cambridge University Press.

————. 1994. *The First Christians in Their Social Worlds: Social-Scientific Approaches to New Testament Interpretation*. New York: Routledge.

————. 2003a. *Conflict and Identity in Romans: The Social Setting of Paul's Letter*. Minneapolis: Fortress.

————. 2003b. Ezra-Nehemiah as a Narrative of (Re-invented) Israelite Identity. *BibInt* 11:413–26.

————. 2005. *New Testament Theology: Communion and Community*. Minneapolis: Fortress.

Evans, Craig A. 2001. *Mark 8:27–16:20*. WBC 34B. Nashville: Word.

Farmer, Sarah Bennett. 1999. *Martyred Village: Commemorating the 1944 Massacre at Oradour-sur-Glane*. Berkeley and Los Angeles: University of California Press.

Fehribach, Adeline. 1998. *The Women in the Life of the Bridegroom: A Feminist Historical-Literary Analysis of the Female Characters in the Fourth Gospel*. Collegeville, Minn.: Liturgical Press.

Fentress, James, and Chris Wickham. 1992. *Social Memory*. New Perspectives on the Past. Cambridge, Mass.: Blackwell.

Festinger, Leon, Henry W. Riecken, and Stanley Schachter. 1956. *When Prophecy Fails*. Minneapolis: University of Minnesota Press.

Fine, Gary Alan. 1996. Reputational Entrepreneurs and the Memory of Incompetence. *AJS* 101:1169–93.

Fitzmyer, Joseph A. 1970. *The Gospel according to Luke I–IX*. AB 28. New York: Doubleday.

Foley, John Miles. 1988. *The Theory of Oral Composition: History and Methodology*. Bloomington: Indiana University Press.

————. 1990. *Traditional Oral Epic: The Odyssey, Beowulf and the Serbo-Croatian Return Song*. Berkeley and Los Angeles: University of California Press.

————. 1991. *Immanent Art: From Structure to Meaning in Traditional Oral Epic*. Bloomington: Indiana University Press.

————. 1995. *Singer of Tales in Performance*. Bloomington: Indiana University Press.

————. 2002. *How to Read an Oral Poem*. Urbana: University of Illinois Press.

————, ed. 1987. *Comparative Research on Oral Traditions: A Memorial for Milman Parry*. Columbus, Ohio: Slavica.

Foner, Eric, ed. 1997. *The New American History*. Philadelphia: Temple University Press.

Foucault, Michel. 1977. *Language, Counter-Memory, Practice: Selected Essays and Interviews*. Edited and translated by Donald F. Bouchard and Sherry Simon. Ithaca, N.Y.: Cornell University Press.

————. 1980. *The Archaeology of Knowledge*. London: Routledge. [orig. 1972]

Freud, Sigmund. 1939. *Moses and Monotheism.* New York: Vintage.

Funk, Robert W. 1996. *Honest to Jesus.* New York: Harper Collins.

Funk, Robert W., and Roy W. Hoover. 1993. *The Five Gospels: The Search for the Authentic Words of Jesus.* New York: Macmillan.

Gamble, Harry Y. 1995. *Books and Readers in the Early Church: A History of Early Christian Texts.* New Haven: Yale University Press.

Gathercole, Peter, and David Lowenthal, eds. 1990. *The Politics of the Past.* Boston: Unwin Hyman.

Geertz, Clifford. 1973. Ideology as a Cultural System. Pages 193–233 in *The Interpretation of Cultures.* New York: Basic.

———. 1983. *Local Knowledge: Further Essays in Interpretive Anthropology.* New York: Basic.

Georgoudi, Stella. 1988. Commemoration et celebration des morts dans les cites grecques: Les rites annuels. Pages 73–89 in Gignoux.

Gerhardsson, Birger. 1998. *Memory and Manuscript: Oral Tradition and Written Transmission in Rabbinic Judaism and Early Christianity,* with *Tradition and Transmission in Early Christianity.* Translated by Eric J. Sharpe. Grand Rapids: Eerdmans.

———. 2001. *The Reliability of the Gospel Tradition.* Peabody, Mass.: Hendrickson.

Gero, Joan, and Delores Root. 1990. Public Presentations and Private Concerns: Archaeology in the Pages of National Geographic. Pages 19–37 in Gathercole and Lowenthal.

Gibblin, Charles H. 1992. Mary's Anointing for Jesus' Burial-Resurrection (John 12, 1–8). *Bib* 73:560–64.

Giddens, Anthony. 1978. *Durkheim.* London: Fontana.

Gignoux, Philippe, ed. 1988. *La commémoration.* Paris: Peeters.

Gillis, John R. 1994a. Memory and Identity: The History of a Relationship. Pages 3–24 in Gillis 1994b.

———, ed. 1994b. *Commemorations: The Politics of National Identity.* Princeton: Princeton University Press.

Goffman, Ervin. 1974. *Frame Analysis: An Essay on the Organization of Experience.* New York: Harper & Row.

Goody, Jack. 1977. *The Domestication of the Savage Mind.* Cambridge: Cambridge University Press.

———, ed. 1968. *Literacy in Traditional Societies.* Cambridge: Cambridge University Press.

Gorman, Frank H., Jr. 1994. Ritual Studies and Biblical Studies: Assessment of the Past, Prospect for the Future. *Semeia* 67:13–36.

Gould, Ezra P. 1975. *A Critical and Exegetical Commentary on the Gospel according to St. Mark.* Edinburgh: T&T Clark. [orig. 1896]

Grässer, Erich. 1965. *Der Glaube im Hebräerbrief.* Marburger theologischer Studien 2. Marburg: Elwert.

Green, Joel B. 1995. *The Theology of the Gospel of Luke.* New Testament Theology. Cambridge: Cambridge University Press.

———. 1997. *The Gospel of Luke.* NICNT. Grand Rapids: Eerdmans.

Grimes, Ronald L. 2000. *Deeply into the Bone: Re-inventing the Rites of Passage.* Berkeley and Los Angeles: University of California Press.

Grimes, Ronald L. , ed. 1996. *Readings in Ritual Studies.* Upper Saddle River, N.J.: Prentice Hall.

Griswold, Wendy. 1994. *Cultures and Society in a Changing World.* Thousand Oaks, Calif.: Pine Forge.

Gundry, Robert H. 1994. *Mark.* Grand Rapids: Eerdmans.

Güttgemanns, Erhardt. 1970. *Offene Fragen zur Formgeschichte des Evangeliums.* BEvTh 54. Munich: Kaiser.

Hacking, Ian. 1999. *The Social Construction of What?* Cambridge: Harvard University Press.

Halbwachs, Maurice. 1980. *The Collective Memory.* Translated by Francis J. Ditter Jr. and Vida Yazdi Ditter. New York: Harper & Row, 1980. [orig. *La mémoire collective.* Paris: Presses Universitaires de France, 1950]

———. 1992. *On Collective Memory.* Edited and translated by Lewis A. Coser. Chicago: University of Chicago Press.

———. 1997. *La mémoire collective.* Edited by Gerard Namer. Paris: Michel.

Halliwell, Stephen. 2002. *The Aesthetics of Mimesis: Ancient Texts and Modern Problems.* Princeton: Princeton University Press.

Halpern Amaru, Betsy. 1983. The Killing of the Prophets: Unravelling a Midrash. *HUCA* 54:153–80.

Hamm, Dennis. 1990. Faith in the Epistle to the Hebrews: The Jesus Factor. *CBQ* 52:270–91.

Handler, Richard, and Jocelyn Linnekin. 1984. Tradition, Genuine or Spurious. *JAF* 97:273–90.

Hardyck, Jane Allyn, and Marcia Braden. 1962. Prophecy Fails Again: A Report of a Failure to Replicate. *JASP* 65:136–41.

Harrington, Daniel J., and Anthony J. Saldarini, eds. 1987. *Targum Jonathan of the Former Prophets: Introduction, Translation and Notes.* ArBib 10. Wilmington, Del.: Glazier.

Harris, William V. 1989. *Ancient Literacy.* Cambridge: Harvard University Press.

Havelock, Eric A. 1963. *Preface to Plato.* Cambridge: Harvard University Press.

———. 1978. *The Greek Concept of Justice: From Its Shadow in Homer to Its Substance in Plato.* Cambridge: Harvard University Press.

Hayden, Robert M. 1994. Recounting the Dead: The Rediscovery and Redefinition of Wartime Massacres in Late- and Post-Communist Yugoslavia. Pages 167–84 in *Memory, History and Opposition under State Socialism.* Edited by Rubie S. Watson. Santa Fe, N.M.: School of American Research Press.

Hays, Richard. 1989. *Echoes of Scripture in the Letters of Paul.* New Haven: Yale University Press.

Hengel, Martin, and Anna Maria Schwemer. 1997. *Paul between Damascus and Antioch: The Unknown Years.* Louisville: Westminster John Knox.

Herndon, William H., and Jessie W. Weik. 1889. *Herndon's Lincoln: The True Story of a Great Life.* 3 vols. New York: Belford, Clarke & Co.

Herzog, William R., II. 2000. *Jesus, Justice, and the Reign of God.* Louisville: Westminster John Knox.

Hezser, Catherine. 2001. *Jewish Literacy in Roman Palestine.* Tübingen: Mohr Siebeck.

Hjärpe, Jan. 1988. La commémoration religieuse comme légitimation politique dans le monde muselman contemporain. Pages 333–41 in Gignoux.

Hobsbawm, Eric. 1983. Introduction: Inventing Tradition. Pages 1–14 in *The Invention of Tradition*. Edited by Eric Hobsbawm and Terence Ranger. Past and Present Publications. New York: Cambridge University Press.

Hogg, Michael A., and Dominic Abrams. 1988. *Social Identifications: A Social Psychology of Intergroup Relations*. New York: Routledge.

Holst, Robert. 1976. The One Anointing of Jesus: Another Application of the Form-Critical Method. *JBL* 95:435–46.

Hooker, Morna D. 1991. *A Commentary on the Gospel according to Mark*. London: Black.

Hopkins, Keith. 2000. *A World Full of Gods: The Strange Triumph of Christianity*. New York: Free Press.

Hornsby, Teresa J. 2002. The Woman Is a Sinner/The Sinner is a Woman. Pages 121–32 in *A Feminist Companion to Luke*. Edited by Amy-Jill Levine with Marianne Blickenstaff. FCNTECW 3. London: Sheffield Academic Press.

Horsley, Richard A. 1987. *Jesus and the Spiral of Violence: Popular Jewish Resistance in Roman Palestine*. San Francisco: Harper & Row.

———. 1995. *Galilee: History, Politics, People*. Valley Forge, Pa.: Trinity Press International.

———. 2001. *Hearing the Whole Story: The Politics of Plot in Mark's Gospel*. Louisville: Westminster John Knox.

Horsley, Richard A., and Jonathan A. Draper. 1999. *Whoever Hears You Hears Me: Prophets, Performance and Tradition in Q*. Harrisburg, Pa.: Trinity Press International.

Hurtado, Larry W. 1999. *At the Origins of Christian Worship*. Grand Rapids: Eerdmans.

Hutton, Patrick H. 1988. Collective Memory and Collective Mentalities: The Halbwachs-Aries Connection. *Reflexions Historiques* 15:311–22.

———. 1993. *History as an Art of Memory*. Hanover, N.H.: University Press of New England.

Irwin-Zarecka, Iwona. 1994. *Frames of Remembrance: The Dynamics of Collective Memory*. New Brunswick, N.J.: Transaction.

Jaffee, Martin. 2000. *Torah in the Mouth: Writing and Oral Tradition in Palestinian Judaism, 200 BCE–400 CE*. New York: Oxford University Press.

James, Wendy. 1997. The Names of Fear: Memory, History, and the Ethnography of Feeling among Uduk Refugees. *JRAI* 3:115–31.

Jenks, Gregory C. 1999. What Did Paul Know about Jesus? *The Fourth R* 12:1.

Jennings, Theodore. 1982. On Ritual Knowledge. *JR* 62:111–27.

Jeremias, Joachim. 1936. Die Salbungsgeschichte Mc 14,3–9. *ZNW* 35:75–82.

Jing, Jun. 1996. *The Temple of Memories: History, Power, and Morality in a Chinese Village*. Stanford, Calif.: Stanford University Press.

Johnson, Luke Timothy. 1991. *The Gospel of Luke*. Sacra Pagina. Collegeville, Minn.: Liturgical Press.

———. 1998. *Religious Experience in Earliest Christianity*. Minneapolis: Fortress.

———. 1999. The Humanity of Jesus: What's at Stake in the Quest for the Historical Jesus? Pages 48–74 in John Dominic Crossan, Luke Timothy Johnson, and Werner H. Kelber, *The Jesus Controversy: Perspectives in Conflict*. Harrisburg, Pa.: Trinity Press International.

Jonge, Marinus de. 1988. *Christology in Context: The Earliest Christian Response to Jesus*. Philadelphia: Westminster.

Jousse, Marcel. 1925. *Études de psychologie linguistique: Le style orale, rhythmique et mnémotechnique chez les verbo–moteurs*. Paris: Beauchesne.

———. 1974. *L'anthropologie du geste*. Paris: Gallimard.

———. 1975. *La manducation de la parole*. Paris: Gallimard.

———. 1978. *Le parland, la parole et le souffle*. Paris: Gallimard.

Juel, Donald H. 1994. *A Master of Surprise: Mark Interpreted*. Minneapolis: Fortress.

Kammen, Michael. 1991. *Mystic Chords of Memory*. New York: Basic.

———. 1995. Some Patterns and Meanings of Memory Distortion in American History. Pages 329–45 in Schachter.

Käsemann, Ernst. 1964. The Problem of the Historical Jesus. Pages 15–47 in *Essays on New Testament Themes*. Translated by W. J. Montague. SBT 41. London: SCM.

Kelber, Werner H. 1979. *Mark's Story of Jesus*. Philadelphia: Fortress.

———. 1983. *The Oral and Written Gospel: The Hermeneutics of Speaking and Writing in the Synoptic Tradition, Mark, Paul and Q*. Philadelphia: Fortress.

———. 1994. Jesus and Tradition: Words in Time, Words in Space. *Semeia* 65:139–67.

———. 2002. The Case of the Gospels: Memory's Desire and the Limits of Historical Criticism. *Oral Tradition* 17:55–86.

Kermode, Frank. 1979. *The Genesis of Secrecy: On the Interpretation of Narrative*. Cambridge: Harvard University Press.

Kilgallen, John J. 1985. John the Baptist, the Sinful Woman, and the Pharisee. *JBL* 104: 675–79.

Kingsbury, Jack Dean. 1989. *Conflict in Mark: Jesus, Authorities, Disciples*. Minneapolis: Fortress.

Kitzberger, Ingrid Rosa. 1994. Love and Footwashing: John 13:1–20 and Luke 7:36–50 Read Intertextually. *BibInt* 2:190–226.

Kirk, Alan. 1998. *The Composition of the Sayings Source*. Leiden: Brill.

Kloppenborg, John S. 1987. *The Formation of Q*. Minneapolis: Fortress.

Knox, John. 1962. *The Church and the Reality of Christ*. New York: Harper & Row.

———. 1987. *Chapters in a Life of Paul*. Macon, Ga.: Mercer University Press.

Koester, Craig R. 1995. *Symbolism in the Fourth Gospel: Meaning, Mystery, Community*. Minneapolis: Fortress.

———. 2001. *Hebrews: A New Translation with Introduction and Commentary*. AB 36. New York: Doubleday.

Koester, Helmut. 1998. The Memory of Jesus' Death and the Worship of the Risen Lord. *HTR* 91:335–50.

Kristeva, Julia. 1969. *Semiotiké*. Paris: Seuil.

Leach, Edmund. 1970. *Claude Levi-Strauss*. New York: Penguin.

Legault, André. 1954. An Application of the Form-Critique Method. *CBQ* 16:131–45.

Lewis, Bernard. 1975. *History: Remembered, Recovered, Invented*. Princeton: Princeton University Press.

Lindars, Barnabas. 1981. *The Gospel of John*. Grand Rapids: Eerdmans.

———. 1991. *The Theology of the Letter to the Hebrews*. New Testament Theology. Cambridge: Cambridge University Press.

Loftus, Elizabeth. 1996. *Eyewitness Testimony*. Cambridge: Harvard University Press.

Lord, Albert. 1960. *The Singer of Tales*. Harvard Studies in Comparative Literature 24. Cambridge: Harvard University Press.

———. 1978. The Gospels as Oral Traditional Literature. Pages 33–91 in *The Relationships among the Gospels: An Interdisciplinary Dialogue*. Edited by William O. Walker Jr. San Antonio, Tex.: Trinity University Press.

———. 1991. *Epic Singers and Oral Tradition*. Ithaca, N.Y.: Cornell University Press.

Louie, Kam. 1980. *Critiques of Confucius in Contemporary China*. New York: St. Martin's.

Lowenthal, David. 1985. *The Past Is a Foreign Country*. New York: Cambridge University Press.

———. 1990. Conclusion: Archaeologists and Others. Pages 302–14 in Gathercole and Lowenthal.

———. 1994. Identity, Heritage, and History. Pages 41–57 in Gillis 1994b.

———. 1996. *Possessed by the Past: The Heritage Crusade and the Spoils of History*. New York: Free Press.

Lukes, Steven. 1973. *Emile Durkheim: His Life and Work, A Historical and Critical Study*. London: Penguin.

MacDonald, Dennis R. 2000. *The Homeric Epics and the Gospel of Mark*. New Haven: Yale University Press.

MacDonald, Margaret. 1999. Ritual in the Pauline Churches. Pp 233–47 in *Social Scientific Approaches to New Testament Interpretation*. Edited by David G. Horrell. Edinburgh: T&T Clark.

MacIntyre, Alasdair. 1981. *After Virtue: A Study in Moral Theory*. London: Duckworth.

Mack, Burton L. 1988. *A Myth of Innocence: Mark and Christian Origins*. Philadelphia: Fortress.

———. 1989. The Anointing of Jesus: Elaboration within a Chreia. Pages 85–106 in Mack and Robbins.

Mack, Burton L., and Vernon K. Robbins. 1989. *Patterns of Persuasion in the Gospels*. Sonoma, Calif.: Polebridge.

Malbon, Elizabeth Struthers. 2002. *Hearing Mark: A Listener's Guide*. Harrisburg, Pa.: Trinity Press International.

Malina, Bruce J. 1996. *The Social World of Jesus and the Gospels*. New York: Routledge.

———. 2001. *The New Testament World: Insights from Cultural Anthropology*. Louisville: Westminster John Knox.

Malkki, Liisa H. 1995. *Purity and Exile: Violence, Memory, and National Cosmology among Hutu Refugees in Tanzania*. Chicago: University of Chicago Press.

Mannheim, Karl. 1936. *Ideology and Utopia*. New York: Harcourt, Brace & World.

———. 1952. *Essays on the Sociology of Knowledge*. Edited by Paul Kecskemeti. London: Routledge.

Marshall, John W. 1997. The Gospel of Thomas and the Cynic Jesus. Pages 37–60 in *Whose Historical Jesus?* Edited by W. E. Arnal and M. Desjardins. Studies in Christianity and Judaism 7. Waterloo, Ont.: Wilfrid Laurier University Press.

McVann, Mark. 1995. Introduction. *Semeia* 67:7–12.

Mead, George Herbert. 1929. The Nature of the Past. Pages 235–42 in *Essays in Honor of John Dewey*. Edited by J. Coss. New York: Henry Holt.

Mead, Margaret. 1970. *Culture and Commitment: A Study of the Generation Gap*. Garden City, N.Y.: Doubleday.

Meeks, Wayne A. 1983. *The First Urban Christians: The Social World of the Apostle Paul*. New Haven: Yale University Press.

Mendenhall, George. 1955. *Law and Covenant in Israel and the Ancient Near East*. Pittsburgh: Presbyterian Board.

Merton, Robert K. 1957. The Sociology of Knowledge. Pages 456–88 in *Social Theory and Social Structure*. Glencoe, Ill.: Free Press.

Meyerhoff, Hans. 1955. *Time in Literature*. Berkeley and Los Angeles: University of California Press.

Michaels, J. Ramsey. 1989. John 12:1–11. *Int* 43: 287–91.

Michnic-Coren, Joanna. 1999. The Troubling Past: The Polish Collective Memory of the Holocaust. *EEJA* 29:75–84.

Middleton, David, and Derek Edwards, eds. 1990. *Collective Remembering*. London: Sage.

Mikolajczyk, Adrzej. 1990. Didactic Presentations of the Past: Some Retrospective Considerations in Relation to the Archaeological and Ethnographical Museum, Lódz, Poland. Pages 247–56 in Gathercole and Lowenthal.

Morrill, Bruce T., ed. 1999. *Bodies of Worship: Explorations in Theory and Practice*. Collegeville, Minn.: Liturgical Press.

Morris, Leon. 1971. *The Gospel according to John*. NICNT. Grand Rapids: Eerdmans.

Mudimbe, V. Y. 1988. *The Invention of Africa: Gnosis, Philosophy, and the Order of Knowledge*. Indianapolis: Indiana University Press.

———. 1994. *The Idea of Africa*. Indianapolis: Indiana University Press.

Munro, Winsome. 1979. The Anointing in Mark 14:3–9 and John 12:1–8. Pages 127–30 in *Society of Biblical Literature 1979 Seminar Papers*. Edited by Paul Achtemeier. Missoula, Mont.: Scholars Press.

Murphy-O'Connor, Jerome. 1997. *Paul: A Critical Life*. Oxford: Oxford University Press.

Namer, Gérard. 1987. *Mémoire et société*. Paris: Méridiens Lincksieck.

———. 2000. *Halbwachs et la mémoire sociale*. Paris: L'Harmattan.

Neal, Arthur G. 1998. *National Trauma and Collective Memory*. Armonk, N.Y.: Sharpe.

Newsom, Carol A., and Sharon H. Ringe, eds. 1998. *Women's Bible Commentary: Expanded Edition*. Louisville: Westminster John Knox.

Nickelsburg, George W. E. 1980. The Genre and Function of the Markan Passion Narrative. *HTR* 73:153–80.

Nora, Pierre. 1996–98. *Realms of Memory*. Edited by Lawrence D. Dritzman. Translated by Arthur Goldhammer. 3 vols. New York: Columbia University Press.

O'Day, Gail R. 1998. John. Pages 381–93 in Newsom and Ringe.

Olick, Jeffrey K. 1999a. Collective Memory: The Two Cultures. *ST* 17:333–48.

———. 1999b. Genre Memories and Memory Genres: A Dialogical Analysis of May 8, 1945 Commemorations in the Federal Republic of Germany. *ASR* 64:381–402.

Olick, Jeffrey K., and Daniel Levy. 1997. Collective Memory and Cultural Constraint: Holocaust Myth and Rationality in German Politics. *ASR* 62:921–36.

Olick, Jeffrey K., and Joyce Robbins. 1988. Social Memory Studies: From "Collective Memory" to the Historical Sociology of Mnemonic Practices. *ASR* 24:105–40.

Ong, Walter J. 1967. *The Presence of the Word: Some Prolegomena for Cultural and Religious History.* New Haven: Yale University Press.

———. 1971. *Rhetoric, Romance, and Technology.* Ithaca, N.Y.: Cornell University Press.

———. 1977. *Interfaces of the Word: Studies in the Evolution of Consciousness and Culture.* Ithaca, N.Y.: Cornell University Press.

———. 1982. *Orality and Literacy: The Technologizing of the Word.* New York: Methuen.

Owen, Stephen. 1986. *Remembrances: The Experience of the Past in Classical Chinese Literature.* Cambridge: Harvard University Press.

Painter, John. 1997. *Mark's Gospel: Worlds in Conflict.* New York: Routledge.

Patterson, Stephen J. 1993. *The Gospel of Thomas and Jesus.* Sonoma, Calif.: Polebridge.

Pelikan, Jaroslav. 1985. *Jesus through the Centuries.* New York: Harper & Row.

Peri, Yoram. 1999. The Media and Collective Memory of Yitzhak Rabin's Remembrance. *JC* 49:106–24.

Perrin, Norman. 1967. *Rediscovering the Teaching of Jesus.* New York: Harper & Row.

Perrin, Norman, and Dennis Duling. 1982. *The New Testament: An Introduction.* New York: Harcourt Brace Jovanovich.

Peterson, David G. 1982. *Hebrews and Perfection: An Examination of the Concept of Perfection in the Epistle to the Hebrews.* SNTSMS 47. Cambridge: Cambridge University Press.

Peterson, Merrill. 1994. *Abraham Lincoln in American Memory.* New York: Oxford University Press.

Prager, Jeffrey. 1998. *Presenting the Past: Psychoanalysis and the Sociology of Misremembering.* Cambridge: Harvard University Press.

Quintilian. 1922. *The Institutio Oratoria.* Translated by H. E. Butler. LCL 4. New York: Putnam.

Randall, James R. 1945. *Lincoln the President: Springfield to Gettysburg.* 2 vols. New York: Dodd, Mead & Co.

Rapport, Nigel. 1997a. The "Contrarieties" of Israel: An Essay on the Cognitive Importance and the Creative Promise of Both/And. *JRAI* 3:653–72.

———. 1997b. *Transcendent Individual: Toward a Literary and Liberal Anthropology.* London: Routledge.

Reid, Barbara. 2002. "Do You See This Woman?" A Liberative Look at Luke 7:36–50 and Strategies for Reading Other Lukan Stories against the Grain. Pages 106–20 in *A Feminist Companion to Luke.* Edited by Amy-Jill Levine with Marianne Blickenstaff. New York: Sheffield Academic Press.

Reinhartz, Adele. 1994. The Gospel of John. Pages 561–600 in *Searching the Scriptures: A Feminist Commentary.* Edited by Elisabeth Schüssler Fiorenza. New York: Crossroad.

Resseguie, James L. 1991. Automatization and Defamiliarization in Luke 7:36–50. *Literature and Theology* 5:137–50.

Robbins, Vernon. 1992. Using a Socio-rhetorical Poetics to Develop a Unified Method: The Woman Who Anointed Jesus as a Test Case. Pages 302–19 in *Society of Biblical Literature 1992 Seminar Papers*. Edited by Eugene H. Lovering Jr. Atlanta: Scholars Press.

Robinson, James M., and Helmut Koester. 1971. *Trajectories through Early Christianity*. Philadelphia: Fortress.

Rosenzweig, Roy, and David Thelen. 1998. *The Presence of the Past: Popular Uses of History in American Life*. New York: Columbia University Press.

Rösler, Wolfgang. 1983. Schriftkultur und Fiktionalität: Zum Funktionswandel der griechischen Literatur von Homer bis Aristoteles. Pages 109–22 in Assmann, Assmann, and Hardmeier.

Sabbe, Maurits. 1982. The Footwashing in Jn 13 and Its Relation to the Synoptic Gospels. *ETL* 58:279–308.

———. 1992. The Anointing of Jesus in John 12, 1–8 and Its Synoptic Parallels. Pages 2051–82 in *The Four Gospels, 1992*. Edited by F. Van Segbroeck, C. M. Tuckett, G. Van Belle, and J. Verheyden. BETL 100. Leuven: Leuven University Press.

Sanders, Joseph N. 1954. "Those Whom Jesus Loved" (John XI. 5). *NTS* 1:29–41.

Savage, Kirk. 1994. The Politics of Memory: Black Emancipation and the Civil War Movement. Pages 127–49 in Gillis 1994b.

Sawicki, Marianne. 1994. *Seeing the Lord: Resurrection and Early Christian Practices*. Minneapolis: Fortress.

Schaberg, Jane. 1998. Luke. Pages 363–80 in Newsom and Ringe.

Schachter, Daniel, ed. 1995. *Memory Distortion: How Minds, Brains, and Societies Reconstruct the Past*. Cambridge: Harvard University Press.

Schmidt, Karl Ludwig. 1969. *Der Rahmen der Geschichte Jesu*. Darmstadt: Wissenschaftliche Buchgesellschaft. [orig. 1919]

Schnackenburg, Rudoph. 1968. *The Gospel according to St. John*. New York: Herder & Herder.

Schottroff, Luise. 1993. *Let the Oppressed Go Free: Feminist Perspectives on the New Testament*. Translated by Annemarie S. Kidder. Louisville: Westminster John Knox.

Schröter, Jens. 1996. The Historical Jesus and the Sayings Tradition: Comments on Current Research. *Neot* 30:151–68.

———. 1997. *Erinnerung an Jesu Worte: Studien zur Rezeption der Logienüberlieferung in Markus, Q und Thomas*. WMANT 76. Neukirchen-Vluyn: Neukirchener Verlag.

Schudson, Michael. 1989. The Present in the Past versus the Past in the Present. *Communication* 11:105–13.

———. 1992. *Watergate in American Memory: How We Remember, Forget, and Reconstruct the Past*. New York: Basic.

———. 1995. Dynamics of Distortion in Collective Memory. Pages 346–64 in Schachter.

Schwartz, Barry. 1982. The Social Context of Commemoration: A Study in Collective Memory. *Social Forces* 61:374–402.

———. 1990. The Reconstruction of Abraham Lincoln. Pages 81–107 in Middleton and Edwards.

———. 1991. Collective Memory and Social Change: The Democratization of George Washington. *ASR* 56:221–36.

———. 1995. Deconstructing and Reconstructing the Past. *QS* 18:263–70.

———. 1996a. Memory as a Cultural System: Abraham Lincoln in World War II. *ASR* 61:908–27.

———. 1996b. Rereading the Gettysburg Address: Social Change and Collective Memory. *QS* 19:395–422.

———. 1998a. Frame Image: Towards a Semiotics of Collective Memory. *Semiotica* 121:1–38.

———. 1998b. Postmodernity and Historical Reputation: Abraham Lincoln in Late Twentieth-Century American Memory. *Social Forces* 77:63–103.

———. 2000. *Abraham Lincoln and the Forge of National Memory.* Chicago: University of Chicago Press.

Schwartz, Barry, and Eugene F. Miller. 1986. The Icon and the Word: A Study in the Visual Depiction of Moral Character. *Semiotica* 61:69–99.

Schwarz, Vera. 1998. *Bridge across Broken Time: Chinese and Jewish Cultural Memory.* New Haven: Yale University Press.

Schweizer, Eduard. 1970. *The Good News according to Mark.* Translated by Donald H. Madvig. Richmond, Va.: John Knox.

Scott, Shaunna L. 1996. Dead Work: The Construction and Reconstruction of the Harlan Miners Memorial. *QS* 19:365–93.

Seim, Turid Karlsen. 1994. *The Double Message: Patterns of Gender in Luke and Acts.* Nashville: Abingdon.

Shils, Edward. 1981. *Tradition.* Chicago: University of Chicago Press.

Shiner, Whitney. 2003. *Proclaiming the Gospel: First-Century Performance of Mark.* Harrisburg, Pa.: Trinity.

Simondon, M. 1988. Les modes du discours commemoratif en Grèce ancienne. Pages 91–105 in Gignoux.

Simmel, Georg. 1903. De la religion au point de vue de la connaissance. Pages 319–27 in *Bibliotheque de congres international de philosophie.* Paris: Colin.

———. 1971. The Transcendent Character of Life. Pages 353–74 in *On Individuality and Social Forms.* Edited by Donald N. Levine. Chicago: University of Chicago Press. [orig. 1918]

Skultans, Vieda. 1997. Theorizing Latvian Lives: The Quest for Identity. *JRAI* 3:761–80.

Small, Jocelyn Penny. 1997. *Wax Tablets of the Mind.* New York: Routledge.

Stanton, Graham. 1975. Form Criticism Revisited. Pages 13–27 in *What about the New Testament? Essays in Honour of Christopher Evans.* Edited by Morna Hooker and Colin Hickling. London: SCM.

Suggit, John. 1985. An Incident from Mark's Gospel. *JTSA* 50:52–55.

Tajfel, Henri, ed. 1978. *Differentiation between Social Groups: Studies in the Social Psychology of Intergroup Relations.* London: Academic.

Tannehill, Robert C. 1986. *The Gospel according to Luke.* Vol. 1 of *The Narrative Unity of Luke-Acts: A Literary Interpretation.* Philadelphia: Fortress.

Taussig, Michael. 1993. *Mimesis and Alterity: A Particular History of the Senses.* New York: Routledge.

Taylor, David Bruce. 1992. *Mark's Gospel as Literature and History.* London: SCM.

Telford, William, ed. 1985. *The Interpretation of Mark.* Edinburgh: T&T Clark.

Terdiman, Richard. 1993. *Present Past: Modernity and the Memory Crisis.* Ithaca, N.Y.: Cornell University Press.

Thatcher, Tom. 1998. Literacy, Textual Communities, and Josephus' Jewish War. *JSJ* 29:127–35.

———. 2001. Introduction. Pages 1–9 in *Jesus in Johannine Tradition.* Edited by Robert T. Fortna and Tom Thatcher. Louisville: Westminster John Knox.

Thelen, David. 1989. Memory and American History. *JAH* 75:1117–29.

Thibeaux, Evelyn. 1993. Known to Be a Sinner: The Narrative Rhetoric of Luke 7:36–50. *BTB* 23:151–60.

Thiessen, Gerd. 1988. Tradition und Entscheidung: Der Beitrag des biblischen Glaubens zum kulturellen Gedächtnis. Pages 170–98 in *Kultur und Gedächtnis.* Edited by Jan Assmann and Tonio Hölscher. Frankfurt am Main: Suhrkamp.

Thomas, Rosalind. 1992. *Literacy and Orality in Ancient Greece.* Cambridge: Cambridge University Press.

Thompson, John B. 1996. Tradition and Self in a Mediated World. Pages 89–108 in *De-traditionalization: Critical Reflections on Authority and Identity in a Time of Uncertainty.* Edited by Paul Heelas, Scott Lash, and Paul Morris. Oxford: Blackwell.

Tolbert, Mary Ann. 1998. Mark. Pages 350–62 in Newsom and Ringe.

Tuchman, Gaye, and Nina Fortin. 1989. *Edging Women Out: Victorian Novelists, Publishers, and Social Change.* New Haven: Yale University Press.

Turner, Max. 1992. Holy Spirit. *DJG,* 341–51.

Valensi, Lucette. 1986. From Sacred History to Historical Memory and Back: The Jewish Past. *History & Anthropology* 2:283–305.

Vouga, F. 1994. *Geschichte des frühen Christentums.* Tubingen: Mohr Siebeck.

Wachtel, N. 1986. Memory and History: Introduction. *History and Anthropology* 12:216–17.

Wagner, Guy. 1997. L'onction de Béthanie. *ETR* 72:437–46.

Wagner-Pacifici, Robin. 1996. Memories in the Making: The Shape of Things That Went. *QS* 19:301–21.

Warner, W. Lloyd. 1959. *The Living and the Dead: A Study of the Symbolic Life of Americans.* New Haven: Yale University Press.

Weber, Max. 1947. *The Theory of Social and Economic Organization.* Translated by A. M. Henderson and Talcott Parsons. Edited by Talcott Parsons. New York: Free Press.

———. 1949. "Objectivity" in Social Science and Social Policy. Pages 49–112 in *Methodology of the Social Sciences.* Edited and translated by Edward A. Shils and Henry A. Finch. Glencoe, Ill.: Free Press.

———. 1952. *Ancient Judaism.* Translated and edited by Hans H. Gerth and Don Martindale. Glencoe, Ill.: Free Press.

Wilken, Robert Louis. 1971. *The Myth of Christian Beginnings.* Garden City, N.Y.: Doubleday.

Wilson, Douglas L. 1990. Abraham Lincoln, Ann Rutledge, and the Evidence of Herndon's Informants. *CWH* 36:301–24.

Winock, Michael. 1998. Joan of Arc. Pages 433–80 in vol. 3 of Nora.

Winsor, Ann Roberts. 1999. *A King Is Bound in the Tresses: Allusions to the Song of Songs in the Fourth Gospel.* Studies in Biblical Literature 6. New York: Lang.

Wire, Antoinette Clark. 2002. *Holy Lives, Holy Deaths: A Close Hearing of Early Jewish Storytellers.* SBLSBL 1. Atlanta: Society of Biblical Literature.

Woll, D. Bruce. 1981. *Johannine Christianity in Conflict: Authority, Rank, and Succession in the First Farewell Discourse.* SBLDS 60. Chico, Calif.: Scholars Press.

Wrede, William. 1971. *The Messianic Secret.* Translated by J. C. G. Greig. Cambridge: T&T Clark.

Yates, Frances. 1966. *The Art of Memory.* Chicago: University of Chicago Press.

Yerushalmi, Yosef Hayim. 1982. *Zakhor: Jewish History and Jewish Memory.* Seattle: University of Washington Press.

————. 1989. *Zakhor: Jewish History and Jewish Memory.* New York: Schocken Books.

Zelizer, Barbie. 1995. Reading the Past against the Grain: The Shape of Memory Studies. *CSMC* 12:214–39.

Zerubavel, Eviatar. 1991. *The Fine Line: Making Distinctions in Everyday Life.* Chicago: University of Chicago Press.

————. 1996. Social Memories: Steps to a Sociology of the Past. *QS* 19:238–99.

————. 2003. *Time Maps: Collective Memory and the Social Shape of the Past.* Chicago: University of Chicago Press.

Zerubavel, Yael. 1994. The Historic, the Legendary, and the Incredible: Invented Tradition and Collective Memory in Israel. Pages 105–23 in Gillis 1994b.

————. 1995. *Recovered Roots: Collective Memory and the Making of Israeli National Tradition.* Chicago: University of Chicago Press.

Zhang, Tong, and Barry Schwartz. 1997. Confucius and the Cultural Revolution: A Study in Collective Memory. *International Journal of Politics, Culture and Society* 11:189–212.

Zonabend, Françoise. 1984. *The Enduring Memory: Time and History in a French Village.* Translated by Anthony Forster. Manchester: Manchester University Press.

CONTRIBUTORS

April DeConick is Assistant Professor of Religion at Illinois Wesleyan University. Her research interests focus on the Gospels (canonical and noncanonical) and early Christian mysticism. She is the author of *Seek to See Him: Ascent and Vision Mysticism in the Gospel of Thomas*, *Voices of the Mystics: Early Christian Discourse in the Gospels of John and Thomas and Other Ancient Christian Literature*, and numerous papers and articles. She may be reached at adeconic@titan.iwu.edu.

Arthur J. Dewey is Professor of Theology at Xavier University (Cincinnati). His research interests focus on the historical Jesus, noncanonical Gospels, and media studies. He is currently co-chair of the Bible in Ancient and Modern Media Group in the Society of Biblical Literature and author of *Spirit and Letter in Paul* and numerous articles. He may be reached at snake@fuse.net.

Philip Esler is Professor of Biblical Criticism and former Vice–Principal for Research at the University of St. Andrews. He is the author and editor of numerous books and articles on social-scientific approaches to the Bible and the Bible and the visual arts, including *The First Christians in Their Social Worlds*, *Conflict and Identity in Romans*, *The Early Christian World*, and the forthcoming *History, Hermeneutics and Communion: Outlining a Socio-theological Interpretation of the New Testament*. He may be reached at pfe@st-andrews.ac.uk.

Holly E. Hearon is Assistant Professor of New Testament at Christian Theological Seminary (Indianapolis). Her research interests include women and Christian origins, the relationship between early Christianity and formative Judaism, and orality studies. She is author of *The Mary Magdalene Tradition: Witness and Counter-Witness in Early Christian Communities* and editor of *Distant Voices Drawing Near: Essays in Honor of Antoinette Clark Wire*. She may be reached at hhearon@cts.edu.

Richard A. Horsley is Distinguished Professor of Liberal Arts and the Study of Religion at the University of Massachusetts, Boston. His research interests focus on Jesus, the Gospels, and their historical context. He has written numerous books and articles, including *Hearing the Whole Story: The Politics of Plot in Mark's Gospel*, *Whoever Hears You Hears Me: Prophets, Performance, and Tradition in Q* (with Jonathan Draper), and *Galilee: History, Politics, People*. He may be reached at Richard.Horsley@umb.edu.

Georgia Masters Keightley is former Chair of the Department of Theology at Trinity College and currently serves with the St. Anselm Institute for Lay Theology. She is the author of numerous articles and papers on ecclesiology, theology of the laity, feminist theology, and early Christian ritual. She may be reached at gk8ly@citcnet.net.

Werner H. Kelber is the Isla Carroll and Percy E. Turner Professor of Biblical Studies and the Director of the Center for the Study of Cultures at Rice University. His pioneering research has focused on rhetoric, hermeneutics, orality studies, and memory. He is the author of numerous books and articles, including *The Kingdom in Mark* and *The Oral and the Written Gospel.* He may be reached at kelber@ruf.rice.edu.

Alan Kirk is Associate Professor in the Department of Philosophy and Religion, James Madison University (Virginia). His research interests focus on memory, orality, and the history of the Gospel traditions. He is author of *The Composition of the Sayings Source* and a number of essays and articles. He may be reached at kirkak@jmu.edu.

Barry Schwartz is Professor Emeritus of Sociology at the University of Georgia. His research interests focus on social approaches to memory and American history. He is the author of numerous books and articles, including *George Washington: The Making of an American Symbol* and *Abraham Lincoln and the Forge of National Memory,* both landmark studies in collective memory. He may be reached at cmsbarry@uga.edu.

Tom Thatcher is Professor of Biblical Studies at Cincinnati Christian University. His research interests include Johannine studies, historical Jesus studies, and interpretive theory. He has written or edited numerous books and articles, including *The Riddles of Jesus in John, Jesus in Johannine Tradition* (editor with Robert Fortna), and the forthcoming *Why John Wrote a Gospel: Jesus—Memory—History.* He may be reached at tom.thatcher@ccuniversity.edu.

Antoinette Wire is former Robert S. Dollar Professor of New Testament Studies at San Francisco Theological Seminary and continues to teach part-time at the Graduate Theological Union (Berkeley). Her research focuses on Gospel traditions, particularly the largely nonliterate people who generated the Gospel stories and who provoked the New Testament letters with their oral prophecies and community leadership. She is the author of *The Corinthian Women Prophets: A Reconstruction through Paul's Rhetoric* and *Holy Lives, Holy Deaths: A Close Hearing of Early Jewish Storytellers.* She may be reached at annewire@hotmail.com.

The editors would like to extend special thanks to Jake Christian, who tirelessly devoted hours to the preparation and formatting of this volume, and to Gale Yee and Richard Horsley for their careful and expert editorial support.

Printed in the United States
3082 7LV S0 0004 B/52-318